Chicago's Block Clubs

HISTORICAL STUDIES OF URBAN AMERICA
Edited by Lilia Fernández, Timothy J. Gilfoyle, Becky M. Nicolaides, and Amanda I. Seligman
Jameo R. Grossman, editor emeritus

Also in the series:

Crossing Parish Boundaries: African Americans, Catholicism, and Sports in Chicago, 1914–1954
by Timothy Neary

The Fixers: Devolution, Development, and Civil Society in Newark, NJ, 1960–1990
by Julia Rabig

Evangelical Gotham: Religion and the Making of New York City, 1783–1860
by Kyle B. Roberts

The Lofts of SoHo: Gentrification, Art, and Industry in New York, 1950–1980
by Aaron Shkuda

The Newark Frontier: Community Action in the Great Society
by Mark Krasovic

Making the Unequal Metropolis: School Desegregation and Its Limits
by Ansley T. Erickson

Confederate Cities: The Urban South during the Civil War Era
edited by Andrew L. Slap and Frank Towers

The Cycling City: Bicycles and Urban America in the 1890s
by Evan Friss

Making the Mission: Planning and Ethnicity in San Francisco
by Ocean Howell

A Nation of Neighborhoods: Imagining Cities, Communities, and Democracy in Postwar America
by Benjamin Looker

A World of Homeowners: American Power and the Politics of Housing Aid
by Nancy H. Kwak

Demolition Means Progress: Flint, Michigan, and the Fate of the American Metropolis
by Andrew R. Highsmith

Metropolitan Jews: Politics, Race, and Religion in Postwar Detroit
by Lila Corwin Berman

Blood Runs Green: The Murder that Transfixed Gilded Age Chicago
by Gillian O'Brien

Chicago's Block Clubs

How Neighbors Shape the City

AMANDA I. SELIGMAN

The University of Chicago Press
Chicago and London

Amanda I. Seligman is professor of history and urban studies at the University of Wisconsin–Milwaukee.

The University of Chicago Press, Chicago 60637
The University of Chicago Press, Ltd., London
© 2016 by The University of Chicago
All rights reserved. Published 2016.
Printed in the United States of America

25 24 23 22 21 20 19 18 17 16   1 2 3 4 5

ISBN-13: 978-0-226-38571-6 (cloth)
ISBN-13: 978-0-226-38585-3 (paper)
ISBN-13: 978-0-226-38599-0 (e-book)
DOI: 10.7208/chicago/9780226385990.001.0001

Library of Congress Cataloging-in-Publication Data

Names: Seligman, Amanda I., author.
Title: Chicago's block clubs : how neighbors shape the city / Amanda I. Seligman.
Other titles: Historical studies of urban America.
Description: Chicago : The University of Chicago Press, 2016. | Series: Historical studies of urban America
Identifiers: LCCN 2016005511| ISBN 9780226385716 (cloth : alk. paper) | ISBN 9780226385853 (pbk. : alk. paper) | ISBN 9780226385990 (e-book)
Subjects: LCSH: Citizens' association—Illinois—Chicago. | Neighbors—Illinois—Chicago—Societies, etc. | Community development, Urban—Illinois—Chicago—Societies, etc.
Classification: LCC HT177.C4 S45 2016 | DDC 307.1/4160977311—dc23 LC record available at https://lccn.loc.gov/2016005511

♾ This paper meets the requirements of ANSI/NISO Z39.48-1992 (Permanence of Paper).

*For all the archivists and librarians who make historical scholarship possible
and in memory of Archie Motley (1934–2002)*

Contents

Acknowledgments

Like the work of block clubs, writing a book of history is by its nature collective labor. I might lay claim to the property, but this book would not be what it is without the work of many others. It is a pleasure to offer thanks and credit to the people and institutions who helped make this book better than I could have done alone.

I am grateful to colleagues who helped me to think through the research, ideas, and prose presented here. Audiences at the Chicago History Museum's Urban History Seminar and the Urban History Association's 2014 meeting in Philadelphia graciously considered key ideas with me. Arijit Sen generously helped me with bibliographic questions and encouraged me to think seriously about the vernacular landscape. Robert Bruegmann asked me some key questions and provided early enthusiasm for this project. Aaron Schutz kindly shared his own research and ideas with me. My colleagues in the Department of History at the University of Wisconsin–Milwaukee have been models of support. I am especially grateful to Margo Anderson, Michael Gordon, Neal Pease, and Merry Wiesner-Hanks for their help with this project. Brad Hunt, Robert Powell, and Timothy Gilfoyle also provided research aid at key moments. Tom Jablonsky read all the chapters in draft form with consummate care. Lilia Fernández provided crucial guidance as I prepared the last draft.

For twelve decades the University of Wisconsin system has been committed to the principle that it "should ever encourage that continual and fearless sifting and winnowing by which alone the truth can be found." I am proud to be part of that tradition. The University of Wisconsin–Milwaukee's support for this project was multifaceted. By providing an institutional home, a research library, and students willing to talk with me about block clubs, UWM made this book possible. An Arts and Humanities Travel Grant from the Graduate

School supported research trips to Chicago. A sabbatical leave in 2013 allowed me to draft the manuscript. The Urban Studies Programs made available the time of several talented graduate student research assistants, including Salman Hussain, Karen Moore, Gestina Sewell, and Lukas Wierer. UWM's cartographer, Donna Genzmer, drew the map. Anita Cathey provided cheerful technical support. Rebekah Bain, a University of Wisconsin–La Crosse undergraduate, volunteered with research assistance and index preparation at a critical moment.

At the University of Chicago Press, I would like to thank editors Robert Devens for cultivating this project in its early stages and Tim Mennel for seeing it through the publication process, ably assisted by Nora Devlin, Ashley Pierce, and Rachel Kelly. Two anonymous colleagues and Elaine Lewinnek provided conscientious feedback on drafts of the manuscript and renewed my faith in the peer review process. I also thank Renaldo Migaldi for demonstrating the Press's high standards in the copyediting process.

I thank my family for allowing this book to be a large presence in our lives for several years. Joe, Sophonisba, and Irene know more about the history of block clubs than they ever hoped, and have patiently let me work when they wanted me to play. I can repay them only with the thrill of seeing their names in print.

It is impossible for me to acknowledge individually all the librarians and archivists whose work undergirds this book. I do not know the names of everyone who acquired and processed the archival collections, staffed the libraries, microfilmed and digitized runs of newspapers, fulfilled interlibrary loan requests, and answered research questions. I am glad to acknowledge a few who offered special assistance at key moments. At the Harold Washington Library Center of the Chicago Public Library, Morag Walsh went above and beyond the call of duty to help me locate documents in the reprocessed papers of Faith Rich. Roslyn Mabry cheerfully opened the reading room to me on an inconvenient day. At the Chicago History Museum, Lesley Martin graciously answered urgent research queries. At UWM, Ahmed Kraima, Tyler Smith, Linda Kopecky, and the interlibrary loan staff all provided excellent day-to-day research support. I would also like to thank Ewa Barczyk for her model direction of the UWM Libraries.

I am especially grateful to the great archivist Archie Motley, who thoroughly transformed the research holdings of the Chicago History Museum in the second half of the twentieth century. I mostly knew Archie at the Chicago History Museum, where he collected and organized so many of their collections and guided researchers to sources we did not know we needed. For several years Archie and I were neighbors in Evanston. I sometimes saw him in the street, dodging between parked cars, picking up garbage. Archie's great gift was to recognize treasure in other people's trash. In the process, he fundamentally changed what researchers can find out about Chicago history.

I literally would not know how block clubs worked to clear their neighborhoods of garbage—or what else they did—if librarians and archivists had not known what to save and how to make it available for researchers. As a small measure of thanks, I dedicate this book to all the archivists and librarians who make historical work possible, and to the memory of Archie Motley.

Abbreviations

AFSC: American Friends Service Committee
ANC: Austin Newspapers Collection
ACC: Austin Community Collection
CANS: Chicago Alliance for Neighborhood Safety
CAPS: Chicago Alternative Policing Strategy
CETA: Comprehensive Employment and Training Act
CHA: Chicago Housing Authority
CHM: Chicago History Museum
CID: Common Interest Development
CPD: Chicago Police Department
CREB: Chicago Real Estate Board
DAV: Disabled American Veterans
EPIC: Every Person Is Concerned
GLCC: Greater Lawndale Conservation Commission
GPWCC: Garfield Park West Community Council
HPKCC: Hyde Park–Kenwood Community Conference
IDOT: Illinois Department of Transportation
IAF: Industrial Areas Foundation
LCNA: Lincoln Central Neighborhood Association
MBSUO: Mohawk-Brighton Social Unit Organization:
NAACP: National Association for the Advancement of Colored People
NACWC: National Association of Colored Women's Clubs
NCO: Northwest Community Organization
NWSCC: Near West Side Community Committee
OBA: Organization for a Better Austin
OCD: Office of Civilian Defense
PHDCN: Project on Human Development in Chicago Neighborhoods
PMN: Park Manor Neighbors

S C C : Southwest Community Congress
S E C C : South East Chicago Commission
S W A B C : Southwest Associated Block Clubs
T O P S : The Organization of Palmer Square
T W O : The Woodlawn Organization
U C C : Uptown Chicago Commission
U I C : University of Illinois at Chicago
U P G : United Property Group
W C M C : Welfare Council of Metropolitan Chicago
W F C W : Winona Foster Carmen Winnemac Block Club

Introduction

In October 1985, the leaders of the 15th Place Block Club urged Chicago Mayor Harold Washington "to expand the city garden program into a much greater source of food and jobs." Active for decades, this West Side group had begun its effort to green the block with planting grass in 1978, and expanded it to vegetable gardening. While her neighbors enjoyed the block's visual transformation, club secretary Faith Rich wanted to introduce her neighbors to organic gardening. Rich and other residents of the block learned many lessons as they turned their block's vacant lots into urban gardens that produced asparagus, collard greens, peanuts, poke salad, snow peas, squash, sweet potatoes, tomatoes, and other vegetables.[1]

In addition to producing foodstuffs for local consumption, the gardens of the 15th Place Block Club provided a wealth of less tangible crops. Local gardens gave southern migrants a chance to exercise their agricultural skills, connected children with community elders, provided both money and healthy food for the block's impoverished residents, and beautified the neighborhood. In the course of nurturing their gardens, club members conducted property title research in city records, enticed a tavern owner as well as the Illinois Department of Transportation to contribute fencing to keep out vegetable thieves, consulted with the city's rodent control office about exterminating the rats that ran rampant in local alleys, and asked the University of Illinois Cooperative Extension Program which vegetables were safe to plant in cadmium-polluted soil. The garden project also moderated the suspicion some of Rich's neighbors felt toward her as one of the neighborhood's few white residents. Although local gardening required a great deal of organization and collective effort, this project was only one of many that members of the block club

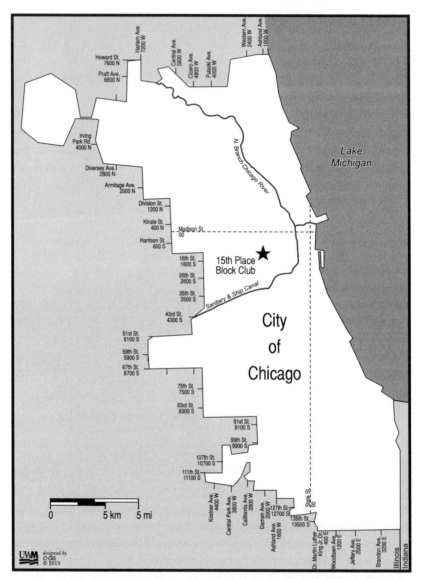

FIGURE 1. Chicago's streets are laid out on a grid. In the early twentieth century, the numbering and naming system was rationalized, with Madison and State Streets serving as the baselines. Addresses "North" appear above the Madison Street line; addresses "South" appear below. Addresses "West" are to the left of the State Street line; addresses "East" are to the right. The street numbers grow higher as one moves farther from a baseline. Approximate locations for specific block clubs can be plotted using the street coordinates that appear around the city boundaries. Map by Donna G. Genzmer, Cartography and GIS Center, University of Wisconsin–Milwaukee.

conducted as part of their effort "to weave together on a limited social level all those individuals of all ages who live within the block."[2]

Chicago's unusually long-lived 15th Place Block Club was also unusual in the scope of its activities. Its programs ran the gamut from beautification projects, such as gardening, to protesting an Illinois nuclear reactor, to helping children get library cards. But it was by no means alone in its work. Chicagoans have been running block clubs for a century. Newspapers, websites, and scholars have also documented the activities of block clubs in other American cities, including Akron, Buffalo, Cincinnati, Cleveland, Detroit, Kansas City, Los Angeles, Milwaukee, Minneapolis, Nashville, New York City, Philadelphia, Pittsburgh, St. Louis, and St. Paul, as well as suburban New Jersey.[3] This book describes the broad range of block clubs' purposes, organizational strategies, and activities in Chicago, where they have flourished. Organized into block clubs, Chicago neighbors cooperatively attempted to make up for the neglect by property owners and municipal government of their shared environment. Despite the ubiquity of block clubs in Chicago, few historians have written about them.

Overview

Block clubs address problems that members see afflicting their immediate surroundings. Neighbors form small-scale organizations devoted to community building and local improvement. Block clubs' essential characteristics are that they are narrow in geographic scope, voluntary in their membership, and composed almost exclusively of immediate neighbors. Membership rosters variously include resident property owners, tenants, landlords, and small business owners. In Chicago, block clubs have been particularly common and visible among African Americans. The Chicago Urban League, devoted to helping black southern migrants acclimate to the city, introduced the first formal block clubs to Chicago in the late 1910s. When its finances allowed, the League supported them over the next several decades. After World War II, the League ran an active, well publicized campaign to cultivate block clubs throughout black sections of Chicago. The prominence of League efforts fed a popular belief that the block club was a particularly African American cultural form. But in multiethnic postwar Chicago, whites, Latinos, and Asian Americans also joined block clubs.

Perhaps inspired by the Chicago Urban League's success, the federal government invigorated Chicago's emergent block club tradition during World War II. Led by Mayor Edward J. Kelly, the Chicago Metropolitan Office of Civilian Defense divided the entire city and the surrounding region into official block clubs. Because of the unusually high population mobility in wartime, participation in federally sponsored, patriotically driven block clubs was uneven. But the designation of twenty thousand Chicago-area block clubs almost certainly marks the historical high point of community organization in the city's history.[4] A relentless barrage of war-related propaganda in neighborhood newspapers familiarized white residents with the idea of block clubs in a way that the Chicago Urban League's laborious but focused organizing campaign could not. When the war ended, the League revived its block club program, making their cultivation part of its "Five Year Plan."[5]

In 1950, the newly formed Hyde Park–Kenwood Community Conference (HPKCC) began organizing its own block clubs. The spark plug for the HPKCC's activity was Herbert Thelen, a University of Chicago professor whose research focused on organizational dynamics.[6] Under Thelen's guidance (and reinforced by his subsequent scholarly evaluations), the HPKCC organized block clubs across its territory. This work served the HPKCC's twin goals of building community and supporting the University of Chicago's plans for neighborhood conservation and urban renewal. In the 1950s, as they explained their success in capturing urban renewal funds, HPKCC speakers spread the gospel of block clubs. Other local urban renewal groups in Chicago followed the HPKCC's model without crediting the origins of block clubs among African Americans. The Chicago Urban League somewhat defensively asserted its primacy in the history of block club organizing. Its 1951 annual report reminded readers:

> The soundness of the block unit idea and method of organization—an Urban League invention—was pointed up many times in 1951. Our community organization staff reports, "We have been impressed and gratified by the number of calls from our block club members who have moved into other areas requesting us to come out and help them organize Urban League–type block clubs in new neighborhoods." The Hyde-Park Community Conference [sic] and other groups are now seeking to organize their areas block by block.[7]

Block clubs appeared most commonly where residents felt problems needed more attention than their neighbors or the city government offered on their own. Chicagoans saw less need to organize where all the buildings were in good condition, the yards were well kept, flowers bloomed, trash was routinely collected, and no nuisances disrupted residents' daily activities. Neighbors might gather for an annual block club party—another Chicago institution closely related to the block club—without sponsoring a formal organization.[8] But on blocks where focused attention could make a difference, Chicagoans did organize, join, and sustain block clubs. For this reason, residents of working- and middle-class areas might participate in block clubs more frequently than the wealthy. Private funds and political clout obviated the need for collective, voluntary improvement efforts.

As organizations of neighbors devoted to solving local problems, block clubs resemble the homeowners' associations that govern "common interest developments" (CIDs) such as suburban subdivisions or city condominiums. Evan McKenzie explains that as many as 20 percent of Americans now live in developments that control property with such homeowners' associations. The crucial difference between block clubs and homeowners' associations is that one is voluntary and the other mandatory. Homeowners' associations "run with the land"; when people buy property in a CID, they must join the homeowners' association and are legally bound by its restrictions. McKenzie explains that it is not only local government regulations, such as building codes, that deny homeowners complete control over their property. Homeowners' associations are designed to be very difficult to alter, even with the democratic will of property owners. Such associations effectively become quasi-official governments that participants cannot contest except by selling their property and moving away.[9]

Block clubs, by contrast, are entirely voluntary. Participants have no legal way to enforce their decisions. Instead, block clubs depend on members' persuasive powers. Notably, homeowners' associations are normally created by a development's original builder to assure prospective purchasers that their investment will retain its value; block clubs come into being on living streetscapes, and are founded by residents who perceive problems that are worth their time and effort to resolve. Because they are voluntary, self-defining organizations, block clubs can have more inclusive memberships than homeowners' associations, sometimes welcoming renters and children into their ranks. Block clubs' purposes are also broader, stretching beyond physical maintenance into social regulation and community building.

Block clubs are by no means the only form of locally based community organization in Chicago. The city has been a breeding ground for formally organized, geographically based associations. In the first half of the twentieth century, both settlement houses and improvement associations brought Chicagoans together with their neighbors in order to create local improvement. Saul Alinsky, regarded as the father of community organizing in the United States, found his hometown such a receptive environment that he based his Industrial Areas Foundation in Chicago. Alinsky's local influence inspired a legion of community organizations and professional community organizers in Chicago, among them a young Barack Obama.[10] Block clubs resembled these larger organizations in their fundamental purpose of uniting neighbors to improve the local environment. Often the creations of larger organizations, their scale was inevitably smaller, their staffing always volunteer, and their goals less prone to controversy.

Block clubs' programs varied from club to club, from neighborhood to neighborhood, and over time. But they consistently reflected members' sensibilities about what needed fixing. Most commonly, block clubs focused on the physical environment. Members worked to beautify their own properties, enhance public spaces, and cajole neighbors into joining the effort. Many block clubs also nurtured a sense of community among neighbors. Their typical concerns and activities were specific to their historical context. In the years after World War II, for example, beautification campaigns attracted broad block club participation in Chicago. At the turn of the twenty-first century, when the Chicago Police Department (CPD) became a major organizer, many block clubs focused on crime prevention.

Block clubs were not all the same, although they had common characteristics. They served different constituencies, had different goals, and pursued different programs. No single block club—not even the busy 15th Place Block Club—engaged in all the activities described in this book. I could qualify every generalization about block clubs with a word like "some," "sometimes," "often," "frequently," "usually," or "many." To avoid larding every page with conditional phrases, I have largely omitted them. Readers should bear in mind that flexibility is a feature of block clubs, not a bug.

The block club is a form without an intrinsic agenda. Because Chicagoans of different races, ethnicities, neighborhood contexts, and class backgrounds organized into geographically distinct groups, their clubs reflected a wide range of aspirations. Some block clubs' goals conflicted with others' purposes. The Chicago Urban League's block club program aimed to demonstrate that African Americans made excellent neighbors. By contrast, the South Side block clubs organized by Father Francis X. Lawlor in the late 1960s and early 1970s explicitly tried to prevent racial integration. Some block clubs hoped to improve troubled relations between resident property owners and tenants, while others sought to leverage the power of tenant numbers to compel absentee landlords to fix their buildings. Still others assumed that only property owners had a vested interest in improvements, and excluded renters from membership altogether.

Block clubs addressed symptoms of urban problems. Members sometimes understood the systemic sources of urban ills, and the resulting problems loomed large in their daily lives. But because they were small, voluntary, and resource-poor, block clubs were not well positioned to address root causes. Their work is a classic example of NIMBYism—"not in my back yard" (or, since many block clubs were organized along facing blocks, "not in my front yard"). Block clubs tried to blunt the effects of broader urban problems on their street. Picking up garbage and disposing of it properly could reduce the numbers of rats born into a particular neighborhood. But a local crimewatch might only divert criminals elsewhere. Block clubs tackled projects that members could reasonably hope to accomplish. They rarely took on problems beyond members' own expertise and energies. Although they routinely agitated for better provision of existing municipal services, they left the unwieldy burden of solving structural issues such as poverty and crime to government, universities, and charities.

Block clubs had two main problem-solving strategies. Most frequently, they defined goals that participants could accomplish on their own. Block clubs beautified untidy parkways and entertained boisterous children with members' ingenuity and resources. Sometimes, however, the clubs' improvement goals overlapped with government responsibilities—often tasks that authorities neglected. Fixing sidewalks, removing garbage, arresting criminals, and clearing blight fell under the purview of government. Block clubs whose projects intersected with public responsibilities sought to attract municipal support. They frequently used local projects to demonstrate that their street deserved extra attention from public programs.

Women conducted much of the day-to-day work of block clubs. The prominence of women in block club work echoed their importance in American crusades for social reform that originated in domestic issues. Often, women's roles resulted from the division in family labor between husbands and wives: in some neighborhoods, adult men earned money to support the family's financial needs, while women worked to raise children and tend the home. In such neighborhoods, the scheduling of events reflected the assumption that block clubs were women's work. The clubs often held meetings on weekdays while children could be expected to be in school and men at work, or after children went to bed. But in neighborhoods where women routinely held down jobs as well as domestic responsibilities, they also often also ran the block clubs. In addition, women's leadership of block clubs stemmed from the significant work of black women in Chicago community institutions. As historian Anne Meis Knupfer points out, "Black women's activism was prodigious." When men were active in block clubs, however, their effort was frequently marked by their holding of the organization's formal offices.[11]

It is tempting to ascribe block club participation to property owners' interest in protecting their financial investment. Protection of property values certainly explains some block club activities. Homeowners in North America have a long history of improving their own properties with an eye toward both present enjoyment and future resale value. They have tinkered with the interiors and exteriors of their homes, installing utilities, upgrading equipment, changing room configurations, cleaning, fencing, seeding, gardening, and decorating. Over the course of the nineteenth and twentieth centuries, urbanites also used a variety of policy tools to sort American cities into districts based on class and function. Lot size standards, zoning, utilities, and service provision combined to build a complexly differentiated urban environment. They separated rich from working-class areas, wealthy residential districts from polluting factories, businesses from homes, and red-light districts from respectable zones.[12] Property owners counted on the legal enforcement of such provisions to increase the value of their land. In the twentieth century, residential racial segregation reinforced the geographic differentiation of property values, a phenomenon that historian Elaine Lewinnek calls the "mortgages of whiteness." "Location, location, location" became the mantra of the real estate industry.[13]

Block clubs, attentive to their immediate surroundings, were well suited to defending the worth of their own small swaths of the city. Through block clubs, property-owning neighbors could encourage one another to make improvements that maintained their mutually dependent property values. Such collective fiscal protectionism was especially important for urbanites who could not relocate at will. Well-off white Chicagoans could isolate themselves by moving to outlying districts and clustering into wealthy enclaves. Working-class white and African American urbanites, however, enjoyed fewer housing choices and benefited from living close to a range of job opportunities. Property ownership was a crucial investment for which working-class Chicagoans were willing to sacrifice all manner of personal comfort.[14] The virulent exclusion of tenants from membership underscores how some block clubs endeavored to shore up property values.

The active participation of tenants in other block clubs, however, suggests that property values cannot fully explain local activism. On some streets, renters joined property owners as equals in running the block club. In other neighborhoods, there were few property owners to participate in block clubs. In some areas, renters like Faith Rich and her neighbors on West 15th Place were the leading block club members. It is conceivable that tenants participated in block clubs out of a sense of solidarity with their landlords, but other reasons are more plausible.[15]

What else explains Chicagoans' propensity to join block clubs? First, participants saw block clubs as a low-cost way to improve their day-to-day quality of life. Sociologists John Logan and Harvey Molotch argued that each parcel of urban land has two functions: its "use value" and its "exchange value."

These values sometimes run together and sometimes conflict. Logan and Molotch explained that "the neighborhood is the meeting place of the two forces, where each resident faces the challenge of making a life on a real estate commodity."[16] Members of the 15th Place Block Club gained no long-term financial benefits from turning vacant lots into vegetable gardens. But they enjoyed the aesthetic, social, and health benefits such improvements afforded, as well as some short-term savings of food costs. Block club anticrime activities made residents—whether owners or renters—feel safer in and around their homes. Property owners may have considered such programs investments in their own property values, but renters and homeowners alike enjoyed the immediate improvements.

A second explanation for participation rests in the politics of respectability. Historian Evelyn Brooks Higginbotham's *Righteous Discontent* demonstrated how southern African American Baptist women deployed education, upright demeanor, and self-sacrifice to benefit the black community and impress their own merits upon white observers. Victoria Wolcott argues that Detroit reformers extended the politics of respectability from individual personal appearance to the cleanliness of neighborhoods.[17] The Chicago Urban League, cradle of the city's block club movement, was steeped in the politics of respectability. Chicagoans' participation in block clubs tangled together their concerns for property values, respectability, and quality of life.

Organization

This book traces how Chicagoans put these related concerns into action through block clubs. Readers might expect a work of history to proceed chronologically, following one block club across a century. But few Chicago block clubs lasted long enough to evolve over time. Because this history draws on fragmentary evidence, the book is organized thematically. Each chapter, however, offers a roughly chronological narrative. I begin with an overview of block clubs' purposes and then discuss the effort required to organize and sustain them. The last four chapters explore how block clubs sought to regulate their physical and social environments.

Following this introduction, chapter 1, "Protect," asks why Chicagoans were receptive to block clubs. The provision of infrastructure in the nineteenth century primed the city for the arrival of the block club approach from elsewhere in the United States. The Chicago Urban League transplanted block clubs into Chicago's friendly soil, hoping to demonstrate African Americans' fitness for urban life. Both the federal war effort and the HPKCC popularized block clubs at midcentury, though with very different goals. Over subsequent decades, Chicagoans discovered that the block club was a malleable form. Despite their origins in the Urban League, antiblack groups used block clubs to fend off integration in the postwar years. In the twenty-first century, the CPD incorporated block clubs into its community policing program. Many block clubs resulted from such top-down organizing efforts, which connected them larger networks of similar groups.

Chapter 2, "Organize," describes how Chicagoans built block clubs. Some such clubs were truly indigenous efforts, formed spontaneously by residents who essentially reinvented the wheel. Many more, however, were laboriously nurtured by umbrella community organizations cultivating local leadership and popular support. The Chicago Urban League occupied the labor-intensive end of the spectrum, while other groups simply declared the existence of block clubs and then activated neighbors, who showed up for a meeting. The founders of block clubs made key decisions about their structure, including membership qualifications, territory, names, dues, and meeting schedules. The clubs were difficult to maintain; they were always low-budget, volunteer-driven organizations. Because of the energy and time required to sustain them, most block clubs were short-lived.

Chapter 3, "Connect," is the first of four chapters that describe block club activities. Many of the clubs tried to create a local sense of community. Events like block parties and other seasonal celebrations were purely social. Block clubs also built group cohesion by excluding undesirables. The umbrella organizations that nurtured the clubs worked to connect participating groups with each other. For their part, block clubs paid special attention to drawing young people into their programs.

Most block club activities centered on the physical environment, efforts explored in chapters 4 and 5. "Beautify," chapter 4, focuses on how block clubs used their own resources to generate local improvement. Block clubs encouraged neighbors to spruce up their own properties and worked collectively to beautify neglected spaces like parkways and streets. Competition was one of the most common strategies for spurring simultaneous participation. Block clubs also converted vacant lots into gardens and "tot lots" for small children.

Private efforts alone could not solve all local problems. Chapter 5, "Cleanse," takes up block clubs' efforts to win government assistance. In theory, public services were available to all, but in practice their implementation varied wildly. When block clubs cleaned up loose garbage from alleys, their efforts availed little unless sanitation crews hauled refuse away. Building code enforcement and urban renewal funds flowed primarily to neighborhoods with active residents who lobbied for municipal attention. Block clubs and their umbrella organizations pushed Chicago's government to direct limited resources to their turf.

Physical improvement efforts could change a block's aesthetic characteristics. But block clubs did not count on an improved landscape alone to transform the local social environment. Chapter 6, "Regulate," explores block clubs' efforts to control their neighbors' behavior. By posting regulations on signs and in newsletters, block clubs in African-American areas of Chicago continued a venerable tradition of instructing residents and visitors on acceptable demeanor. Members sought to drive away legal nuisances such as taverns. Less commonly, block clubs also attempted to reduce criminal and gang activities, such as drug dealing, that threatened residents' safety. Until the CPD launched a community policing program in the 1990s, however, such efforts gained little traction. In the twenty-first century, however, the CPD revitalized Chicago's century-old tradition of block clubs by becoming one of the largest organizers in the city's history.

When block club members worked together on common goals, they were operating from a special relationship; they were acting as *neighbors*. Neighbors may be strangers, acquaintances, friends, or enemies. People who live near each other in cities are not automatically associated. Yet their daily proximity means that neighbors often know one another by sight, or by the traces they leave on the streetscape. Members of Chicago's block clubs used their relationships as neighbors to undertake goals together that were too daunting to try alone. But in doing so, they also frequently found themselves at odds with other neighbors over the future of their shared streets. In the process, they confronted important limits to their collective capacity.

Neighboring is a distinctive human relationship. This book's conclusion argues that neighboring offers promise as a conceptual tool for understanding how urbanites relate to one another and mutually affect the fate of the cities they inhabit. Scholars have overlooked neighboring's analytical power, understanding it simply as an aspect of community—a concept that has undergirded urban studies for more than a century. Instead, I suggest, neighboring should be recognized as a fundamentally important relationship, alongside analyses that foreground family, employment, religion, and friendship. This book maps one path to understanding how neighbors shaped the city.

Researching Block Clubs

Systematically researching block clubs presents several obstacles. Block clubs are primarily oriented to action. Most generate little documentation of their efforts. Fewer still spend energy reflecting on their own histories, producing the celebratory accounts used to study urban community institutions such as churches and fraternal organizations. The most common kinds of surviving evidence associated with block clubs are organizational records, like meeting minutes and newsletters, and ephemera such as flyers announcing cleanup afternoons and block parties. Block clubs also sometimes publicized their activities in local newspapers and, in the twenty-first century, on websites and blogs.

Historians must be able to access such documents to conduct research. Happily, archives and libraries have preserved many materials from block clubs. But because the clubs have not yet been studied much, their records can be hard to identify. Archivists rarely use "block club" as a keyword in finding aids, making them difficult to zero in on even in rich, well-described collections. Block clubs are often lumped together under the more general term "neighborhood associations," which covers a broad range of local social and improvement activities. In Chicago, which has a strong geographic orientation, archival records are often arranged by neighborhood. Thus, a scholar in search of block club records must comb through dozens of distinct archival collections and drill deeply to find relevant materials. Appendix 1 further discusses strategies for discovering archival records about block clubs.

The nature of the preservation process creates an additional analytic difficulty for the researcher surveying archival evidence about block clubs. Block clubs were sometimes top-down, sometimes bottom-up groups. Some came into being because of the efforts of larger, professionally staffed organizations. The Chicago Urban League, for example, cultivated block clubs throughout its first four decades. Thus, the League's records, which are well organized, cataloged, and preserved in the Richard J. Daley Library of the University of Illinois at Chicago, provide excellent access to information about its block club program. Other block clubs remained fiercely independent of the larger organizations that are more likely to have their records archived. Their work is, therefore, harder to uncover. It is impossible to estimate with confidence how many unaffiliated block clubs existed in Chicago's history, precisely because their records were unlikely to end up in archives. The uneven preservation of block club records can lead to what social scientists call "survivor bias" in the evidence base. Thus, the analysis of block clubs may inadvertently overemphasize the importance of those that were connected to larger organizations, while understating the significance of autonomous groups.

The exceptional case is the 15th Place Block Club, an independent group. Its records offer a wealth of detail, cover many years, and reveal a broad variety of activities. The records are available because of one member, Faith Rich, who understood the importance of collecting and preserving them. Rich herself was as remarkable as the club she joined. She was a leftist white woman who earned a PhD in classics from Bryn Mawr College in the 1930s. In the 1950s, she and her husband, Ted Rich, deliberately moved into North Lawndale as it was transitioning from white to black. Rich's education and personal energies meant that the activities of the club she belonged to were exceptionally well documented. After Rich died, her widower toted grocery bags full of her papers on Chicago's elevated train to the Chicago Public Library, which accepted and eventually processed her archive.[18]

The extraordinary character of Faith Rich's papers and the records of the 15th Place Block Club raise the question of how representative they are. How many clubs were active and influenced their immediate environs without creating records at all, much less having them preserved for future study? How many other long-standing, active, independent block clubs simply do not show up in archives available to historical researchers? How many people who created and lovingly preserved their group's records lacked the cultural capital or the institutional trust to get them archived? Block clubs' action orientation, professional archival preservation practices, and time constraints on the research process may all combine to skew analysis toward block clubs associated with larger organizations such as the Chicago Urban League. The richly detailed and fascinating records of a group like the 15th Place Block Club are clearly unique, and illuminate the scope of what block clubs are capable of. But researchers must take care not to interpret their activities as essentially representative of other, less vibrant block groups.

Because of their inward focus, their small scale, and the problems of researching them systematically, block clubs have largely escaped scholarly attention. Block clubs are a form of neighborhood association, a subset of community-based organizations, about which more is known. Historical studies of local activism are attracted to the magnet of Saul Alinsky, the abrasive father of community organizing, and his successors. Organizers in the Alinsky tradition focus on "develop[ing] multi-issue organizations in order to build power." Tiny block clubs, oriented to local improvement, receive little attention or are dismissed outright as insignificant.[19] Studies of Chicago have largely failed to dwell on the presence of block clubs. For example, St. Clair Drake's 1940 book *Churches and Voluntary Associations in the Chicago Negro Community* was exquisitely attuned to the variations of black associational life in Chicago up to the Great Depression. Drake omitted block clubs entirely, even though he carefully documented the existence of thousands of social clubs among the city's estimated 250,000 African Americans.[20]

Contemporary urban scholars do know about the existence of block clubs,

and mention them at least in passing. Often, however, authors and their publishers have not considered such clubs sufficiently important to draw systematic attention to them. My personal library includes many books in which
I have scrawled emendations in the "B" section of the index, listing pages
where the author has referenced one block club or another. Only a few master's theses, dissertations, and published books and articles have explored
block clubs in any depth.[21] The urban sociologists Mary Pattillo and Sudhir
Venkatesh offered the most detailed observations about block clubs in their
treatments of black Chicago communities, emphasizing how local leaders
used them to ameliorate troubling conditions and bind neighbors together.[22]
Other social scientists have also explored social and psychological aspects of
block associations.[23]

Very few professional historians have written extensively about American
block clubs. They all examine local Urban League affiliates, which pioneered
the form. In an article and a book chapter, Sylvia Hood Washington claims
that the Chicago Urban League's block club program exhibited conservation-
ist and environmentalist sensibilities previously unrecognized among African Americans. Immersed in the literature about African Americans' social
reform efforts of the first half of the twentieth century, Priscilla Dowden-
White argues that scholars should not dismiss block organizing and social
welfare efforts in St. Louis as less politically important than efforts to confront
segregation in employment and housing. "No one strategy" for improving the
condition and civil rights of African Americans, she argues, "worked in isolation from another strategy." Touré F. Reed and Jeffrey Helgeson both examine
Urban League block club programs alongside the League's more often studied
industrial employment programs. Like Dowden-White, Reed and Helgeson
emphasize the pragmatism of block clubs as part of the continuum of the long
black freedom struggle.[24]

The evidence undergirding this book draws primarily from block clubs
on streets of private housing. As other scholars have noted, public housing
residents in Chicago and elsewhere also actively tried to shape their living
conditions by participating in official and unofficial tenant groups. Organizing in public housing reflected two important relationships: residents' common status as tenants of the public housing authority and their proximity to
each other as neighbors. Some organizations encompassed all residents of a
particular complex of the Chicago Housing Authority's (CHA) properties,
while others, such as "floor clubs," more closely paralleled private housing's
block clubs.[25] The women religious of Marillac House conducted community
organizing in nearby West Side neighborhoods, work that included encouraging floor clubs in the newly constructed Rockwell Gardens.[26]

In academic terms, then, block clubs amount to what David Horton Smith has called the "dark matter of the non-profit world."[27] They are hard to see, but their effects can be observed. They leave traces on the urban environment, but we do not know much about how they work. This book is an effort to chart the history and significance of Chicago's block clubs for the first time.

Block clubs' activities raise two broader questions about life in modern American cities. How have city residents related to government? How have neighbors managed each other's space?

First, the history of block clubs reveals their pragmatic relations with municipal government. Since the 1930s, the Democratic Party machine has dominated Chicago's formal politics. The machine routinely exchanged city services and government jobs for votes. Its influence peaked with the administration of Mayor Richard J. Daley (1955–76). Its low point came with the mayoralty of Harold Washington (1983–87), whose efforts to connect city government with the neighborhoods were stymied by the "Council Wars," systematic opposition from an aldermanic majority. Daley's other late-twentieth-century successors, including his son, Richard M. Daley, continuously reconfigured the party coalition to keep up with Chicago's changing demographics.[28] Throughout the twentieth century, block clubs sought to extract city services from the government without being co-opted by the machine.

The Chicago Urban League set an early tone for block clubs' relationship with the political system, insisting that its own affiliate groups remain entirely nonpartisan. Its strict abstention from formal politics derived from fear that even a whiff of radicalism could alienate the wealthy white philanthropists who underwrote its operations. Yet block clubs' major activities were political in a fundamental sense, in that they were concerned with the state of the *polis*, the city. Many of their aspirations—for cleaner streets and local amenities—brought them to City Hall's doorstep. How could block clubs win services without becoming subservient to the Democratic machine, which controlled the perquisites of city services through its aldermen, ward committeemen, and precinct captains?

For most of the twentieth century, block clubs angled to attract public resources. They did not try to influence the larger shape of city policy or the outcome of elections. They did not try to transform the underlying political order. They rarely suggested new policies or programs. I have uncovered no evidence, or even hints, that they promised to turn out Democratic voters in exchange for political benefits. Block clubs limited their formal political involvement to getting the city to fulfill its acknowledged, existing obligations. They represented themselves simply as citizen groups petitioning for the services to which they were entitled. In this sense, block clubs were pragmatic, collective extensions of individual citizens' efforts to draw on municipal resources. They manifested what historian Jeffrey Helgeson calls the "politics of home," which he describes as "the diverse efforts of black women to engage with the institutions of the city in order to improve the quality of life in their local communities."[29]

Block clubs presented carefully constrained expectations. They were unsuited in scale and character to promote systemic change. No less a light than Jane Jacobs commented on the limited utility of block clubs in her masterwork *Death and Life of Great American Cities*. Jacobs noted that city dwellers formed key relationships in "street neighborhoods and . . . among people who do something else in common and belong to organizations with one another." She listed "block improvement associations" in her lengthy enumeration of such groups (which concluded with the phrase "ad infinitum," implying there was no end to urbanites' creativity). Small organizations proliferated and were crucial to the overall process of creating change in the city. But they were by themselves insufficient to achieve important policy and governance goals. In Jacobs's analysis, the littlest organization that could make substantive change was a "district," which had "to be big and powerful enough to fight city hall. Nothing less is to any purpose."[30]

Although Jacobs was writing about New York City, she might have been commenting on Chicago's block clubs. Block clubs walked a delicate line. In Chicago, only larger community organizations embraced the quixotic quest of challenging City Hall. Block clubs were sometimes constituent members of such reform-oriented community organizations, but they were too small to take on such activity alone. Furthermore, engaging in formal politics could disrupt tenuous relationships among neighbors and could threaten a group's very existence.

Many block club programs were designed to demonstrate that members' turf merited municipal attention. Block clubs' self-improvement efforts showed that they were willing and eager to put sweat equity into their surroundings. They did not seek handouts or ask the city to deliver anything they did not deserve. In a context of limited city budgets and targeted programs, the block clubs' role was to show that public funding and equipment would not be wasted on their streets. They invited government to invest in their blocks because residents had already invested in them.

Block clubs' traditional distance from elected officials dwindled in the twenty-first century. Although it was influenced by the Chicago Urban League's model of block club organization, the HPKCC's work heralded an alternative relationship with electoral politics. As early as the 1950s, it built a working relationship for its block clubs with neighborhood alderman Leon Despres. Elsewhere in the city, however, block clubs' appeals to their aldermen for assistance or meetings often went ignored. In the early twenty-first century, a few Chicago aldermen began reaching out to their constituents through block clubs. The CPD's organizing program under its community policing strategy signaled a new phase in the relationship between city government and block clubs.

A second major theme of this book is how urban dwellers dealt with their immediate neighbors' spaces. Historians have explained much about large-scale transformations in American cities since the eighteenth century. Innovations in transportation enabled cities to spread out. As cities attracted large populations and new productive functions, they also accumulated lots of waste. Sidewalks, paved roads, electrical infrastructure, and sewer and water systems ameliorated much of the basic filth. Such improvements were unequally distributed, however, with poor people consistently confined to districts that received worse services. Demographic shifts facilitated by annexation and suburbanization insulated wealthier populations from the sectors of the city that were never fully cleaned up. Urban historians have devoted significant attenion to understanding how municipal and federal governments changed cities' physical environments. Systems for regulating zoning, buildings, and sanitation and programs such as conservation, urban renewal, and historic preservation contributed to an unevenly but definitely transformed twentieth-century urban landscape.[31]

For all that we know about macrolevel changes in American cities, we know much less about microlevel variations within neighborhoods. How did ordinary residents, on their own and in small collectivities, manage their environs? By looking closely at the block clubs' activities, we can learn both what urbanites cared about and how they thought microprojects could help. In the course of their daily activities, city dwellers come into repeated contact with their neighbors' properties. They often develop firm opinions about how their neighbors should manage the exteriors—and sometimes the interiors—of their homes.[32] While they were not suited for causing fundamental transformations in the urban environment, block clubs could create modest changes that affected the quality of life precisely where it mattered most to participants.

Urban residents who want public improvement face a conundrum: how to manage areas over which they have no authority. Land owners may change their own property—enhance it or let it deteriorate—within the limits of municipal code enforcement. Their neighbors may not enter or change it without express permission. Yet the conditions of nearby public and private properties affect urbanites' health, safety, and daily pleasure. As they escape hot, crowded homes, walk to their cars or to public transportation, and spend leisure time outside, residents encounter spaces they cannot control. Looking at block clubs—whose activities have targeted proximate troubles—provides a sustained opportunity to learn about how urbanites have addressed the problem of managing neighboring places. Block clubs have had many discussions about what problems have bothered their members, and have made choices about which of those problems to address. Their conversations reveal what aspects of urbanites' surroundings have mattered to their daily lives.

Individual action against recurrent problems such as litter and gang violence might have appeared fruitless. But working with neighbors promised solutions to bothersome issues. Neighborly cooperation could make big problems manageable, draw official attention to issues beyond local remediation, and inspire others to take care of their own properties. A Chicago Urban League staff organizer encouraged a block club president to conduct conspicuous efforts, explaining, "I know that you have many people living on your block who just have not had the time or energy to take on another activity. But when they find that there is another who is willing to help do this big job of getting neighbors interested in keeping the block beautiful they will cooperate 100 per cent."[33] The prospect of collectively leveraging local improvements has been enough to push many Chicago residents into joining block clubs. Studying their successes and failures provides a historical window into how city residents have managed their surroundings.

The history of Chicago block clubs across a century reveals the persistent efforts of residents to control their environment. Improving blocks cooperatively has bypassed the limits of individual action without depending on the city government to initiate change. The block club was an intermediate, collective, voluntary tool to address those problems that residents identified as key to their quality of life. Although most block clubs have had at their core the relatively benign purpose of beautifying the physical environment, some groups have leaned more toward social control. Block clubs were rarely effective at achieving all their goals, but they could accomplish more than residents working alone. Despite their shortcomings, block clubs have the capacity to address immediate problems and connect neighbors without large outlays of capital, time, or political influence. This book explores their potential and explains the limits of how Chicago neighbors protect their surroundings with block clubs.

Protect

In March 1952, a staff member from the Chicago Urban League visited the 2200 block of West Maypole Avenue to check up on a block club she was trying to organize. Her notes reflect frustration. The block had great potential as "one of the best where we could have shown concrete results." In the past, its resident homeowners had demonstrated their ability to maintain their properties to high aesthetic standards. Newer, younger residents, however, showed less inclination to put their energies into their immediate surroundings. The League worker could not entice the older residents to put forth any more effort. She observed that the long-standing homeowners "resented the apathy of the young people and the new residents who were not concerned about beautifying." Her notes complained, "This, the worker does not really understand because some of the people the[r]e are those who are termed as the better type Negroes, who are in the higher economic bracket and it seems to her that, if for no other reason, that they have decided to remain in the block, they ought to organize and beautify." She concluded that prospects for organizing a successful block club were grim: "It seems to be an impossible task to get the two groups together."[1]

Implicit in the staff worker's brief notes were a range of assumptions that informed the League's program: block clubs should improve the physical environment; established, property-owning black Chicagoans should teach more recent southern migrants their standards for community upkeep; and the resulting beautiful blocks could be used as a public demonstration that African Americans were responsible urban residents who made good neighbors. In the middle of the twentieth century, Chicago's majority white population reflexively interpreted black settlement as signaling a block's inevitable decline.

Demonstrating that blacks did not automatically damage their neighbors' goodwill or property values was an important Chicago Urban League goal.[2] While the League's tactics—including fruitless trips, like the worker's visit to the 2200 block of West Maypole—were particularly-time consuming, the organizing of block clubs served the League's overall mission to acclimate the urban north and migrant African Americans to one another.

The League's program laid the foundation for the spread of block clubs across Chicago in the twentieth century. From the first, organizers and participants understood the protection of their immediate surroundings as a central purpose of block clubs. At a minimum, street cleanups and gardens elevated the character of the landscape. The anticipated consequences of physical improvement were numerous and sometimes spectacular. Improvement could signal local upkeep standards to residents and other interested observers such as potential neighbors, outside critics, gang members, and criminals. At various times, participants believed that communicating local vigilance demonstrated the high quality of the blocks' residents, encouraged good neighbors, fended off decay, protected property values, improved children, deterred crime, and warned away undesirable residents.

No single block club generated all of these expected benefits. As Chicagoans through the twentieth century adopted the Urban League's block club structure, members infused the clubs with meanings and goals consistent with their own specific concerns about contemporary urban life. The activities of block clubs reveal how Chicagoans' concerns shifted during the twentieth century.

At the same time, while block club members' collective actions suggested solidarity among participants, they also reflected tensions among neighbors. For example, the visit of the League's organizer to the 2200 block of West Maypole illuminated the class fractures among Chicago's African Americans. The League's organizing staff quietly struggled with block clubs dominated by property owners, who resisted participation by their home-renting neighbors. On the South Side, the Hyde Park–Kenwood Community Conference (HPKCC) spread the Chicago Urban League's model of block organization among its largely white constituency and to similar Chicago organizations that sought urban renewal. While HPKCC members refrained from the outright objections to residential integration that were common in Chicago's all-white neighborhoods, their block clubs largely embraced the goal of ridding Hyde Park of its deteriorating buildings—and, consequently, their often poor and black occupants. By the late 1950s, whites on Chicago's South and West Sides adopted the block club as means to control and protest the arrival of

black residents on their streets; whether the interlopers were renters or property owners did not matter to segregationist groups. In the 1970s, by contrast,
North Side block clubs consisting almost entirely of renters tried to remedy
the neglect of absentee property owners who were unresponsive to the requests of individual tenants. In the twenty-first century, the CPD organized
block clubs that used both social and environmental approaches to drive out
criminals. All of these differences among neighbors revolved around two central questions: Who had the right to occupy a block, and who had the responsibility for its maintenance? A shared interest in a particular block did not
imply consensus on the answers to these questions.

The cleanliness and social order of any given block depended on multiple parties: its various property owners, residents, visitors, local commercial and industrial enterprises, and urban service workers such as garbage
collectors and police. While some stakeholders fulfilled every responsibility
their positions implied, others did so imperfectly, or actively produced further disorder. Block clubs allowed members to push their neighbors and the
city government to live up to the formal and informal commitments that they
believed residence, property ownership, and governance entailed. They often
pressured government to fulfill its promises. For example, when they endorsed
neighborhood efforts to attract urban renewal funding, or petitioned for increased police patrols, they were attempting to extend the influence of government on their streets. At two key moments, government officials also used
block clubs to try to induce local improvement efforts from city residents. The
high point of block club participation in Chicago almost certainly occurred
during World War II in response to the federal government's organization of
a war-supporting club for every block in the region. Beginning in the 1990s,
the CPD's community policing program and a few aldermen encouraged
residents around the city to form block clubs to improve public safety and
beauty—two things which contemporary social science theory suggested were
interrelated.

Deficiencies in the urban landscape reflected shortcomings of both residents and the municipal government. Neither kept order perfectly. Block club
members stepped into the gap between the prerogatives of private owners and
the duty of municipal government to protect the urban environment. They
manifested organizers' recognition that neither individual efforts nor municipal action alone were sufficient to create a cityscape in which they wanted to
live. From the early twentieth century onward, many Chicagoans put their efforts into collective, voluntary action as an appropriate middle way to shape
their residential neighborhoods.

Antecedents

Proximity foisted common concerns on neighbors. In the nineteenth century, people who owned property in developing parts of Chicago formed the earliest antecedents of block clubs. Neighbors who shared adjacent street frontage created associations to build local infrastructure. Historian Robin L. Einhorn's *Property Rules* argues that up to 1865, Chicago's politics were characterized by a "segmented system." This form of municipal "privatism" was designed to prevent the use of taxes to redistribute wealth, even for ostensibly public purposes. Only "abutters," owners of adjacent properties, had the right to petition for the installation of specific local improvements such as sidewalks under this system. In return for the privilege of deciding whether they wanted an amenity, they were taxed for its cost. Even though in theory all Chicagoans enjoyed the public good of infrastructure, landowners benefited particularly from any resulting increase in their property values. Thus, it was reasoned, they should have to pay for its expense. This system resulted in an uneven distribution of such improvements across the city. As Einhorn observes, the relative wealth and local interests of property owners were "visible in macadam, plank, and mud and recorded in the high death rates in working-class neighborhoods."[3]

The formally segmented system ended with the Civil War, industrial pollution in the Chicago River, and the arrival of street railways. These events dramatically demonstrated that the public interest serves multiple constituencies. But remnants of this system survive in the twenty-first century in the use of special assessment taxes for local municipal improvements.[4] The circulation of petitions and "remonstrances" (counterpetitions) among neighboring property owners—who may well not live nearby—is not the same thing as a formal (or even informal) block club. Ann Durkin Keating points out, however, that the process of special assessment on a "block by block basis" made the street a natural unit for nineteenth-century improvement associations.[5] The segmented system established for Chicago the principle that adjacent property owners could act collectively for their common, sometimes narrow, local interests.

In the twentieth century, the circulation of racially restrictive covenants reinforced the idea that property interests depended on the neighbors. As African Americans migrated north in the years during and after World War I, white property owners built up a system of racial segregation to forestall black neighbors. In addition to fears about the social consequences of interracial contact, two related sets of concerns about property informed whites' prejudices. First, they asserted that the presence of nonservant African Americans as neighbors would depress the value of their real estate property when they tried to sell it. Second, they claimed that black Southerners would not maintain their homes in accordance with acceptable standards, thereby exacerbating their unwelcome effect on their neighbors' property. Although nineteenth-century black Chicagoans often lived intermingled among the city's white population, racially segregated neighborhood residential lines formed and hardened with the onset of the Great Migration around World War I. Violence directed against black "pioneers" who attempted to integrate white areas of the city sent a very clear message that African Americans should not venture beyond the established residential districts on the South and West Sides.[6] To reinforce the segregation of the housing market, the Chicago Real Estate Board encouraged the formation of all-white block organizations.[7] The pressure of a dramatically increasing black population in a restricted housing supply, however, meant that African Americans continued to search for new places to make homes.

Some white property owners eschewed violent tactics for keeping blacks from occupying nearby property. Instead, they relied instead on a pair of related legal mechanisms: racially restrictive deeds and covenants. A racially restrictive deed was language written into the legal document that described a particular property. It specified that no matter who owned the land, African Americans and other unwelcome neighbors were not permitted to occupy it—unless they were servants. A racially restrictive covenant, by contrast, was a binding agreement among a group of neighbors that they would sue anyone who permitted nonwhites, or other enumerated undesirables, to live in the area.[8] Creating a racially restrictive covenant required locating and communicating with the people who owned property in the covered area, whether they lived on the street or elsewhere. A covenant was not the same as a block club; it was a legal arrangement. Signatories did not hold regular meetings or spin off other events. Its purposes were limited, as when abutting neighbors agreed to invest their money in common improvements such as sidewalks. But the practice of creating restrictive covenants provided Chicagoans with the precedent of local, voluntary collective action rooted in proximity and property ownership.

In 1948, the US Supreme Court ruled in the case of *Shelley v. Kraemer* that it was unconstitutional for courts to enforce the provisions of racial restrictive covenants and deeds. But Chicagoans did not immediately abandon covenants. In the early 1950s, a few block organizations in the Hyde Park–Kenwood area created "conservation agreements." These extralegal covenants committed property owners to using their buildings only as single-family homes, as defined by Chicago's zoning code. In keeping with the HPKCC's preference for combining racial liberalism with class exclusivity, an agreement signed by members of the 5200 Greenwood Avenue Block Group specified: "The parties hereto desire to protect property values in the above described area and to develop and improve the said area and the surrounding community for themselves and all persons irrespective of race, creed, or national origin." A similar "property owners agreement" in the nearby 5200 block of South Ellis Avenue committed signatories to communicating with neighbors about any planned substantial alterations or sales. The document, however, was explicit that it was a nonrestrictive covenant: "It involves no legal obligations. The whole point of it is to build mutual confidence and to permit cooperative activity."[9]

On the national level, the idea that the block was a basic organizing unit of urban life gained intellectual traction in the first quarter of the twentieth century. Patricia Mooney Melvin's *The Organic City* documents a formal experiment in block organization conducted in Cincinnati, Ohio, between 1917 and 1920. Mooney Melvin credits Stanton Coit of New York City's Neighborhood Guild settlement house with originating the idea of block-level local governance in the late 1880s. Coit intended to organize block residents into delegations that were to "oversee all municipal services in the neighborhood and to raise sufficient money for a 'variety of economic, educational and recreational activities'" and "eventually to federate them in a single city guild."[10] Coit failed to implement this vision in New York City, but the idea survived.

In 1914 the progressive reformer Wilbur C. Phillips elaborated Coit's concept into a detailed "social unit plan" to support delivery of public health services. With the support of an initial $63,000 raised from wealthy New York City donors, in 1916 Phillips founded the National Social Unit Organization. This group funded a pilot of the "social unit" idea in Cincinnati's Mohawk-Brighton neighborhood. The Cincinnati experiment's major focus was provision of health and welfare services to infants and small children. Under Phillips's guidance, beginning in December 1917 the Mohawk-Brighton Social Unit Organization (MBSUO) designated thirty-one block organizations, held local elections, and compensated local "block workers" for their labor connecting residents to the organization's services. Phillips also organized occupational councils for physicians, nurses, social workers, teachers, clergy, businessmen, and trade unionists to interact with the residents' council. Although the effort to provide health care was successful, in 1920 the MBSUO fell under attack from Cincinnati's mayor, who interpreted the organization as a threat to his power base. The mayor derided the concept of such local governance as socialism, a potent charge in the wake of the Red Scare in the United States and the Russian revolution. In November 1920, the MBSUO dissolved itself.[11] Because the block organizations were created and funded from above rather than built from the ground up, it is unlikely that they survived the demise of the larger group.

The Chicago Urban League

Roughly simultaneously with Phillips's social unit experiment, local chapters of the National Urban League also began cultivating block clubs. Although sporadic, the Urban League's program was the first serious block organization effort in Chicago. The ultimate influence of the Chicago Urban League's block organization program far surpassed the numbers of its clubs. The League's work among middle-class African Americans established block clubs as a Chicago institution. A century after the National Urban League's affiliates began their work, a block club organizer employed by North Side Alderman Ameya Pawar said simply, "It's in our DNA."[12]

Founded in New York City in 1910,[13] the National Urban League and its affiliates were devoted to helping Southern black migrants adapt to life in the urban north. The Urban League operated on a model of class-based racial self-help. Middle-class African Americans transmitted their values and behavior to others, thereby "uplifting" them and the race as a whole. For its first half century, the League's primary program was "industrial" work, connecting black migrants with job opportunities and training them in appropriate workplace behavior. Several League chapters around the United States also engaged in block organization work, which they pointed out with pride in publicity materials.[14] But whenever affiliate finances were strained, block work was sacrificed to sustain the industrial work.

Surviving sources make it difficult to parse precisely when and where the National Urban League's block club organizing program originated, and how it spread.[15] Its journal, *Opportunity*, which routinely documented the activities of the national office and its local affiliates, was not launched until 1923, well after block work had begun at the local level. The National Urban League's affiliates' initial activities are difficult to trace. The historian Nancy J. Weiss explains that the League's early records are sparse, and that the relationships between the central organization and the affiliates were "hopelessly jumbled" until 1918.[16]

Early in the 1910s, the National Urban League spread the model of block group organizing to several cities. A 1925 article in *Opportunity* credited Mrs. John Hope of Atlanta, Georgia, with having pioneered the "neighborhood union" form in 1908. Mrs. Hope and instructors from her husband's Atlanta Baptist College (now Morehouse University) organized residents of five black sections of the city. Also during the 1910s, the National Urban League, operating in its first several years as the National League on Urban Conditions among Negroes, organized neighborhood unions in New York City.[17]

Other sources suggest that the League's block organization idea originated in Pittsburgh, where it appears that the neighborhood union model narrowed to the block level. Scholars of the League's history credit the Pittsburgh affiliate's first executive director, John T. Clark, with promulgating the block club idea, although it appears that women did the organizational heavy lifting. During Clark's tenure in Pittsburgh, which began in 1918, Margaret Mann organized groups of mothers within specific geographic areas. She volunteered her services until the chapter found money to pay her a salary in 1920. Mann's successor, Grace Lowndes, transformed the mothers' groups "into full-fledged neighborhood units." These groups "pledged themselves to make 'a better home for (their) families, a better neighborhood for (their) homes, and a better land of this, our America.'" Pittsburgh's model of block club organization spread to other cities, including Chicago. Clark oversaw their development in St. Louis, where he moved to direct that city's Urban League in 1926.[18] Chicago's Urban League affiliate first began organizing block groups in the late 1910s.

For the first several decades of its existence, the Chicago Urban League's precarious financial position undermined its ability to offer any sort of consistent programming. When it had funds available, the organization's major tactics were what League historian Arvarh E. Strickland later criticized as the "old handmaiden approach" of direct service through case work, mass placement in industrial jobs, and block organization. In contrast to the National Association for the Advancement of Colored People (NAACP), which pushed for legal expansion of civil rights, the Chicago Urban League's casework and industrial placement services were firmly in the tradition of racial uplift. Industrial services were focused on adjusting black Chicagoans' demeanor and expectations to improve their odds of winning jobs in a narrow, racially defined employment market. The historian Jeffrey Helgeson argues that League staff members in Chicago saw the potential for a broader program for social change, similar to that of the NAACP. But as Strickland's analysis reveals, the Chicago Urban League was dominated by its board and funders for the first half of the twentieth century. These funders, many of whom were wealthy white industrialists, effectively hemmed in any threats of radicalism or militancy from the League's leadership.[19]

The League's conservative approach to improving black Chicagoans' lives was not limited to the industrial realm. African American residential communities appeared chaotic to observers because of the racist housing market,

racial segregation, and poverty. Rather than directly addressing the underlying causes of Chicago's crowded and dirty black neighborhoods, the League
made "community organization" work an important goal. The historian Priscilla Dowden-White's analysis of the St. Louis Urban League emphasizes the
distinction between "community organizing" and "community organization."
The latter, she explains, reflected the St. Louis Urban League's goal of using
up-to-date, scientifically validated social work methods to create "organization" that remedied perceived "disorganization" among black migrants.[20] Until 1956, whenever staffing levels permitted, the Chicago Urban League focused
on a similar strategy of community organization.

"Block work" was among the League's earliest activities in Chicago. As in
Pittsburgh, mothers represented its entering wedge into block club organization. According to Strickland, the Chicago Urban League's early block work
aimed at supporting a broad program of social welfare work. Its first annual
report explained, "Club women have carried advice about health, cleanliness,
deportment in public places, care of children, overcrowding and efficiency,
into the homes of the newcomers in this section where most of them live."
Block-level efforts soon narrowed to focus on physical improvement, and
shifted toward more formal organizations. In 1926, the League's Civic Department reported relationships with seven "neighborhood clubs" federated into
a council that was planning to "assist in the forming of new clubs next year."[21]

In the 1930s the Chicago Urban League experimented with generating
local improvements. In 1934 it revived its block club program in the area
bounded by 47th and 51st Streets and Cottage Grove and South Parkway. It
hoped to provide "a demonstration of the effectiveness of community organization procedures in accomplishing neighborhood improvement." Its 1938 annual report boasted of the reorganization of several clubs, highlighting "The
Annual Flower Show and Neighborhood Improvement Fair . . . preceded by a
parade through the district." In 1941 the League boasted that "for four years the
League's Department of Civic Improvement has used all the known processes
of civic education in order to stimulate Negro citizens to action. . . . Beautification contests, flower shows, motion pictures, exhibits, newspaper articles,
radio talks, pamphlets, lectures—all of these methods have been used." The
work of the John R. Lynch Model Community Council was especially promising. Due to its efforts, "hucksters were persuaded to use the alleys; janitors
took greater pride in their buildings; abandoned cars and trucks and ugly signs
on lawns disappeared; streets and alleys were better cleaned." The group organized successful votes to remove taverns from the area, though it failed in its
effort to make a dent in "policy," a numbers-running gambling system.[22] The

Chicago Urban League's organization effort continued during World War II, probably in cooperation with the program of the federal Office of Civilian Defense.

Beginning in 1947, the League's restaffed community organization department began to develop the model of block club organization that eventually spread throughout Chicago. Under the leadership of Alva B. Maxey, a small staff pursued a vigorous program of block club organization beginning in 1950. They worked not only among relatively established black neighborhoods of the South Side, but also on the West Side, where migrants from the South were expanding a small African American enclave. The League's 1952 report enthusiastically explained:

> The Block Club technique, an Urban League invention, is fast becoming the accepted method of involving the average citizen in civic improvements. Block clubs have shown themselves to be ideally suited to combating social problems which are peculiar to urban living. While they aim directly at the physical problems of the neighborhood, their very method of operation attacks. [*sic*] The deeper psychological factors involved in social disorganization. The tendency of city-dwellers to feel lost, not a part of the community, temporary, hostile, suspicious, isolated, fearful, and defeated, is overcome when they meet in intimate groups and share their feelings. In these Block Clubs, neighbors can communicate and come to know their mutual hopes, plans, and problems. Class clashes and feelings are compelled to operate in any city block, but in the Negro community the tensions are exaggerated because forced ghettoization causes a highly hetergeneous [*sic*] group to live together.

Jeffrey Helgeson summarized the accomplishments of the postwar Chicago Urban League's community organization staff. From a base of ten affiliated clubs in 1940, the numbers rose to ninety-three block clubs and five councils by 1947, dropping to thirty-seven in 1950. Maxey's guidance increased the number of clubs participating in seven area councils to 141 in 1953, and to 175 by 1955.[23] Most of the information about League block clubs reported in this book comes from the period of Maxey's leadership when staff organizers wrote unsigned but detailed and sometimes acerbic reports about the ups and downs of their labors.

When the Chicago Urban League organized block clubs in the early 1950s, staff workers took great pains to interpret their goals to recruits. When they called on potential Leaders, they explained their purposes; they also routinely re-explained the League's goals again at the initial meetings of new groups, and reiterated those explanations in their notes. Because the League's approach demanded a significant volunteer time commitment, staff tried to convince

potential leaders that the effort devoted to the club would be worth the investment of their energies. For example, a staff organizer explained to members
of the 1500 Block Group on Drake that they had "one goal—beautification
and better neighborhood." The apparent simplicity of this point was decep-
tive, for League staff organizers had "intangible" as well as concrete goals. In
an article published in 1957, after the suspension and revival of all League operations in Chicago, Maxey summarized the purposes of the block club program in eight points:

> In brief, block clubs are attempting to teach people to (1) develop and main-
> tain cleanliness, (2) subdue, restrain and sublimate their hostilities, (3) assume
> their proportionate share of civic responsibility, (4) be thrifty and dependable,
> (5) develop aesthetic tastes with regard to their surroundings, (6) adopt and
> extend good manners, (7) strive for upward mobility by conforming to pre-
> vailing norms of behavior, and (8) learn the ways to become acceptable to a
> diverse urban population. Thus, these organizations are striving to educate
> their members and neighbors in the direction of middle class ideals.

In the article, Maxey explicated the League's goal of inducing migrant African
Americans to behave more like members of Chicago's established middle-
class black community. She explained that "the un-urbanized behavior of the
Negro newcomer is just as disturbing and unacceptable to the older urban
Negro residents as it is to the whites." In order to transform the migrant into
a desirable neighbor, Maxey continued, "these clubs are striving to educate
newcomers to understand, accept, adopt and integrate middle class norms
and behavior patterns, while at the same time stimulating individual growth
and development." A reporter for the *Chicago Defender* reinforced the connection between block clubs and the racial uplift of Southern migrants, arguing, "Just as the European emigrants to America are taught the language, laws
and traditions of America, someone must teach the migrants from the farms
and small towns of the Southland how to live in a large city. No organization
is better fitted to do this type of work than a 'BLOCK ORGANIZATION.'"[24]

As Maxey's unapologetic language about "middle class ideals" suggests,
the Chicago Urban League's efforts were infused with an attitude that the
historian Evelyn Brooks Higginbotham has dubbed "the politics of respectability." Educated, elite African Americans sought to elevate the reputation
of "the race" among whites by bringing the behavior of other blacks into line
with middle-class values and norms. Higginbotham explains that "there could
be no transgression of society's norms. From the public spaces of trains and
streets to the private spaces of their individual homes, the behavior of blacks

was perceived as ever visible to the white gaze." Erica Ball's study of the antebellum period broadens Higginbotham's interpretation of the politics of respectability, explaining that "its power stemmed not . . . solely from its effects on whites but also, and more important, from its effects on the individuals who embraced it." While Higginbotham's analysis focused on Southern churchwomen at the turn of the twentieth century, the politics of respectability traveled to the urban North along with black migrants. Victoria Wolcott explains that in the context of interwar Detroit, reformers "repeatedly stressed dress, demeanor, and neighborhood cleanliness."[25] In Chicago as well, the politics of respectability directly informed the Urban League's aspirations for using block clubs to transform the city's black population into a model.

The League envisioned block clubs transforming their participants at the same time as they improved the local environment. Maxey explained that development of civic responsibility helped create the "grass-roots leaders" whom cities needed to "fill a vacuum and become the medium for furthering the democratic process in a complex, changing society." The League cultivated leadership skills because, "through block clubs, people learn to work in groups, to follow leadership and, in turn, to become leaders. Each member of the group learns to work according to his own capacity, to overlook peculiarities in others, and to be tolerant of individual differences in the interest of larger aims. Each learns to do, by doing; to follow, by following; to lead, by leading; and to cooperate, by cooperating." Indeed, as chapter 2 explains, when Chicago Urban League staff began organizing a block group, they paid careful attention to clues about the leadership capacity of potential participants. The block club, Maxey concluded, offered a "natural and popular vehicle for developing an element of community cohesion in the otherwise disorganized neighborhood." The historian Touré Reed elaborates that, "from the Urban League's perspective, the active participation of black neighbors in their own uplift was necessary both to demonstrate blacks' worthiness of inclusion and to counteract the damage inflicted on black institutions by the migration."[26]

When internal political conflicts forced the shutdown of the entire Chicago Urban League operation for six months in 1955, active block organization efforts ceased as well. After the League's reconstitution in 1956, the new executive director, Edwin C. Berry, reoriented its work away from direct services like block club organization. Berry instead emphasized approaches that critiqued the unjust treatment of black Chicagoans, arguing that block clubs were "unable to effect fundamental changes in the problems bearing down on the Negro throughout the community." In contrast to his predecessors, Berry shook off the dominance of white philanthropists on the board. He led the organization into the territory of civil rights protests, especially in the public school system, and with startling forthrightness denounced Chicago as "the most segregated city in the country." Berry's shift to an activist, rights-oriented stance reflected a broader change in the Urban League's approach across the country, as the organization responded to pressure to add civil rights work to its traditional social welfare agenda. Hints, however, suggest that the Urban League did not abandon block clubs altogether. Parris and Brooks' history of the organization reports that in 1968, affiliates in at least thirty cities were using block clubs as a mechanism to combat "ghetto conditions." A few of the block clubs that the Chicago Urban League seeded in the early 1950s persisted in their efforts even without professional support staff.[27]

Historians have debated how to understand the significance of the League's block organization effort in Chicago, with its rootedness in the politics of respectability and its focus on the environmental aesthetic of residential neighborhoods. As Strickland's dismissive "old handmaiden" comment suggests, scholars have criticized early Urban League programs for attending to the symptoms rather than to the structural causes of urban poverty, residential segregation, and employment discrimination. Historian Christopher Reed's introduction to the 2001 edition of Strickland's classic history of the Chicago Urban League, for example, observes that until the 1955 reorganization, white funders threatened to withdraw their support if League "activities appeared too militant and similar to what was to be expected from a civil rights organization." Landmark federal legislation such as the Voting Rights Act and the Civil Rights Act, which permitted "recognition of African Americans as full-fledged citizens enjoying their full civil rights—as neighbors, students, consumers, voters, workers, competitors," were ultimately achieved only through "protest activity" in the 1960s.[28] Even while it considers the inability of the Urban League's service-focused program to create systemic change, scholarship about the organization tends to pay more attention to its job placement programs than to its community organization efforts. Because at first blush block club organizing appeared to have little political or economic meaning, analyzing its importance has been ancillary.

As historians have recently begun to reconsider the Urban League's significance, they have also rediscovered its block club program. Touré F. Reed's *Not Alms but Opportunity* argues that it is time to stopping judging the League in dichotomous terms. Previous scholars have tried to discern whether its philosophy was "conservative," in the tradition of the educator Booker T. Washington, or closer to the "bourgeois militancy" of the scholar W. E. B. DuBois. Touré Reed acknowledges that the League's approach to racial uplift clearly prioritized programs to benefit the "talented tenth" over poor blacks' needs,

and he agrees that "in some respects, the League's strategy of treating organized activities as a means of improving the character of black neighborhoods
was an accommodation to residential segregation." But it is more significant,
Reed continues, to see the League's analysis as grounded in the traditions of
the Chicago School of Sociology, the discipline's center in the early years of
the twentieth century. While the Chicago School's stodgy liberalism failed to
challenge "the hegemony of industrial capitalism," it is unfair for us to expect
too much of them. "Leaguers, like all of us, were products of their historical
moment," Reed concludes. "They used the intellectual and institutional tools
at their disposal both to understand their world and to try to create a more
democratic society."[29]

Both Jeffrey Helgeson and Priscilla Dowden-White sympathetically interpret the League's pragmatism on a continuum of political responses to African Americans' struggle in the urban north. Helgeson acknowledges that the
Chicago Urban League's block club program was "entirely non-controversial,"
but argues that it was part of "important pragmatic efforts to grapple with the
problems of everyday life." Dowden-White's analysis of the St. Louis Urban
League similarly treats its conservative approach as part of a broader campaign to advance the position of blacks in American society. She argues that
pragmatic improvement and overt advocacy were not diametrically opposed
strategies. Instead, they were necessarily complementary tactics in the effort
to improve African Americans' political and economic statuses.[30] Block clubs
demonstrated blacks' worthiness as citizens, while rights campaigns aimed to
secure legal protections.

Sylvia Hood Washington's analysis of Chicago Urban League block clubs
is an outlier to these debates. In the only extended historical consideration of
the League's block organization program, Washington argues that the block
clubs' work to clean up Chicago's impoverished neighborhoods was a necessary response to the dangerous environmental conditions that segregation
imposed on black residents. She claims that the clean-up campaigns, rather
than being a patronizing middle-class effort focused on achieving respectability, manifested a previously unrecognized conservation sensibility among African Americans.[31]

The Chicago Urban League's strategy of organizing block clubs served
multiple goals that supplemented civil rights aims without contradicting
their goals. Their difference rested in means and timing, not in ends. Local improvement efforts like those run by League-cultivated block clubs were
meant to serve as a demonstration of African Americans' collective fitness
for urban life, to cultivate a cohort of local leadership, and to improve poor

living conditions. In the short run, local improvement programs could foster environmental conditions that money and attention from the municipal
government reflexively supported in wealthier white neighborhoods. In the
long run, block clubs illustrated that participants were willing and able to take
responsibility for activities that would make a concrete difference in each other's daily lives.

The Chicago Urban League intended this message to reach two audiences,
one black and one white. First, the demonstration of block clubs' capacities
might persuade their immediate neighbors to participate. Maxey suggested
that block club programming affected even neighbors who appeared "highly
mobile and indifferent to neighborhood affairs." She claimed that after migrants developed a stable enough personal situation to put down roots and
become "sufficiently motivated and interested," they "often take the new ideals with them when they move to another location."[32] Although this assertion
may have been more wishful than empirically grounded, the League's organization work did lay a foundation for the development of block clubs as a
familiar form of civic life in twentieth-century Chicago.

Second, the insistence on blacks' respectability was aimed at white Chicagoans who doubted that African Americans could maintain their homes
decently. Maxey was explicit about the block clubs' purpose in "improving
race and intergroup relations." Residential segregation meant that whites
rarely observed how African Americans lived. Only in the days before they
moved out of transitioning neighborhoods and "on their casual trips through
the Negro slum areas" did white Chicagoans get a close look at black neighborhoods. Block clubs demonstrated that a well-tended black block could
be a pleasant environment. According to Maxey, the League's clubs invited
"groups from the larger community to be the guests of the block clubs, and to
come in for a tour and inspection of organized blocks. Some clubs also ar-
range tours for members of their own block to visit and see the work of organizations in other blocks and to exchange ideas." As chapter 4 shows, when
the Urban League ran cleanup contests, its staff recruited white judges. Visitors could take the message of African American fitness for urban living back
to white social circles.[33]

The reaction of white Chicagoans to blacks' attempts to find housing in
white neighborhoods in the postwar period suggests that the Urban League's
message of black respectability largely fell on deaf ears. What white Chicagoans did glean from the League's efforts was that block clubs were a useful organizational form. In the early 1950s, as the HPKCC began organizing
block clubs in its South Side territory, the League expressed enthusiasm about

its own influence while somewhat defensively claiming credit as the form's inventor.[34]

Civilian Defense

The spread of block club organizing received a major lift during World War II, when the federal government's Office of Civilian Defense (OCD) established block clubs throughout Chicago. During the war years, Chicago was a city of migrants. Whites from around the country and African Americans from the South poured into Chicago in search of employment in defense industries; some Japanese Americans from the West relocated to the interior of the continent when liberated from wartime concentration camps. Despite the transformations of city life wrought by wartime, the OCD turned to a Chicago institution—the block club—as an instrument for inculcating patriotic support for the war effort. If the Chicago Urban League's program first established the suitability of block club organization for Chicago, the OCD familiarized the entire city with its potential.

New York Mayor Fiorello LaGuardia directed the federal OCD. LaGuardia recognized Chicago as a separate "special defense unit," with Chicago Mayor Edward J. Kelly as the area's civil defense coordinator. Under Kelly's leadership, the Chicago OCD turned to the block as an essential unit for coordinating universal participation in the war effort. It is unclear why Kelly's OCD office decided to complement employer-based civilian defense efforts with block groups. Because his success as mayor during the Great Depression rested in part on careful cultivation of black voters, Kelly's frequent public appearances on the South Side may have familiarized him with the Chicago Urban League's block organization program.[35]

Chicago's planning for civil defense began in late 1940. Shortly after the United States formally entered the war in December 1941, the OCD divided the entirety of Chicago into "block units." Block leaders disseminated official information about their neighbors' expected role in supporting the federal war effort. The reflection that "the minute men of yesterday are the block captains of today" points to the perceived necessity of total civilian mobilization. By late January 1942, one section on Chicago's West Side elected captains for an estimated 95 percent of blocks. At a ceremony in March, the OCD swore in approximately sixteen thousand Chicagoans as block captains. Every block where neighbors could be aroused formed block units and elected residents to a variety of offices. Chicagoans became block captains and "wardens" in charge of morale, victory gardens, local preparations for air raids, conservation of scarce materials, salvage of grease and paper, and sale of war bonds. Children delivered messages.[36]

As this list of responsibilities suggests, the purpose of the OCD block unit program was more to harness civilians' energies to national defense than for local welfare. As a part of the effort, the OCD conducted a census of Chicagoans. Residents 12 years old and older were expected to "be registered on a roster card which will be brought to every home by the block captains." This demographic information may have been used to set proportional block-level quotas for bond sales. Block units tracked their participation with illustrative "thermometers" set up on corners so that passersby could see whether their blocks measured up. As in other communities, the air raid wardens were responsible for controlling resident behavior during simulated attacks. In one 1942 experiment, for example, the air raid wardens instructed their neighbors to turn their lights selectively on or off in order to create an illuminated "camouflage pattern" confusing to potential enemy pilots.[37]

Some OCD block groups prioritized boosting the morale of soldiers from the block with communications and small gifts from home. The Very Good Club, serving zone 21's block 7, produced a monthly newsletter including health and wedding news, lists of blood donors, and the deployments of soldiers. The newsletter featured a lengthy "alley report" describing neighbors' gardens in loving detail. The club distributed the newsletter to residents and sent it out to soldiers, using a carefully maintained list of addresses. One soldier serving in France wrote to the club that after he read the newsletter, he forwarded it to his English bride, who "honestly is thrilled each time your sheet gets to her." He continued, "She feels, and its [sic] because of the paper, that she knows you all as real neighbors and old friends. Rightly enough some day soon we hope to be coming home so that she can really meet you instead of the paper being the medium of a distant friendship."[38]

Despite early enthusiastic participation, by 1945 most of Chicago's civil defense block clubs were exhibiting significant war fatigue. After Germany's surrender, and anticipating victory over Japan, President Truman abolished the OCD in June. Mayor Kelly kept his Chicago staff employed after the OCD closure, but only a few block units continued their federally nurtured association after the war. The Very Good Club decided not to cease its activities until 1946, because "the war isn't over till the last man is out and home again." The most notable lasting OCD group was a division on the city's North Side, whose members regrouped after the war to form the Old Town Triangle Association and run an annual art fair that persists into the twenty-first century.[39] The OCD's block organizing program was not structured to create lasting social networks in Chicago. But it did ensure that residents through-out the city had experience with their immediate neighbors as possible allies in protecting their common interests.

Urban Renewal and Conservation

By 1950, a substantial portion of Chicago's population had seen block clubs in action. In addition to whatever direct benefits it brought to participants and their immediate environs, the Chicago Urban League's program was fundamental in demonstrating that the block club was a workable form in Chicago. The OCD's program familiarized Chicagoans, for a brief and focused period, with the idea of the working cooperatively with block-level neighbors for common ends. In the post-war years, the HPKCC was instrumental in spreading the idea of block club organizing as a civilian, non-emergency activity.

The HPKCC brought two significant innovations to the cultivation of block clubs. First, it harnessed block club organizing to a broader neighborhood transformation project, urban renewal. This approach differed from the Chicago Urban League's strategy, which was directed toward development at the personal and block level rather than to engaging government powers. In addition, Hyde Park organizers concluded that a pragmatic approach to organizing was more effective than idealism in persuading residents to participate in a block group. One of the lead advocates of block organization declared, "As long as there is willingness to work on problems, ideological differences can be avoided or settled." In contrast to the abstract goal of racial uplift that informed the League's work, the HPKCC used improvement both as an end in itself and as the means to that end. Although the HPKCC deserved its reputation for being interracial, liberal, and middle-class, not all residents subscribed to the unusual combination of values that the organization advanced. Its vision for interracialism proved particularly controversial in postwar Chicago, where many white neighborhoods rejected even a hint of integration. HPKCC director Julia Abrahamson explained that participants discovered "that it was fruitless to debate about ideas or differences, that approval of a neighbor's origin or philosophy was not essential; working with him to get the street cleaned was."[40]

In Hyde Park, the South East Chicago Commission (SECC) organized the city's first major push for urban renewal on behalf of the University of Chicago. Hyde Park was a neighborhood with wealthy origins and a housing stock that mixed mansions and apartments. After World War II, it began to attract middle-class professional African Americans seeking distance from the poor black Southern migrants who were moving into neighborhoods to the north and west. Two organizations with complementary visions worked to blunt the effects of this population shift. An interracial, interreligious group founded the HPKCC in 1950 to protect Hyde Park and southern Kenwood. The HPKCC's aim was to preserve the area's existing character and protect it from the deterioration, crowding, and deferred building maintenance that seemed inexorably to accompany the arrival of poor blacks in Chicago neighborhoods. The HPKCC's liberals welcomed racial but not class integration in the neighborhood. Second, from 1952 forward, the University of Chicago backed the SECC, which coordinated the area's pioneering appeal for authority and funds to tear down and rebuild large stretches of Hyde Park's less desirable properties. The HPKCC's community mission was broader than the SECC's focus on urban renewal, but the two organizations' goals coincided. The HPKCC consistently supported the SECC's redevelopment program. Arnold Hirsch explains that "the genius of the symbiotic relationship between the HPKCC and the SECC extended beyond the fact that one dealt with the 'grass roots' and the other moved the levers of power. It was also that the latter staunchly defended the community's interests and permitted the former to articulate its highest ideals."[41]

Right from the start, the HPKCC incorporated block clubs as a key element of its work. The block club program was the brainchild of Herbert Thelen, a University of Chicago professor whose research focused on group behavior in organizations. Thelen first encountered the idea of block clubs at a citywide "human relations" program in 1948, likely featuring the Chicago Urban League's efforts. Attending the founding meetings of the HPKCC, Thelen ensured that they incorporated block-level organizing. He provided educational materials for organizing block groups, and conducted some of the HPKCC's early training. With his wife he participated in a club on their home block of 5600 South Drexel Avenue. With his colleague Bettie Belk Sarchet, Thelen also wrote both practical and scholarly evaluations of the HPKCC's block club organizing program. Although the structure of the block clubs' relationship with the HPKCC changed several times over the next decade and a half, Thelen's basic program of organizing flourished.[42] Because it was financially well supported, in part through the block group network, the HPKCC was able to employ a dedicated staff organizer as well as a full-time building inspector who assisted clubs in monitoring their neighbors.

The HPKCC block clubs served many functions that supported both members' interests in their blocks and the Conference's larger goals. Clubs organized activities for their own blocks, provided a mechanism for HPKCC fundraising, targeted properties for building code enforcement, and vetted the SECC's proposed program of urban renewal—thereby creating a veneer of community review of plans that very selectively transformed Hyde Park's built environment. In her book about the organization's early years, HPKCC executive director Julia Abrahamson explained the "triple purpose" for the process that started at the club level and then brought neighboring groups together under the Conference's aegis:

> (1) giving recognition to the thinking and contributions of each of the block groups, (2) providing evidence that residents were actually affecting the planning, and (3) deepening perspective as block groups came into contact with the views and interest of other blocks, sometimes in conflict with their own, and learned the necessity of finding solutions on a wider basis than the self-interest of individual blocks.

In retrospect, Abrahamson lamented the separation of the HPKCC and SECC functions into distinct organizations as a mistake made by an inexperienced group. She asserted "that a single strong organization *supported by all community forces and keeping their interests in proper balance* could have combined the strengths and methods of the conference and commission and might have achieved more with less conflict, less cost, and greater speed."[43]

Historian Arnold Hirsch brought a more critical eye to Hyde Park's urban renewal program in *Making the Second Ghetto*. Urban renewal exiled many of the poor, black, migrant residents who occupied Hyde Park's less expensive, deteriorating properties. No one carefully tracked where they found replacement housing. Many displaced people probably ended up occupying the deeply segregated ghetto of the city's public housing system, which was intended in part to shelter Chicagoans displaced by urban renewal. In Hirsch's view, the separation of organizations that Abrahamson lamented allowed HPKCC members to enjoy "the luxury of their liberalism"[44] without having to feel directly responsible for the eviction of their poor neighbors.

The educated elite who made up the HPKCC leadership did not go about their business quietly or modestly. They made frequent appearances around the city, and wrote about their efforts. They received frequent coverage not only in Chicago's daily newspapers, but also in such popular national venues such as *Reader's Digest*. Inspired by the HPKCC's model, several other Chicago community-based groups seeking to attract federal urban renewal funding to their local neighborhoods founded block clubs in the 1950s and 1960s.[45] In the twenty-first century, many people remember urban renewal as a deeply flawed mechanism for urban improvement. Bitterly nicknamed "Negro removal" and "the bulldozer," urban renewal often broke up impoverished but striving working-class communities, unhousing residents and uprooting small businesses without adequately assisting in their relocation. Established neighborhoods of individual owners and renters were replaced by highways and large, forbidding, corporate-owned modernist buildings.[46]

But in the 1950s, many groups in Chicago, especially local business interests, saw urban renewal as a promising way to redevelop their own communities. Especially enticing was the prospect that urban renewal programs could "conserve" an area. This attractive term implied the selective preservation of existing resources rather than the wholesale destruction of large swaths of buildings. The procedures for winning urban renewal funds were onerous and complex; in 1958 the process required twenty steps, including creating a community conservation agency like the SECC, winning designation as a "conservation area," conducting surveys and public hearings, and receiving approval from multiple local, city, and federal authorities. Despite the organizational obstacles and urban renewal's increasingly ominous reputation, a 1962 study by the Metropolitan Housing and Planning Commission found that more than two hundred "'conservation oriented' civic organizations" were at work in Chicago.[47]

Thanks to the division of labor with the SECC, the HPKCC's network of block clubs was several steps removed from the process that brought urban renewal programs into the neighborhood. This was not the case for other Chicago areas that followed Hyde Park's lead. One of the less complex and controversial steps of winning approval for urban renewal was to show that the local conservation agency enjoyed community approval. A local network of block clubs effectively demonstrated an organized and supportive local constituency. Conversation groups in Uptown and North Lawndale, for example, heeded Abrahamson's admonition that block clubs demonstrating community support for urban renewal should be part of the same organization that spearheaded the larger effort. With varying degrees of competence and success, they cultivated block clubs to show that their proposals represented the desires of the community's residents as well as business leaders' interests.[48] In the common event that the group failed to win urban renewal funding, the president of the Greater Lawndale Conservation Commission observed, block clubs could still be harnessed for "do-it-yourself" demonstration purposes and other goals that supported the mission of their parent organizations.[49]

Organizational Networks

As the approaches of the Chicago Urban League and the HPKCC suggest, many Chicago block clubs were created by larger organizations pursuing an agenda for a broader constituency. As the block clubs spread across Chicago, some emerged spontaneously as truly indigenous organizations. The 15th Place Block Club is the rare example of a vigorous, long-lived, independent block group with a rich and accessible documentary record. Such autonomous groups are the hardest for historians to identify and track, because their records are the least likely to be archived. Most block clubs were organized and cultivated by larger groups that had their own motivations for encouraging local residents to join forces. As the list of umbrella groups below shows, the kinds of organizations that devoted staff time to organizing block clubs ranged from community associations to the city of Chicago itself and the US federal government:

American Friends Service Committee
Associated Block Committees of Garfield Park–Austin
Austin Tenants and Owners Association
Between-the-Tracks Council
Beverly Heights Associated Block Clubs
Blocks Together
Chicago Alliance for Neighborhood Safety
Chicago Commission on Human Relations
Chicago Housing Authority Citizens Committee
Chicago Police Department
Chicago Real Estate Board
Chicago Urban League
East Humboldt Park Planning and Conservation Commission
Edgewater Community Council
Garfield Family Council[50]
Garfield Park West Community Council[51]
Greater Lawndale Association of Block Clubs
Greater Lawndale Conservation Commission
Healthy South Chicago Coalition
Highburn Associated Block Clubs
Hyde Park–Kenwood Community Conference
Kenwood Ellis Community Center
Marillac House
Midwest Community Council
Near West Side Planning Board
Neighbors At Work
North Ken-Oakland Community Conference
Northwest Community Organization
Office of Civilian Defense
Organization for a Better Austin

Organization of the Southwest Community
Park Manor Neighbors
Pilsen Neighborhood Community Council
Southwest Associated Block Clubs
Southwest Lawndale United Block Club Council
The Organization of Palmer Square
The Woodlawn Organization
Town Hall Association (Austin)
Triangle Community Organization
United Block Clubs
United Friends
United Property Group
Uptown Conservation Commission
West Side Community Committee
Woodlawn Block Club Council
Woodlawn Community Conference[52]

Organizations cultivated block clubs as logical extensions of their mission. A block club could support the parent organization, carry out its work, and nurture talent and community among residents. The HPKCC's founders, for instance, charged its initial block club committee to "consider ways and means of helping individual citizens, with their neighbors, to diagnose their neighborhood problems and to take action; to build a greater sense of community throughout the neighborhood."[53] In its most crass form, the reason for cultivating block clubs was entirely self-interested. Some umbrella groups created a network of block clubs to support the organization: dues contributed financial support, and raw constituency numbers bolstered the organization's account of its own representativeness. Less cynically, community organizations nurtured block clubs as the best mechanism for creating results, such as beautification or safety, that could benefit the wider neighborhood.

Despite the broad range of goals that inspired block club cultivation, umbrella organizations granted block clubs a great deal of autonomy to set their local agendas. Parent organizations often regarded the active participation of block club members as more important than their conformity to institutional purposes. Whatever their shortcomings, a shared commitment to democratic, voluntary participation prevented parent organizations from imposing predetermined outcomes on affiliated block clubs. Any block club activity—even activity that contradicted the stated purposes of the umbrella organization— was better than no activity. Block clubs occasionally left their parent networks, but I have found no evidence of larger associations expelling member block groups; more often, parent organizations such as the Chicago Urban League lamented the inactivity of groups they had laboriously nurtured. To keep block clubs connected with each other and the umbrella group, parent organizations routinely collected block club leaders into larger agglomerations.

The Chicago Urban League's federation of block clubs set the baseline against which to consider other organizations' networks. The League expected member block clubs to send representatives to their local "council," which represented several nearby groups. At a meeting of the Princeton Avenue Civic Club, League staff member S. T. Turner explained the purpose of the Parker Council:

> to promote projects within a specified area; to interpret wholesome civic pro-grams so that all the residents within this area will be able to receive maxi-mum benefits from all the resources that can be used to meet common goals; to secure better police protection, clear streets, better housing and, in short, just plain community improvement; and if after a good period of time the residents would come to know each other, then the council would seek to promote better citizenship. In this manner, the residents would have a better idea of protecting other people's property.[54]

After League organizers succeeded in creating block clubs, they pushed the groups' leaders to participate in their local council. Chapter 3 describes the gentle and pushy tactics that the League used to induce block clubs to share in their councils' work.

Influenced by the League's model, several other Chicago organizations cultivated block clubs to support a broad agenda of "community improve-ment" without describing a more specific set of goals. Approximately seven-teen block clubs allied themselves with the Garfield Family Council in the mid-1960s. The organizers used the slogan "People can unmake slums" to rally participants around such projects as "a solution for vandalism, a coop-erative purchase of grass seed to substitute green lawns for grassless areas, the planting of privet hedges and trees, insisting on lids on garbage cans to prevent papers being lifted by winds, urging one school and the local adja-cent candy store to impress upon sweet-toothed youngsters to deposit candy wrappers in trash cans, and a campaign among those who use the streets as garages to tread elsewhere than adjacent lawns." The American Friends Ser-vice Committee (AFSC), the Quaker service organization, operated Project House in the East Garfield Park community area. In the summers, Project House often hosted student interns seeking an urban experience. Work with the AFSC was a practical application of the Quakers' religious bent toward social justice. Starting in 1965, Project House VISTA volunteers worked with several neighboring block clubs. In the process, according to the VISTA su-pervisors, "many people began to feel a need for a larger neighborhood organization to work on problems common to the various blocks." Participants created a United Block Club that outlasted the summer's effort. The group "unit[ed] representatives from six blocks and individuals from other blocks to work together on street sanitation, inadequate housing, local school problems, and individual family difficulties."[55]

Creating autonomous, democratically constituted organizations had some clear upsides for umbrella groups. But children do not always do what their parents want. In Hyde Park, for example, the HPKCC supported the urban renewal program promoted by the SECC. Expecting approval and endorsement, HPKCC encouraged member block clubs to scrutinize the plans carefully. After such deliberation, a few member groups came out against the plan—objecting either to the anticipated demolition of properties in their own bailiwick or to the larger approach to local problems.[56] The Greater Lawndale Conservation Commission (GLCC) found itself similarly at odds with board member Gloria Pughsley, to whom it had delegated the responsibility of organizing a network of block clubs in North Lawndale. Pughsley was so influential within her network that it refused to cooperate with the GLCC's agenda. As chapter 5 explains, eventually the GLCC gave up and hired a staff organizer to restart the effort.

Because of their formal autonomy, block clubs' histories (and occasionally their records) are distinct from those of the organizations that cultivated their existence. Without consistent support, some dissolved; but others flourished. After its Steering Committee of Block Clubs foundered in 1964, the HPKCC sent out representatives to discover whether the affiliated clubs still existed, what they were doing, and how their members felt about their relationship to the HPKCC. By the last quarter of the twentieth century, one analysis suggested, most block clubs had dissolved, dropped their HPKCC affiliation, or lost their membership to condominium-level organizations. In 2013, with assistance from the CPD's Chicago Alternative Policing Strategy program (discussed below), the HPKCC renewed its effort to cultivate block clubs. In its call to participate, organizers invoked the importance of Hyde Park's block club tradition. By contrast, the Winona Block Club was founded in 1962 under the aegis of the Uptown Chicago Commission. By 1973 the club expanded its territory to include streets to the north and south, encompassing residents on Foster, Carmen, and Winnemac as well. Renamed for all those streets, the Winona Foster Carmen Winnemac Block Club continued its existence in 2015, with more than five hundred participants "liking" its active Facebook page. It offered a substantial range of local activities, but had little apparent connection to the Uptown Chicago Commission, which was also still operating.[57] Most Chicago block clubs, although brought into existence by larger organizations, sank or swam because of their own participants' efforts.

Exclusion

Not all Chicagoans wanted to build connections with a wide range of their neighbors. Block clubs sent messages of exclusion as readily as they called for inclusion. The block club was an organizational form pioneered in black neighborhoods to demonstrate African Americans' value as urban neighbors. But in the postwar decades, white Chicagoans discovered block clubs' utility for neighborhood racial defense.

Many whites believed that when blacks moved into their neighborhoods, the physical environment would deteriorate and homeowners' property would lose its resale value. Newly black neighborhoods became crowded and dirty, experienced spikes in crime and declines in school quality, and received fewer city services. In retrospect, it is possible to see that the migration of blacks into white neighborhoods did have deleterious effects on an area's quality-of-life indicators. This occurred not because blacks were intrinsically bad neighbors, but because the segregated housing market shaped the experience. Because of the scale of the Great Migration and white resistance to residential integration, blacks' need for housing far outstripped the available, segregated supply. As a result, when blacks did gain a foothold in a new neighborhood, they arrived in numbers far greater than those of the departing white population. Once well-off African Americans opened a neighborhood to blacks, the housing vacuum provided an opportunity for poorer blacks to move in as well. The arrival of both groups was often accompanied by a local decrease in political influence. In Chicago's patronage-driven political system, this routinely meant the provision of fewer city services. The combination of overuse and official neglect that followed black in-migration caused a steep decline in the quality of the environment—a decline that whites could observe even when they did not grasp the underlying mechanisms. Middle-class blacks frequently tried to move out of neighborhoods where poor blacks followed, thus starting the cycle over.[58]

Hyde Park's influential residents parsed the process of racial transition with enough clarity to separate out the consequences of class and race. The Hyde Park urban renewal program aimed to retain residents and properties that enhanced the neighborhood's prestige. Impoverished recent migrants who were struggling to gain a foothold in the city often accepted housing in accommodations that owners allowed to run down. It was such buildings that the HPKCC and its block clubs targeted for city housing code inspections.[59] Middle-class and wealthy African Americans who shared the goal of keeping out the poor were welcome to stay in postwar Hyde Park. Whites in working-class neighborhoods could not leverage the city's tools of building inspection, urban renewal, and selective demolition. Instead they tried to preserve their neighborhoods by keeping blacks from moving in at all. Keeping blacks out, they reasoned, prevented the advent of deterioration and crime. A racially homogeneous neighborhood provided an environment that was both socially and aesthetically desirable for white occupancy.

In 1948, whites lost a key tool protecting racially exclusive neighborhoods with the US Supreme Court decision in *Shelley v. Kraemer*. In a master's thesis completed in 1951, Zorita Mikva traced the rise in the neighborhood improvement association as a replacement for the now unenforceable covenants. Mikva identified several hundred Chicago organizations that were federated into approximately a dozen larger networks. Such neighborhood associations were substantially larger than most block clubs. They each typically encompassed at least eight blocks and could range up to more than eighty blocks. Improvement associations used the leverage provided by their members' numbers to block public housing from white neighborhoods.[60] By the late 1950s, when all the locations had long since been determined, no more public housing was being planned in Chicago. Yet it was clear that African Americans were continuing to move into privately owned housing in white neighborhoods.

In 1959, the abruptly formed United Property Group in West Garfield Park used block clubs to express nonviolent but hostile white solidarity in the face of black in-migration. When the Hargraves family purchased a house at 4338 West Jackson, they became the first African American residents of the block. As often happened in this period, the immediate response of white neighbors was to form an angry mob around the Hargraves' home.[61] Neighbor Gordon Mattson, however, argued that "mob action and violence is [*sic*] no way to solve the problem. It only plays into the hands of the speculators who want the neighborhood to panic so that they will be able to make big profits in buying and selling property." Mattson disavowed the tactics of violence, but shared the goal of keeping more blacks from moving into the neighborhood. In an alternative plan published in the community newspaper, the *Garfieldian*, he called on his neighbors to work cooperatively within the law to stop more African Americans from purchasing homes in their area. The fifth point in his eight-point plan was "Organize a block committee to work out means of cooperation in your block." The larger community organization he was proposing, the United Property Group (UPG), would serve as a source of accurate information and rumor control to keep white homeowners from "panicking" and selling their homes to blacks. In Mattson's vision of organization, the block club was an arm of the larger network. If neighbors knew each other better and understood that the UPG was distributing reliable information, then they might not leave. The UPG and its associated block clubs persisted until 1965, when West Garfield Park had become almost entirely black.[62]

A decade later, Father Francis X. Lawlor, a Roman Catholic priest in the Augustinian order, similarly turned to block clubs to spread the message that blacks were unwelcome in the South Side's West Englewood neighborhood. Perhaps because his effort took in a larger swath of the city and played on his personal charisma and public defiance of archdiocesan authority, Lawlor's Southwest Associated Block Clubs received much more attention from the city's daily newspapers than the UPG ever had. Before he launched his organizing career, Lawlor had spent twenty years as a teacher at St. Rita's High School. He gained organizing experience in campaigns against sexual indecency and communism. Beginning in December 1967, starting at 67th and Honore Streets, Lawlor turned his energies toward organizing whites into block clubs to keep African Americans out of West Englewood. The UPG's rhetoric reflected their assumptions about the degrading effects of blacks on property values. Lawlor and the Southwest Associated Block Clubs (SWABC) expressed a more naked racism, ignoring the emerging American practice of coding racial hostility in neutral terms. Geographer Brian J. L. Berry explained that the SWABC's antipathy toward blacks was cultural in its focus. Lawlor expressed the belief that until basic "socioeconomic, cultural" disparities between blacks and whites were remedied, they could not live near each other.[63]

The SWABC's immoderate racism drew a swift response from Chicago's archbishop. In February 1968, John Cardinal Cody stripped Lawlor of his authority to preach and administer the sacraments in Chicago and ordered him into exile in Tulsa, Oklahoma. In late March, Lawlor announced that he was returning to Chicago in defiance of Cody's orders. Lawlor resumed organizing block clubs, and, thanks to his notoriety, received numerous invitations to address other groups sympathetic to his approach. In the wake of the conflict with his superiors in the Catholic Church, Lawlor enjoyed great personal support from the whites in West Englewood, who posted signs proclaiming that "Jesus loves Father Lawlor." They also elected him their alderman in 1971.[64]

Lawlor's influence extended beyond West Englewood. Initially working within a boundary of Ashland Avenue on the east, Western Avenue on the west, and 59th and 75th Streets on the north and south, Lawlor rapidly built an expansive network. By 1971, its boundaries stretched northeast to Wells and 43rd, and south to 109th Street. Before he was sent to Tulsa, he had started 14 clubs; on his return in March 1968, the SWABC's press chairman reported that the group had 65 clubs in its network. By late summer 1968 she estimated that there were more than 150, although her count of the number organized before Lawlor's Tulsa sojourn had jumped to 50. Even if the raw numbers were exaggerated, Lawlor's organizing efforts enjoyed considerable success. By 1970, related groups—the Highburn Associated Block Clubs and the Beverly Heights Associated Block Clubs—were also receiving publicity in the SWABC newspaper.[65]

Lawlor saw as particularly significant the protection of Ashland Avenue, a commercial thoroughfare that formed the symbolic eastern boundary of white occupation. The South Lynne Community Council spent a decade failing to keep blacks from crossing Ashland Avenue; in Lawlor's view, their tactics of racial reconciliation were too moderate, geared to improving whites' attitudes towards blacks. It was more important, he asserted to Cardinal Cody, to "hold the line at Ashland av." Unless they did, "it would be only a matter of time till every Catholic parish and school, built at great sacrifice by the people on the Southwest Side of Chicago, would be empty. Non-Catholic whites would suffer the same fate." Reinforcing this claim, SWABC members posted signs in their windows reading, "Ashland is the line."[66]

Lawlor acknowledged that there were some African Americans who shared the desire to live in "good, clean, law-abiding communities." But he asserted that even such decent people should be kept out of white neighborhoods, and that whites should stay in their homes. "When they [blacks] move in," Lawlor claimed, "the ghetto closes in around them again and they're in the same bad predicament they left and you're in a worse one because you've left your friends, your security, your community." Lawlor believed that block clubs created solidarity among white neighbors. He urged his constituents to "get out, meet your neighbors, share some time together." If block clubs connected white residents, they would not move out quickly, "creating another vacancy," when blacks seemed poised to move in. At a public meeting on Chicago's West Side, Lawlor seemed to raise the possibility that blacks might live among whites—but only if they could tolerate hostile neighbors. He claimed that the racial solidarity generated by white block clubs would serve as an additional protective mechanism: "Once you have unity, you will find that when persons of a diverse nationality or race move in, you will be able to accept this and not feel threatened. You have every right to stay here and if they don't like your community, they should move."[67]

Although Lawlor occasionally hinted at the possibility of racial coexistence, the Associated Block Clubs' range of actions and speech showed clearly that peaceful integration was not on their agenda. Lawlor wrote long columns in the group's newspaper explaining the fundamental incompatibility of African American and whites. In one overwrought article, complete with a headline printed in large capital letters, SWABC argued that "CRIME STATISTICS

FIGURE 2. Father Francis Lawlor and the Southwest Associated Block Clubs were adept at borrowing tactics from the other side of the American racial divide and adapting them to their own ends. This cartoon, published in the April 10, 1970, edition of the SWABC's newspaper, the *ABC News*, plays on Black Panther Eldridge Cleaver's rhetoric to argue that whites should participate in block clubs to protect their neighborhoods against African Americans. Courtesy of the Chicago History Museum.

SHOW NEED FOR POLICE HELP FOR SOUTHWEST RESIDENTS." Despite having one of the lowest crime rates in the city, West Englewood was unsafe. Lawlor's article declared, "The rights of homeowners and apartment dwellers in a stable, law-abiding community are being challenged by government bureaucrats, biased and incompetent clergymen, unscrupulous real estate speculators and agents, the Administrative Staff and Members of the Chicago Board of Education, leaders of the Black and pro-Black Civil Rights organizations and a highly vocal handful of pseudo-intellectuals, teachers and laymen who erroneously believe that de facto segregation is necessarily evil or an injustice to the Black people." Lawlor's network of block clubs focused on blunting the effects of black migration by finding white buyers for houses that did go on the market, policing crimes committed by blacks in the so-called fringe areas, chasing storefront churches from commercial streets, and stopping school integration efforts.[68]

Police and Politics

Father Lawlor's dual roles as block club organizer and alderman signaled an important shift in block clubs' relationship with Chicago politics and government. Early-twentieth-century block clubs under the Urban League's influence kept themselves carefully nonpolitical. The clubs' reticence derived from what historian Arvarh Strickland calls a "cardinal principle" of the Urban League movement, keeping "reference to politics" out of both "League philosophy and statements on policy and purposes." To pacify funders, the Chicago Urban League avoided all suggestions of radicalism. It was explicit with affiliated block clubs that it was nonpartisan, and that they must be nonpartisan too. One League block club member who demanded that members clear their plans with the precinct captain was so offended by their adamant refusal that he stalked out of a meeting and resigned from the group.[69]

This avoidance of political involvement limited what League block clubs could accomplish in Chicago, whose government has been controlled by the Democratic political machine from the 1930s on.[70] Allocation of local government services was the prerogative of the precinct captains and aldermen, who doled out perquisites to constituents. For example, to schedule a pickup of bulky garbage, Chicago residents had to ask their ward superintendent, who was almost always a political appointee.[71] Despite their emphasis on local improvement, League-influenced block clubs tended to shy away from incurring debts to politicians with the power to leverage better local services. Faith Rich, who actively participated in her local block club and observed others around the city, noted that in defining their boundaries, most clubs sought to evade control by precinct captains.[72]

Minimizing partisan connections offered some advantages for block clubs. Getting bogged down by members' political differences had the potential to fracture a group so that it became nonfunctional. Additionally, a 1962 report on the state of organizing in Chicago noted, "Experience has proven,

in general, that these groups are too small in size to influence public policy."[73]
Flying under the political radar gave block clubs the leeway to pursue their
autonomous goals without interference from a structure on which they had
little natural purchase.

Block clubs that developed outside of the Chicago Urban League's tradition had fewer compunctions about cultivating political relationships. In
Hyde Park, where the HPKCC and its block clubs maintained close ties with
independent Alderman Leon Despres, the relationship worked in two directions. Not only did the urban renewal program involve major enabling legislation and public financing, but block clubs also felt comfortable asking for
assistance with their projects. Despres reciprocated by asking block clubs to
cooperate with such efforts as tending newly planted street trees. Beginning
in the 1960s, Chicago block clubs became much less inhibited about engaging
in overtly political activity. The wedge that opened up the relationship was
the issue of civil rights. As the example of Father Lawlor's SWABC suggests,
whites rallied around the alderman-priest who promised to protect them
from integration. For their part, African Americans lent their block clubs'
energies to promoting the civil rights movement, in both its Southern and
Northern iterations. In the early 1960s, many black block clubs sent money
south to support civil rights activists. Similarly, when Rev. Martin Luther King
held a major civil rights rally at Soldier Field in 1966, several West Side block
clubs raised money to hire buses to transport residents to the rally.[74]

Block clubs' connection with government grew even stronger in the 1990s,
when the CPD began promoting new approaches to crime prevention. Before the advent of the Chicago Alternative Policing Strategy (CAPS) in 1993,
block clubs concerned about local crime had little leverage with the CPD.
Chicago policing was geared to dispatching police in automobiles to answer
calls that arrived via the 911 emergency telephone number. In the 1990s, however, Mayor Richard M. Daley split the CPD's focus between 911 and CAPS. A
national trend with some distinctive Chicago touches, the community policing approach harkened back to the era of the "beat cop" who was personally
familiar with the public he served. The central idea of CAPS was for a cadre of
officers to develop relationships with local residents and institutions that promoted public safety before crimes occurred. Under the CAPS strategy, which
continued under Daley's successor, Rahm Emmanuel, Chicago is divided into
districts and subdivided into thousands of walkable beats, each with its own
dedicated officers and regular "beat meetings." Community members are invited to share their views of local needs and get to know their officers before
crimes occur.[75]

As CAPS developed over its first two decades, organizing block clubs became an increasingly important activity for CPD staff. Two important social science theories informed CAPS's cultivation of block clubs. First, George Kelling and James Q. Wilson's influential "broken windows" theory, published in 1982, decried the shift in police goals from maintaining order to enforcing laws. They argued that small flaws in the physical environment encourage crime. When criminals see untended, vandalized property, they recognize opportunities. Therefore, protecting property is critical to keeping the public safe. Kelling and Wilson also strongly urged that police officers be deployed on routine foot patrols to build local relationships, instead of remaining in cars and responding only to emergency calls. CAPS also draws on the sociologist Robert Sampson's theory of collective efficacy, which he developed in the same turn-of-the-century context where the CPD worked out community policing in practice. The theory of collective efficacy argues that groups of neighbors can act together to reduce violence.[76] Both of these lines of argument pointed logically toward block clubs' potential for deterring crime. If residents could work together to create an orderly physical environment, then their labors might also reduce levels of community violence.

The CPD did not arrive instantly at the idea that CAPS should budget for the civilian side of community policing. But, starting around 1998, the department hired permanent, professional, civilian staff to organize block clubs. In the 1990s, CAPS especially encouraged block club members to participate in their local beat meetings, where police officers invited residents to discuss community concerns. The CPD publicly praised civilian block club organizers and publicized their anticrime efforts. In the twenty-first century, the CPD website encouraged the creation and registration of block clubs. On the assumption that any association was better than none, CAPS organizers experimented with "vertical block clubs" in high-rise buildings, which are especially common in Chicago's lakefront areas; "virtual block clubs" in wealthy areas where residents were too busy to meet face-to-face; and "walking clubs" and "garden clubs" that engaged residents in healthful outdoor activities that demonstrated local interest in public spaces. By 2013, the CAPS office employed a cohort of twenty-four full-time community organizers to encourage residents to develop stronger connections with one another, take actions to signal that crime was unwelcome, and improve the environment. This number represents only a small fraction of the CPD staff of more than 12,500 sworn officers, but it makes the CPD one of the largest employers of community organizers in Chicago's history.[77]

In the same period that CAPS began organizing block clubs, a few Chicago politicians began to use block clubs to connect with their constituents. Forty-seventh Ward Alderman Ameya Pawar, first elected to the City Council in 2011, treated organizing block clubs as a service. Pawar was influenced by the outreach practices of other contemporary and former aldermen, including Dick Simpson, Mary Ann Smith, and Joe Moore. Simpson, who became a professor of politics after leaving office in 1979, organized a "ward council" populated by representatives of the precincts to advise him on priorities. Forty-eighth Ward Alderman Mary Ann Smith routinely consulted with the existing network of block clubs that served her North Side constituents. She asked them to help her decide how to allocate certain funding, and bound herself to vote on certain City Council items in accordance with their recommendations. Forty-ninth Ward Alderman Joe Moore runs a "participatory budgeting" election, in which "all 49th Ward residents age 16 and over, regardless of citizenship or voter registration status," are invited to vote on how he will allocate his discretionary infrastructure budget.[78]

Rather than simply respond to residents' views as expressed through their groups, Alderman Pawar has taken the additional step of organizing block clubs. His ward service staff members organize them to perform a variety of local functions. Their activities range from traditional beautification and other self-help projects to more overtly political tasks, such as conducting an annual "block audit" that enumerates local infrastructure improvement needs, and attending Ward Council meetings with the alderman. Pawar, who holds a Master's degree in threat and response management, and whose professional background includes working for Northwestern University's Office of Emergency Management, also sees disaster management as a potential benefit of the neighborly connections fostered by block clubs.[79]

Pawar's conviction that neighbors are critical allies in moments of disaster reflects an emerging twenty-first century consensus. The deaths of hundreds of elderly, poor, and socially fragile Chicagoans in the 1995 heat wave convinced some observers that if neighbors had known each other better, fewer deaths would have occurred.[80] During heat events after 1995, Mayor Richard M. Daley and other officials repeatedly urged Chicagoans to check on their neighbors who lived alone. Terrorist incidents in US cities, most notably the hijackings of September 11, 2001, and the Boston Marathon attack of April 2013, added to the sense that in emergencies, urbanites must rely on vigilant civilian neighbors for aid even before "first responders" arrive on the scene. Budget-driven reductions in police service in places such as Camden, Detroit, and rural Oregon pushed residents to experiment with volunteer emergency management measures.[81] Block clubs cannot substitute for professional policing, but both the CAPS program and Pawar's approach to organizing in the Forty-seventh Ward reflected a new relationship between block clubs and Chicago governance. Although Chicago Urban League organizers rejected political involvement, in the twenty-first century the city has reached out to block clubs in the hope that an engaged citizenry can enhance the normal functions of governance.

Conclusion

During the century after the Urban League pioneered block club organizing, Chicagoans tested reasons to participate. They hoped to improve their own and their neighbors' properties, to create a congenial climate on their blocks, and, above all, to protect their home turf. Block clubs, they often found, could reach goals that money achieved for the wealthy. Rich neighborhoods enjoyed well-maintained physical environs and comparatively unrestricted access to public services such as garbage collection and policing. In neighborhoods where most residents could not pay for a desirable environment, block clubs could inexpensively impose aesthetic standards held by a group of energetic and organized residents. A participant in a Los Angeles block club observed,

> It's no accident that block club events, and block clubs themselves, are most active among neighborhoods that struggle and almost nonexistent, or simply invisible, amongst neighborhoods that don't. For the latter, there is no need to prove anything. Besides, as anybody who's been to Pacific Palisades or upper Brentwood knows, such places frown on even having sidewalks because just walking around is considered déclassé, potentially criminal. Holding a party in the middle of the street is completely off the radar.

A Hyde Park block club member laconically affirmed this view in 1964. Explaining why his club existed in a latent state—able to activate if needed, but otherwise doing nothing—he commented: "Block is in good condition really no need for a block meeting."[82]

In Chicago, as in California, most block clubs emerged in working- and middle-class neighborhoods, not in the enclaves of the rich. A central goal of the clubs was to create an acceptable street environment, something that neither individuals nor government were accomplishing on their own. The clubs cajoled neighbors to bring nearby public and private spaces into compliance with their shared vision for a desirable streetscape. They used a host of incentives to induce cooperation. They also tried to regulate how people

Organize

In May 1966, under the headline "Future of Block Club Movement Depends on Austin Residents," the *Austinite* newspaper recounted interviews with Eugene Leonardi and Marcella Kane. Leonardi and Kane were organizing block clubs in their southeast Austin neighborhood. In addition to founding their own club on the 5000 blocks of West Washington Boulevard and Madison Street, they also seeded several more block clubs. Although their initial group had no apparent sponsor, Leonardi argued forcefully that "block clubs can't be islands unto themselves." Instead, they should be part of a "network of block clubs with block chairmen forming a Block Senate with a director at the head." In Leonardi's view, block clubs were easy to start—founders needed only "plans for the future and one person from the block to spark the effort." As many block club organizers discovered, however, developing sustainable block clubs was harder. In Austin, designated block captains called personally on each of the homes along their streets "to explain the purpose of the club and what it can accomplish." Keeping block clubs going was also difficult, for "there must be projects to sustain interest in order to keep members alive and alert to what is going on in the community and to provide activities." Expressing pride in the success of their own group, Leonardi believed that its nine years of existence "may make it among the oldest block clubs in the United States."[1]

Leonardi's claim about his group's superlative longevity may have been correct at the moment he spoke to the *Austinite* reporter in 1966. But nine years did not set a record. In 1957, Chicago Urban League organizer Alva B. Maxey reported one group that had lasted for twenty-five years. In the postwar years, several exceptional Chicago block clubs persisted for decades. The 15th Place Block club, documented in Faith Rich's personal papers, lasted from 1967 until at least 1987. On the North Side, at least three block clubs have even

LEADERS OF BLOCK CLUB MOVEMENT—Group of block club captains present picture of unity as they gather on a sunny Sunday afternoon to discuss setting up clubs. They are from left Mrs. Frank Cortese, Cortese, Mrs. J. P. Olson, Mrs. John Fischer, Mrs. John Navin, Mrs. John Middleton, Mrs. William McMahon, Mrs. William Fouser, Mrs. Leroy Beagley, Thomas Kenny and Mrs. Walter McCaffrey. All but Mrs. Middleton and Kenny are leaders in Central Austin's growing block club network.

FIGURE 3. Austin neighborhood block club leaders in May 1966. Source: "Future of Block Club Movement Depends on Austin Residents," *Austinite*, May 25, 1966. Austin Newspapers Collection, box 7, Special Collections and Preservation Division, Harold Washington Library Center, Chicago Public Library.

longer track records. The Lakewood-Balmoral Residents Council, founded in 1969, was struggling to find leadership and problems to focus on in 2013, but continued to stage activities such as its annual block party. Founded in 1975, Every Person Is Concerned (EPIC) continued with an active program in 2013. For its part, the Winona-Foster-Carmen-Winnemac Block Club, which started in 1962, has reached the half-century mark and is probably the oldest continuously existing block club in Chicago.[2]

Leonardi's pride in his group's durability reflected the challenges of organizing and sustaining a block club. It was not opposition or budget constraints that made it hard to nurture block clubs. They rarely faced competition and could easily scale their activities to suit members' capacities. But block clubs consisted of volunteers whose only certain common ground was shared residence on the same street. Being neighbors provided a foundation for organizing such a club, but not always the reasons to keep one going. The same qualities that made block clubs simple to start also made their existence precarious. The willingness of neighbors to participate, their dependence on volunteer efforts, and competing personal demands all affected whether block clubs got off the ground and how long they lasted.

How organizers went about creating block clubs depended on their goals. Umbrella networks aspiring to achieve both a sense of community and common improvement goals expended considerable effort. Professional or volunteer organizers knocked on doors or made telephone calls, hoping for the chance to explain their purposes, identify participants, and motivate potential leaders. They called the initial meetings and proposed organizational schemas, while encouraging those who attended the meetings to make critical decisions about their groups' structure. By contrast, parent groups that were oriented toward specific, immediate outcomes tended to announce actions without worrying about organizational sustainability. Quick results were supposed to motivate the group's continuity. A few umbrella organizations simply used local newspapers or flyers to announce the creation of block clubs, confident that motivated residents would respond.

Once organizers rounded up potential members, participants faced a series of choices about how to shape their shared activities. Key decisions included geographic boundaries, eligibility for membership, dues commitments, meeting patterns, leadership structures, and larger network affiliations. Some groups took the definition of these commitments seriously, spelling them out in legalistic detail and voting on official charters. Others simply pursued their goals, neither worrying about organizational niceties nor leaving paper trails for future researchers.

Block clubs' longevity rested directly on their participants' efforts. Umbrella groups often hoped for the long-term durability of the groups they founded. To keep track of their activities, they expected block club leadership to report upward periodically and participate in a larger community network. If a group faltered, sometimes the parent organization lent a hand in stabilizing it. But the burden of sustaining a block club over time fell to its membership. A group with a residentially stable and deeply committed leadership core, such as the 15th Place Block Club, could indeed last for decades. But clubs that depended too much on one strong leader fell apart if that person lost interest. Creating a block club could be as easy as calling a meeting. But creating a structure that would outlast particular residents was a task that most block clubs were not equipped to manage. Groups such as Leonardi's nine-year old club were exceptional in Chicago's history.

Organizing Methods

A block club is not a complicated organization. Creating one requires no special expertise. In its simplest form, neighbors meet together, agree on an action, and carry it out. Some organizations created pamphlets or manuals describing how to go about forming block clubs, but no single established method described their establishment. John Brister Turner, the author of a 1959 doctoral dissertation on block clubs in Cleveland, explained, "Sometimes the formation of such groups is under the initiative of outside agencies like a District Council. Sometimes they are initiated by contagion from other clubs, or they may even emerge spontaneously."[3] In Chicago, some block clubs were declared into existence by fiat. In other cases, they were carefully cultivated as part of a campaign to build what in the twenty-first century might be called "community capacity."

The Chicago Urban League's block club campaign in the early 1950s illustrates the labor-intensive end of the organizing spectrum. In this period, when it was relatively well funded, the League devoted several staffers to organizing block clubs in the South and West Side neighborhoods where African Americans lived. League workers provided a great deal of guidance for starting clubs and logistical support for their ongoing efforts. In return, as will be explained in chapter 3, it expected reciprocal participation in block club federations called district councils. Because of the deep investment in their cultivation efforts, League staff struggled to get block clubs to exhibit what they considered a sufficient level of autonomy.

The League began by assigning a staff member to a particular block. The worker traveled to the block from the League offices at 3032 South Wabash Avenue, and spent hours trying to identify residents who might be induced to lead a new club. Leaders were residents who were already connected to some neighbors and could be role models for others. The organizer's initial goal was to find three potential leaders, each of whom was to invite three neighboring acquaintances to the block club's first meeting. In the parallel experience of the HPKCC, leadership was more than just the willingness to organize a meeting. Director Julia Abrahamson found that block clubs benefited from several kinds of leadership. In addition to the willingness to call meetings and plan activities, other important leadership skills included "imagination and sensitivity with difficult group members or . . . a gift for quietly stimulating others to act." An early error some block clubs made in intellectual Hyde Park, Abrahamson observed, was "the tendency . . . to think of group leadership in terms of verbal proficiency. Gatherings of residents were thus sometimes subjected to hours of interminable theorizing and talk which alienated busy people." League organizers, by contrast, regarded the ability of potential leaders to define local problems as a crucial skill. Maxey explained: "Each brings into the open his particular 'gripe' and problem and from these a neighborhood group evolves."[4]

In locating potential leaders, an organizer might have only a few dozen or upwards of a thousand residents to contact. On streets of single-family houses, only a few residents might be home if the organizer visited during weekday business hours; on blocks whose housing stock was primarily apartment buildings, the organizer was confronted with hundreds of residences to visit—if she could get inside the building. Ringing doorbells could be a difficult way to meet people. If occupants were at work or were unwilling answer their doors for a stranger, the organizer could become demoralized. One League staff worker offered this account of her effort to short-circuit the obstacle of ringing a stranger's doorbell in a multi-unit building:

> I tried a technique that occurred to me earlier, in the office. I went into several entrances of buildings along one side of Calumet Avenue. I copied names from the mail boxes, noting the proper address. I selected the names of those persons in whose name I thought the apartment or telephone might be listed. When I returned to the office late that afternoon, I looked up the names in the telephone directory to get phone numbers of the names I had listed from the mail boxes. Out of ten names, only three were listed in the phone book. The purpose of this technique is to enable the worker to make an initial contact in a new block without the disadvantages of door to door contact.[5]

In the twenty-first century, the identification of occupants might be accomplished almost instantly using a "smart phone" connected to an address database, or it might be complicated by residents' abandonment of landlines. In the 1950s, the organizer had to travel to the target block and then back to the office, where there was a telephone book, in order to find the information she sought. But even counting the travel time, collecting this information was worthwhile.

In some cases, identifying local leaders was easy; in other cases, winning residents' cooperation was onerous. In the 4400 block of Langley Avenue, for example, an enthusiastic prospective leader explained that "she had lived in the neighborhood a number of years and they had always been envious of the block club on 44th Street. She felt that with the help of worker and neighbor Mrs. Robinson she might be able to call together a committee." Potential recruits did not always volunteer that they were sparkplugs. The League worker's notes on the effort to organize the 600–700 block on 46th Street suggest the difficulties of cajoling reluctant leadership to follow through. The initial prospect, Mrs. William Jones, agreed to provide the names of potential members who might welcome the organizer's calls, but then she fell ill. The possibility of being hospitalized meant that she could no longer host the first meeting. For her part, Mrs. Gunn acknowledged that she "had been very busy but promised that she would try to contact other people that week." Mrs. Heath, who also had made no further contacts, "wanted to know if men were invited too," reflecting her assumption that block club work was primarily for women. They were fortunate finally to stumble upon Mr. Long, a self-described "very busy man" who seems to have talked himself into taking up a leadership role. After offering to donate supplies—as a substitute for the time he lacked—he ended up volunteering "to knock on doors and talk to neighbors because he is in a selling business and he thinks that anything can be sold, even the block club."[6]

The League facilitated its recruits' efforts to contact their neighbors. West Side organizer Rachel Ridley provided Durwood Monroe with a letter of introduction:

> This letter comes in order that you might have an official authorization to show to persons you contact, to work with you as residents of the 2300 block of West Monroe Street for a better community.
>
> We are anxious that all persons know you as President of the 2300 block club on West Monroe.

The organizing task was complicated by people who feigned cooperation. One League staff worker was appalled by a visit to a one-room apartment that was at the "height of uncleanliness." According to the organizer's notes, the occupant "said she would come to the meeting but one could assume from her expression that she would not." The worker wrote off that prospect, noting, "From all indications, she was trying to make us think she was interested in the club when she was not."[7]

As the worker's observations about hygiene suggest, the class status of the organizers and the organized shaped the League's effort. The politics of respectability determined whom League organizers saw as potential leaders, and which neighbors they regarded as being the problems to be solved. By and large, League staff assumed the classical model of racial uplift. Settled members of the middle class would demonstrate the standards of living expected in Chicago for newly arrived working-class neighbors. The organization's class-based assumptions may have predetermined the outcome of their efforts. A League staff report about the mixed-income blocks of 3500 and 3600 South Wentworth in 1952 shows how misleading early impressions could be:

> Since the persons referred to me previously were not productive leads, I decided to visit homes and businesses which looked good from the outside. After talking to the owner of a candy store, I was referred to a Mrs. Lux who was the owner of the building. She agreed that the block could use an organization

formed for the purpose of improving its appearance and suggested several names of owners to me. She was not overly enthusiastic but said she would try to attend a meeting when called. Since she works nights, she pointed out that it might be difficult for her to give much time in forming a club. I talked next to a Mr. & Mrs. Wills. They too were interested but thought that for either, the time would be a factor. Mrs. Wills was not physically well but said she would try to attend a meeting.

Mrs. Lux assumed that only other property owners were suitable block club participants, but the League organizer encountered only a tepid response from her referrals. The staffer was fortunate to stumble across a renter with an activist temperament:

As I rang other door bells, I met tenants who recognized the need for some improvements in the area. They were not too articulate about their wishes, but had much feeling, primarily of a hostile nature about their neighbors. A Mrs. Burton (3617 S. Wentworth) who is active in the Eastern Star Movement felt strongly enough about the idea of block improvement to offer her home for the first meeting. Her home happened to be one of the poor ones visited but she is obviously making an effort to beautify it. She had planted grass and flowers in her front yard and felt quite bitter about the way her neighbors trampled the flowers. While talking with her, she called in several of her neighbors to have me explain the Urban League program. They all listened politely and plan to attend the meeting on Monday, Oct. 20th at 10:30 a.m.[8]

The planned meeting time, during business hours on a weekday, suggested that the expected participants were probably women. It implied that the participants did not work standard business hours and were available to devote themselves to community labor. Although they may have been tenants and not property owners, their presence at home during the day meant that they were respectable enough to have leisure time available for block club work.

When a meeting time was finally set, the League mailed notices to potential club members, relying on the names provided by the successful initial contacts. For example, Rachel Ridley sent a letter to Mrs. Clementine Stewart, explaining, "Mrs. Addie Bryant has informed me that you are interested in improving your block. For this reason I am calling a meeting Monday, October 2nd., at the home of Mrs. Bryant, 1939 West Washington Blvd. . . . for the purpose of planning a program to meet the needs of your block."[9]

Setting a meeting, however, did not guarantee that people would attend. A 1985 study in Nashville, Tennessee, conducted with funding from the Ford Foundation's Block Booster project, suggested that block club participants had to see problems as solvable locally. Block club members were more likely than their neighbors to have a high estimation of their own skill level, their sense of civic duty, and the value of their block, while regarding local "problems as only moderate." Block club participants needed to feel both that there were problems worth their time and that they had the capacity to solve them. The League worker trying to organize the reluctant residents of the 3500 and 3600 blocks of South Wentworth in 1952 reported that "attendance . . . was extremely poor" at the October 20 meeting. Only the flower-planting Mrs. Burton had showed up. She and the League organizer went back out into the block and tried to round up other attendees. The organizer "did make some attempt to bring people to the meeting but none of them were home when I rang their bells." Mrs. Burton, by contrast, succeeded in dragooning two of her neighbors. The League organizer, "therefore, spent most of the hour and a half talking with Mrs. Burton and attempting to interpret the lack of attendance. She was extremely disappointed and seemed to feel it very personally." Although this was a time-consuming and often frustrating method for organizing block clubs, contemporary practitioners thought it was the best method of cultivating participation. Thelen and Sarchet observed of organizing in Hyde Park: "For getting people to an initial meeting, ready to go to work, there is no substitute for personal contacts."[10]

Once a League block club gained some traction and started meeting on a regular basis, the staff worker pulled back. The League still provided logistical support and attended the occasional meeting if the club experienced problems and notified the office. The League staff worker also mailed out announcements of upcoming meetings for clubs that provided lists of their members' names and addresses. Before the age of home computers, printers, and e-mail, duplication of notices usually required an investment in capital equipment beyond the reach of most block groups. When given sufficient notice, the League used its mimeograph machine to help clubs announce events; if club members had personal access to such equipment, the League encouraged them to use it instead. The 1500 Drake Block Club, disappointed with the turnout at an early meeting, specified to the League office their preferred format for the communication "explaining the purpose of the organization" to prospective participants. They politely requested "that a letter be sent out rather than a card."[11]

Delivering such a high level of services to block clubs was not without its own costs, as the HPKCC discovered. In 1962, its block director refused a duplication request from one club, abashedly explaining, "Our mimeograph machine is old—and as you have learned, tempermental [sic]. We are afraid such an additional monthly load might kill it completely." She also assuaged the club's leaders' fears that the HPKCC was spying on them. When they reacted with suspicion to a request for a copy of their monthly minutes, she explained, "I did not meant to imply that I intend to watch over every detail of you[r] group's business; you have a highly intelligent and experienced executive committee fully capable of doing that. However, it is generally mutually useful for me to know what block group's [sic] are doing since I sometimes know how other groups have handled similar problems, or that additional information can be obtained from a certain agency. Since I cannot attend every block meeting in our community, I ask each block group to send me written reports."[12]

Clubs did not always realize that the League's support for new groups was meant to taper off. Startup assistance sometimes spilled over into ongoing demands. In a semiannual report a League staff worker concluded, "It has proved impossible for me to give adequate service to the individual block unit to the extent that the members in the blocks wish. They seem to feel that because the Urban League has sent an individual to organize the units that the person should be free throughout the months to visit their block club meetings and to help them to plan and carry out their programs." A staff worker reported with asperity a gender-specific request from one club: "Mrs. Lydia Taylor called the office several times requesting a *male* worker to come to the meeting of her club. Having an acute staff shortage, plus our one male worker being assigned to the Westside, she had to settle for a woman."[13] The League aspired to be a mother bird tending hatchlings; fledglings were supposed to fly on their own.

While its community organization program lasted, the Chicago Urban League staff showed extraordinary dedication to nurturing new block clubs. Other groups that wanted to cultivate block clubs got them started with less time-intensive methods. Several umbrella organizations hired staff organizers, as the League did, but only the HPKCC rivaled the level of logistical support that the League provided to its clubs. HPKCC organizer Peggy Wireman estimated in 1964 that "one staff person could handle ten active block groups."[14] Depending on the purposes of each sponsoring umbrella group, some put less emphasis on formal organization, democratic processes, and community building, and gave more attention to action.

In the 1960s, the Organization for a Better Austin (OBA) also relied on knocking on doors. Its organizers used insights gained about one person's perception of problems as a tool for gaining entrée with the next person they talked to. Ed Shurna, who worked for the OBA under the guidance of Shel Trapp, described to scholar Aaron Schutz how this process worked:

I would go and knock on every door on the block [in my assigned area]. And I would say, "I'm with St. Catherine of Sienna Church, and I'm knocking on doors to find out if there are any problems in the community." And we'd start

conversations on the front porch. And then somebody would bring up an issue: "Curbs are falling apart, and I blew two tires while I was trying to park my
car, and the city never cares about this neighborhood." So I knock on the door
next door and I used this same rap, "Hi, I'm Ed Shurna. And I was just talking to your neighbor, and he was complaining about the damn curbs that are
cutting up his tires. And we were talking to see if there's an interest in people
getting together to see if they could do something about this." And then I'd go
to the next door. And maybe by then I'd have identified some woman who was
willing to walk with me and knock on the doors so that I'd get more credibility.
[So] that I wasn't just some outsider. It's the neighbor down the block and I.

And after I had knocked on as many doors as I could, I would ask three
or four people that seemed the most interested if we could get together and
talk with their neighbors about what we might do about the curbs, or what we
might do about the abandoned building on the corner, and we would have a
small planning meeting.

In contrast to the Chicago Urban League's approach, block club organizers in
Austin were more focused on provoking residents to act on their own behalf
than in structuring a formal organization. The OBA organizing staff was concerned that if left to their own devices, block clubs would quickly deteriorate
into social groups rather than stay action-oriented. In an earthy description
typical of organizers in the Alinsky tradition, Shurna continued:

[Shel] Trapp would say [that] you shouldn't have more than two planning
meetings before you do an action, otherwise people are just masturbating or
something. And so I knew when I had a planning meeting I had a plan for a
bigger meeting where we can invite the whole block out, and then we'd have a
strategy from that [bigger] meeting. We wanted to get the city department of
sanitation, or the city police, or the building owner on the corner to come out
to that meeting. So the building process was pretty simple that way.[15]

The HPKCC's approach to block club organizing was similarly top-down.
In contrast to the Chicago Urban League and the OBA, however, the HPKCC
regarded staff-run door-to-door organizing as impractical. For its first year,
the organization designated twenty "zones" within its territory, and dispatched
"zone coordinators" to cultivate leadership and block groups within those
areas. In 1952, however, it abandoned this approach and launched a series of
"community clinics" where block group leaders could network, rehearse recruiting and problem-solving tactics, learn about larger community issues, and
model block organization for visitors from other neighborhoods. A "block
steering committee" met monthly to link block groups together. Director Julia Abrahamson reported that as the HPKCC's staffing increased, so too did
the services they offered to area block groups.[16]

Explicit instruction helped inexperienced organizers practice tactics for connecting with their neighbors. The Garfield Park West Community Council (GPWCC), a community improvement association, aimed to "end the creeping blight which has been attacking the area." Its leaders made the creation of block clubs an integral part of their initial organizing drive. Within a few months of the GPWCC's first meeting in spring 1954, it launched a membership drive spearheaded by 150 "block captains." Residents who joined a block club also became members of the GPWCC. By the end of the summer, the GPWCC netted two thousand members from the approximately twelve thousand families within their geographic scope of two hundred blocks.[17]

A "block captains' manual" written by one of the GPWCC's founders facilitated this successful organizing campaign. The manual explained the role of the block captains, interpreted the relationship between block clubs and the GPWCC, described how to organize block meetings, and offered a "suggested sales approach" to persuade neighbors to join the clubs. The manual instructed block captains in precisely how to recruit new members:

1. Contact personally *each* good family (not just one to a building) in your block that is attempting to live up to the responsibilities and duties of good citizenship.

2. Get the Council's message across to these neighbors in a clear, concise way so that no possible misunderstanding of the Council's program can ensue.

3. Enroll these families in the Council. Dues are $2.00 a year.

4. Ask these member families to display our membership certificate.

5. Welcome newcomers to your block immediately. Explain the Council's standards and enroll these families as members of the Council.

6. Make a listing of all block members for personal use and a duplicate for the Council office. Turn in all census type cards to your Block-Captain Coordinator.

7. Make maps for personal use and the Council office of all property in your block, noting particularly vacant land, structures, size, the numbers of families in each, the number of units, whether or not the structure is converted (legally or illegally, if known), the name of the owner and whether or not the owner lives on the premises, and the specific use of the property, i.e., rooming house, convalescence home, family residence, owner plus one family of tenants, etc.

The manual's "suggested sales approach" elaborated that the "good citizens" were "not those who have littered property, inadequate garbage facilities, disreputable tenants, illegal conversions, overcrowded premises, dilapidated garages, rat infestations, or those who are hostile and contemptuous of their neighbor's rights, or those who disregard the welfare of their neighbors by speeding through the alleys and streets." The manual also provided specific domestic hygiene instructions for members, who were to set a good example for their neighbors:

1. Keep the home area clean, i.e., the parkway, steps, porches, yards, and street gutters.
2. Provide adequate garbage facilities, a covered can per family. A covered can will prevent rats from feeding on discarded refuse.
3. Keep your alley line swept. Stop others from littering your property, etc.[18]

Most of the GPWCC's subsequent activities focused on the state of the entire neighborhood of West Garfield Park, which was undergoing transition from white to black. The organization treated the block clubs as constituents to be activated for specific purposes, rather than as neighbors to be cultivated for their long-term community leadership potential.

The approach employed by the Northwest Community Organization (NCO) in the early 1980s exemplifies more action-oriented organizing. The NCO did not simply count block club members as latent supporters. Instead, it used block clubs to undertake actions that advanced organizational goals. To start a block club, NCO staff created and distributed flyers announcing meeting times and locations; little evidence in the organization's records suggests the kind of deliberate, preliminary cultivation of leadership that the Chicago Urban League routinely employed. For example, to encourage attendance at the initial meeting of a new club for the 2100 block of West Crystal Avenue, the NCO distributed a flyer with the headline "How long do we have to put up with abandoned buildings on our block??" It argued that "our community needs more housing, and instead we have abandoned, dangerous buildings." The flyer elaborated, "We are trying to get together a block club to work on these abandoned buildings and other problems of the block." It invited residents to a meeting at the People's Missionary Baptist Church.[19]

On occasion the NCO organizers went from door to door to scout a block's potential. On a visit to the 1700 block of North Francisco, an organizer spoke to residents who ranged from young adults to the elderly. Many of them, the organizer discovered, could identify problems on the block, but were afraid to act. The problem was that "most of the block . . . seem intimidated by the teenagers that live in the red apartment building on the east side of the street." As will be discussed in chapter 6, some block clubs that saw youth as a problem found strategies to address generational divides; but this street was paralyzed by fear. The organizer identified the possibility of "tapping Joyce Hudson and her network" in order to "produce as many as 6 people, as well as some potential leadership" for a block club. But Mrs. Hudson was "very clear that she won't act if she feels there is a possibility of retaliation on the part of the teenagers." Brief notes suggest that the NCO may also have directly recruited residents to their events, but in general their records do not document the kind of systematic, labor-intensive organizing that characterized the Chicago Urban League.[20]

In service of their efforts, some community organizations created guides to interpret the work of block clubs to local residents. The manual published by the GPWCC was only one of many. This documentation allowed professional staff to focus their time on identifying leaders who, in turn, would volunteer to organize their blocks using the printed tips. Although the manuals mostly contained pragmatic instructions, they also sometimes pointed to the larger issues that organizers believed would resonate with potential members. According to the historian Benjamin Looker, for example, an organizing manual provided by the federal government's Office of Civilian Defense during World War II "stressed the importance of the smallest residential units to the largest geopolitical struggles. As one explained, 'Overseas they are fighting block by block, from house to house'; hence, in the U.S. 'Each home must be a fighting squad; each block or neighborhood is a fighting battalion.'"[21]

Printed materials allowed residents to learn about the importance of block clubs in private and come to meetings primed to participate. Organizers for Neighbors At Work in Garfield Park felt strongly that they could not proceed with revitalizing defunct block clubs "until we can get the proper LITERATURE needed to let the people know of their importance in the community and how they can help to strengthen it by participating in a block club." The Greater Lawndale Conservation Commission, which had a tenuous relationship with its block clubs, reported in 1963: "Up until 1957 GLCC published a small leaflet entitled 'What Is a Block Club.' Today there is so much block club activity that a leaflet of this kind is no longer needed." A new GLCC pamphlet explained the block clubs' purposes and the block leaders' responsibilities without detailing an organizing method. The East Humboldt Park Planning and Conservation Commission's flyer introduced potential block club members to its expectation that the block club's "chairman (or representative) attends the regular monthly meeting of Block Leaders of the East Humboldt Park Planning and Conservation Commission," and that "he in turn keeps his Block informed of the Commission Activities and Program, which he learns at these meetings." An explanatory pamphlet issued by the Residents Councils of the Midwest Community Council mentioned that one club responsibility was "To hold one fund-raising project a year for the Council." It also provided several pages of "ready reference"—primarily contact information for city government offices where clubs could request help, such as removal of dead animals and sanitary violations. Attendees at a 1997 city-wide conference of block clubs hosted by the CPD's CAPS program received an official binder that included an instructional pamphlet published by the Mayor's Office of Inquiry and Information. Although established block clubs were unlikely to require instruction in *How to Form a Block Club*, members could photocopy it to share with curious residents on neighboring blocks.[22]

In the twenty-first century, umbrella organizations have used the Internet as a passive recruitment tool. Forty-seventh Ward Alderman Ameya Pawar's website published a map of district block clubs, where curious residents could discover which territory they lived in. Pawar's website also featured a Power-Point presentation with detailed guidance about how to start a block club. The site included sample scripts, by-laws, and meeting agendas, as well as checklists and strategies for organizing. The Edgewater Community Council similarly published a map and e-mail addresses for all of the groups in its area. The CPD's website offered general organizing tips. It suggested that volunteer organizers recruit in person instead of simply leaving flyers. The CPD also advised that organizers keep records about who said they would attend a meeting and what their concerns were. It concluded, "Always remember to be inclusive. Chicago is one of the most diverse cities in the country. In some instances, you may need to identify a bilingual neighbor who would be willing to translate for neighbors who do not speak English."[23] Using the Internet to describe organizing tactics did not obviate the importance of street-level recruitment, especially in neighborhoods with few computers. But it did provide a handy reference point for entrepreneurial volunteers.

The organizational techniques employed by bottom-up block groups are more difficult to discover than those of umbrella organizations. The historical traces left by self-organized groups tend to be ephemeral rather than institutional; announcements of public events may appear in newspapers, but groups' origins are rarely documented. Even the creation of such a historically-minded group as the 15th Place Block Club might have remained obscured had the founder not died while the club remained active. The newsletter of the 15th Place Block Club memorialized her in 1972, noting that "Mrs. Charles Nowling who lived at 3136 West 15th Place was the founder of our present block club. Mrs. Nowling called the first block club meeting in her home June 28, 1967. . . . She succeeded in getting cooperation from both sides of 15th Place for the first time in 20 years, some said, there was grass on both sides of the street where before in many places there was only mud and dust."[24] It is likely that most other bottom-up groups were started just as simply, by one or two residents who knew about block clubs elsewhere in Chicago. If organizers grasped that a block club was a simple, adaptable concept, all they had to do was invite their neighbors to sit together and figure out what they could do collectively to improve their block.

Spatial Considerations

Even for block clubs on the informal end of the organizing spectrum, deciding on the group's spatial territory was a fundamental decision. A group's coverage area determined its basic constituency—who might participate and who might benefit from its actions. As the label "block club" suggests, for most groups this decision appeared straightforward: they served the block. The block, however, required definition. Clubs variously encompassed only one side of one street of a given block (the "block strip"),[25] buildings on both sides of a street, all the buildings occupying a shared square block, or two or more adjacent streets. In 1942, the OCD divided Chicago into numbered square blocks. An official explained that the square block was "bounded on four different sides by four different streets, for example, the block between Crawford and Karlov, Washington and Madison.'" For its part, the HPKCC used the block strip as a unit for calculating the extent of organization in the neighborhood "because of the variation in size of block organizations." The St. Louis Urban League defined the "block unit" as "people living on both sides of a street in a single block."[26] Chicagoans appear generally to have favored the approach used in St. Louis. The frequently-used front entrances of buildings brought neighbors on facing sides of the street into visual contact with one another, while residents on different sides of a square block might be unaware of each other's existence.

The Chicago Urban League wanted its affiliated clubs to enjoy some initial confidence-building success. Its staff discouraged participants from starting out too large or ambitiously. One League worker encountered a group that hoped to build a playground for local children. Urging them to work with another club instead of tackling this undertaking alone, the League worker cautioned that "individual block units usually work out best and that cooperation between the blocks could be used for large projects such as the playground." Once, a League staff organizer heard that two neighboring groups were about to join together. She "tried in every way to intercede that the 1500 and 1600 blocks on south Central not merge." Ultimately, however, the worker had to acknowledge that "it has been a futile request because the blocks have merged and they are doing a marvelous job in increasing the attendance." One successful club leader reacted "indignantly" when he heard that a League worker was organizing on a block near his. He had planned "to expand his club into that block." The League worker rushed to soothe his ruffled feathers, explaining "that the League had no objection and indicated we welcome his expansion"; they merely wanted to know about his plans to avoid "duplication of work." Such territorial disputes were rare, but they could generate hurt feelings. One Hyde Park block club's meeting signs were torn down by the leader of a neighboring group who resented their "trying to poach on his territory." A group in Uptown opted for cooperation rather than merger, noting that "each block has its own, unique problems (such as a 'problem building') and that the two streets could always work together on a temporary, informal basis for special projects."[27]

The general preference for using the sides of the street that faced each other did not prevent significant variations. Organizers recognized that a crucial part of nurturing stable groups was honoring members' local expertise. A representative of the HPKCC observed, "The block program is flexible. A block decides what its boundaries will be: one side of the street, all the way around the block, a four-square block area, etc." In Hyde Park, Thelen and Sarchet found one group where "dwelling units with rear entrances facing on the alley came together to form a block organization."[28] This group's decision about their geography probably reflected participants' shared concerns about the alley. In the more loosely organized, action-oriented block clubs affiliated with the NCO, clubs tended to occupy several adjacent blocks.

Faith Rich encouraged her neighbors to organize the 15th Place Block Club around the square block rather than around the two sides of the street that faced each other. Although she respected local customs, as a PhD she also wanted to be able to conduct empirical research to support the club's interests. She hoped to use a US Census publication called *City Blocks* to gather information about the area. Such data gathering was difficult for members of the general public, since "very few other statistics are kept by the block—most by the census tract only which typically includes about 20 blocks." In investigating the club's options, Rich learned that "many Chicago block clubs use the two sides of the street rather than the square block. Some did this deliberately to avoid coincidence with the precinct and possible political domination." Because of the 15th Place Block club's unusual choice to cover the square block rather than opposite sides of the street, its boundaries overlapped with the club just to the north. Its newsletter clarified them in 1986: "Although the 15th Place Block Club's charter covers the rectangular block from 15th Place to 15th Street, Albany to Kedzie, the south side of 15th Street is also in the 15th Street Block Club. Members may belong to both Block Clubs if they wish."[29]

Tall buildings proved hard to organize. Although much of Chicago's housing stock consists of low-rise apartment buildings and single family homes,
many residents lived in high-rise buildings in Hyde Park, on the North Side
(especially along the lakefront), and in public housing constructed in the
1950s and 1960s. Julia Abrahamson thought that in Hyde Park, proximity to
the ground made a difference in people's willingness to participate; residents
of "elevator buildings" were resistant to being organized into block groups,
"and the higher people were removed from the ground the less interested they
seemed to be in the community." In an effort to engage residents removed
from street level, the CPD's CAPS program experimented in the twenty-first
century with organizing "vertical block clubs" in high-rise buildings. The sociologist Sudhir Venkatesh found that tenants of the Chicago Housing Authority's infamous Robert Taylor Homes sliced the problem a different way.
Residents' self-support networks became "quasi-block clubs," and the CHA's
Citizens Committee organized "floor clubs" that selected tenants for janito-
rial and security responsibilities.[30]

Most Chicago block clubs were physically small, covering only one or
two blocks. The major exception to this generalization occurred on the city's
North Side in the last quarter of the twentieth century. In the Edgewater and
North Center areas, "block clubs" covered much larger swaths of territory,
some with as many as two dozen blocks in their purview. The large size of such
groups mirrored the scale of the early-twentieth-century "improvement associations" that were often used to defend racial segregation.[31] But organizers
of these groups used the term "block club," not "improvement association" or
"neighborhood association." This choice aligned them with the city's block
club tradition, even when they explained themselves as serving a "neighborhood."[32] To manage governance in these larger groups, local blocks selected
representatives to interact with governing councils and report back to their
immediate neighbors.[33]

Variations in the size of block groups' territories mattered less than whether
they were active. Maps produced by umbrella organizations suggested carefully delineated, stable groups and failed to convey the extent of resident participation. Some of these groups enjoyed continuous histories of activity. Others, however, were paper organizations that awaited energetic leadership and
member participation to make them locally meaningful.[34]

Naming Practices

Once participants were committed, they selected the club's name. In a few
instances, umbrella organizations kept track of block clubs by numbering

them. The St. Louis Urban League, for example, referenced its block units with numbers designating the order in which they had affiliated with the city-wide federation. Similarly, most OCD block clubs simply used their assigned geographic zones and block numbers. Members of the Very Good Club, however, decided on their catchier name by pulling it out of a hat.[35]

Most Chicago block clubs gave themselves specific, descriptive titles. A club's name usually referenced the number and name of the street where participants lived. Chicago was initially organized on the gridiron system. The city's street naming and numbering system was further rationalized early in the twentieth century. Most streets run at right angles to each other and are numbered sequentially, using the downtown's prominent State and Madison Streets as the north-south and east-west baselines, respectively. North-south street names are also theoretically clustered in alphabetical groups from A to Z according to their distance from the Illinois-Indiana boundary in the southeastern portion of the city, although numerous exceptions make that rule difficult to infer from observation in some locales.[36]

As a result of the city's easily comprehensible geography, Chicagoans carry these geographic references in their mental maps and can readily recognize where in the city a given address lies. Many block clubs simply used their street names to identify themselves. Perhaps because of their intensely local orientation, most block clubs omitted more generic information from their names. Few used the directional designation, referring to themselves simply with the block number and street name. Most clubs also left the designation "Street" or "Avenue" off of their names as well. Such information was only necessary for groups like the 15th Place Block Club, which needed to distinguish itself from the neighboring West 15th Street Block Club.[37]

Not all clubs felt constrained by the city's grid. Members instead imaginatively designated themselves with other aspects of their local geography, history, or purpose. The whimsical name of the Mary K Club in West Garfield Park "was arrived at by the fact that the club boundaries are Keeler to the east and Kenneth to the west. The K stands for Keeler, Kildare, Kolin, Kostner[,] and Kenneth. The Mary stands for Maypole, the north boundary." The Chicago Beach Area Block Group acknowledged a prominent feature in the Hyde Park neighborhood's environment. This group explicitly voted against calling itself a "club," opting for the word "group," which carried a less social connotation. The R. A. Crolley Block Organization, for its part, was named after a founding member's father. The names of the Spic & Span Block Club and the Civic and Neighborhood Club underscored the members' goals. Members of a club organized in the 3500 and 3600 blocks of South Princeton Avenue debated whether to include a reference to the Urban League in its name, "because of its prestige value." The group could not decide between "Prince-ton Avenue Civic League" and "Princeton Avenue Civic Improvement Club," but the League organizer reassured them that they could reference them-selves as "affiliated with the Urban League."[38]

Most block clubs' names were important primarily to the members them-selves, who consulted their own priorities in deciding on them. The partici-pants did not expect to receive the kind of publicity that made the twenty-first-century preoccupation with branding a critical consideration. Block club names projected either their locales or some characteristics that animated their founders.

Structure

Once a block club called itself into existence with a name and boundaries, it faced an array of additional preliminary decisions. Some groups did not bother with details of organizational structure, but simply met as was con-venient and acted. But other block clubs set up more formal organizations. Once again, the Chicago Urban League took the most structured approach, with block clubs specifying their leadership, dues, and meeting schedule in written constitutions. Yet even the Chicago Urban League's detailed organiz-ing structure was dwarfed by that of the St. Louis Urban League, which set out rigid requirements for its block units, specifying that they qualified for mem-bership only if they could show ten participating households.[39]

Many Chicago Urban League clubs, though not all, adopted constitutions and by-laws. Agreeing on governance could build relationships among club members, or test their ability to cooperate. To ease matters, the League pro-vided a template constitution that clubs modified to reflect their priorities. Many League-organized clubs took seriously the task of constitution writing, and spent weeks at the task. The group at 6800 Prairie Avenue even formed a By-Laws Committee to examine the proposed constitution. Their debate was "stormy," and the proposed contents were criticized as "rigid." The League urged using *Robert's Rules of Order* to maintain decorum at meetings. After a period of inactivity, revisiting the constitution could also help rejuvenate a dormant club.[40]

Not all participants regarded a constitution as a prerequisite for an effec-tive club. Julia Abrahamson noted that in Hyde Park, formal constitutions were optional. She observed that "blocks which had responsibility for com-mon property and a continuing project, such as the establishment and opera-tion of a playground, usually found it useful to organize formally, with char-ter, constitution, bylaws, and the regular election of officers. Some formally

voted on a full complement of officers and committees, while others asked for
volunteers." Surveying HPKCC block club members, an investigator spoke
with one resident who thought his block's organization was far too complicated. The investigator reported:

> Mr. Clark is not happy with the work of the Steering Committee—he says,
> "there are too many presidents." It is hard to get them to agree on meeting
> dates, items of business, etc. He assigns tasks, they don't do them, he does
> them, they tear apart his work. He says—too many people not doing anything
> and then criticizing what is done. And he says their block constitution is more
> involved than the one in Washington, which doesn't help matters any.[41]

The looser organizing approaches preferred by some umbrella groups implicitly reflected Clark's sentiment that too much structure interfered with the
club's work.

Clubs with a formal structure almost universally elected a president, or
recognized its top-level volunteer with the title of block captain. After real-
izing the insult implied by their original title "block head," one North Side
club instead designated captains. The president typically acted as both the key
coordinator on the street and a liaison with other block clubs and umbrella
organizations. A block club's ability to accomplish its goals depended on both
the leader's personality and the participants' willingness to contribute their
labor.

Organizers had different ideas about what qualified as good leadership. As
Chicago Urban League staff workers explored a block, they carefully assessed
not only whether potential leaders could bring their neighbors to a meeting,
but also how they would perform in a group setting. Their notes are dotted
with observations about residents' personalities and the search for "persons
capable of leadership." Visiting with one prospect, a staff worker noted that
she "was very talkative and she has the possibility of being a good worker. No
apparent leadership ability was noticed." At another club, which started itself
up without external encouragement, the worker observed that the president
"impresses me as a domineering 'know-all.'" By contrast to the League's approach, reports of initial meetings of block clubs under the umbrella of the
NCO in the 1970s and 1980s describe groups' discussions but do not mention
identification of leadership as part of the organizing task.[42]

The Chicago Urban League's insistence on formal organization could dis-
tract a group from its primary purpose. The block club at 7100 South Eberhart Avenue factionalized into competing parties, interfering with its ability to
function. More commonly, however, League organizers encountered difficulty
recruiting officers. Some clubs were full of eager participants but reluctant

leaders. At a visit to the organizing meeting of the 4800 block of Prairie Avenue, the worker watched in frustration as the person targeted for the presidency refused the honor: "The club was interested in electing Mrs. Caldwell as president. Mrs. Caldwell declined and as a result every person nominated declined." The staff worker knew that Mrs. Caldwell, a thirty-year resident of the block, was its first black inhabitant and had spent many years working alone for improvement. It was possible that her efforts had alienated her recently-arriving neighbors, so the League staff worker worried that the impasse threatened to derail the group's entire future. The staff worker "explained that there could be no club unless people were willing to take responsibilities for leadership, and asked each person to give reasons why they did not want to hold office. Worker emphasized the fact that Mrs. Caldwell should especially give her reasons." In response, Mrs. Caldwell "stated that she had not been able to maintain a friendly relationship with most of her neighbors. She thought something about her personality caused this unfriendliness and thus would damage the club." As a result of the League organizer's gentle intervention, the group elected less potentially divisive members to its leadership positions.[43]

Faith Rich, probably the most educated member of the 15th Place Block Club, consistently served as its corresponding secretary, not its head. Rich wrote to a relative about her neighbor Pearlie Mae Robinson, who was the club's president. Robinson was "a black woman who is now president of the Howland PTA, the 15th Place Block Club and several more organizations." A tenacious woman, Robinson had given birth to seventeen children and had managed to purchase her house outright despite having bought it on the onerous terms of a contract sale. Robinson was, Rich wrote, drafting "her autobiography although she is only semi-literate."[44] Rich, whose personal papers contain coded suggestions that she was a committed leftist, was conscious of the racial dynamics at play on her street. She probably recognized that holding the top leadership position herself would have reeked of white privilege. Status seeking would have undermined the relationships she was trying to build on the block. Being corresponding secretary capitalized on her literacy and her typewriter, permitted her to serve her neighbors, and allowed her to document the group's activities without alienating skeptics. Despite her demurrals, when Rich traveled to her home state of Vermont on holiday, block club members offered the warm testimonial that "the 15th St. block club operates whether there is an elected President or not because of Faith Rich."[45]

Especially in the case of the Chicago Urban League's block groups, the leadership ranks extended far beyond the presidency. Before they agreed on by-laws, some groups elected "temporary" officers responsible for convening the club until permanent leadership could be chosen. In addition to the president, some groups elected multiple officers, including vice presidents, secretaries, treasurers, and chaplains. An observer of North Lawndale block clubs in the 1960s thought that giving members these mantles of responsibility had an additional purpose. If elected to formal office, participants were more likely to turn out for meetings.[46]

Although many Chicago block clubs instituted formal rules and structures, few bothered to notify government agencies of their existence. They may have registered as federal 501c(3) organizations for tax purposes, or filed incorporation papers with Illinois. The Lakewood-Balmoral Residents Council, whose members had some ambivalence about whether it was a block club or a larger service organization, incorporated as an Illinois nonprofit organization in 1969, but it was a rare exception. Most block clubs lacked the legal knowledge and funds required for even routine document preparation and official recognition.[47] The bylaws of the 70th Place and Crandon, Oglesby, Paxton Block Club Inc., incorporated in 1995, ran to twenty-three pages of legal prose, with fourteen articles and dozens of sections. In the late twentieth century, the Chicago CAPS program sought a way to capture information about the existence of block clubs. The 1997 pamphlet *How to Form a Block Club* encouraged organizers to file articles of incorporation with the Illinois Secretary of State (for fifty dollars), register with the Cook County Recorder of Deeds, and apply for a tax identification number from the federal Internal Revenue Service. Perhaps because few block club volunteers bothered with onerous paperwork that promised so little return, CAPS later dropped the suggestion.[48]

Chicago block clubs tended to be internally organized, but had little incentive to share that information with the wider city. They enjoyed their under-the-radar existence without any formal relationship with any level of government. Even the CPD, which has organized hundreds of block clubs in the twenty-first century, does not routinely publicize how many there are, thus suggesting their independence. In contrast, Buffalo, New York, had 559 "registered and certified" block clubs on its books in 2013 (although officials estimated that up to three-fourths of that number were not active).[49] The quasi-legal status of Chicago block clubs allows their members to pursue their goals without worrying about external interference. The dubious advantages of formal registration outweigh the disadvantages of paying for recognition.

Membership

While drafting their charters, block club founders asked themselves who was eligible to join. Although membership usually required some stake on the

FIGURE 4. In organizing a block club, participants confronted questions both logistical and philosophi-
cal. Drawing by Clyde White. Source: Herbert A. Thelen and Bettie Belk Sarchet, *Neighbors in Action:
A Manual for Community Leaders* (Chicago: Human Dynamics Laboratory, Department of Education,
University of Chicago, 1954).

block, the answer was not always straightforward or inclusive. A study of
participation in Nashville, Tennessee, argued that the usual indicators—race,
education, and high social economic status—did not determine who joined
block clubs. A dissertation in New York City, however, found that block club
members generally had more education and income than their nonparticipat-
ing neighbors.[50] As the block club founders debated their structure, they considered what race, property ownership, and age implied about which people
had a legitimate interest in the area. The greatest divide fell along the status
of property ownership. Residents of some blocks never had to ask themselves
whether everyone counted, because all residents lived in owner-occupied
single-family houses. But blocks with multiunit housing almost inevitably
hosted at least some renters. When property owners started a block club, they
often considered tenants to be second-class denizens.

The debate over whether renters could join block clubs played out most
visibly in the efforts of the Chicago Urban League. Black property owners in
Chicago were amenable to being organized among themselves, but they did
not willingly embrace their renting neighbors. For example, the Five Hundred
Club on 42nd Place, formed in the 1920s, consisted solely of property owners.[51]

The Chicago Urban League consistently encouraged clubs to take an inclusive approach toward membership qualifications. But the politics of respectability embedded in the League's organizing method privileged homeowners. In selecting participants for a club's first meeting, League staff zeroed in on well-networked residents of spruced-up properties. Because League workers interpreted well-kept building exteriors as an indicator of leadership and civic interest, by default, property owners set the terms for club membership. Instead of assuming that all neighbors had an equal right to join, property owners often acted as though they had the right to decide whether to include or exclude renters.

League staff workers frequently encountered potential leaders who refused to participate at all if the new clubs admitted renters. Historian Jeffrey Helgeson points out that middle-class black homeowners, who had overcome the odds against African American property ownership, were often "antagonistic" toward both renters and absentee landlords. One black property owner sympathetically admitted that renters desired to improve their surroundings, but nonetheless found them disappointing neighbors. Ignoring the constraints of the segregated housing market, she explained that renters often had large families and so could not afford to improve property that they would abandon when the rent increased. Other clubs grudgingly included renters, who for their part correctly perceived that "many of the members, because they are landlords, prefer not to have the tenants at meetings." Renters who knew themselves to be unwelcome often declined the opportunity to participate.[52]

Property owners' hostility to renters derived from both class distinctions and a broader American ideology about the social value of homeownership. Americans tend to believe that home ownership is a positive good, both for property owners themselves and for their neighbors. The federal tax code's deduction for interest on home mortgages reflects this consensus. A 2013 literature review found that such beliefs were robust even in the wake of the twenty-first-century housing foreclosure crisis that undermined many Americans' hold on homeownership. The study's authors examined both popular beliefs and social science assessments of the relationship between homeowning and such conditions as psychological and physical health, children's behavior and success in school, and engagement in politics and community organizations. Even the steep decline in housing values after 2008 did not shake most Americans' aspirations to own a home, or their confidence in the benefits of property ownership.[53]

In the context of the United States, the ideology of property ownership implies that financial investment in lots and buildings also gives owners a moral stake in their neighborhoods. Owners care about the physical state and future condition of the block in a way that transient renters do not. The president of the block club on the 200 block of North California Avenue, Mrs. Creola Fuller gave voice to this belief when she accounted for her club's inactivity by referencing the apathy of tenants. She explained "that many people who live within this block are tenants and it is very hard to impress upon them the need to join a block club as they feel that they will only be living within this block for a short time."[54] Such theories about the consequences of tenant mobility, however, rarely manifest explicitly in the records of Chicago's block clubs. Instead, the sources show a combination of latent and active hostility between black property owners and black tenants. Property owners tended to be long-established members of the middle class, while renters were working-class, more recent migrants, or both. Owners of single-family properties also resented local black owners of multiunit buildings who rented apartments to poorer tenants. The structures of racial segregation in Chicago prevented blacks of means from moving into white neighborhoods. Segregation also kept the black belt integrated by class—often to the chagrin to middle-class property owners who would have preferred a more homogeneous environment.

African Americans shared in the "American Dream" of homeownership, a cliché that captures the hope that real estate serves as a buffer against the vicissitudes of the housing market and as an investment with reliable dividends. As historians Andrew Kahrl and Beryl Satter have shown in different contexts, blacks' ability to retain property is often tenuous. African Americans often lacked access to the federally guaranteed self-amortizing thirty-year mortgages that has made homeownership widely available to whites since the New Deal. Instead, African Americans often turned to risky contract sales or lost their homes to predatory real estate experts who led them afoul of complicated and unfamiliar laws governing property relations.[55] The fragility of their own grasp on real estate may have exacerbated black property owners' sense that their neighbors' improper behavior threatened their own security. An observer encapsulated the feelings of a group of Hyde Park's black landlords, who resented that their tenants were "destructive, non-interest[ed] in the community, unwilling to cooperate."[56]

Established black Chicagoans harbored two kinds of resentments against their more recently arrived neighbors.[57] First, homeowning block club participants criticized how other property owners managed buildings that were occupied by tenants. Black Chicago's cramped housing stock could not expand quickly enough to absorb increasing numbers of residents. Landlords in black neighborhoods employed a variety of tactics to accommodate tenants' need for spaces to sleep and eat. In the first half of the twentieth century, many landlords subdivided large apartments into smaller units. With the encouragement of the city government during World War II, apartment owners often installed a "kitchenette," a group of small-sized appliances that fit into a small kitchen space. Such "conversions" afforded family units a modicum of privacy. The kitchenette technology enabled families to prepare food without having to share the equipment with neighbors.[58] The property owners rarely bothered to deconvert their apartments after the war ended; the increase in black Southern migration made it easy and profitable to find tenants hungry for housing in any condition. Resident property owners worried that the increased population of converted buildings nearby endangered the value of their financial investments.[59]

In addition to harboring concerns about the physical state of neighboring properties, middle-class blacks resented how occupants of crowded apartments put their personal lives on view in public spaces. Conflict over appropriate public behavior and use of public space has a long history in black Chicago. James Grossman's *Land of Hope* documents instructions the *Chicago Defender* provided for migrants uncouth enough to "use vile language in public places" and otherwise violate middle-class cultural norms. Mary Pattillo's *Black on the Block* traces the continuation of that conflict into the twenty-first century, as residents disputed whether barbecuing on the grassy space of parkways was acceptable.[60] When block clubs promulgated standards prohibiting certain public behaviors such as repairing cars on the street, they were often imposing rules on neighbors who could not comply. Chapter 6 details how block clubs attempted to regulate the undesirable behavior of their neighbors. Tensions between resident property owners and tenants on a block were often palpable to the League organizers who tried to bring them together in block clubs.

Although their organizing methods were complicit with property owners' prejudice against renters, Chicago Urban League staff did not let exclusion of tenants pass entirely unchallenged. League executive director Frayser Lane explained to a prospective president, "Successful block clubs include property owners and tenants in their membership. Everyone who lives in a block is a trustee of that section of Chicago and is responsible for what happens in the block." League staff reinforced this inclusive message verbally. One worker spent a fruitless hour conversing with Mr. Merrill of the 4000 block of South Calumet Avenue, who was willing to work to revive the block club and give the worker "the credit for forming it"—but only if renters were excluded. The League organizer wanted "to try to help him see that the inclusion of tenants could be a means of overcoming what hostility there was between tenants and landlords." But she left the meeting feeling that "he was definitely hostile toward me as a person who could threaten his status on the block . . . and in order to assuage his feelings [I said] that I would withdraw from the block." When included in a discussion with a newly formed club at 4300 South Champlain, the League organizer argued that it "usually was advisable to have membership open to any persons in the block who are interested in the general conditions of the neighborhood." The club's new members disregarded this advice and voted that tenants could not join.[61] The Chicago Urban League's inclusive impulse could not override the combination of class bias and commitment to democratic processes that informed their methods: they sought out the people—often property owners—who appeared most invested in the block. Those who were interested enough to show up for meetings set the terms; those terms often meant that non–property owners were not invited to participate.

In neighborhoods with few resident property owners, the exclusion of tenants was not up for debate: the tenants were the block club. "Floor clubs" organized in Chicago public housing, for example, by definition consisted of tenants. Faith Rich's research on the demographics of West 15th Place in the 1960 census suggested that only 23 of the block's 233 dwelling units were occupied by their owners. Tenant-run block clubs sometimes targeted the shortcomings of absentee landlords, a term that reflected the gap between their physical presence and financial stake in the block. In the 1970s the Northwest Community Organization and The Organization of Palmer Square fostered block clubs in order to encourage action against local buildings that were neglected and abandoned by their owners. Because squatter settlements frequently caused fires in legally untenanted properties, the block clubs asked owners to either tend the buildings or have them demolished.[62] Such groups sometimes assumed an adversarial stance toward property owners rather than regarding them as possible stakeholders in the block club.

Assumptions about age and race also inflected block club membership. Older members routinely regarded young people as both potential participants in and targets of block club activities. Most block clubs, however, did not make youths eligible for formal membership. Some groups set up youth auxiliary clubs that recognized young people as significant local residents without expecting them to function like adults. The 1960 agenda of the 3200–3300 Carroll Block, for example, included "organizing of youth to be junior block clubbers."[63] Junior auxiliaries provided young people with the opportunity to be helpful to their neighbors without subjecting them to the tedium of formal, adult-oriented meetings.

The Chicago Urban League's key role in popularizing block clubs created an impression that block clubs were the special province of African Americans.

Officers and staff of the Greater Lawndale Conservation Commission (GLCC), who were familiar with the League's block club model, believed that previous experiences made blacks especially receptive to being organized. The flip side of black openness to block clubs was the assumption that whites were not interested in organizing them. Mrs. Vinegar, who occupied one of only three black households on the 3300 block of West Fullerton Avenue, was interested in organizing a block club. Perplexed by the small number of black neighbors, she asked the advice of the local League council. The council suggested that she try to organize a club that included her white neighbors—a step which had not occurred to her. In the GLCC's organizing experience, however, it was difficult to persuade whites in racially transitioning neighborhoods to cooperate with newly arrived black residents.[64] Such assumptions did not stop organizers in white neighborhoods from trying to head off black arrival using block clubs.

Elsewhere, residents tentatively explored interracial block club membership. In Hyde Park, an early block club meeting that turned on white response to black neighbors became a touchstone story. It was later repeated in many venues, taking on the quality of myth. Hints in the different versions of the story suggest that if it actually happened, it likely occurred in January 1950, on the 5600 block of South Drexel Avenue, where block club scholar Herbert Thelen lived. Stripped to its essential elements, the tale involved an all-white block club debating what to do when a black family moved onto the block. One participant finally posed three contrasting alternatives to the group. In HPKCC executive director Julia Abrahamson's telling, the options were:

> We could form a mob to try to drive the Negroes out.
> We could ignore them.
> We could visit them and ask them to join us in preventing deterioration and keeping the block a pleasant place to live in.

Faced with such stark and loaded contrasts, the group decided to invite the black family to join in their block club effort.[65]

Over the years, HPKCC partisans provided several different versions of the story in different venues, retelling it to local audiences, placing it in a lengthy pamphlet of the national neighborhood organization ACTION, and seeing it reprinted in *Reader's Digest*. Although the details and emphases changed with each context, narrators consistently reiterated the moral that white residents should calmly welcome their black neighbors. In Abrahamson's optimistic version, the black family graciously accepted their neighbors' somewhat reluctant invitation: "Fortunately, the newcomers were sensitive people who recognized at once the committee's embarrassment and helped them to talk about block problems. They appreciated the visit, thought a block organization was a fine idea, would be happy to cooperate." In the gloomier version offered by Bettie Sarchet, Herbert Thelen's academic collaborator, the black family remained on the block, but aloof from the white residents: "The new family was not sure of their welcome; block residents did not find that they had much in common with the family, nor understand their way of life. The newcomers have never attended the block meeting, and apparently they live their own lives on the block but apart from it."[66]

With a story that takes on such mythic proportions, however, it is difficult to tell whether it actually happened or whether it was simply used as a dramatic illustration of a larger point that the organization was trying to make. The tale was so often told, and so influential, that a significant variation appeared in a very different context. Father Francis Lawlor, organizing antiblack block clubs in the Englewood neighborhood, rhetorically echoed the HPKCC story to make the contrary argument that integration was impossible. In his version of the story, Lawlor explained:

> The 59th to 67th–Ashland to Western Community has only three choices if it is to survive despite pressure from outside. The choices are:
>
> [1] Violent rejection of all Negroes.
> [2] Mass exodus and leave the community to Blacks.
> [3] Organize Block Clubs and let the cultural, social and economic standards of individuals determine the future as to whether there will or will not be any racial integration.[67]

In contrast to Hyde Park's class-stratified racial integration, Lawlor's suggestion of voluntary racial reconciliation was a sham. He consistently argued that inherent cultural and social differences between the racial groups made the prospect of integration completely undesirable for whites. The block clubs he organized were meant to keep blacks out, not to encourage racial reconciliation.

Block club membership could have been defined straightforwardly: anyone who lived on a block could join a club. However, block clubs rarely used such an inclusive approach. Instead, as they organized, block club founders considered the intrinsic worth of each category of their neighbors. They made decisions about whether tenants and property owners, whites and blacks, children and adults could belong to the group. These choices reflected important undercurrents in each club's mission and circumscribed the limits of what it could accomplish.

Logistics: Schedule, Meetings, Dues

Block clubs set their own meeting schedules according to the convenience of members as well as the urgency of their projects. While some met as often as twice a month, most met less frequently. As part of a reorganization effort, the Robert S. Abbott Neighborhood Club set "fourth Wednesday nights of each month" for meetings. Mrs. Ethel Jones, the president of the club at that served the 5100–5200 blocks of South Michigan Avenue, was sensitive to the fact that her small club included only a "faithful few." She planned regular meetings in warm weather. But to prevent them from becoming "overworked," she held only "call meetings" in winter. She arranged these "when any member felt that there was a problem in which they needed the entire club's attention." A member of a Hyde Park block club decried the practice of holding meetings simply to keep a club in existence. He explained, "Experience here proved that an attempt to have this neighborhood meet with the same frequency as neighborhoods having acute immediate problems, tends more to kill off the block organization than to vitalize it. We are a rather exceptional neighborhood in which most people are involved in important professional business of their own, and can be induced to continue giving time only if they see problems worth the amount of time involved."[68]

Turnouts for meetings reflected the group's health. Annabelle Bender, investigating OCD block clubs, identified a club in Hyde Park that held several successive meetings to elect a series of presidents. Each president failed to organize neighbors to implement any civil defense efforts. At the other end of the extreme, Sarchet reported meetings of a few HPKCC block clubs that attracted as many as 150 neighbors. For the most part, an active, well-supported block club might see between eight and twenty people attend any given meeting.[69]

On a practical level, block clubs' meeting schedules determined who could take part. The timing of meetings and activities sometimes reflected the assumption that block clubs were women's work without making a gendered standard explicit. Programs held on weekday mornings or afternoons effectively precluded participation from men. Because more men than women worked regular business hours, daytime meetings accommodated women's schedules. The first meeting of the 1500 Drake Block Club, for example, was called for a Wednesday at one-thirty in the afternoon, a time when people who worked during the day could not attend. Apparently even homemakers found this time "inconvenient," so the meetings were rescheduled for seven-thirty in the evening. On the 5000 block of South Drexel Avenue, where many members of the block group were mothers, members decided to hold their meetings between eight and ten in the evening, after children were put to bed. The 2300 West Adams Street Block Club scheduled a "party" for sweeping the sidewalk and raking up leaves for two p.m. on a Thursday. Although the invitation omitted reference to gender, the organizers did note: "In case your neighbors are at work we will all pitch in and sweep and rake for the Bread winners."[70] Meetings that were held on evenings and weekends could accommodate both women and men—at least those whose jobs occupied them during regular weekday business hours.

An initial problem for block club organizers was that of identifying meeting locations. Programs usually took place in outdoor public spaces targeted for improvement. But activities had to be discussed and planned first. The CPD's website advised twenty-first-century block clubs: "There is no hard and fast rule on where you should hold your meetings. Some people prefer to meet on their block, rotating the location among participating neighbors. Some people prefer to find a neutral location, such as a park, library, church or police station to hold their meetings." In practice, few clubs looked beyond their own block for an indoor meeting site, so members were constrained by the opportunities in nearby buildings. Residential neighborhoods constructed after the rise of zoning in the 1920s often had homogenous building types, so a residential street might consist entirely of single family homes. Older residential districts, by contrast, included a mix of multiunit apartment buildings and nonresidential structures such as taverns, corner groceries, other commercial enterprises, or churches.[71]

Many block clubs met in members' homes. Some clubs, however, preferred to meet in public spaces. The Friendly Neighborhood Club moved its meetings from members' homes to the nearby Jubilee CME Church. Some groups regarded public meeting spaces as superior to private homes. The block clubs associated with the NCO met frequently in spaces such as local churches or a local American Legion hall. Members of the 4600 and 4700 Monroe Block Club were willing to leave their block to meet in the headquarters of the Austin Tenants and Owners Association, which occupied a storefront around the corner at 29 South Cicero Avenue.[72]

Public spaces had their limits. Members of the 2900 W. Adams block club were reluctant to meet at the nearby Catholic settlement house. But they were enthusiastic about the space made available by the settlement-sponsored neighborhood organization. One HPKCC block club met in the lobby of an apartment building; a critic suggested that the place was "too public" for such a purpose, presumably because any passerby could overhear the discussion. Some facilities charged for the use of their meeting rooms, requiring block clubs to dip into their modest treasuries.[73]

To pay for such expenses, block club members taxed themselves. As clubs discussed their charters, they also debated the proper amount for member-ship dues. In the 1950s, League-affiliated clubs usually charged dues between twenty-five and fifty cents per meeting. Members of the 7300 South Calumet Block Club decided to get the group activated by charging dues of one dollar a month for the first three months and then reducing the monthly fee to fifty cents. The 15th Place Block Club leadership sent neighbors a letter explain-ing, "We do not make an issue of dues; but some persons have said that they would like to pay dues even though they cannot attend meetings very often. The dues are $1 a month." Although the club did not insist on payment, it did celebrate Faith Rich's tactic for gently inducing the owner of a deteriorating eighteen-flat building to pay his annual dues a year in advance. She earned his gratitude by rounding up the neighborhood children to reseed his grassless yard. Typically, members submitted dues payments to the treasurer as part of monthly club meetings. Thelen and Sarchet identified one club that "set up a rule that the treasury should never be accumulated to more than $100 unless funds were earmarked for a special project which would cost more than that amount."[74]

Block clubs used their collective funds to pay for expenses. Many of their programs relied primarily on volunteer labor and individually owned sup-plies such as rakes, but some activities required the outlay of money. When clubs held parties, for example, their members might pitch in with food and drinks, but turn to the club for disposable paper goods such as plates and napkins. Although club leaders anticipated that there would be expenses, they did not always know at the outset what their needs would be. A newly formed club on South Indiana Avenue set a dues payment without specifying what the funds were for. When one participant shyly questioned the purpose, the new leaders responded expansively that the money would be used for "Christmas beautification, block incinerators, unfortunate children, etc." In addition to regular dues, clubs raised money for special goals though fund-raisers such as socials and teas. Faith Rich wrote to her father about her block club president's desire to send a poor girl from their street to a summer camp. Thelen and Sarchet found some block clubs whose leadership "believe[d] that paying regular dues gives the members a responsibility for the on-going pro-gram of the group and helps to create a sense of belonging."[75]

Having money to spend sometimes created problems. A club on the 4300 Block on St. Lawrence Avenue disbanded after a dispute about "florals." According to the memory of a longtime block resident, the club's habit had been to send flower arrangements to members. When members moved away but continued to expect flowers from the club, the subsequent "disturbance" caused the remaining group members to quit. This memory was so discouraging that, seventeen years later, residents were reluctant to organize a new block club under Chicago Urban League auspices. The 7200 South Michigan Avenue block group similarly broke up over the proceeds of money raised in a Thanksgiving turkey raffle. The club bought chairs with the funds, but as the group dissolved, members argued about who should keep the chairs.[76]

Block clubs also exacted an invisible toll from their individual participants. In addition to volunteering for activities, members contributed personal funds and labor toward meetings. Father Francis Lawlor explained that one of the advantages of hosting a meeting was that it could "be a good excuse to clean one's house." The Chicago Urban League gave some thought to how hosting a meeting could burden members. The hostess of a League club meeting might feel obliged to provide refreshments for her guests. The League prodded presidents to keep the snacks "small or modest" in order "to avoid embarrassing any of the members who may not be able to serve much, if at all when it is their turn to host the meeting. Remember, people differ as to the size of their income, size of family, even though their interest in the group and the community are equal. Of course, it would be alright to have big or fancy refreshments on special occasions; then too, such affairs might be financed by the whole group." Expectations for clean meeting venues and the provision of food put much of the hidden costs of block clubs' efforts onto women, who were primarily responsible for indoor domestic labor in the United States in the twentieth century.[77]

Block club dues also supported the umbrella organizations that cultivated their existence. The Community Pride Block Club, located in the 1300 block of South Lawndale Avenue, asked their League organizer "whether or not the club owed Mr. Turner anything for his services." Turner explained that the League assisted them without charging for his time, but that "it would be good if at the time of the membership campaign that this block club made a contribution to the Urban League." To his surprise, three months later the club contributed fifteen dollars to the League's general operations.[78]

Despite its insistence that the clubs did not directly owe money in exchange for organizing them, the League nonetheless expected them to affiliate with their district councils and contribute to their logistical and financial support. Both HPKCC and League block clubs sometimes resisted generating financial support for the larger organization. Members of the 2900 West Fulton Street Block Club, with monthly dues of fifteen cents, heartily resented their district council's expectation to receive two-thirds of those funds. In response to their objections, the League staff worker urged them to attend a council meeting so that they could "discuss this matter openly on the floor."

The councils, for their part, also supported the larger organization—again through its member block clubs. The ways and means chairman of a district council wrote to the block club presidents in her area explaining that the council had voted to contribute one hundred dollars to the Chicago Urban League. She flatly informed them that each block club was responsible for coming up with a share: "To raise this one hundred dollars, I am asking that each and every Block Club to contribute at least $5. As President of your Block Club, I'm depending upon you to stress the importance of this project to all your members. Here are a few things that can be done: A small party, sell dinners or merely tap your resources." This recommendation drew on African Americans' long tradition of small-scale, sacrificial financial support for organizations they were committed to.[79]

That tradition was strained when the umbrella group's fundraising goal overrode other organizational purposes. The Woodlawn Organization (TWO), the first black group that Saul Alinsky's Industrial Areas Foundation organized, treated its fundraising needs with less subtlety than did the Chicago Urban League staff. A memorandum from a block club organizer to Alinsky's assistant Ed Chambers suggests that block clubs may have been created in order to build a financial network for the organization, rather than for their own sake. When reporting on several nascent block clubs, the organizer was careful to comment on how much money each had raised to support TWO. In order to belong to TWO, a block club had to pay a fifty-dollar membership fee. Groups also received tickets to a fundraising banquet, which they were expected to sell. Frustrated with the 7300–7400 Blackstone-Essex group, the community organizer wrote that "they are going to give some sort of block club party or if they have to, take the money out of their treasury to pay the balance of $75 that they owe T.W.O."[80]

Logistical considerations, such as meeting locations and dues, were not ends in themselves; they facilitated the larger work of block clubs. Leaders nonetheless took them seriously, for their terms conditioned the ability of members to participate with the enthusiasm and goodwill necessary to sustain the organization. Members disgruntled by matters such as financial obligations or inconvenient meeting schedules could not be counted on to use their energies to improve their neighbors' lives.

Sustaining Block Clubs

Block clubs were hard to sustain for many of the same reasons they were difficult to organize. They were vulnerable to the personalities and personal circumstances of their leaders, and they depended on volunteer labor. Formal

LEADERS OF THE COMMUNITY GROUP MUST BE
WORKING MEMBERS OF THE TEAM, NOT INDIVIDUAL BOSSES.

FIGURE 5. Ineffective, domineering, or absent block club leaders often failed to sustain their neighbors' cooperation. Drawing by Clyde White. Source: Herbert A. Thelen and Bettie Belk Sarchet, *Neighbors in Action: A Manual for Community Leaders* (Chicago: Human Dynamics Laboratory, Department of Education, University of Chicago, 1954).

nonprofit organizations register with the state for tax purposes, create boards of directors, engage in systematic fundraising, and may hire (often small) staffs. In contrast, block clubs lacked the kinds of infrastructure that facilitated self-perpetuation. Members of clubs without successful activities drifted away, allowing the club to wither. Some clubs did forge close ties between neighbors, and could be called into action or reinvigorated if prompted by an outside organizer. On some streets, the only remnant of a block club is an annual summertime block party, where neighbors get the city's permission to close off the street and share beverages, frozen treats, potluck food, and children's games. On other streets, especially after active participants have moved away, the block club has left no visible sign.

Block clubs were especially dependent on the enthusiasm of their presidents, who did much of their legwork. Researchers in Hyde Park found that "domineering" personalities were ill-suited to sustain block clubs. Chicago Urban League staff members expended much of their early organizing energies identifying participants who could plan activities and catalyze broad participation without dominating a group. Leadership implied willingness to both work for the good of the block and spread out responsibility. A League staff worker worried, for example, about the 2100 West Maypole Avenue Block Club, where the president "is really a one woman block club. She calls meetings at will and decides projects at will and sets about to attain what she has in mind. In reality, we know this is not the best way for a club to operate." The block club columnist for the *Garfieldian* newspaper criticized "a common practice of civic followers who elect officers to hide behind them." He argued that the residents with "complaints" should not simply lay their problems at the feet of the block club president. Instead, all members should "make the same sacrifice" as their elected leaders. If they did not, then "their property values will continue to drop and their block and community continue to deteriorate." The downside of depending on a single strong leader became apparent when that person was no longer available. When a president grew old, fell ill, lost interest, or moved away without cultivating a replacement, the club failed. Other clubs simply "disintegrated" as members lost interest.[81]

Clubs that faded out of operation usually did not leave records that allow scholars to search for causes of their decline. A 1987 doctoral student found that only a quarter of New York City block associations whose most recent contact information she obtained to conduct her research still existed.[82] The informal organizational approach of block clubs means that their records are selective. Their activities and programs were sometimes reported in newspapers or preserved in personal archival collections. But most club endings are marked by the absence of documentation. Only when parent organizations followed up on their constituent clubs can we get glimpses of their dissolution. Both the Chicago Urban League and the HPKCC did check up on their block clubs. Even in cases where an outside organizer came around to ask, however, former participants did not necessarily know why their clubs had fallen into inactivity. Ida Summers provided a variety of hypotheses to a Chicago Urban League staff worker investigating the collapse of the homeowners group at the 4300 block of South Vincennes Avenue: "We discussed the fact that the former club had failed because of lack of continuous leadership and possibly because of the expense involved on their first project. This first project had been an attempt to prevent a liquor store from opening on the corner of their block. She felt that the failure to include tenants as members of the club was also a reason and that a woman would perhaps be a better leader than a man." Some, all, or none of those explanations might actually have explained the group's demise. Mrs. Oscar Davis, the acting chairman of the 5200 Drexel Block Group, similarly offered a Hyde Park surveyor a number of reasons for the "discouragement" of her group, which had stopped doing much after her predecessor moved away. She explained that it was "not lack of interest but lack of interest in communicating about problems" and tenants' fears about being evicted with only five days' notice if they were marked as "habitual complainers." She felt that the "group in this area will work if responsible leadership is recruited; someone with the time to devote to it and the interest and ability to get people to talk." But because she herself was in school four evenings a week, she was not well suited to assume that responsibility.[83]

Most Chicago block clubs were, in short, ephemeral. Rare were the block clubs, like those on the 5000 block on West Washington or West 15th Place, that lasted as long as a decade. Those clubs enjoyed patient, committed leaders and were residentially stable enough to continuously reinvigorate themselves. In a city as mobile as Chicago in the twentieth century, that combination was unusual. The Winona-Foster-Carmen-Winnemac Block Club, the EPIC Block Club, and the Lakewood-Balmoral Residents Council, all of which are near the half-century mark, may be unique in Chicago's history. Frank Cherry's dissertation about black Southern migration to Chicago found high attrition among block club members. Cherry suggested that block club organizing might have been a last-ditch effort among homeowners who later regretted that they had not just moved out of the community when they saw undesirable residents moving in.[84] Block club leaders, however, did sometimes strive to connect neighbors to one another. Creating community was an abstract goal, but it was one that block club leaders dedicated much effort to.

3

Connect

In December 1951, the Chicago Urban League staff member assigned to the city's West Side visited a meeting of the club covering the 3100 block of 15th Street. The leaders, Pearl Rodgers, Emmett Waters, and Doris Nesbitt, had already sustained the club for three years without support from the League. The group ran its own newspaper, called *Street Scene*, planted stories about its programs in the *Chicago Defender*, and ran a vibrant slate of activities. Although the League organizer's notes suggest a lack of familiarity with Judaism, they approvingly documented the group's intentionally interreligious programs: "This is an unusual club in that all of its activities are planned to bring in Jewish and Christian belief. They are planning a big Christmas Celebration December 23rd. The adults will go caroling and they will sing Christian and Homika [sic] songs. The Homika [sic] songs were taught to the group by the Rabbi in that area."[1]

The simultaneous presence of African Americans and Jews in the territory of the West 15th Street Block Club reflected the neighborhood's demographic past and future. Historically a center of Jewish population in Chicago, North Lawndale was experiencing racial transition in the early 1950s. For many whites and blacks in the United States, hostility characterized this fraught experience.[2] The block club at West 15th Street, however, seemed determined to expose members to each other's faith traditions as a way to forge relationships across race and religion. If the club's goal was to slow the progression of racial change, there is little to suggest that it succeeded. Between 1950 and 1960, North Lawndale's population shifted from 13.1 to 91.1 percent African American.[3] But the club's effort to forge bonds among neighbors paid less quantifiable dividends. Between its work and that of the 15th Place Block Club, just one block south, residents enjoyed at least two generations of formal and informal programs intended to promote a sense of community among local residents.

Community is a foundational topic in urban social science scholarship. At first blush, the sheer numbers of people and diversity of opportunities appear to make sustaining intimate neighborly ties in cities impossible. Sociologists and historians have spent well over a century trying to figure out whether and how community can exist in the urban context. Scholars from Ferdinand Tönnies to Thomas Bender to Robert Putnam to Robert Sampson have all weighed in on the questions. If community does recur or persist, social scientists remain bedeviled by the question of how to measure it and how to recognize its effects. By the twenty-first century, scholars have answered Tönnies's initial skepticism about the prospects for *Gemeinschaft* in the context of *Gesellshaft* by repeatedly identifying community in urban industrial contexts. But they have not come to consensus on a straightforward, universally acknowledged standard for recognizing community when confronted with it. Most recently, sociologist Robert Sampson's book *Great American City* argues for the simultaneous complexity and possibility of approaching this task through study of "neighborhood effects."[4] This book's conclusion considers the potential for using the term "neighboring" as an alternative to "community" for examining how urbanites have related to one another.

Block club members, however, were undaunted by social scientists' difficulty with operationalizing the concept of community. Throughout the twentieth century, local leaders fostered communal ties on their streets, organizing a variety of activities with an eye toward connecting neighbors with one another. Club newsletters directly reinforced community bonds. On the premise that unstructured time together builds relationships, they often scheduled purely social programs. The most prominent example of the socially oriented block club program is surely the block party—which on some blocks represents the sole collective activity. Creating communal ties with a block club served sometimes as means, sometimes as end. For many block clubs, projects such as the beautification efforts described in the next two chapters anticipated the enhancement of neighborly ties as a side effect. For organizers in the tradition of Saul Alinsky, however, community spirit was mere sentiment; what mattered was harnessing neighbors' connections to the power to create change.

In his important book on community, *Bowling Alone*, the political scientist Robert D. Putnam distinguished between "bonding" and "bridging" forms of social capital. "Bonding" social capital reinforces connections among in-group members, while "bridging" forms forge connection across group boundaries.[5] The West 15th Street Block Club's performance of both Hanukkah songs and Christmas carols reflected bonding and bridging impulses. The group endeavored to connect members across the religious and racial boundaries that otherwise separated them, and to build up alternative relationships based on their identification as neighbors. Many Chicago block clubs likewise worked on both of these fronts. While their activity was necessarily centered inward, on the block itself, most block clubs were networked beyond their immediate boundaries to larger organizations. These networks were especially important to Alinsky organizers as the means for leveraging participants' concerns into action. The extent to which block clubs enhanced Chicagoans' sense of community with their neighbors cannot be measured scientifically. But the consistency with which they pursued programming to connect neighbors suggests that block club members sincerely found the effort of building community to be worthwhile.

Bonding

Organizers, members, and leaders often asserted that block clubs built a sense of community among neighbors. A commissioner of the Greater Lawndale Conservation Commission (GLCC) explained that the purpose of block clubs was to cultivate "a sense of cohesiveness and identification with the community." In the Austin neighborhood, block club organizer Marcella Kane reflected on how hard urban life made it for neighbors to meet each other. She told a reporter that block clubs "kind of take the place of the old-time general stores," where, according to nostalgic tradition, townspeople gathered to share local news. Father Francis Lawlor said that his white South Side groups were "formed to help the area maintain its identity as a neighborhood and as a cultural center." Emphasizing that whites should show their unity by refusing to sell their homes or leave the community, he elaborated, "All that a block club asks is that people act like neighbors." Without invoking sentimental language about community, Quaker leaders affiliated with the American Friends Service Committee's block club organizing program pragmatically declared, "The block is where people feel secure and can attack their problems most easily." They interpreted the efflorescence of neighborhood activism in the 1960s as a possible "trend away from big city-wide efforts."[6] The frequency with which block club leaders invoked a sense of community as the foundation of their actions suggests how tenaciously they held this belief.

There is no reliable way to measure how block clubs affected whatever sense of community residents felt, or whether participants developed long-term relationships as a result of membership. Information about block clubs is too scanty—preserved in fragmented sources from scattered times and places—to allow any sort of systematic study of this question. To rigorously demonstrate a causal relationship between block clubs and the sense of connection that members felt with each other, we would need more than systematic information about block clubs themselves. We would also need carefully designed survey data that operationalizes perceptions of "community" before and after the period of block club activity while meaningfully isolating other causal factors. But, as sociologist Robert Sampson points out in *Great American City*, "discussion around community is normative and nostalgic rather than analytical, impeding progress on how research should proceed."[7] Block club leaders, however, acted as though the connection between the community spirit and their activities was so obvious that no justification was required. They did not wait for an academic study to tell them whether gathering neighbors together for fun or improvement would increase their long-term sense of community. They just organized those connections and assumed the desired results would follow.

Parties were a popular and easy way to build residents' connections. A pamphlet about the Hyde Park–Kenwood block clubs explained why they programmed social events. Parties "would provide a welcome break in a program of hard work, and would further strengthen community loyalties." Although putting on a party required labor for the organizers and hosts, block clubs staged an inventive array of social gatherings. Many block clubs routinely celebrated holidays such as Christmas and Valentine's Day together. For example, the 3600 Calumet Block Club's Christmas Party featured the chance to play keno and enjoy a meal of "baked ham, potato salad and cold drinks." Members reported that the "highlight of the event was a 'grab bag' in which each person deposited a present costing not more nor less than 50¢. These were in turn, distributed among the group."[8] Such an approach kept individual costs low while creating a slender bond of property exchange among participants.

Clubs required only a modest pretext to create social opportunities. The Lorel Street Block Club's "Come Together Party" invited neighbors to socialize for no special reason. The Wendell Phillips Improvement Club held a party to celebrate the eighth anniversary of its founding, not a decimal anniversary but nonetheless a long tenure by block club standards. The similarly successful 7100 Eberhart Block Club ran an annual street carnival. The Progressive Twin Block Club added some friendly parental competition to its tea party by featuring a "baby contest" as part of the festivities. Such sociability earned scorn from organizers in the Alinsky tradition, who regarded the tendency of block clubs to lapse into being "social clubs" as a failure rather than a strength. But most block clubs organized programs that brought neighbors together for fun.[9]

Even ostensibly social events sometimes carried an ulterior motive. One major purpose was to cultivate participation in the block club. Leaders hoped that neighbors who were not initially inclined to work for a local common good might change their minds after socializing with active members. The leadership of the Chicago Urban League–organized 500 Bowen Improvement Club, for example, thought that holding a party might "stimulate neighborhood interest" in its efforts. Participants in the Cosmopolitan Neighborhood Improvement Association similarly thought that a social gathering in a neighbor's backyard would support their "effort to further build the membership of the organization" by attracting both landlords and their tenants. In 2012, the Winona Foster Carmen Winnemac block club hosted a "Holiday Gathering" at a local bar, which incidentally provided the opportunity to renew group memberships. Continuously refreshing the core of engaged participants enabled a club to sustain itself.[10]

Charging for admission to social events raised modest sums to support clubs and their programs. The Miller-Carpenter Street Block Club organized a "Bunco & Card Party" for the dual purposes of getting people interested in the club and raising funds for its 1955 "Pompeii Camp program." Ticket sales were so strong that organizers moved the party to a larger venue. The 3200 West Polk Street Club extended an invitation to other local block clubs to attend its "first annual affair" in 1964. The event was reported to be "well attended and profitable," suggesting that the club charged a fee for attendance or snacks. The president of the 2800 West Wilcox Block Club, by contrast, thought that its 1965 tea was a failure due to "lack of cooperation among the neighbors, and lack of interest." This event appeared to break the fragile group, which the Neighbors At Work community association later attempted to revive.[11]

Groups of federated clubs organized more elaborate occasions that combined sociability with financial support for the larger organization. The Chicago Urban League's Westside Community Improvement Council sponsored a fundraising tea featuring a play, and split the proceeds with the host club. Organizers spent considerable effort working out the perfect price point for admission. Ultimately they decided to have low-cost tickets in the hopes of attracting the maximum number of participants; they additionally tried to incentivize member block clubs to do their part by offering a prize for the group that sold the most tickets. For several years, the Greater Lawndale Association of Block Clubs ran an annual "Villa Venice" dinner and dance in suburban Northbrook to support the Greater Lawndale Conservation Commission. GLCC staff organizers expected one thousand people to attend the first occasion. They reached such large numbers by distributing tickets to board members, who were then expected to purchase whatever they were given and to attend the festivities. They also raised money through the sale of advertisements in the program. Such tactics were not uniformly well received. James Walton, an African American judge and GLCC board member who was active on the West Side, returned his tickets. Walton explained, "I see no way in which such an affair can demonstrate 'an awareness of the fact that it is an awakened community'[;] in fact I see little evidence of any awakening which has affected the lives of those who live in Lawndale. In keeping with my conscience I cannot attend such an affair." Hyman Levine, a GLCC board member representing North Lawndale's Mount Sinai Medical Center, also returned his tickets to the event, which conflicted with the onset of the Jewish Sabbath on Friday evening.[12]

After hosting events, some block clubs published news about their activities, further reinforcing the bonds they hoped participants had built. Hyde Park–Kenwood Community Conference (HPKCC) executive director Julia Abrahamson explained that the "theory of group dynamics on which the block program was based" was one of replacing conflict with connection. She argued "that since conflict is due to misunderstanding and ignorance it can be largely eliminated by information and discussion." Newsletters, which conveyed information that readers could digest in private, complemented the public work of block club meetings. For block clubs with skilled writers, self-published newsletters helped communicate the group's projects and kept neighbors apprised of local activities. A widely disseminated report on the block club program in Hyde Park–Kenwood emphasized the importance of both written and personal communication among members. The author observed, "Neighborhood newsletters, a welcoming committee to acquaint new homeowners with the community program, block parties and picnics, kept all residents informed of activities and gave them an increasing sense of community loyalty."[13]

Few such newsletters survive, but those that remain provide a wealth of information about block club activities. Most block club newspapers are preserved only in scattered issues rather than in continuous runs. The papers of the HPKCC, for example, contain many files with one or two examples of a block club's newsletter. By contrast, thanks to Faith Rich's devotion, the unusually active 15th Place Block Club ran a newsletter that reached at least issue number 79, making it possible to trace its activities over many years. While some newsletters were straightforward reports of block club doings, creative editors tried to inform their neighbors of local events in an entertaining fashion. For example, the *Chips off Our Block* newsletter, published for the 5500–5600 Dorchester block, borrowed poetic meter and verbal structure

REPORT*

The BLOCK asked the
Chairman, and
The Chairman asked the
ALDERMAN, "Could
We have a STOP sign
At 56th and D........?"

The Alderman said,
"CERTAINLY," I'll go
And tell my SECret'ry
To write the City
Engineer and see
If he is free."

The secret'ry said,
"OF COURSE" and wrote
To the Engineer, "There're
SO many accidents, they'd
like to have a STOP sign
At 56th and D........"

The Engineer said, "Bother,"
And the engineer said,
"Dearie me, I'm SUCH a
BUSY man and I wish they'd
Let me be.

Many people think
That a SLOW sign is
Just as good, COULDN'T
They keep their slow sign
At 56th and D........?"

The Secret'ry said, "OH?"
And went and told the
Alderman. The ALDERMAN
Said, "OH," and
"Well, it seems to Me

There's really such a LOT
of Screeching of Auto
Brakes and QUITE a
Lot of Crashes
At 56th and D........,

That a Study of the Corner
Can't do us very MUCH
Harm, though it may not
Do much good--
I think we'll all agree."

So the city Engineer
Agreed to make a STUDY
Of the Traffic situation
At 56th and D........

And it DIDN'T do any harm,
in FACT, it really did some
Good, for we've got a bright
New STOP sign
At 56th and D........

*With Thanks to A. A. Milne

THEATRE PARTY

The date has been set for the
COMMUNITY THEATRE PARTY, which
will, we hope, raise the final
$4,000. needed for the 1957
Conference Budget.

The Date is June 13; the Place,
The Harper Theatre; the Prices,
$.50 for the 4 o'clock show,
and $1.00 for the 7:15 and 9:15
P.M. shows.

The Feature will be "Mr.
Hulot's Holiday, a delightful
comedy without social significance.

The 1957 Conference MEMBERSHIP
DRIVE did so well that both the
Conference and our block are
entitled to that fine glow which
comes with the feeling of a task
well done.

The CONFERENCE membership is
now over the 3,000 mark--last
year's membership was about 2,000.
The BLOCK membership is 114--
43 of these are new members.
(This does not include those members who have not yet sent in
their renewal checks or those
who intend to join the Conference but have overlooked sending in their applications.)

In all, 300 people worked on
the drive. Our block provided:
Mrs. William Baker, Mrs. Edna
Costigan, Mrs. Ralph Cowan, Mr.
George Daigneault, Mrs. Maurice
Donohue, Mrs. William Doyle, Mrs.
Dave Fultz, Mrs. Seward Hiltner,
Madge Lorwin, Mrs. Hans Morgenthau,
Mrs. Jerome Sloan, Mrs. Paul
Talalay and Mrs. Garth Thomas.

FIGURE 6. The newsletter *Chips off Our Block* borrowed from poet A. A. Milne's "The King's Breakfast" to narrate the lengthy effort involved in getting a new stop sign for the corner of 56th and Dorchester. Source: *Chips off Our Block*, May 1957, folder 5, box 96, HPKCC records, Special Collections Research Center, University of Chicago Library. Courtesy of the Hyde Park–Kenwood Community Conference.

from A. A. Milne to explain the complications involved in its successful effort to obtain a stop sign for the street corner.[14]

Most newsletters were decidedly amateur affairs, running to just a page or two. In the days before desktop publishing, many block club newsletters were produced on personal typewriters, featured hand-drawn illustrations and hand-lettered stencils, were reproduced using mimeograph machines, and were distributed by hand. The club at 3100 West 15th Street, however, was fortunate to have a professional journalist as a member. Enoc P. Waters, Jr., *The Chicago Defender*'s national editor, volunteered to edit the club's monthly newsletter, *Street Scene*. The newsletter exhorted readers: "It is hoped that every resident of the block will regard himself as a reporter."[15]

Like a small town newspaper, the newsletter of the Greater Progressive Property Owners Club of Millard Avenue reported local gossip in addition to club news. Items in the January 1962 issue included block club social activities, crime reports, and members' travel. It warned that a neighbor's purse had been snatched on nearby Ogden Avenue, and expressed regret that "the Dozier boys were delayed in leaving Chicago for Las Vegas because their instruments and clothing were stolen from their station wagon which was parked on a neighborhood street." The newsletter also reiterated the pleasure that members had experienced as they celebrated at the annual Christmas party, editorializing, "The members sang carols, exchanged lovely gifts and feasted on the delicious repast. How good and how pleasant it is for neighbors to dwell together in unity."[16]

The Block Club News of the 700–800 South Kilbourn-Kolmar and Fifth Avenue Block Club, with a reported circulation of sixty homes, took a more serious tone. One issue included a lengthy injunction from editor A. L. Dixon to his middle-class African American neighbors to stop "running" when poorer blacks moved on to the block. Instead, they should "maintain this neighborhood." While sounding remarkably like whites' admonitions to neighbors in racially changing areas, Dixon's editorial reflected the block club's larger aspiration to maintain the street's residential stability. Reports from the club's Sick Committee also helped residents keep up on their neighbors' needs; in the same issue it announced: "There was no report of any sick in the block this week. However Mrs. Wilson of 764 Kilbourn is still confined to the house with an arthritic condition. Mrs. McShan of 4510 Fifth Avenue is home from the hospital and has returned to her job."[17]

Networks of block clubs enjoyed deeper resource pools than did individual groups, and they also benefited from the logistical support of umbrella organizations. They could publish more elaborate newsletters than the homemade efforts of individual block clubs. The Chicago Urban League's *Volunteer*, for example, billed itself as "The Voice of the Federation of Block Units and Neighborhood Groups." The Greater Lawndale Conservation Commission similarly published *The GLCC NewsNotes* to keep members apprised of its efforts to attract urban renewal. Block clubs reported on their programming in a regular monthly column.[18]

The Southwest Associated Block Clubs (SWABC), spearheaded by Father Francis Lawlor, published one of the thickest and most professionally designed of the surviving newsletters for a block club network. In 1968 it was produced twice a month, with a reported eight thousand copies distributed free to members of affiliated block clubs. Even in its original format as a newsletter, a single issue ran to sixteen pages. By 1970, when the newsletter had switched to a newspaper format published on newsprint and changed its name, the SWABC was charging ten cents per copy. The *Southwest Associated Block Club News* (later *ABC News*) carried a wide variety of items ranging from friendly gossip about local residents to opinion columns to crime statistics received from the CPD. The newspaper also provided Father Lawlor a forum for elaborating his arguments about the impossibility of harmonious racial integration.[19]

Other block clubs, instead of publishing their own newsletters, disseminated news about their activities through commercial outlets. In addition to several daily newspapers, Chicago also enjoyed a strong tradition of local and ethnic newspapers that kept select audiences informed about topics the mainstream papers ignored. Neighborhood newspapers were a natural outlet for publicizing information about block clubs. In the one-square-mile neighborhood of West Garfield Park, for example, the *Garfieldian* alerted white residents of the United Property Group's plan for creating block clubs. In the wake of racial transition, it also provided regular column space to Rufford Milton, who kept readers apprised of the doings of the block clubs associated with the Garfield Community Council. *The Chicago Defender*, the citywide black paper, was an especially good venue for publishing announcements of block club events. In addition to keeping members informed, the *Defender* advertised a block club's good works to the broader Chicago community. Such publicity about club programming modeled possibilities for other groups. It also provided a wealth of evidence for skeptics that black residents worked to improve their neighborhood's conditions, contrary to racist assumptions about automatic black degradation of the urban environment. Recognizing the significance of the *Defender*, in 1964 the GLCC started feeding reports of its block clubs' activities to the paper.[20]

But publicity also carried some risk. The HPKCC developed an "unwritten rule" that its block clubs needed to obtain advance clearance for press

releases. Its leaders felt their efforts undermined by block club news that contradicted their stands or distracted from larger goals. In response to block
club leaders who ignored the hierarchy, HPKCC staff recommended the creation of a handbook to institutionalize the main office's authority.[21]

In the twenty-first century, block clubs kept their members connected and
engaged through new digital communications methods. They circulated the
e-mail addresses of their leaders to provide convenient lines of communication. Some groups posted local information, especially crime alerts, on their
websites. For example, the NET Block Club, which served residents of Elmdale and Thorndale on the North Side, invited readers to subscribe to its news
blog. Other block clubs took advantage of the social media website Facebook,
which allowed users to "like" the pages of organizations, see their updates,
and share information. The Winona Foster Carmen Winnemac Block Club's
Facebook page announced local social activities, meetings, and community
improvement opportunities, and shared links of potential concern to members. In November 2013, the Lakewood Balmoral Residents' Council's Facebook page featured photographs of children dressed for Halloween, advertised information about lost and found house cats, and alerted readers to a
spike in burglaries and the presence of a coyote in the neighborhood. The
CPD organized "virtual block clubs," mostly in lakefront high-rise buildings.
Second Ward Alderman Bob Fioretti interpreted the definition of virtual
block clubs for his constituents: "For some people with their busy schedules,
a club that has no face-to-face meetings is what works. Members meet and
have dialog via the Internet."[22]

Youth

Although they aspired to connect with a broad range of their neighbors, block
club participants worried especially about young residents. In the twentieth
century, American youth set themselves apart culturally in a variety of ways—
not all of them embraced by adults. Seeing youth as a group needing specialized attention, many block clubs tried to draw children and teenagers more
tightly into the fabric of the local community. Their programming either focused on youth directly or attracted children as helpers to adult projects such
as cleaning and gardening. It is tempting to interpret attempts to bring youth
into block club programs as a form of social control. Indeed, that was often the
case, as young people's behavior on the street often troubled block club members trying to create an uplifting local environment. In the years after World
War II, Americans were particularly concerned about teenagers' disruptive-
ness. Chapter 6 explores how block clubs responded to complaints about the

undesirable behavior of neighborhood young people. This section examines more benevolent attention to youth. Block clubs tried to make young people feel connected to their neighbors, just as they sought for adults.[23]

Block club leaders hoped engaging children while they were young would preempt later trouble. Juliette Buford, a block club organizer for the GLCC, focused on involving youth. She argued that block clubs depended on youth participation: "*Only* if young people are involved can there be stability in organized efforts to improve a neighborhood through citizen action." Chicago Urban League organizer Alva B. Maxey similarly claimed that lavishing direct attention on youth spurred their involvement in the adult concerns. Block clubs, she claimed, "have found that children cooperate more willingly in neighborhood maintenance and beautification projects, along with their parents, when they feel that the adults are interested in them per se. Methods for including the children include neighborhood athletic teams, special drill teams for boys and girls, play-lots, better conduct training courses, thrift clubs, shop and handicraft classes, and junior warden groups for cleaning up litter."[24] Accordingly, block clubs tried to create activities of real interest to young people. Although the overt purpose was to provide fun for children, community building for the sake of local improvement was a significant covert goal.

Block club leaders reached out to children using tactics that shielded them from tedious adult business. They assumed that children and youth did not want to sit through meetings where adults discussed local problems. A Chicago Urban League block club serving the 2600 block of West Adams Street named itself the Youth Progressive Club. Members explained that because "much work needs to be done concerning molding the characters of the youth and since the youth of today will be the leaders of the world tomorrow, the adults decided that it would be very good to have a mixed official slate composed of children and adults." Despite this inclusive aspiration, all of the elected officers used the title "Mrs.," suggesting that the leaders were all grown women. Block clubs found other ways to connect with young people. Many created "youth auxiliaries" or "junior" block clubs, to allow young people a structured, semiautonomous way to participate in community improvement efforts. The GLCC, for example, reported in 1959 that twenty-five of its fifty-five clubs had affiliated youth groups.[25]

Block clubs offered children social and competitive activities. Parties allowed them to connect with one another under the watchful eyes of adult block club members. The clubs also sought to engage youth in constructive activities. The 500 Bowen Club used a Halloween party to gently introduce young people to the responsibilities of block club membership. Adults praised

FIGURE 7. Participants in the Marillac Unit of Block Clubs enjoyed a sack race and other recreational activities aimed at children. Photograph by Sister Jane. Source: Sister Jane, "Marillac Unit of Block Clubs," *Voice of the Midwest Community Council* 11, no. 7 (October 1958): 3. Near West Side Community Committee Records, box 39, folder 524, University of Illinois at Chicago Library, Department of Special Collections.

adolescent participants for providing snacks for the younger children. The club organizers were hopeful that "the children's parents had expressed appreciation and they believe that they will be able to get their cooperation in the block club." The West Side Community Improvement Council considered whether young people from member clubs would enjoy taking part in a talent show. This activity sent a message that youth had skills and abilities that should be showcased and applauded. The 4300 Wilcox Block Club organized a baseball team for boys up through age eighteen, and softball for girls. For its part, the 15th Place Block Club sponsored a baseball team called the Sparks. Both the boys on the team and the cheerleaders wore green and white uniforms while participating in the Chicago Park District's summer baseball program.[26]

When block clubs successfully captured children's attention, they could enlist them in the improvement projects that will be described in chapters 4 and 5. The teenage members of the Junior 4800–4900 Monroe Block Club noticed when the adult group held a cleanup program in their alley. The junior group tidied up the public street. On the 3000 block of West Cullerton Street, both adults and children participated in North Lawndale's Operation Pride improvement campaign. The youth block club accepted responsibility for collecting "all paper and refu[s]e on the front and rear of the premises." Adopting the spirit of the Operation Pride program, the children made their responsibilities a friendly competition. They divided their territory by gender, assigning girls to patrol one side of the street and boys the other.[27]

As the persistent cleanup activities suggest, block clubs recognized that city streets were not always ideal places for children's play. To protect youth from real and imagined dangers, some block clubs sent youth away to more wholesome locales. The 1600–1800 Drake Improvement Block Club, whose leaders the Marcy Center staff regarded as "capable and aggressive," sent local children to a day camp. The 2800 Adams Block Club took its children apple picking in Libertyville, a wealthy agricultural suburb far north of Chicago. In 1954, the 4700 South Evans Avenue block club organized parents on the block in sponsoring a bus trip to Riverview Amusement Park, which was famous for its roller coasters. Although Riverview later shut down in the wake of intense interracial conflict among its patrons, the Chicago Urban League received no report that this outing was anything other than a chance for the children to enjoy themselves together.[28]

Bridging

Umbrella groups hoped to connect their block clubs with one another and the larger organization. Formalized relationships helped with many goals. Vertical and horizontal connections allowed parent organizations to steer potential members toward established groups, deploy experienced leaders to inspire new clubs, and attract municipal attention that was difficult for small groups to attain. For many block clubs, connection with a larger organization allowed them to leverage resources to help their street. Indeed, Shel Trapp explained to researcher Michael Westgate that he organized block clubs in the Austin neighborhood into "civics" in order to translate participants' concerns into powerful actions: "I formed street clubs so we could keep dealing with issues. And I formed the civics so we could deal with issues that covered the whole area, whether it was crimes, bad buildings, panic peddling, whatever." Thelen and Sarchet, who studied the HPKCC's block clubs, assumed that all block clubs arose from some larger organizational effort. Interpreting the psychology of that relationship, they observed that the block clubs "react in different ways to [the debt to the parent organization]. Some will deny it; others will accept it gladly and look to the parent organization for much help; still others will feel little one way or the other about this fact. Some block groups develop jealous loyalty to themselves; others, to a larger community. In any case, the way a block group feels toward the parent organization changes from time to time." However, the 15th Place Block Club's vigor showed that block clubs did not depend on connections with larger community organizations for success.[29]

The HPKCC believed that both block clubs and the larger organization enjoyed synergies from their relationship. It saved its block clubs time and effort by sharing its files of sample newsletters and meeting notices, documentation of city government departments and functions, and explanations of the HPKCC itself. Keeping the HPKCC apprised of block club meetings and ongoing activities allowed "coordination of effort and maximum effectiveness for the conference program." When the leaders of a block club let the HPKCC's main office know their meeting schedule, "there could be public announcement in all the community newspapers (thus increasing attendance) and a staff member or volunteer observer could be present." The staff's "careful monthly reports on every block group" provided the organization's leadership with "a bird's eye view of problems, failures, progress, and successes."[30]

Some block groups were not persuaded that this connection was valuable. Echoing Thelen and Sarchet's reading of block club psychology, Julia Abrahamson noted that the HPKCC's benefits did not guarantee that member groups affirmed the connection:

> Several blocks behaved as if the conference were not in existence. These had organized themselves without any assistance and resented the suggestion that they cooperate with the conference. Certain others, brought into being by the conference staff, became alienated for one reason or another: disapproval of action or lack of action by the central organization; fear of domination by the conference; insistence on engaging in generalized activities not directly related to the block program; the use of methods opposed by the conference; refusal by the conference to allow its name to be used to further the private projects of individuals.

The imperfect relationship between the HPKCC and its block clubs prompted several reorganizations of the central group's leadership structure in the 1950s and 1960s. For a while, the HPKCC's groups cooperated with its block steering committee. Abrahamson reported that an average of forty of the fifty-two participating block clubs sent representatives to the steering committee's monthly meetings in 1958. Participants may have seen the steering committee as a ladder to local status and power. Explaining why block club leadership had to be constantly replenished, Abrahamson noted that "the best of leaders moved on and up in the conference organization." But by 1963, participation was so poor that the block steering committee voted to dissolve itself, leaving Hyde Park's block clubs largely to their own devices.[31]

The Chicago Urban League set very clear expectations for the block clubs it cultivated. But, as in the HPKCC, its block clubs did not fully cooperate. The leaders of those clubs were supposed to attend local federation meetings and report their activities upward to the League. As it built a network of block clubs in the early 1950s, the League also organized them into seven

subregional networks. These local "councils" gave block club leaders the opportunity to connect with one another and to organize events for their collective memberships. One of the League staff workers, Mr. Turner, explained
that the purpose of the council was "to promote projects within a specified
area; to interpret wholesome civic programs so that all the residents within
this area will be able to receive maximum benefits from all the resources that
can be used to meet common goals; to secure better police protection, clear
streets, better housing and, in short, just plain community improvement; and
if after a good period of time the residents would come to know each other,
then the council would seek to promote better citizenship."[32]

League staff members told block club leaders that their commitment included writing reports of their clubs' activities and attending local council
meetings. Organizers sent a letter to West Side block club presidents, organizers, and "potential organizers," explaining, "It is the aim of the Council and
the Block Clubs that are already organized and functioning very well to help
organize additional Block Clubs this year and the[y] do all in their power
to push activity among the clubs that have sort of dropped by the way." The
League's Rachel Ridley argued to the membership of the Westside Improvement Council that the clubs' regular reports to the council were "of vital importance in maintaining control" of their efforts.[33] But council leadership depended substantially on volunteers who had already been pressed into service
as presidents of their block clubs. Getting them to participate in the councils
as well was a challenge.

The League's postwar efforts to organize federated groups were less successful than those of the St. Louis Urban League in the interwar years. In
St. Louis, despite meeting only twice a year, the Federation of Block Units
engaged in a variety of political, consumer, and civic efforts. In Chicago, volunteers who were enticed to lead block clubs felt fuzzy about the reasons
for participating in the League's larger network. A letter cajoling delinquent
presidents to attend the meetings of the West Side Community Improvement
Council hinted at vague consequences of their absence: "You will find that if
you personally attend the Council meetings you will realize just how necessary it is for every officer and every block club to give time and energy to
fulfill the obligation you have assumed. We are looking forward to having
representatives from 27 block clubs present. If you do not come there is a possibility that your block will not be represented." It was especially "important
and urgent" to attend a meeting where officers would be elected. The League
staff was particularly eager to entice the active but aloof 3100 West 15th Street
Block Club to share their energy and leadership experience with the West

Side Council. They even resorted to public shaming, commenting pointedly in the block club news section of the council newsletter, "We are wondering why the 3100 Block Club never sends a representative to the regular meeting. We know you are one of us." Perhaps inspired by athletic leagues' practice of rotating trophies among their champions, the West Side Council used an added spur to participation. It owned a "membership cup," which it sent home to "the block club who has the most members or representatives present" at each monthly council meeting.[34]

Neither carrots nor sticks could ensure that block club representatives attended the council meetings. The League staff set out on a frustrating mission to persuade block clubs to participate. Mrs. Hicks, of the 500 Bowen Improvement Club, told her League organizer that "she had never understood the purpose of council in the first place, that she had attended meetings, there were few people present and there seemed to be no plan." A League staff worker noticed that the Washington Park Court Property Owners Association was similarly "not too cooperative in regard to supporting the Council's program," and so planned to commit "much time in working with the president and other members of the group." A League staff organizer visited the established and independent-minded 4900 Vincennes Avenue Improvement Club four times before it agreed to associate with the League. The staff worker was gratified when the club finally agreed to support both the League's fund-raising and its Block Beautiful contest. For its part, the members of the 3200 West Fulton Block Club "apparently were so pleased with the situation within their block that they could not see any need for participating in the council." A League staff worker's report enumerated their points of pride: "The members were proud that their block club was interracial and that there was no strain between the members. They were proud that the city had recently installed new lights. Their neighbors took pride in maintaining their property." Having determined that appeals to self-improvement would not persuade them to join the council, the organizer cleverly appealed to their sense of duty for racial uplift, explaining "that no man is able to live by himself and that since they were so successful, why not attend council meetings and try to impress upon others the need for doing the same." This tactic, the staff member reported a little smugly, did the trick.[35]

Affiliated groups did not automatically remain in the network. In July 1953 the League staff received a terse letter from the 2900 Walnut Street Block Club. The club's assistant secretary, Mrs. L. Montgomery, explained that they had "voted to sever its affiliation with the Urban League and [that she was] hereby returning the By Laws." Montgomery's return of the original charter was probably meant to sting the feelings of the League staff. Although the League customarily provided new block clubs with a model charter to modify or adopt, if it no longer wished to be connected with the League, the 2900 Walnut Street Block Club could have voted to disaffiliate and send notice without a gesture of rebuke. Maxey, the director of the League's community organization department, responded with a letter of her own. She acknowledged that the group had not gotten along with Rachel Ridley, the organizer originally assigned to get the group going. Maxey continued:

> We had heard indirectly, that there was some confliction [*sic*] and dissatisfaction within the organization but we had hoped that with the assignment of the new worker, whatever there was disturbing the group could be worked out satisfactorily to all concerned.
>
> It is obvious from your letter that this has not been the case. Since Mrs. Ridley helped to organize this group, the Urban League would at least, like the privilege of visiting with you at your next meeting in order that we might hear, first hand, the reason behind this recent action of the group.[36]

League records do not indicate the outcome of this request. This dramatic severing of the umbilical cord, however, appears to have been a relatively rare occurrence. Block clubs were much more likely to fade out of existence than to divorce their parents.

Like the block clubs, council operations required a small fund of money to operate. The staff worker explained to the Princeton Avenue Civic Club that the Parker Council had "no dues in order to join[,] but each block club is requested to pay the sum of one dollar to maintain the costs of the council. These funds will be used during the Block Beautiful Contest, securing of postage and stationery supplies and for any incidentals such as a member of a block becoming ill or dying, and then condolences and a wreath would be sent to the family." Even after the League stopped supporting block club work, the Park Manor Neighbors (PMN) retained a carefully structured system of inclusion: "To receive a charter the block group must have at least twenty members who pay 50¢ a piece per year. The block group pays $10.00 annual dues to PMN. Block groups must have at least four meetings a year, must have officers and operate as a going organization. Each block group sends two representatives to the Block Council which is the top policy making group of PMN. Block Council meets monthly. A new block group desiring a charter applies one month, and is issued or refused a charter the following month."[37] As explained in chapter 2, block clubs taxed themselves to support both their councils and the Chicago Urban League.

The councils, when functional, provided volunteer services to block clubs beyond what the League's small staff could accomplish. The Westside Community Improvement Council offered block club presidents a workshop in organizing and operating methods. It also wrote to the mayor in search of "valid information" about rumored plans for urban renewal in the area. Member clubs of the DuSable Council, on the South Side, coordinated its children's Christmas parties. They created a "council-wide party" on one day without having to rent a large space or provide transportation away from their members' homes. The councils also provided direction for club participation in League-sponsored improvement competitions (a topic taken up in depth in chapter 4). For example, in 1953 the West Side Council "decided to discontinue the Better Homes and Yards Program for this year and emphasize the Block Beautiful idea in our organization program."[38] The councils, then, did require additional labor from both organizers and volunteers. When the councils worked, however, their network helped block clubs leverage their small-scale efforts into broader community connections and neighborhood improvements.

The Chicago Urban League's effort to federate its network of block clubs was not entirely successful. Many blocks remained missing from the orderly pyramid of block clubs, councils, and central federation that the League envisioned. The councils were as difficult to organize and sustain as were block clubs themselves. The Abbottsford Council, which covered territory directly west of Washington Park, stopped meeting in 1954, rendering it effectively dead. A League staff organizer strategized with the president of the 5300–5400 Indiana Avenue Improvement Club about using the annual Christmas lighting contest to revitalize the Abbottsford Council, but it is not clear that this idea bore any fruit. The League's major organizational crisis in 1955, and the six-month shutdown that followed, brought to an end its lavish cultivation of block clubs and councils.[39]

Even without an ongoing effort, however, the federation model was among the Urban League's legacies to other Chicago block organizing efforts. When later, larger community organizations created block clubs, they often sought to connect them following templates laid down by the League and the HPKCC. The GLCC, for example, built an "association" of block clubs to support its urban renewal program. While it hoped to mimic Hyde Park's success in attracting conservation funding for the neighborhood, its approach to organizing among North Lawndale's African American residents mirrored the League's network of clubs. When the American Friends Service Committee initiated its organizing effort in 1965, it quickly created a "United Block Clubs" group as well as individual block clubs. AFSC staff reported that "many people began to feel a need for a larger neighborhood organization to work on problems common to the various blocks."[40]

The white defense networks of the United Property Group (UPG) and Father Francis Lawlor's SWABC adapted the federation model to their aims. Block groups connected through the UPG and the SWABC had a functional relationship with the central organization, but were not expected to work cooperatively with each other. The UPG asked participants to provide information when they suspected blockbusters might be trying to move African Americans into the neighborhood. It wanted to provide rumor control for the network as a whole. Founder Gordon Mattson explained that members should consider the UPG "the only reliable source of information concerning buildings in the area." The SWABC disseminated information and ideas through its newsletter, and occasionally turned members out for rallies and demonstrations. Its surviving records, however, do not suggest that participating groups worked together. In fact, the SWABC leadership refused an opportunity to send delegates to a convention of the Southwest Community Congress (SCC). SWABC president Mary Boyte explained that the SWABC voted against acknowledging "the SCC as a legitimate organization working in the best interests of the people." They specifically objected to the SCC because it had been organized by Saul Alinsky's Industrial Areas Foundation.[41] The purpose of the antiblack federations was less to get participants to connect to each other than it was to communicate the group's numbers and potential strength to outsiders. Their members wanted to be left in what they saw as racial peace, not to build a sustainable network for political change.

As the SWABC's rejection of the SCC suggests, a different set of assumptions about the value of connecting block clubs underpinned Saul Alinsky's model of community organizing. Alinsky, operating in Chicago out of the Industrial Areas Foundation (IAF), is widely recognized as the founder of modern community organizing in the United States.[42] Alinsky himself lived in Hyde Park; although he must have been aware of the HPKCC's block club program, he stayed aloof from the organizing effort in his own neighborhood.[43] The Alinsky model organized participants to generate power. An abstract sensibility of community spirit was merely a side effect, not a central goal. Block clubs were one tool for creating effective collective action, but they were not enough.

Alinsky had learned organizing methods from the American labor movement. In his practice, he translated those insights into geographically bound urban spaces. He organized communities himself, trained professional organizers, and published such influential works as *Reveille for Radicals* and *Rules for Radicals*. American groups Alinsky organized through the IAF included the Armourdale Neighborhood Council in Kansas City, Kansas; the South St. Paul Community Council in Minnesota; and FIGHT in Rochester, New York. Much of his organizing work occurred in Chicago. His first Chicago effort was in the Back of the Yards neighborhood, where Joe Meegan organized the Back of the Yards Neighborhood Council. Under Alinsky's supervision, the IAF staff also organized The Woodlawn Organization, the Campaign Against Pollution, the Northwest Community Organization, and the Organization of the Southwest Community. Alinsky's model and staff also influenced the creation of other groups in Chicago, including the Organization for a Better Austin (OBA) and United Power for Action and Justice. While he became notorious for advising activists to "rub raw the sores of discontent," Alinsky's method of encouraging community residents to acquire power was broader and more complicated than that provocative phrase suggests. A key element of his philosophy was that participants must perceive in the community organization a way to advance their own self-interests; abstract, altruistic public benefits were insufficient motivators.[44]

Alinsky's approach required community organizers to spend months on the ground in a target neighborhood, discovering local concerns and identifying influential local people. His team entered a neighborhood to organize it only after having been invited and hired by an existing institution in the area. Alinsky demanded a steep contractual fee and a three-year commitment; in 1965 he charged approximately three hundred thousand dollars for three years of IAF service. His goal was to ensure that the inviting community could muster sufficient resources to make organizing success likely. Alinsky's organizing staff described their fieldwork in weekly memoranda, which they pored over together to ascertain the area's existing and potential power structure. After discovering the local basis for a successful community-based organization, Alinsky convened the residents identified as prospective leaders. He helped them to build a group that could sustain itself after his organizing team withdrew.[45]

Alinsky organizations in Chicago had three distinguishing features. First, they were structured as organizations of member organizations, not as organizations of individual members. Second, the groups convened annual community congresses using democratic voting methods to determine their central agendas. Third, they focused on leveraging their numbers into power and action. Block clubs often provided a base of participants in IAF organizations, but Alinsky's staff never relied on them alone; they were dubious about the clubs' potential for creating the kind of change and power they were working for.[46]

Thomas Gaudette, who later directed IAF organizing in the Austin neighborhood, argued as early as 1959 that block clubs were too insular to be effective on their own. Referring to his own experience in the Chatham–Avalon Park Community Council on Chicago's South Side, Gaudette explained, "The block club is unable to handle the larger problem. Its self interest is complete with clean lawns, street sweepers, controlled dogs, a policeman for each block, clean alleys." Shel Trapp, who worked under Gaudette in Austin and went to found National People's Action, was similarly skeptical of the long-term potential of autonomous block clubs. Trapp explained, "They usually start around one bad building or a pothole, something very small. As soon as that's done, it usually becomes a social club." Although he organized block clubs for the Organization for a Better Austin (OBA), he also grouped them into "street clubs so we could keep dealing with issues." Atop the street clubs, Trapp created a layer he called "civics." The civics incorporated eight square blocks and met monthly. These groups conducted much of the day-to-day action associated with the OBA in the 1960s, such as running "kangaroo courts" to intimidate slum landlords and blockbusting real estate dealers.[47]

Block clubs served as delegates to the larger community groups that IAF staff organized. Because of their indisputably local base in the neighborhood, they were well positioned to provide broad popular representation. Not everyone in a neighborhood belonged to a local church or civic organization, and not every local organization consisted exclusively of locally based members. While Roman Catholics worshipped and went to school in geographically-based parishes, Protestant churches and Jewish synagogues were not necessarily local in the same sense. Indeed, during neighborhood racial residential transition (a phenomenon many Alinsky groups experienced), congregants routinely moved away but retained their memberships in their old neighborhoods.[48] Religious affiliation did not guarantee a local stake. By contrast, in the US urban context, residence in an area defines a person as belonging there. Because block clubs drew most of their membership from residents, when participants attended community congresses they were incontestably local.

The involvement of block clubs established a democratic foundation for the larger community organization. Mark Santow's analysis of metropolitan segregation in the United States explains that it was crucial to the Alinsky model that individuals, with their personal and idiosyncratic ideologies, did not hold direct membership in community organizations. Rather, groups such as block clubs were better able to represent the collective interests of their constituencies. They were compelled to sort out their positions through democratic processes.[49] Each organization wrote and ratified its own constitution describing which local groups were eligible to participate, and on what terms. In the OBA, for example, member groups could send delegates to the annual congress in proportion to their size.[50] In this model, block clubs functioned as peers. They enjoyed the same kinds of representational status, voting rights, and voice as other local organizations such as churches, lay organizations, and civic groups. The scale and diversity of Alinsky-model organizations contrasted with the Urban League approach to federation. Block clubs helped set the agenda for the larger organization, but the success of both groups did not depend on the time of the same few overcommitted volunteers.

Block clubs appear on the membership rolls and as active participants in the annual congresses that determined the Alinsky organizations' priorities. For instance, block clubs provided much of the OBA's membership. In 1969, when the OBA held its third annual congress, an estimated 700 delegates from 201 member organizations participated; some three-quarters of those member organizations were block clubs. Many of those block clubs probably predated OBA, because in the mid-1960s the Austin neighborhood was a hotbed of community organizing efforts. The Woodlawn Organization (TWO) allowed block clubs to send delegates to its annual constitutional conventions in exchange for annual dues of $125. But observers thought that Woodlawn block clubs were weaker, and that, in contrast to Austin, "TWO sustains the block clubs. It isn't the other way around."[51]

Block club participation in Alinsky-style community groups such as the OBA and TWO worked in two directions. The block clubs voted on the larger organization's agenda, and then their members helped carry it out. Block clubs, like other member groups, had voting rights at the annual community congresses. Their delegates could offer, debate, and vote on resolutions, elect the larger organization's leaders, and hold office themselves. Membership and leadership in block clubs were credentials that suggested qualification for higher office in the OBA. At the OBA's founding convention, delegates from block clubs were elected as its corresponding secretary and recording secretary. Also, resolutions passed at the OBA congresses expressed the collective views of delegates. In 1971, block clubs offered resolutions condemning the perceived increase in crime in Austin and calling for weekly block club cleanup efforts and the implementation of a "citizens radio patrol" throughout the neighborhood. The meat of the OBA's work was then carried out throughout the year by its standing committees, also staffed from the network of block clubs that were crucial to its day-to-day work. In keeping with the abrasive style of Alinsky's activism, many OBA activities were public protests that required large numbers of people to be visible and effective. When the OBA demonstrated at the homes and offices of blockbusting real estate dealers, they turned out scores of protesters who paraded with signs

FIGURE 8. Block club delegates to the 1962 congress of The Woodlawn Organization. Source: *Woodlawn Booster*, July 25, 1962, folder 5, box 1, TWO papers, Chicago History Museum. Courtesy of Hurley Green.

and chanted slogans. To recruit picketers, they tapped the network of member organizations, which were dominated by block clubs.[52]

Other scholars provide a fuller accounting of how Alinsky organizations translated their numbers into collective action and change.[53] As geographically based local groups, block clubs provided one of the bases for such community organizations. But Alinsky organizers did not cultivate block clubs with any more altruism than they expected from participants. For organizations such as the Chicago Urban League, the block clubs merited attention in and of themselves; the bonds forged among neighbors had social and cultural dividends beyond measure. But for Alinsky organizers, the clubs were only a means to larger ends.

Conclusion

Historical sources do not reveal how much these efforts to connect neighbors bore fruit. Block clubs and the people who belonged to them left few records of their activities; the long-term, intangible consequences of their programs are essentially impossible to unearth. "Before and after" photographs of an alley can illustrate the rewards of a morning spent on cleanup, but block clubs could not document the network of relationships or the web of good feelings built. Certainly, Alinsky groups persistently brought neighbors together to work for political change; but because block clubs themselves were not direct actors in their programs, their further contributions remain obscure. Social activities were their own evidence for whatever enhancements to community spirit they brought about. Document-based historical evidence cannot tell us whether neighbors greeted each other more often, helped each other out in times of need, or developed lasting friendships because of block clubs.

Only hints of such sustained relationships appear in archival sources. Faith Rich's papers, for example, contain many carbon copies of letters she wrote on behalf of neighbors who needed copies of their birth certificates.[54] Did Rich's neighbors on 15th Place learn to rely on her literacy, typing skills, and good will because of her commitment to their block club? They might have trusted her in the absence of its organized efforts; but, without the block club, they also might have seen her only as the sole white woman on the block, without grasping other possibilities for their relationship.

Block clubs routinely turned their neighborly connections to local improvement. They ran many voluntary programs to transform their surroundings using only local contributions. Frequently, however, they discovered that they needed assistance from the government to fulfill their visions. In accessing public support, they framed their efforts in pragmatic, not ideological terms. As Benjamin Looker explains in his important article on the neighborhood movement of the 1970s, "the romantic language of neighborhood communalism is a place where traditional distinctions among left, liberal, and right often blur or collapse." The National Association of Neighborhoods tried to build a "Neighborhood Platform Campaign" in 1979. It held votes in favor of "a checklist of traditional left-Democratic policy items, all envisioning a substantially increased role for central government." But it quickly ran up against the religious and political views of the organization's substantial Catholic constituency, who resisted using their connection for ordinary partisanship.[55] Perhaps intuitively sensing the discord that deep engagement in traditional partisan policy issues could bring to their carefully built neighborhood bonds, block clubs confined their engagement with government to the task of accessing their fair share of existing programs. They did not take the next step, of advocating for new policies that might have further transformed urban life.

Most block club efforts focused on their immediate surroundings. As Alinsky's organizers noted, their intensely local focus kept most block clubs from looking outward. The few moments when block clubs did break out of the local mode came in unusual contexts. In 1986, the often exceptional 15th Place Block Club wrote a letter to the Illinois Commerce Commission, petitioning them to stop construction on the Braidwood Nuclear Reactor, more than sixty miles away. Similarly, in 1987, members sent a letter to Paul Simon, US senator from Illinois, about their discussion of the federal minimum wage.

But most block clubs lacked interest in commenting on matters so far from home. Much more typical was the response of the Winona Foster Carmen Winnemac (WFCW) Block Club to Chicago's 2013 plan to close many of the city's public schools, including one nearby. The school closing plan was rooted in a deep history of the city's demographic changes, the chronic underfunding of public education, the national rise of charter schools, and the strained relationship between the mayor and the teacher's union. But the WFCW's Facebook page simply urged members to advocate for local schools to remain open. It did not try to unpack the deeper problems of the Chicago Public Schools.[56]

Block clubs did not try to shape public policy; they simply tried to use it. They called for local improvements that capitalized on existing government tools and their own energies. When they considered the problems of local garbage collection or housing conditions, their members possibly could have interpreted their deep causes. They might have explained the reasons for uneven city services or shelter inequity in partisan or racial terms. But the block clubs straightforwardly attended to the business of making concrete, immediate changes to the environment. As historian Jeffrey Helgeson suggests, the clubs' pragmatic approach to improvement does not mean that their participants opposed structural change, but only that the block club was not the ideal vehicle for leveraging policy transformations.[57] Their members remained free to participate individually in politics and policy aimed at underlying social structures. In the interests of achieving modest local transformations, block clubs kept their attention on goals that were achievable without engaging ideological debate.

4

Beautify

The alley between the apartment buildings was dark. In Chicago, alleys running behind buildings provide access to garbage containers, laundry rooms, utilities, storage lockers, and parking spaces—unsightly but important functions in the dense twentieth-century city.[1] The alley's darkness troubled the tenants of the Hyde Park buildings that backed onto it. They wanted the space lit, but as renters they could not unilaterally make desired changes to the property. A delegation from their block club went to the building's owners with a proposition: If they could raise the funds to install new electrical equipment in the alley, would the owners provide the electricity? The owners agreed to pay for the ongoing costs. With a subscription of fifty cents from each affected tenant, the block group lit the alley.[2]

The Hyde Park–Kenwood Community Conference's (HPKCC) story about installing alley lighting underscores the complications that renters faced in controlling their environment. Tenants occupied the block, but property ownership conveyed the right to control a site's use. Without their landlords' agreement to cover the ongoing expenses of electrification, they could not have banished the alley's darkness. The block club could impose a voluntary tax on current members for the one-time expense of installation, but it lacked a mechanism to support its indefinite costs beyond their tenancy. Landlords, however, could build the ongoing costs of electricity into the rents they charged. Property ownership provided twentieth-century Chicagoans with great latitude to establish living conditions for themselves and their tenants. Within the broad limits of the city's haphazardly enforced building code, owners could do what they wanted with the appearance of the interior and exterior of their own properties.

Like the Hyde Park tenants, property owners sometimes turned their improvement energies beyond their own plots of land. Working through block clubs and larger neighborhood associations, they prodded their neighbors and the city government to fix broken infrastructure, provide services, and invest in local beautification. It is tempting to ascribe their desire to improve the urban environment to ownership. The idea of "property values" offers an intuitively satisfying explanation for why people who own land want it improved. Real estate developers recite the mantra of "location, location, location" to explain why similar buildings in different parts of a city sell for different prices. Although separate properties have discrete sales prices, embedded in the modern notion of property values is a belief that neighboring land uses are crucial to a given lot's ultimate sale price. The historian Carl Nightingale has argued that the primacy of property values amounted to an ideological claim that developed when "London land speculators invented the driving principle of class segregation, the idea that having poor people as close neighbors brought down the property values of the rich."[3] According to this belief in property values, the price that a landowner can command at the moment of sale depends not only on the intrinsic merits of the lot and building, but also on the qualities of nearby properties and the class status of their inhabitants.

This belief shaped housing costs. The importance of neighboring properties was inscribed into US public policy in the 1930s, when the Federal Housing Administration's *Underwriting Manual* set standards for insuring houses that included a calculation of the risk presented by their neighbors, with poor and African American residents assumed to degrade housing values automatically.[4] In the modern US real estate market, a beautiful building amid other well-kept buildings sells for a higher price than one surrounded by decay. A building in a black neighborhood usually sells for less than one in a white neighborhood. Property owners' interest in the quality of their neighbors' properties thus stems directly from their financial interests. This belief was so firmly held in the United States in the twentieth and twenty-first centuries that it seemed commonsensical, a scientific law of property relations rather than an idea that human action translated into a consistent practice.[5]

The strong financial interests of property owners in their neighbors' land might explain why block clubs so consistently sponsored local improvement efforts. As chapter 2 has suggested, property owners dominated many block clubs. Notably, the Chicago Urban League routinely failed to persuade block clubs to admit renters on an equal basis with property owners. League organizers also learned that property owners did not agree on what counted as desirable land use. Owners of single-family homes found themselves at odds with owners of neighboring multiunit buildings who crowded many tenants into their properties while allowing them to deteriorate. Dominance by property owners surely conditioned some block clubs' activities, but by itself it cannot account for the broad range of local improvement efforts Chicago residents organized.

Tenants like the members of the Hyde Park alley block club held firm opinions about their environment and devoted their energy to local improvements. In Chicago neighborhoods where most residents were renters, block clubs also flourished. Tenant-run block clubs were as concerned with local improvement as were those comprised of property owners. In poor neighborhoods, in fact, property owners were the main target of block club activity. Tenant-run block clubs pushed landlords to bring their properties up to their standards of decent living. Renter-dominated block clubs, however, faced different constraints. On a day-to-day basis, for instance, members of the Hyde Park block club were more aware than their landlords were of the need for safe alleys, but they could not enact their lighting plan without permission. While property owners had to work within the limits of Chicago's loosely enforced building code, renters who wanted to improve their living quarters needed the consent of their landlords to make changes to their homes. They routinely lacked the means to improve a building's fixtures or structural soundness.

The idea of "property values," in short, is insufficient to explain local activism for beautification. Instead, participants' desires to improve their daily surroundings drove block club programming, although certainly long-term financial gain may also have informed the participation of particular property owners. In the Los Angeles suburb of South Gate, historian Becky Nicolaides argues, both the "use value" and the "commodity value" of properties affected how homeowners perceived their worth.[6] Members of Chicago block clubs likewise sought beautification not only to protect their investments, but also because their surroundings mattered to their daily lives.

In their quest for beautification, block clubs pursed a broad range of improvement activities responding to specific local problems. For some clubs, beautification meant adding decorations to an orderly environment. To others, improvement meant eliminating eyesores. As a first resort, block clubs engaged in beautification projects that members could complete on their own. Often, however, volunteer efforts brought block clubs into contact with government regulations or services.

Most club projects were specific to the blocks where they took place. Residents worked to slow down local traffic or ameliorate a problem site. Often, block club members worked to beautify local spaces, such as vacant lots, that were effectively public, even when they remained privately owned. A common way to deal with a menacing vacant lot was to transform it into a children's play space or community garden. Block clubs also participated in beautification programs sponsored by larger organizations, such as summer-long, citywide improvement campaigns and Christmas-decorating competitions. Coordinated beautification campaigns sought to demonstrate to neighbors that a small, organized effort could make a substantial difference to the appearance of the block. By simultaneously fixing up their buildings and beautifying their lawns and gardens, participants hoped to beautify their own homes while inspiring neighbors to invest their time and energy in the block as well.

Local Concerns

As the Hyde Park alley example suggests, Chicago block clubs addressed intensely local concerns. They cleaned up some problem areas and improved other spaces to the point of beauty. Block clubs ran a wide range of activities to ameliorate decay and promote beautification. Members scaled their projects to fit the people and institutions who could make their desired improvements. Often, only local residents were positioned to recognize patterns of neglect. Public officials and absentee landlords failed to notice their needs, and had to be persuaded to be part of the solutions. Many block club beautification projects focused solely on a block and required the cooperation only of immediate neighbors.

The inward focus of block club beautification efforts provides historians with an unusual opportunity to grasp how Chicagoans experienced the landscapes they traversed daily. Excellent scholarship from architects, historians, and geographers analyzes the built environment to reveal what the static cityscape meant to its inhabitants. By combining the research techniques pioneered by scholars such as Kevin Lynch and Grady Clay with print and digital resources such as Sanborn Fire Insurance Maps, the 1942 Chicago Land Use Survey, and Google Street View, it is possible to reconstruct residents' experiences of the vernacular urban landscape. The choices block club members made about what to fix adds dynamism to these established research methods. By scrutinizing the successes and failures of residents who sought small-scale changes in their surroundings, we can begin to trace how city dwellers dealt with the rents in the urban fabric left by large-scale processes of capitalism and American democracy.[7]

Examining block club projects also reveals features of their streets: first, that a given condition was present—to some degree or another—on the block;

second, that it seemed manageable enough that residents could hope to fix it. For example, a pair of West Side clubs pooled their funds to buy a snowplow for common use. Heavy snowfall in wintry Chicago was routine enough that most residents kept shovels or snowblowers and coped with snow individually. A shared snowplow, however, could save members money, time, and effort, especially easing the burden of heavy labor for elderly or disabled neighbors. Similarly, a club in Hyde Park worked with the neighboring osteopathic hospital to reduce the noise from its new heating and air conditioning unit. This probably necessitated collective action. Unaffiliated people who lived near the hospital might have suffered in angry, isolated silence; but a shared concern presented by a group could get the attention of hospital administrators. Many of the topics that concerned block clubs were so specific that no public policy, charity, or government agency would have thought to address them. What one block club focused their efforts upon might have seemed insignificant to a different group. Only by illustrating that there were local eyes on a problem and a collective will to fix them could block clubs generate solutions that required more than an individual to accomplish.[8]

Chicago block club members were troubled by a broad variety of problems endemic in the twentieth-century urban environment. Technological, economic, and demographic transformations left their marks on the landscape, where residents endured their consequences. Some groups were concerned about traffic; they agitated for stop signs at busy street corners, slowed local cars, and diverted parking lot traffic from residential alleys. The Springfield Avenue Community Club educated members about the "'smust'—smoke and dust—that is gradually blanketing our city, dirtying our homes, and creating an unhealthy atmosphere in which to rear our children." The 4100 Van Buren Block Club worried for years about an abandoned house. When it looked as though a tree was about to fall on it, the precinct captain finally responded to their complaints and had it torn down. Other block clubs won benches for their local playgrounds and new streetlights—outright improvements for their areas.[9]

Of course, not every effort was successful; even active block clubs had to live with bothersome environmental conditions. The 4700-4800-4900 Kimbark Avenue Block Group, for example, reported "no real luck in getting trees sprayed" to combat pest infestations. A club on the 7300 Calumet block checked on the status of an abandoned car they had asked to have removed. Both the Chicago Urban League and the HPKCC cautioned new block clubs against starting with problems that were too big for small, inexperienced groups. They feared that early failure would discourage any further efforts. HPKCC director Julia Abrahamson explained that her organization "constantly encouraged newly organized blocks to begin on projects simple enough to promise success. As residents tackled one problem after another and learned that it was possible to solve them by working together, their confidence grew, and with it their ability to overcome the inevitable frustrations. . . . The beginning of collaboration by block groups on neighborhood and community-wide projects was a welcome sign of increasing maturity."[10]

The successes and failures of the Drexel Strip Block Group illustrate the variety of issues that a block club might focus on. In 1964, a HPKCC representative interviewed Ernest Clark, the Drexel chairman. He reported multiple accomplishments, despite difficulties with the group's organization. The group had managed to persuade the owners of several local apartment buildings to provide better lighting and lawn care. Clark claimed that "there has also been some improvement in the teenage behavior because of threatened action," but did not explain his block club's methods. The club had also won the demolition of the "old Chicago Hospital" after "much pressure from residents." On the other hand, school officials had ignored the club's offer to renovate a vacant lot into a playground. The group also had not found a solution for dealing with local teenagers who bothered their neighbors, especially the "pranksters" who disturbed the peace of the neighborhood convalescent home.[11]

The struggle of the 3800-3900 Monroe Block Club with a nearby branch of the Disabled American Veterans (DAV) organization reveals its persistent efforts to ease a local nuisance. DAV trucks routinely parked in the alley, trapping residents' cars in their garages. The club president told the local newspaper that residents "can't get to the garages in day time. If they park in the garages at night they can't get out in the morning." When the residents asked the drivers to allow them access to their garages, they "got such reply as wait or no response at all." The DAV foreman's promise to construct a loading dock went unfulfilled. Club members' exchanges with the DAV also reveal how urbanites selectively read minute elements of their environment through the screen of race. Frustrated club members suspected that racism was to blame for the DAV's unresponsiveness, "complaining that this could only be done in a Negro community." When members wrote to the parent DAV organization, they received another promise of cooperation and a reminder that the DAV employed many African Americans. This commentary caused them to scrutinize that letter in search of "the relationship between the DAV Negro employment and the infringement of the 3800 Monroe block residents' property rights."[12]

The residents of the 3800-3900 blocks of West Monroe Street learned that volunteer organizations could not coerce neighbors' cooperation. An alternate strategy for rallying neighbors was to model the desired action without explicitly asking anyone to participate. A twenty-first-century block club in

Buffalo, New York, transformed a vacant lot into a garden by tending flowers in inexpensive planters made from used tires and parking lot bumpers. In a video segment about the effort, Olga Ruiz of the Oxford Square Block Club explained, "People that would normally not volunteer come and help. If I'm here by myself sweeping, it never fails where there's a kid that comes up to me and says, 'Can I help you?'" Faith Rich wrote to her sister about having similar experiences while planting grass on Chicago's West 15th Place. When local children saw Rich "digging up soil, lugging wire for fences, planting or bringing seeds to people," she told her sister, they "flock around and help me and then the adults get interested and the whole block and a piece of the adjoining block has got in motion." With perhaps a dash more authority than Faith Rich employed, the president of the block club on the 3900 block of West Monroe Street recruited his three sons to join him in picking up trash on Sunday mornings. He explained to a reporter, "The reason more don't pitch in to help isn't because they're lazy or don't care. . . . But you have to understand that there are old people who can't do the work, men who work odd hours six and seven days a week and just don't have the time or energy to do all the things that should be done." Block club activists worked conspicuously, hoping their neighbors would recognize the value of their project and contribute what they could.[13]

Even as block clubs focused on particular problems, they also aimed at wider effects. They hoped to inspire similar efforts that might improve their own blocks as well as the broader neighborhood. To this end, block clubs sometimes publicized their events. An especially common tactic was for a club to report an event to its parent network, resulting in a brief notice in the larger group's newsletter. Neighborhood newspapers and the citywide African-American *Chicago Defender* also routinely covered block clubs' beautification projects. Block clubs devoted their energies to the activities themselves, not to detailed documentation of their efforts; the trace that block clubs left for historians is the fact that the activities occurred, but not information on how well they succeeded or whether they had long-term effects.

Vacant Lots

Block clubs did not work only to eliminate problem spots. They also worked to transform local liabilities into amenities. Vacant lots troubled many city neighborhoods in the postwar years. Much of Chicago had been built up by the mid-twentieth century, but not all structures stayed up. In flourishing neighborhoods, developers swooped in on older buildings and replaced them, sometimes to the chagrin of residents who felt the new buildings' aesthetics were inharmonious with the existing neighborhoods. In impoverished neighborhoods, residents often felt themselves lucky just to get decaying and abandoned structures torn down. But even that solution posed new problems.

Many neighbors saw untended lots as threats. Often unmown and unpoliced, vacant lots accumulated unsightly weeds and garbage. Some became gathering spots for unemployed men who hung out in them for hours at a time, sometimes leaving behind dangerous debris like broken bottles or drug paraphernalia. In the 1980s, illegal "fly dumpers" abandoned loads of refuse in vacant lots, often in black neighborhoods, instead of depositing it in officially sanctioned garbage dumps. The accumulated garbage attracted rats, which reproduced under the shelter provided by trash. To the dismay of the block club on the 1900 block of North Humboldt Boulevard, neighbors routinely parked their cars in a vacant lot with a convenient entrance ramp. Faith Rich complained that the same problem "plagued" the 15th Place Block Club when buildings were torn down. Sometimes block clubs dealt with nuisance lots by decorating them. The 5600 Drexel Avenue Block Group fenced in and planted shrubs on a lot left vacant after a building was demolished. Other block clubs, bothered by the appearance of vacant lots and the behavior they fostered, launched projects to repurpose them as community resources. Community gardens and small playgrounds that Chicagoans called "tot lots" were two of the most common new uses.[14]

Changing a hazardous vacant lot into a play spot for children solved two problems at once. It both rid the street of a menace and contained potentially troublesome children whose behavior might otherwise disturb their neighbors. For instance, concerned that the children on her block lacked a convenient place to play, a "childless woman" elected chair of the 6900 Wabash Avenue Block Club put up play equipment in her own yard. The Chicago Urban League staff worker worried, however, that "her extreme dedication to these interests may alienate some of the block people." She prompted the club to consider remaking the block's empty corner lot into a play area.[15]

Transforming a vacant lot, however, was not as simple as just installing equipment in a private yard. Members of a group on the Near West Side outlined the steps they thought would be necessary for the "development of lot south of Miller St. playlot with grass, trees and benches for the purpose of providing seating space for the Mothers." In order to make the transformation, they concluded that they would have to

1. Find owner of lot.
    (a) Secure his permission for use.
2. Get residents to clean lot.

3. Prepare for planting.
    (a) May need funds for black dirt etc.
4. Get benches.

Tracking down owners was a difficult task, but block clubs could not simply
co-opt abandoned lots and repurpose them. They had to secure the owners'
permission first. Sometimes the owners refused. The block club at 2900 West
Walnut Street proposed to rent a vacant lot for a play area, using funds donated for the purpose. The owners declined the club's offer, citing the desire
of tenants in adjacent buildings not to be disturbed by children's games. In
other cases, block clubs sought help from aldermen and from the Chicago
Park District.[16]

Hyde Park scholars Thelen and Sarchet noted that a community-sponsored
playground required maintenance and periodic equipment replacement, as
well as the effort of construction. Surrounding informal playgrounds with
fencing kept children from running into traffic. To pay for a fence around a
vacant lot on their block, members of the 4400 Adams Block Club conducted
a small fundraising campaign, netting more than one hundred dollars from
five-dollar pledges. The group that organized a tot lot for the vicinity of South
Drexel and 56th Street issued regulations for its members. Residents could access the locked tot lot using a combination lock, but children were not permitted to play in it without adult supervision. Gendered assumptions informed
postwar tot lot construction and use. According to Thelen and Sarchet, "usually, a group of fathers got together to clear the lot and level it off. Fencing
and other equipment was built by father's groups. A mother's committee was
organized to provide supervision, with two mothers on duty whenever the lot
was open." A publicity photo for an exemplar project, however, showed a man
helping a child down the slide.[17]

On blocks with few small children, building a tot lot was not the most
sensible use of block club resources. Transforming a vacant lot into a garden
presented an alternative strategy for local beautification. Urban agriculture
has a long history that scholars are just beginning to unpack. Chicagoans
became familiar with urban gardening on a broad scale during World War II,
when the Office of Civilian Defense (OCD) encouraged city block clubs to
join other Americans in tending "victory gardens." The OCD matched volunteer gardeners with plots of nearby land designated for food cultivation. Decades after the war's end, urban vegetable gardening enjoyed a revival.[18]

Like a tot lot, a garden improved a street's aesthetic quality and occupied
older children who enjoyed working in dirt. The nutrition offered by fresh
vegetables also had the potential to improve the health of block residents

Neighbors tackled their trash littered vacant lots--

To produce this playground where small children may play, supervised by mothers.

FIGURE 9. A study of block clubs in Hyde Park credited fathers with creating tot lots and mothers with supervising them. In an illustration from the study, however, a man helps children down a slide. Photographs by Mildred Mead. Source: Herbert A. Thelen and Bettie Belk Sarchet, *Neighbors in Action: A Manual for Community Leaders* (Chicago: Human Dynamics Laboratory, Department of Education, University of Chicago, 1954).

across ages. With these three goals in mind, the 15th Place Block Club, ener-
gized by the indefatigable Faith Rich, devoted enormous efforts to community gardening. Its gardening project began in the late 1960s, with "a veritable
madness of buying dirt and planting," and evolved by the mid-1980s into a
large-scale project. To support their work the club members wrote a letter
to Mayor Harold Washington petitioning for help from a "city garden crew
with access to heavy equipment for digging out the bricks prior to preparing
the soil for planting."[19] In the intervening two decades, the gardening project taught the club's participants much about growing grass and vegetables;
revealed pollution in their physical environment; brought them into contact
with local proprietors, property owners, and city officials; and cultivated community life.

The 15th Place Block Club's project started in 1968 when the club's president, Pearlie Robinson, became concerned that "we have been planting either
no grass or just poor weak grass which quickly gets trampled by the children
and does not come back the next year." Residents were discouraged in their
efforts to get property owners to establish perennial grass. One janitor never
followed through on his promises, and "there was nothing in the leases o[r]
[c]ustoms to make the landlords plant grass." The owners of nearby buildings experienced the same difficulty, explaining that "it [wa]s useless to plant
[grass] because the children will wear it off anyway. When they did supply
grass seed it was annual and had of course to be planted over again each year."
Nonetheless determined to green the environs, Robinson asked the resource-
ful Rich if she knew how to find what she called "'Come Back' grass." The
block club took the task upon itself, purchasing grass seed with its own funds
and committing to the labor of tending it. Residents turned out twice a day
for two weeks to water the initial plantings. The club "gradually established
perennial grass" over the next several years, developing "our goal of grass all
around the block" by seeding all the lawns, "something which was generally
thought to be impossible." By 1973, some of the local building owners had
agreed to purchase dirt for the project, although one such donated lot of soil
left "even more stones than there were originally."[20]

Rich wrote to her sister that the grass wrought "a great change." It not
only improved the appearance of the area the block club officially tended,
but also provided the neighbors with an incentive to transform their home
environments—even if they were not property owners. Rich explained, "In
the house next to us one of the tenants who had never done anything about
grass before suddenly bought flowers, dug up part of the grass and put the
flowers there, planted grass around the side of the house. She even set up a
bird bath. If this keeps up we will be practically suburban."[21]

At roughly the same time as the grass project, the block club also began encouraging neighbors to plant food crops. Faith Rich and her husband, Ted Rich, had a vision "to cover Chicago's west side with organic gardens on the vacant lots." Their model was the 3300 block of West Flournoy Street, where several residents kept gardens in their backyards and "many vegetables were donated to block club affairs." For her part, block club president Pearlie Robinson was "dreaming of the country in the city, where fruit and nuts grow in the yards and in the parks and the children can pick and eat as they did the persimmons and pecans when she was a girl." Tending lawns and several gardens was enough work so that the two activities sometimes competed for attention, but club members persevered.[22]

One of the first obstacles to gardening on vacant city lots was the poor quality of the soil. The club tried to remedy its deficiencies. Faith Rich attempted to create compost with enough nutrients to grow healthy plants. She buried her garbage next door to her home in the hope of helping a neighbor's vegetable garden. The block club voted to include leaves in the compost, since the addition of yard waste to kitchen refuse makes for more fecund soil. Rich asked the Chicago Department of Streets and Sanitation and the Chicago Park District to contribute dead leaves to the effort; because the block abutted Douglas Park, one of the city's largest parks, suitable leaves were not far away. But she found that they "could not dump leaves on private property without specific permission from the city." The city refused to help identify the property owners so that the block club could seek their cooperation. In one case, a frustrated Rich later discovered, the city itself owned the lot. Further, when the block club members had their soil tested in 1986, they found excessive levels of cadmium contamination. This discovery sent them to the University of Illinois Cooperative Extension Program for information about which vegetables could be safely grown and consumed. The group also took advantage of an offer from the Metropolitan Sanitary District of Greater Chicago for free sludge. As a result of this difficulty in obtaining soil good enough for gardening, the 15th Place Block Club urged the city to update its laws so that building wreckers would be required to leave three inches of soil on the site of a wrecked building.[23]

Despite the troubles with the soil, the 15th Place Block Club ultimately supported five vacant lot gardens on its block. Rich wrote, "At first most of the people thought I was crazy and only the children worked with me, picking up the stones and planting the seeds. But then some things grew, many more began to be interested and a few actually worked so that last year I did hardly anything." The gardening effort attracted several older men on the block. Rich described them in loving, wry detail in a letter to her sister:

Two men, both tenants, in the Kedzie building, a 24 apartment building on one corner of our block, became interested in the garden and go out there as early as six o'clock in the morning I am told. They spaded it up and planted it . . . One of the men doesn't really do any work because he has a bad heart and is not supposed to lift a finger or do anything but he contributes companionship for the other man and a great many ideas, many of them inconvenient. He also goes out and buys things for the garden. He says he often spends much more for liquor and why shouldn't he put the money in the garden instead. Why indeed?

The garden received tending from "Mr. Fane . . . a former Mississippi farmer who has some disability and cannot work." He told Rich that he was "delighted" that the block club's garden provided him an opportunity to spend time outside. Fane even devoted himself to the garden during the winter, starting plants in his basement for early spring transplantation. The gardeners received additional help from "Mr. Robert Simms, age 12, a student at Johnson School, [who] came over with his father's tractor and disked and leveled the garden." Perhaps more than other sporadically offered block club programs, gardening depended on the continuous energies of participants to prepare, plant, weed, and harvest. In 1987, the 15th Place Block Club debated inconclusively on whether to turn one of its collective plots over to a church for a parking lot, because Robinson, the club's president, "said she could no longer be responsible for a garden." A fallow garden presented as much potential trouble to a block as an abandoned building or an unused lot.[24]

City gardening created some new problems for block clubs. On West 15th Place, thieves of both human and animal varieties made gardening frustrating work. While suburban and rural gardeners may fume about rabbits and deer stealing their food, the 15th Place block club contended with rats. Overflowing refuse in the alleys attracted rats to the neighborhood, so the club asked the city's rodent control program to make extra sweeps of their gardens. People hungry for the vegetables grown in the gardens also snuck in at night to steal the fresh food.[25]

The ability of unauthorized mammals to get at the tender produce engendered a debate on West 15th Place about whether to fence in the gardens. The leftist Rich was opposed to fencing the lots, "but some of those who worked on it do want it fenced so they can eat according to their labor." Despite her own lack of enthusiasm for fences, it probably was Rich who wrote in the club's newsletter about its decision to control access to the garden plots. She reported that three young brothers put up a fence around one of the gardens "to safeguard the wonderful work Mr. Brown and Mr. Fane are doing." The club also persuaded a tavern owner on the block to donate some fencing he owned. He agreed, but only on the condition that the club return the fencing if the lot was ever sold and the garden built over. Rich also corresponded with the Illinois Department of Transportation (IDOT) on behalf of the club, in hopes of obtaining free fencing and steel posts. IDOT granted the request, but only on the condition that the club would be charged for materials that were vandalized or not returned. The club declined the offer, explaining, "We do have a small Treasury but in the event of extensive vandalism we could not afford to pay for the damages."[26]

With the donated labor of residents and the fencing protecting their produce from poachers, the West 15th Place gardens produced asparagus, snow peas, squash, collard greens, peanuts, tomatoes, sweet potatoes, and other vegetables. While residents (and thieves) consumed the vegetables, the club calculated the value of their labors. Rich reported that, "The gardeners on Albany near me figured out that they had got $500 worth of food from their garden." She found another multifamily garden whose tenders estimated that it saved them one thousand dollars in food costs. Once block youths were involved in cultivating the patches, Rich also compared the value of their produce to the wages they could earn through city programs sponsored by the federal Comprehensive Employment and Training Act (CETA). She concluded that "a young person could make more money from garden produce than from CETA work; that is, the estimated value of the garden produce was greater than the CETA wages." From the club's point of view, the value of the gardening project was not only in what it produced, but also in what it saved. They sent a letter to their US Congressional representative, Cardiss Collins, advocating for the continuation of city gardening subsidies and programs: "We found that the value of the garden was greater than the prized CETA work of the young people. We believe that losing these programs will cost more in relief and medical bills, and trash accumulating on the unused vacant lots than would be saved by eliminating the programs."[27]

When members of the 15th Place Block Club and their neighbors reflected on the importance of the gardens, they emphasized more than their pragmatic value. Rich learned that her gardening had initially aroused some suspicions among her neighbors, who "thought I had been sent by Mayor Daley to make fools of them! They apparently believed that whites did not garden." But she noted with amusement that when a television camera crew came to film the garden, previously skeptical neighbors "who had never done any work before came and took up forks and hoes." Publicity about the garden made their block look good. In a short essay in the club newsletter, Rich reminded readers that Chicago's motto was "Urbs in horto," Latin for "City in a garden." She argued that the city ought to support gardening efforts with demonstration gardens, aid to aspiring gardeners, and vegetable plantings around the city. Gardens would provide food for residents, take advantage of young people's energies and cultivate their skills, and provide some income. Rich noted a special role of urban vegetable gardening in combating poverty: "Since it appears that high unemployment and poverty will continue we should wage the war on poverty of which we have had only a few skirmishes so far. Gardens are one way to do this." On working class and poor blocks like West 15th Place, aesthetic considerations combined with the economy of food and labor to make gardening attractive on many levels. In more solidly middle-class neighborhoods, residents believed that flower gardening—alongside other decorating and ornamental schemes—made important aesthetic contributions to their quality of life.[28]

Improvement Campaigns

To enhance the cosmetic and structural condition of city neighborhoods, Chicagoans turned to improvement campaigns in the postwar years. Organizers believed that simultaneous improvements offered neighborhood- and citywide benefits that sporadic, individually focused efforts did not. In many ways, improvement campaigns resembled cleanup campaigns, which are taken up in chapter 5. They differed in focus and methods, but not in intent. In cleanup campaigns, participants removed garbage and other hazards from their surroundings, especially public spaces such as alleys and streets. Improvement campaigns, for their part, promoted upgrades to private properties such as buildings and yards. These programs were often structured as competitions. Although contests rewarded the best entrants, as far as organizers were concerned, the goal was to spur large numbers of residents to spruce up their homes and surroundings. Recognizing the important role of organized groups, such competitions encouraged both individual homeowners and block clubs to enter. Block clubs responded enthusiastically, often functioning as the competitions' linchpins.

The historian Benjamin Looker differentiates two kinds of improvement campaigns undertaken in the 1950s. On the one hand, real estate companies sponsored improvement campaigns in hopes of preventing further governmental involvement in the housing industry. From the time of New Deal, leaders of the private housing industry felt threatened by the federal government's involvement in urban renewal and public housing. In dozens of cities that participated in campaigns run by the real estate industry, "organizers strove to ensure that the solution to neighborhood blight would be rooted 'within the framework of our free-enterprise system.'" Black clubwomen, however, used the same strategies to encourage neighborhood cleanliness while offering different analyses of their significance. Organizers from the National Association of Colored Women's Clubs (NACWC) and other groups believed that improvement campaigns "might help discredit entrenched assumptions about the inevitable link between darker skin and blighted communities." Participants in NACWC campaigns "identified the discriminatory practices that underpinned deficient residential environments, while casting self-initiated rehabilitation as a way to stake a political claim as a community." Rather than demonstrating the value of the capitalist system, cleaning up black neighborhoods demonstrated residents' legitimacy and stake in the city.[29]

Mid-century Chicagoans were familiar with both corporate and civic campaigns encouraging residents to improve their homes and streets. Both the Chicago Urban League and the Chicago Real Estate Board (CREB) sponsored improvement campaigns in which block clubs participated. These programs probably influenced other smaller organizations to run their own local programs. Operation Pride, a program aimed directly at block clubs in North Lawndale, inspired Mayor Richard J. Daley's administration to sponsor a citywide campaign of the same name. While CREB's 1958 campaign focused especially on property owners, the other programs tried to maximize public participation, offering outreach and support to residents, local merchants, schools, employees, and civic institutions. Chicago groups also ran Christmas decorating contests in winter. Although such programs were not run exclusively by or for block clubs, they took advantage of the united action that block clubs made possible. Sponsoring organizations communicated with participants through block clubs, sending instructions about planning and rules for the groups to disseminate to residents.

Improvement campaigns incentivized participation with awards of cash and honor, recognizing both individual properties and the best blocks. One award-winning Chicago Urban League club achieved its distinction by spurring participation with its own block-level prizes. An archivist recalled her family's participation in the block-club-centered "Clean-up, Fix-up, and Paint-Up" campaign held annually in Indianapolis. Years later she reflected, "Like patriotism, this was understood to be a vertebra of good citizenship." Sponsors understood the real reward to be the time and money residents invested in improving their properties. The results were not intended to be confined to the winners, but rather were aimed to spread the effects of improvement as far as the campaign reached.[30]

Organizers valued the widespread benefits of competitions over the potential divisiveness of setting neighbor against neighbor. The League's annual

Christmas decorating contest even united a group suffering from internal strife. Despite the leadership tensions in the 7100 Eberhart Block Club, the League staff organizer reflected that it remained "known as the number one block club." It repeatedly won "first award for Christmas decorations and each year [they] have been head and shoulders above the other contestants." The Midwest Community Council's newsletter praised the 2700 Monroe Club for decorating a vacant lot. In at least one case, where block clubs were active but their coordinating federation was moribund, the League used a competition to try to revive district-level activity. West Garfield Park's United Property Group, aiming to hold white residents in the neighborhood, sponsored a lighting competition in 1959. Organizers explained that they hoped "to prove that a city community can give itself just as much of a holiday air—by simple and tasteful outdoor decorating—as some of the suburban areas with their big lawns and rambling ranch houses." The Midwest Community Council newsletter observed spillover effects from its 1961 Christmas decorating contest, noting with pride that "many blocks were well decorated that had not officially entered the contest."[31]

As was the case with block clubs more generally, the Chicago Urban League led Chicago's way into improvement campaigns. Working squarely in the uplift model of the black clubwomen Benjamin Looker describes,[32] the League's improvement campaigns had two goals. First, the League wanted residents of participating blocks to enjoy a pleasant environment. It also wanted to show outsiders that African American neighborhoods could be as attractive as those in which white Chicagoans lived; blacks could be good neighbors, just as whites could. To support both of those goals, the League often worked in partnership with the *Chicago Defender*, which encouraged widespread participation and publicized contest results.

Until it suspended operations in 1955, the Chicago Urban League and its affiliated councils ran a confusing array of improvement competitions. The names and competitive elements shifted over time as the organization and councils experimented, but the central purposes were constant. During the Depression years, League civic secretary Maude Lawrence organized "beautification contests." Beginning in 1937, the League sponsored a "Better Block Contest." In 1946, when block club programming became more important to the overall menu of League activities, it relaunched the idea on the South Side with a "Block Beautiful" competition, which the *Chicago Defender* also sponsored. Starting in 1949, West Side clubs participated in their council's "Better Homes and Yards" competition; but in 1953 the West Side Council abandoned the Better Homes and Yards approach in favor of Block Beautiful. In 1951 the League added a Christmas decorating contest for winter beautification. An annual "Mrs. Block Beautiful" pageant, with an award given to a married female participant, provided further incentive to get involved.[33]

The Community Improvement Council's Better Homes and Yards competition offers a window into the kinds of improvements the League hoped participants would make. The contest encouraged residents to focus their improvements in four areas, awarding individual prizes for "best flower box, best front yard, best back yard, and best general appearance"; in its second year, the council designated a "window box" competition especially for children. League staff organizer Rachel Ridley scheduled the West Side competition to coincide with the Midwest Community Council's cleanup parade in the same area, underscoring the synergies of broad local improvement. The Community Improvement Council gave out awards at a celebratory event held in Garfield Park's Gold Dome Building. In toting up the results of the competition on the racially changing West Side, Ridley was especially pleased to note that whites as well as African Americans (who could be expected to participate in League-sponsored events) entered the competition.[34]

League staff members were mindful of the racial implications of their improvement campaigns. The League's 1948 annual report singled out for praise the 4700 block of Calumet, where members carefully tended grass seed. Reflecting on residents' recent history as Southern cotton farmers and their deeper history as slaves, the report observed, "It's something of an achievement for a voluntary organization to persuade people who have fought grass up and down cotton rows literally for centuries so completely to change their old habits of thinking about grass as to be willing to make a bed for it, plant it, nurture it, and to protect it from those whose backs ache at the very sight of it." League staff members carefully organized their program to get the word of Southern blacks' adaptability to urban life out to a white audience. Without mentioning the race of the judges, the League's 1952 annual report explained, "A variety of people served as judges, some of them coming from suburban areas. They found it an excellent opportunity to see some of the work which the Negro community is doing."[35] As African Americans were largely confined within Chicago's city limits in the 1950s, the phrase "suburban areas" served as a code for whites. An illustrative photograph showing an interracial group of judges inspecting a spruced-up yard highlighted the existence of white witnesses to black achievements in property upkeep.

Outdoor improvement campaigns flourished in summer, when warm weather enticed Chicagoans into the sunshine. But block clubs did not forgo beautification during snowy and cold Midwestern winters. In early winter, parent organizations sponsored programs and contests encouraging block club participants to put up Christmas decorations and lights. As in the

".... children and parents and grandparents get together."

"We've made our homes beautiful — for ourselves and our children . . ."

"On August 28th, judges will make the rounds. Neighbors will point with pride . . ."

FIGURE 10. This series of images from the Chicago Urban League's 1950 annual report accentuated three distinct functions of their cleanup competitions: intergenerational communal effort, local beautification, and the opportunity to impress white judges. Source: "Together . . . the Reporter of the Chicago Urban League," August 1950, folders 1–20, box 1, series 1, Chicago Urban League records, University of Illinois at Chicago Library, Department of Special Collections. Courtesy of the Chicago Urban League.

warm-weather competitions, organizations used the campaign to reach potential supporters. Some League block clubs made putting up lights on their
homes a regular winter expectation for members, and did so without having to run competitions. The leadership of the 7100 Rhodes Block Club felt
that Christmas decorating helped ease racial tensions on the still-integrated
block. The club's leader explained to a League staff member, "The turning
point came with the Christmas decorations. Everybody helped and a friendly
spirit grew out of this. Several of the white people in the block who had
seemed unfriendly or indifferent, contributed to the Christmas decorations
and seemed to have changed their attitudes." Where they did hold competitions, League district councils taxed member clubs a small fee to pay for
prizes. While more ephemeral than gardens and paint, Christmas decorations indicated to passersby that the inhabitants had discretionary income,
spare energies, and house pride—all signals of a neighborhood where people
might want to plant themselves and their families.[36]

Sponsoring organizations learned to set the terms for group contests carefully, lest they arouse more suspicion than cooperation. The CREB's "Better
Neighborhood Crusade" ran afoul of black Chicagoans' worries about real estate dealers' ulterior motives. To commemorate its seventy-fifth anniversary
in 1958, CREB's advisory board decided to focus on "the field of neighborhood conservation . . . because of its close relationship to realtors." The Better
Neighborhood Crusade offered twenty thousand dollars in prize money—
including five thousand for the best block—to encourage Chicago property
owners "making the greatest improvement in appearance, maintenance and
rehabilitation of buildings and compliance with city building and housing
standards." A total of 485 blocks from fourteen different Chicago neighborhoods signed up to compete by submitting "before and after" photographs
and their properties for inspection.[37]

Black participants in North Lawndale, however, were startled to discover
that awards committee inspectors expected to enter their homes to check on
their compliance with the housing code. A Lawndale representative wrote
to CREB, explaining that this procedure aroused "resistance on the part of
homeowners, especially Negroes, who were suspicious of real estate men." In
the postwar period, CREB members refused to broker properties for African
American homebuyers. Further, housing code inspection results requiring
costly repairs could effectively drive property owners out of their homes. Expecting black residents to give white real estate dealers entrance into their
homes to count transgressions crossed the bounds of reasonable contest terms.
When Lawndale launched its own Operation Pride competitions, it took a

lesson from this example and specified in its publicity materials that inspections would be limited to building exteriors.[38]

Participants understood that the competitions demanded the investment of both sweat and money. Cash prizes of several hundred dollars awarded to individuals and groups seldom repaid personal investments. Instead, the awards provided a symbolic motivation alongside the satisfaction of enjoying an improved home and streetscape. The improvements themselves were usually uncontroversial, but organizers and participants did find points of disagreement. Despite confining judgment to exteriors, the Greater Lawndale Conservation Commission's effort in the late 1950s generated a number of different complaints. Gloria Pughsley, the head of the GLCC's block club program and also the organization's frequent antagonist, reported the discontent of residents who took out loans to finance major renovations for their properties. They felt slighted when the judges honored cosmetic changes, rewarding "those who planted pretty gardens and had painted flagstones." Joseph Guinta, whose Midwest Community Council ran a cleanup parade, suggested to the GLCC staff that they should consider devoting staff and funds to programs rather than competitions. Guinta argued that competitions did not encourage additional improvements, asserting, "People who are so inclined, will 'cleanup and maintain their property whether prizes are awarded or not.'" The mail-order giant Sears, Roebuck, and Company, which was headquartered in North Lawndale until 1974 and was the GLCC's largest funder, also criticized its approach. Although the Sears-Roebuck Foundation contributed fifty thousand dollars to the NACWC's improvement campaign, in Lawndale Sears wanted to generate the broadest possible community participation from inexpensive efforts. Citing high Chicago unemployment, higher black unemployment, and the uncertainty of financing for home improvements, Sears staff suspected that "costly improvements would not bring great results." Instead of using cash prizes, they recommended instead that "certificates of honor . . . be awarded at the conclusion of the campaign." To incentivize small improvements rather than costly structural repairs, Sears permitted participants to purchase paint and grass seed at cost.[39]

The GLCC launched the "Cleaner Lawndale" campaign in 1955 and changed its name to "Operation Pride" in 1961. Over time, organizers continuously tinkered with the specifics of the program, adding new categories for awards and expanding the repertoire of related activities. While the basic competitive categories were for "home owners, tenants, block clubs, and vacant lots," the GLCC experimented with different ways to motivate participation. In 1966, for example, the competition included a special contest for janitors, while in 1962 merchants from Lawndale contributed "merchandise gifts" for "housewives who showed ingenuity in housekeeping and decorating skills." Organizers expressed the beautification theme in motivating slogans, such as "Putting lawn back into Lawndale" and "Fix-up, paint-up, keep-it-up."[40] Whatever the language used to describe the contest, the consistent purpose was to encourage residents to invest their own funds and energies into beautification—regardless of whether they won the formal contest. To help participants understand the inexpensive possibilities, the GLCC provided a checklist of improvements they could make, including the following:

> Mow lawn and trim hedges.
> Sweep sidewalks and steps.
> Ask neighbors to move their automobiles and remove debris from the curb.
> Paint window frames, replace and broken glass [sic], and wash plate glass doors.
> Repair or remove dilapidated fences, sheds, and garages from the premises.
> Pay attention to rear yards, alleys, and fences, as well as to property fronts.
> Paint fences and remove dilapidated ones.[41]

In 1962, the GLCC calculated that the program had inspired ten million dollars of investment in North Lawndale properties. A few years later, it estimated that "a typical winning entry involves spending about $1,800 on painting, roofing, pruning hedges, repairing porches, and tuckpointing." These estimates contradicted Sears's assumption that Lawndale residents lacked the capacity to spend on their homes. By 1962, Operation Pride was so established in North Lawndale that Mayor Richard J. Daley agreed to attend the awards ceremony.[42]

Daley must have been impressed with what he saw in North Lawndale. Within two years, the Mayor's Office of Inquiry and Information began sponsoring its own Operation Pride in other Chicago neighborhoods.[43] Mayor Daley's program's goal was "community re-education and consciousness of the need for rehabilitation and pride in their neighborhoods."[44] Over the course of the 1960s, the city government spread Operation Pride to communities across Chicago, many of them also aspiring to attract urban renewal. Community-based groups in Lincoln Park, Uptown, South Shore, Logan Square, Woodlawn, West Garfield Park, South Lawndale, and Wicker Park all coordinated with the city on local Operation Pride events.[45] As the program spread, the Mayor's Office of Inquiry and Information took credit for inventing Operation Pride; the Chicago Tribune reported in 1969 that the office's director, John Billings, had "devised the program in 1962," which happened to be the year in which Daley attended Lawndale's closing ceremony. During President Lyndon B. Johnson's tenure, Daley attached federal War on Poverty monies to Operation Pride, involving the Chicago Committee on Urban Opportunity and the Model Cities program in funding salaries for support staff. The Mayor's Office of Inquiry and Information eventually began stressing that Operation Pride should be a year-round activity rather than having a special focus in the summer. Perhaps this dilution of the program into routine neighborhood maintenance explains why it stopped receiving newspaper publicity after 1973.[46]

In its decade of operation, each participating community added local touches to Operation Pride. In the wealthy Lincoln Park neighborhood of Park West, for example, organizers held an "antiques fair" to order to raise funds for worthy community programs, among them Operation Pride. By contrast, in the much poorer West Garfield Park, participants received information about improvements they could make without having to pay for city permits or risk property tax increases. A community that was home to numerous white southern migrants, Uptown held a 1972 program that included children's health screenings and immunizations for diseases such as measles, polio, and tetanus. Several communities made parades the centerpiece of their summer-long Operation Pride programs. Most parades included the standard fare of marching residents and musical entertainment, but Logan Square's joint Flag Day–Operation Pride parade in 1965 featured an elephant, a chimpanzee, and a lion.[47]

Although each Operation Pride program took on the specific flavor of its local community, the key role of block clubs in generating physical improvement remained a consistent theme. The benefits of block club involvement were two-fold. First, block clubs were excellent vehicles for publicizing the program. They were not only a useful communication network, but also inspirational. Residents who believed that their neighbors' improvements would amplify the benefits of their own work were more likely to participate. Second, block clubs' collective work leveraged broader improvements than individual residents working alone could achieve. Block groups in North Lawndale, for example, shared the costs of repairing sidewalks, purchasing sod, and repairing gutters and porches.[48] Despite the presumed benefits of block club participation, Operation Pride's results produced temporary improvements, rather than long-term local transformations. Like most cleaning activities, cosmetic changes affected residents' immediate quality of life without altering the underlying conditions that caused neighborhood decay.

Many block clubs' programs to improve their environment were initiated and completed at the local level, contingent only on members' efforts. Larger programs, such as the Better Homes and Yards competition and Operation Pride, nominally connected the block clubs' work with other groups' efforts.

But their implementation remained completely local in focus; participants expended elbow grease only in the areas immediately around their homes. Many local problems, however, had deeper roots than publicly sponsored, individually implemented programs could handle. Persistent problems such as garbage, building deterioration, and neighborhood decay were too big to address with private energy alone. Effective solutions demanded both local attention and the weight of public policy and politics. In addition to beautification programs, block clubs worked on local problems by harnessing the power of government to their streetscapes. The solutions that government offered, however, only incompletely addressed the problems they were theoretically designed to solve. Block clubs complemented and sometimes completed the work of government in neighborhood problems.

afford sidewalk repairs than residents in other parts of Chicago. In 1964, the City Council budgeted one million dollars for a program to split the costs of sidewalk repair between petitioning property owners and the city. But even shared expenses were too much for poorer communities, especially those with old vaulted sidewalks that were prohibitively expensive to repair. The Dickens-Winchester Block Club's formal appeal for assistance through a special program illustrates how Chicagoans needed special expertise in the operations of city government to maintain their common spaces.[2]

Because of their small size and unofficial status, block clubs' resources were insufficient to achieve all that members envisioned as possible. Collective beautification exercises took advantage of concentrated time and local elbow grease to create relatively small-scale and temporary solutions. Yet, as Chicago entered its second century, residents faced problems that required more intensive treatments than block club members could provide with their own labor and funds. In twentieth-century Chicago, working-class residents such as those served by the Dickens-Winchester Block Club could not construct new sidewalks themselves; nor could they afford to pay assessments for them like their well-off counterparts in Hyde Park. They lacked the expertise and authority to compel the rehabilitation of abandoned buildings or the clearance of deteriorated infrastructure. But just as property owners believed that the quality of nearby buildings affected the value of their land, so too did block club members feel that the physical environment on their blocks conditioned their quality of life every day—whether the responsible parties were public or private, and whether the scale of the problem was large or small.

Block clubs in working-class areas could not execute large-scale rehabilitation projects on their own. As informed members of the polity and through their links to larger organizations, though, they often knew about the city, state, and federal governments' approaches to remediating urban deterioration. In the twentieth century, urban redevelopment programs were not universal improvement efforts, applied evenly throughout the city. Instead, they were targeted at particular neighborhoods and were funded according to political priorities. In order to attract desirable improvement, block clubs had to become squeaky wheels. Like larger community-based organizations, they demonstrated that they deserved assistance by working on their own behalf and lobbying for programs to supplement their efforts. In working cooperatively to pressure government officials to bring rehabilitative efforts home, block club members were exercising a venerable American right: the freedom of association, as guaranteed by the US Constitution's First Amendment. Neighbors worked together not as ideologically bound partisan allies, but as pragmatic, temporary cooperators. They complemented the work of government officials, drawing attention to areas that could benefit from existing remedies.

Many problems that plagued block club members resulted from inadequate provision of city services, owners' neglect of their own properties, and the natural decay of physical infrastructure. Especially between World War II and the mid-1980s, block clubs sought to harness the power of government to magnify their local efforts. In the early postwar years, block clubs often focused on garbage collection, participating in citywide projects to address unsanitary conditions. Large-scale cleanup efforts faded from fashion in the later postwar years, but block clubs continued with local antigarbage campaigns. Block clubs were also troubled by deteriorating buildings, a problem that became acute in Chicago in the last quarter of the twentieth century. When owners allowed their properties to conflict with city codes or abandoned them altogether, block clubs tried to bring them into compliance with the city's rules.

Block clubs, however, were poorly suited for dealing directly with larger problems. Small, volunteer-driven organizations lacked the resources to effect large-scale transformations in their environments. Block clubs had an interest in larger midcentury programs that affected their landscapes, such as antigarbage campaigns and urban renewal and conservation. They were not, however, perfect partners for their parent organizations' plans. Block clubs' preferences were vulnerable to the agendas of more powerful institutions, and discord between clubs and sponsoring organizations could undermine the effort. Some causes, such as mayoral cleanliness campaigns, were relatively benign efforts that offered only benefits to residents. But especially in the 1950s and 1960s, umbrella organizations sought to use their block clubs' approval as evidence for bringing urban renewal to their neighborhood—whether or not all of their constituents welcomed such redevelopment. This effort worked in Hyde Park, where the HPKCC's program of advocacy for urban renewal was structured to defuse the objections of block clubs that opposed their plans. In North Lawndale, however, the organization sponsoring urban renewal fumbled its attempt to win residents' support. Block clubs worked most effectively when their efforts complemented those of city officials, accorded those of umbrella groups, and were limited to their territory alone.

Garbage

Nineteenth-century Chicago property owners had to figure out how to dispose of their own garbage. Some disposed of it tidily, but others dumped it wherever most convenient—including city streets and waterways. A portion of the

South Branch of the Chicago River was notorious as "Bubbly Creek," a nick-name referring to the noxious effects of industrial pollution. Over the course of the twentieth century, Chicagoans assigned responsibility for city sanitation to a combination of public officials and private scavengers. Small property owners' taxes paid for municipal garbage collectors, while the city required owners of large buildings to pay for private scavenger services. Gaps in collection meant that sanitation was imperfect at best. While residents with clout and wealth made sure their streets were clean, waste often went unchecked in poor and minority neighborhoods. Block clubs sometimes tried to fill in the holes of this fragmented public order through programs that pushed their neighbors into more sanitary habits and harnessed additional public services.

Loose garbage was a perennial problem in Chicago's streets and alleys. Refuse historian Martin Melosi explains how urban waste disposal practices differ from other utilities that make modern cities relatively clean, safe, and convenient. Most utilities are infrastructure systems dedicated solely to their tasks. Sewer and water systems and telephone, electrical, and cable utilities deliver their services and remove by-products through exclusive networks. Those systems may break down (with potentially disastrous results), but they do not depend on human operators to conduct the moment-to-moment manual labor of service delivery. By contrast, the infrastructure system used to remove garbage from its point of origin is the combination of staffed trucks and roads that have multiple users and purposes.[3] The dependence of the garbage collection and disposal system on roads means that the people who operate the garbage trucks enjoy a great deal of discretion about how thoroughly they do their jobs—with consequences for neighborhood residents.

Chicagoans began to regulate the collection and disposal of waste products as early as 1849. The historian Craig E. Colten explains that the city's evolving sanitation regulations focused on where to deposit garbage, refuse, ash, and industrial solids once they were collected. In the nineteenth century, much waste was dumped on the lakefront to create landfill. In the twentieth century, the city turned to dumps within and beyond municipal limits and then to incinerators for solutions to its growing garbage problem. With policy focusing on the disposal of waste rather than its thorough removal from the streets, city neighborhoods were rarely uniformly clean, even after collection days. Municipal garbage collection was often "erratic," prompting the wealthy to pay private garbage scavengers to haul away their waste. Colton points out that "other neighborhoods had to rely on 'more or less' faithful and 'more or less' regular municipal crews."[4]

The uneven collection of garbage did not go unnoticed by people who frequented poor neighborhoods. Residents certainly observed the conditions near their own homes. Tenement neighborhoods suffered not only ram-shackle buildings, but also children playing amid refuse in alleys and on streets. Upper-class reforming women also noticed garbage in the streets, and pushed city government to remedy the hazard. In 1892, in advance of the World's Columbian Exposition, the Municipal Order League persuaded the Chicago City Council to make street sweeping a municipal function. As Suellen Hoy points out, however, only the downtown area enjoyed consistent attention from cleaning crews. Jane Addams, the founder of Hull-House, fa-mously prodded city government to improve its garbage collection process by deploying neighborhood women to inspect "backyards, alleys, and the huge wooden garbage boxes that were fastened to street pavements." Dissatisfied with the results, Addams bid unsuccessfully for a scavenging contract. She settled instead for a position as a salaried garbage inspector. In keeping with the nationwide move away from private garbage collection in the Progres-sive Era, in 1914 the Woman's City Club successfully pushed Chicago to end the "franchise" system for garbage disposal. The city launched a municipally owned approach to garbage collection. But these collection and disposal sys-tems were not enough to keep trash off the streets. Cleanliness required per-petual vigilance.[5]

Regulations defining whose garbage was a municipal responsibility com-plicated control of the waste spilling into Chicago streets and alleys. After World War II, a city ordinance differentiated whether garbage collection was a public or private responsibility according to building size. Buildings con-taining four or fewer residential units were eligible for public garbage col-lection. Owners of apartment buildings with more than four units had to contract with a private scavenger to pick up their trash.[6] According to one report, by the 1980s an average of four different private haulers served each Chicago block.[7] Negligent tenants and landlords compounded the garbage problem by failing to dispose of their waste neatly. In 1986, a representative of the 15th Place Block Club explained how these uncoordinated efforts left their alley a mess:

> Some landlords do not provide enough cans and the garbage is thrown on the ground.
>
> When the city tries to ticket the landlord, manager, or janitor the city has trouble finding him. He is an absentee landlord.
>
> Or the landlord provides the proper cans but the tenants do not bring their garbage down to the alley. They may pile it on the porch where it feeds the rats. Or they may send a young child who is not tall enough to get it into the can. He or she drops it on the ground where it is appreciated by the rats.
>
> Or bulky trash is stuffed in the cans, leaving too little room for the garbage.[8]

In other words, multiple parties were responsible for removing garbage from the same place. If any one of them fell short, filth followed.

Chicago blocks that mixed large and small residential buildings were vulnerable to both the municipal crew that hauled away garbage and also the private trucks hired by landlords. The city might do a fine job with the buildings for which it was responsible, but the street could still be a mess if the residents and private scavengers allowed garbage to accumulate. For example, the *Austin News* neighborhood investigative reporter reported that the private scavenger hired by the owner of a nine-flat on her block failed to pick up the building's garbage for two weeks, leaving "the refuse . . . piled up high against the fence, drawing rodents and insects." The city had the power to issue a ticket to the building owner, but it did not pick up the accumulated garbage. Alternatively, the residents and private scavengers might handle their trash carefully, but if the municipal garbage crew was not regular in its rounds, the street might still be unclean. When the chairman of the Central Austin Block Clubs complained to the city that his garbage had not been picked for two weeks, they finally sent a truck to do the job. "But I'm a taxpayer," he lamented, "and I should not have to call to get garbage picked up." Even when supplemental programs provided garbage pickup, as occurred when Chicago's Model Cities program ran an extra truck on West 15th Place in 1986, it made only selective stops. To address the deficiencies stemming from dependence on multiple garbage haulers, the 15th Place Block Club proposed that "the city should take back the responsibility for all garbage collection regardless of the size of the building, subcontracting to private scavengers where desirable." Whatever advocacy Faith Rich and her neighbors conducted in favor of making public garbage collection universal was unsuccessful, however; the building-size differentiation remained Chicago public policy in the twenty-first century.[9]

Because of the shortfalls in municipal and private sanitation, Chicago block clubs made it their business to deal with the garbage that fell onto the streets and alleys somewhere on its journey between a home and a dump. The work of the Miller-Carpenter Street Block Club exemplified block clubs' orientation to garbage. The group was formed under the auspices of the West Side Community Committee and the Near West Side Planning Board in late 1953 as part of their preparation for urban renewal and conservation. The Miller-Carpenter Street Block Club made garbage its first priority. Its antigarbage program used a variety of approaches to cleaning waste from the streets. It educated neighbors in the reasons to clean up, provided tools for individual use, ran activities for group "demonstrations," and worked with local institutions, businesses, and officials to clean up particular problem sites.

Neighborhood clean up days often involve the whole family--

Parks and business streets are often included in the general clean-up.

FIGURE 11. Groups of Hyde Park residents engaged in a cleanup of their streets. Photographs by Mildred Mead. Source: Herbert A. Thelen and Bettie Belk Sarchet, *Neighbors in Action: A Manual for Community Leaders* (Chicago: Human Dynamics Laboratory, Department of Education, University of Chicago, 1954).

RAT CONTROL METHODS
Chicago Health Department—Division Environmental Sanitation
Rat Control Section

DON'T GIVE THE RAT A FREE MEAL

REFUSE

For each FAMILY living in a house there should be STANDARD LEGAL REFUSE
CANS with tight-fitting covers—like these (20 gallon to 32 gallon capacity).

Placed on racks
such as these

TODAY : Make sure you have enough cans

EVERY DAY : Use them

Garbage and rubbish should go IN the
cans, not just NEAR them.

But certainly
not like this

GARBAGE IS RAT FOOD

Bird food should
be placed on
raised platforms

Why feed him ?   No   Yes

Make sure that all garbage, rubbish, and ashes in the
yard and alley are picked up and placed in containers.

FIGURE 12. The Miller-Carpenter Block Club distributed educational flyers like this one in hopes of
persuading their neighbors to participate in a collective effort to clean up the streets and alleys. Source:
box 39, folder 527, Near West Side Community Collection, University of Illinois at Chicago Library, Department of Special Collections. Courtesy of the Chicago Department of Public Health.

The club began by encouraging residents to get rid of older, unsanitary
refuse storage boxes made of cement. To replace them, it sold more than one
hundred modern cans and covers. It distributed flyers to neighbors explaining how to "protect the health of your family by keeping your alleys clean."
One flyer's advice included:

1. Don't feed Rats and Flies.
2. Rats carry rabies, plague, typhus and other diseases.
3. Flies spread dysentery, tuberculoses [*sic*] and possibly *Polio*.[10]

Following up on the sales campaign, the club conducted a usage survey, asking the city to ticket neighbors who had not replaced their outmoded cement boxes with cans. Pragmatically recognizing Chicago municipal corruption, leaders of the Miller-Carpenter Street Block Club also considered what they could do to prevent officials from dismissing the tickets. The group sent follow-up letters to people who had purchased the metal containers, inquiring why they were not being used. In the early spring of its first year, the club held its first annual "clean up demonstration," turning out seventy-five residents who were supplied with "brooms and shovels" to clear garbage out of the alley. After a few years of experience, the club developed a more sophisticated approach, scheduling the demonstration for Saturday rather than Sunday, so that "the people could not have any excuses like going to church etc., and they feel that Saturday the city will be able to send us a Dump Truck to pick up the dirt after we clean."[11] The club leaders hoped that the city's prompt removal of accumulated refuse would enhance their neighbors' confidence that the effort of cleaning up the streets was worthwhile.

In addition to educating and turning out residents for cleanup events, the Miller-Carpenter Street Block Club also forged relationships with local institutions. Working in cooperation with the Parent-Teacher Association (PTA) of a nearby school, members cleared rubbish from a vacant lot and transformed it into a "play-tot-lot" for children. The club also reached an agreement with a business owner whose property tended to accumulate rubbish. He agreed that his staff would dispose of "wood and large corrugated boxes" properly, as long as neighbors were instructed to stop "using *his property* as a dumping ground." The resulting letter that the block club sent out to residents admonished: "Cooperation is a two-way proposition; let's be sure we do our part." The group appealed to the ward's garbage superintendent and alderman to work with it on a list of specific projects, including sidewalks, street sweeping, street lighting, the purchase of a vacant lot by the city, the paving of another lot, and, of course, garbage inspection. The alderman, however, was preoccupied by an upcoming election and refused to meet, instead promising vaguely to "look into" their requests.[12]

In elite Hyde Park, block club members were more concerned with the cleanliness of the streets than with loose garbage dropped in alleys. Parked cars prevented city street sweepers from capturing litter hidden between tires and curbs. If residents removed their cars on a regular basis, then the city street sweeping service could take care of the problem. The HPKCC, the alderman, the ward sanitation office, and block clubs collaborated to develop a system for leafleting residents in advance of a planned sweep and locating the owners of unremoved cars on the day of the cleaning. According to Julia Abrahamson, this systematic approach was so effective that the city took over the notification tasks, posting permanent signs bearing the cleaning schedule, and fining the owners of unmoved cars before the sweeping.[13]

Block clubs creatively asked their neighbors to contribute to cleaning up their common surroundings. A common strategy was to call an event that demonstrated the dramatic difference a few hours' collective work could make to the appearance of the street. The Neighborhood Conservation Council, which served the 5000 blocks of West Madison and Washington Streets in the early 1960s, held an "assault on dirt and debris" in their shared alley twice a year.[14] The Chicago Urban League staff reported on an event held by the 1200 Block Springfield Club on May 1, 1954:

> At 10:30 a.m. the streets had been properly blocked and the residents had gathered in front of their homes with rakes, picks, shovels, etc., to spade their lawns. Mr. Turner requested that they gather in the center of the street to receive instructions on how to seed their lawns. After completing the task, each person felt that they had accomplished a good days [sic] work and they now felt that since the neighbors had seen their efforts they would be able to secure better cooperation in keeping their property, streets and alleyways clean.[15]

In a variation on this approach, the Associated Block Committees of Garfield Park–Austin linked picking up litter with weeding. The 2100 West Crystal Block Club sent a special notice to a landlord to participate in their cleanup, inviting him to take care of "the refuse that has accumulated around your building at 2151 W. Crystal." The club suggested that "if you can't make it that day but could get things picked up in the day or two immediately before that, it would be a big help." Members of the Ohio-Ashland Block Club felt their first cleanup event was a particularly notable success because of the participation of a normally absentee landlord, who brought along a crew of four assistants. The 5400 South University Block Club in Hyde Park underscored its satisfaction by sending members a newsletter recounting their activities, including the accomplishment that "900 pounds of dirt and rubble was collected in 4-½ hours."[16]

Some block clubs preferred not to organize common cleanup demonstrations. For example, the Unity Block Club eschewed holding cleanup events at fixed times. Instead, the members invested the club's funds in brooms that were available to all neighbors. It publicized the location where the brooms were stored and advised residents: "Do not be afraid to ask your neighbor to let you borrow the broom to sweep the front of your home or residence, the street or the alley."[17] Whether block club members worked collectively or individually, the message was the same: The more neighbors who worked to clean up the street, the better.

Some block clubs celebrated successful clean-up events. The Dickens-Winchester Block Club invited residents to join in "cleaning the sidewalks, parkways, and gutters and helping people to clean their yard." Participants should "bring rakes, shovels, brooms, and garbage bags if you can." The effort was to be followed immediately by a picnic "with *Free Hotdogs and Lemonade for any children who participate*. Adults are invited to bring cookies, cupcakes, etc." The 15th Place Block Club newsletter reported in 1976 that as part of Clean-Up Week, the club helped children who lived on the block to get library cards. While most children "brought home armfuls of books," the event was not without hitches. The report continued, "One little girl in kindergarten was disappointed because she could not get a card not being able to write her name. We will put her name in later when she succeeds."[18]

Many block clubs gave children a special role in keeping local areas tidy. Officers of the 1300 Kedvale-Keeler Block Club sent out a note to landlords and tenants reminding them of the importance of their assistance: "We cleaned your street and alley Saturday morning. Didn't it look almost clean enough to eat off? The children played a big part, too, by helping to sweep. Won't you please cooperate with your Block Club and refrain from littering up your street with all kinds of trash? Train your children as well as yourself to use the trash baskets." In Hyde Park, residents expressed irritation with children who dropped their trash on the ground. In response, several block clubs adopted a multipronged strategy to turn the problem around: The clubs purchased trash cans, held monthly litter patrol activities for the children, threw them a reward party, and then taught them to use the trash cans. By contrast, a newly forming group in the West Town neighborhood reported that their work was minimized when area children preempted their effort. The block club chairman reported, "They really knocked themselves out. I saw little kids not more than five years old picking up garbage with toy shovels and pails." They rewarded the children's initiative with a trip to a new ice cream store for banana splits. Two Chicago Urban League clubs even managed to make cleanup part of a party. They planned to conclude their block party with "a bubble bath ceremony in which part of the street will be scrubbed."[19]

The 15th Place Block Club ran a summer project in 1970 that addressed three problems at once. It consolidated into a single effort the empty bottles discarded on the street, the excess energies of children, and the chronic hunger of poor urbanites. President Pearlie Mae Robinson explained:

> I collect bottles from children. I am very happy about the project bec[au]se it gives the children some way to make money, not to have to beg for a penny or a nickel from any one on the street. It gives them something to do. They look forward to work every day. They learn about time.
>
> When I first started it I went out one day and told the children to give me any kind of bottle you can find. I will give you one cent for it. I don't care what kind it is. So for about one week I took bottles when they brought them. After a while they were at my house at 6 A.M. on Sunday. So I set a time which was 4 P.M. every day except Sunday. I thought that after about three weeks I would not have to do anything because I thought that in this ghetto where I am people did not have money. They could not buy that much whiskey or beer or wine. But after three weeks I was taking in about 2000 bottles a day. So you can understand why I can truly say there is more money in the ghetto than people say there is. Now at this time I yet have not been able to complete my total figures for the year 1970; but I can say that I took in over 45,000 bottles.
>
> I have seen children put their money together and buy food. They didn't buy all candy as people say they would do. They would buy meat and crackers, milk and cake. Three or four children would put their money together and buy meat and crackers and one big bottle of pop so they all could drink. They would go on a back porch or some other place and get a knife and fruit such as cantaloupe and cut and eat it. I would still be in my yard buying bottles from other children so they could do the same. So when I saw this it encouraged me to go ahead with the project because this meant they did not have to steal to eat. I know how it feels to be hungry.[20]

Faith Rich reported on this project in her annual holiday letter, telling her friends and family, "Every afternoon you could see the children lining up with bags, boxes and armfuls of bottles. She paid them a cent for each bottle of any kind. People noted with amazement that the broken glass on the streets practically disappeared."[21]

Groups of block clubs similarly coordinated community-wide cleanup events. Marillac House, a Catholic settlement house run by the Daughters of Charity religious order, organized a modest block club program. In 1959 it set aside a July day for an "Alley Fair," explaining, "Block Clubs entering this project will be cleaning, repairing, painting, and planting in order to get their yards and alleys ready for that date." The next year, they sponsored a cleanup week in April. The United Block Clubs, consisting of half a dozen clubs on the West Side, "held street cleaning rallies [and] approached the city for street-corner litter baskets and better cleaning services." In an instance of joint municipal–block club planning, the 28th Ward in 1966 worked with block clubs to organize the removal of bulk refuse from the area. According to a newspaper report, the plan developed by the block club presidents "involves the block clubs canvassing their blocks, instructing block residents to put out all bulky garbage on a given date. The bulk is picked up on the following day by 28th ward open trucks."[22]

Other block clubs tackled garbage in their alleys with less coordination but no less fervor. In spring 1953 and 1954 the 7200 Rhodes Avenue club rounded up local children to clean its alley. In 1977 the Ohio-Ashland Block Club asked its ward superintendent to provide more garbage cans; a member followed up by posting signs in English and Spanish reminding residents to use the lids to keep out rats. Several months later, a church group from Lansing, Michigan, learned about this effort from a newspaper clipping and sent a delegation of members to aid in the effort of "painting garages, porches, fences and garbage cans, filling rat holes and planting grass." Such sporadic efforts could not maintain absolute cleanliness in the alleys, but they had the capacity to temporarily reduce nuisances.[23]

Block clubs made special efforts to rid their streets and alleys of rats, which often lurked in excess garbage. Rats were notorious villains in urban areas across the United States. They swarmed through piles of unkempt refuse, and sometimes grew bold enough to bite sleeping children. In Washington, DC, in 1969, the innovative Anacostia Neighborhood Museum put on an exhibit called "The Rat: Man's Invited Affliction." According to Benjamin Looker, exhibit "visitors were confronted with graphic displays on the community's rodent problem, children's skits depicting daily existence in rat-infested housing projects, and, as capstone, a display case filled with live rats, which scurried about in a simulated backyard strewn with garbage and debris." Chicagoans likewise understood that rats brought a whole host of ills associated with filth and disease. Block clubs simply wanted to be rid of them.[24]

Although garbage cleanup efforts helped control vermin as a side effect, block clubs also singled rats out for focused attention. Any given resident's attempt to clean up his or her own mess was fruitless unless neighbors coordinated their sanitation efforts and municipal staff killed the rodents. Many block clubs associated with the Northwest Community Organization in the 1970s and 1980s appealed to the city and their neighbors to remedy rat infestations in the West Town area. Rats so plagued the neighborhood that they served as a problem around which to organize. The NCO called an initial meeting for the 1500 block of West Erie, charging, "The rats are out of control and the city is not doing anything about it. Let's get together and do something to better our block." One block club pushed a landlord to follow through on promised rat-control steps; when its efforts failed, it appealed to its alderman to add pressure. Members of the Ohio-Ashland Block Club asked their ward supervisor to provide more garbage cans for their alley, and volunteered to create a bilingual flyer reminding residents to keep garbage in the cans and lids on the cans. Citing a "superabundance of rats in our neighborhood," the Albany Avenue Block Club asked the Department of Streets and Sanitation to provide a speaker on the "subject of rat control." When the city created the Department of Rodent Control in 1978, the Shakespeare-Dickens-McLean and Mozart-Francisco block clubs held a joint public meeting with the department's "big cheese" as a guest. Block clubs counted any cooperation from the city as a "victory." The residents of 1800 North Mozart Street and Francisco Avenue celebrated the news that "our area will be baited for rats." They also won promises that their sewer would be cleaned and a bulk trash pickup provided.[25]

Cleanup efforts could backfire if club members did their part but some other link in the chain broke down. Roberta Wilson organized the 4200 Wilcox Block Club to pick up garbage and place it in the alley. She was disappointed by her alderman's failure to send out sanitation crews. Without removal, the neatly organized litter remained an eyesore. Wilson fretted, "This is the easiest way to lose the cooperation of the block members" who invested considerable personal effort without seeing a meaningful change. The Wells-Princeton Neighborhood Improvement Club decided to petition the precinct captain and the alderman for improved garbage collection in their area. They expressed their frustration to the Chicago Urban League staff organizer. They had tried "to contact the alderman for a hearing in connection with getting adequate garbage collection and cleaner streets," but were "unable to get an audience with him." Under a cheery headline, "Clean-Up Week a Good Start," the 15th Place Block Club commented in its newsletter on how hard it was to keep garbage contained. The article noted that just "one week after Clean-Up you can walk through the alleys and still see many overflowing cans without covers." Sometimes crews responsible for collecting garbage made it worse. The newsletter continued, "One private scavenger even strewed part of the garbage he was supposed to pick up in the alley and when a block club member asked him to pick it up, he refused. The owner of the building was called and promised to speak to his scavenger. This owner said he did need more cans and asked where they could be got." Loose garbage could not be contained to one problematic property; wind and cars easily spread it to neighboring lots. Because cooperation was essential to resolving local garbage issues, block clubs also participated in programs promoted by citywide organizations and institutions.[26]

In the middle of the twentieth century, Chicago mayors spearheaded a series of citywide cleanup campaigns. Chicago's programs drew on a longer national tradition of public programming against garbage. Martin Melosi relates the broad history of drives to promote cleanliness in American cities. Especially in the first two decades of the twentieth century, institutions across the United States sponsored "civic education" campaigns to raise awareness of and support for sanitary methods of domestic waste disposal. The goals were twofold: to improve individuals' garbage disposal habits, and to put pressure on public officials to improve city services. Reformers made children special targets of these campaigns. According to Melosi, children "inspected streets and alleys, reported litterers, held meetings, and, of course, conducted parades." In addition to whatever efforts they made themselves, the children could educate their parents. The fervor for generating individual responsibility for sanitation efforts was such that "cleanup campaigns reached the proportions of a movement in the 1910s, spreading so rapidly that almost every city and town conducted at least one spring campaign."[27] While the public focus in other cities shifted toward improving municipal service after World War II, in postwar Chicago citywide cleanup campaigns flourished, with block clubs enlisted as key participants.

In keeping with the progressive tradition, in the early 1950s the Midwest Community Council sponsored an annual cleanup parade on the West Side, and recruited hundreds of children to participate. Before the parade, school principals involved students in a poster competition. In 1952 the parade route ran along Jackson Boulevard and featured "a larger refuse collection truck and street sweeping machine" contributed by the city's Bureau of Sanitation. Other public events included a talk by Chicago's fire chief about how rubbish could lead to fires. According to a newspaper report, "Highlighting the program were short Clean-Up sketches by students from Beidler, Emerson, and other local grade schools, pointing out the necessity for clean homes and streets in dramatic skits." The Midwest Community Council's parade was one link in a chain of mid-century municipal events encouraging residents to contribute to local sanitary improvement.[28]

Mayor Martin Kennelly (1947–55) treated a cleanup campaign as a "pet project." Kennelly promoted a "Campaign for a Cleaner Chicago" that combined public education and threats. The United States Steel Supply Company's John C. Cushing served as chairman of the Mayor's Committee for a Cleaner Chicago, which organized the campaign. Kennelly dramatized the importance of a clean city by personally scrubbing State Street. The Mayor's Committee's immediate focus was on residents' role in garbage disposal. The goal was to inspire compliance with a recently passed but unenforced city regulation requiring the use of "standard" garbage cans between twenty and thirty-two gallons in size, covered with tight-fitting lids. On one block, to illustrate the importance of the lids, actors dressed as housewives and a rat pantomimed the difficulty rodents had in opening properly covered garbage cans. According to 1949 estimates, only about one-seventh of the city's households had standard garbage cans, and nearly a quarter lacked any refuse containers at all. Because the 1949 campaign resulted in the identification of only a few thousand additional approved containers, Kennelly hinted that the city might begin arresting garbage can scofflaws.[29]

Although garbage was at the core of Kennelly's Campaign for a Cleaner Chicago, the organizing committee folded in a range of related municipal sanitation concerns. In 1949 the campaign shifted its focus monthly, variously highlighting garbage, litter, flies, weeds, fire, snow removal, and street cleaning. In July and August, for example, the campaign focused on reducing ragweed, whose pollen was the scourge of Chicago's allergy sufferers. Organizers especially emphasized clearing ragweed plants from vacant lots, which the committee recommended replanting with attractive shrubs and trees. Over the remainder of Kennelly's term, the Mayor's Committee for a Cleaner Chicago engaged in modest experiments to broaden its reach. In 1950 several cooperating West Side businessmen's associations sponsored a "Miss West Side Cleanup Queen" beauty contest. A 1953 contest invited Chicagoans to write letters explaining why they deserved to have two hundred house painters converge on their home to repaint it in just half an hour. Several programs encouraged civic organizations and commercial groups to purchase rubbish bins for their neighborhoods. Chicago Urban League organizer Alva B. Maxey explained how several block clubs worked in conjunction with the Mayor's Committee for a Cleaner Chicago, the Bureau of Streets and Sanitation, and the CPD in a model street-cleaning program. To illustrate how block clubs could aid official cleanup efforts, the clubs explained street cleaning machinery to their neighbors, posted and later removed "no parking" signs, and assisted in the removal of cars from the streets while the cleaning was in process.[30]

Kennelly's campaign faltered in his last years as mayor. After succeeding Kennelly in 1955, Richard J. Daley reinvigorated the idea under the joint auspices of the Citizen's Committee for a Cleaner Chicago, the Chicago Board of Education, and the Chicago Association of Commerce and Industry. Like Kennelly's campaign, Daley's employed events such as parades to publicize the message of resident responsibility for cleanliness. In contrast to that of his predecessor, Daley's campaign encompassed a wider array of activities within its scope, including beautification and safety. In 1958, for example, the campaign featured a "good garden month" competition. In 1961 the Citizens Committee for a Cleaner Chicago turned to automobiles, distributing litter bags for cars and encouraging safe driving.[31]

Daley's Citizens Committee was as much about boosting Chicago's national reputation as it was about cleaning the city. At the 1956 kickoff meeting, the commissioner of streets emphasized that "for the first time in his 15 years with the city bureau, he felt that he was able to prepare a budget that would give the city adequate trash and garbage service."[32] Daley sought to leverage garbage collection into good publicity for the city. The National Clean Up–Paint Up–Fix Up Bureau, a public relations group funded by the National Paint, Varnish, and Lacquer Association, organized an annual national competition recognizing America's cleanest big city. The association's corporate goal was to persuade Americans to buy more paint, so its competition encouraged them to spruce up the exteriors of their homes as well as collect garbage.[33] In Kennelly's last year in office, Chicago had been recognized as the competition's third-place finisher. For most of the 1960s, however, Chicago won first place in the national contest celebrating America's cleanest big city, losing once (to Detroit) in 1964.[34]

Melosi points out that not everyone received cleanup campaigns well. A short campaign was insufficient to make up for deficiencies in municipal efforts to create a sanitary environment. Even at their best, these interactive information campaigns were "cosmetic activities, short-term substitutes for effectively enforced ordinances and efficiently conducted collection and disposal practices."[35] Further, as Benjamin Looker notes, some black activists regarded cleanup campaigns as a tactic oriented against the wrong problem. Instead of doing cleanups themselves, African Americans should have been organizing protests to compel the city government to live up to its acknowledged responsibility for creating a sanitary urban environment. Looker points out that the famed *Brown v. Board* psychologist Kenneth Clark chastised the leader of a cleanup campaign in a black New York City neighborhood for failing to protest the city government's neglect:

> She did not understand that it is not the job of the people to sweep the streets; it is the job of the Department of Sanitation. It had not occurred to her to advise these women to organize to gain these services to which they were entitled. In a middle-class neighborhood, the people see to it that government does provide services. To lecture the miserable inhabitants of the ghetto to sweep their own streets is to urge them to accept the fact that the government is not expected to serve them.[36]

The civil rights activist Bayard Rustin similarly argued that such campaigns confirmed "one more of the white man's stereotypes about the Negro," referring to beliefs that blacks created unsanitary living conditions and therefore should be left to remedy them on their own.[37]

Such critiques reasonably pointed to real shortcomings in urban sanitation programs and cleanup campaigns. But sponsors rarely regarded midtwentieth-century Chicago cleanup campaigns as ends in themselves. As a paint industry trade group's sponsorship of the national competition to determine America's cleanest city suggests, they carried either overt or covert purposes beyond sanitary improvement. An American Friends Service Committee observer reflected on the reluctance of residents to participate in a local campaign on the West Side. Neighbors resisted the club's "efforts at community clean-up" because they perceived it as "primarily benefitt[ing] landlords" through increases to property values.[38] By making residential areas seem more attractive on the surface, such campaigns echoed the Chicago Real Estate Board Better Neighborhoods Crusade's underlying purpose of selling real estate. Finally, as the Miller-Carpenter Block Club's effort suggests, many cleanup campaigns were connected to larger efforts to remedy other neighborhood problems.

Despite these reasons for opting out or choosing other forms of activism, block club members nonetheless willingly cleaned up their blocks. Sometimes the presence of an active block club was itself the signal needed to persuade responsible parties to complete their tasks. Lewis James, of the 6300 block of South Ingleside Avenue, recalled how officials took the very existence of their block club as a sign that residents deserved basic services:

> The neighbors felt that soon after Negroes moved into the area, they stopped getting adequate garbage collection and other city services. One of the first things the block did was to check these things with the alderman and the Ward Superintendent's Office. They wrote letters as a group, and they decided one day that if the garbage was not picked up on a stated day, each individual on the block would call the Ward Superintendent's Office and plague them. This brought results. They stated that later the garbage collectors themselves stated that where blocks are organized, they are much more careful to keep to schedule. They even sweep the alleys. Where there is no block organization, they don't feel that they have to do anything.[39]

Such efforts reflected block clubs' pragmatic accommodation to Chicago's unbalanced distribution of power and perks. If residents wanted a clean block, they had to make it happen by initiating the change themselves. At the same time, they clamored for the services that city officials reserved for those who asked often enough.

Code Compliance and Abandoned Buildings

One of the most perplexing problems that block clubs faced was that of how to respond to neighbors' properties that did not meet their standards. While block clubs could turn out members with great enthusiasm and energy for sprucing up their own residences and cleaning up refuse spilled in public places, private property was another matter. Private property rights gave owners full authority over their own buildings and lots as long as they complied with city regulations. This system protected property owners from interference by strangers and neighbors alike, who theoretically could not even enter the grounds without permission. Block club members certainly noticed when a property's use seemed to violate the city's zoning or occupancy codes, or when a building was abandoned without being properly boarded up. But they were not permitted to alter someone else's holdings. Even block clubs that would have been willing and financially able to fix their neighbors' properties could not do so without consent from the owners.

Despite the legal notion that property was private, the effects of problem properties were public. Block clubs did not sit by helplessly when problem buildings diminished their day-to-day experiences and their confidence in their own property values. Instead, they asserted their interest in safe and attractive environs by bringing violations to the attention of appropriate authorities. Especially in the 1950s and 1960s, block clubs run by property owners researched whether troublesome homes and businesses conformed to city zoning codes. They hoped that public officials could compel noncomplying owners to change how their buildings were used. In the 1970s and 1980s, tenant-run block groups used the court system to address buildings that were neglected and abandoned by their owners.

In the mid-twentieth century, Chicago property owners were especially concerned by how "conversions" allowed crowding of residential buildings. In periods of population boom, Chicago neighborhoods attracted more families and unattached adults than the housing supply was built to hold. As European immigrants flooded Chicago in the late nineteenth and early twentieth centuries, families took in boarders and lodgers, sharing their living quarters with relative strangers in exchange for money.[40] In the twentiethh century, however, American expectations for privacy changed. The introduction of occupancy regulations defined crowded homes as illegal, and lodging became less common. But Chicago's growing population needed places to sleep and cook. Conversions let building owners house more residents than intended for a structure, while still offering individual living quarters.

When a residential unit was "converted," an apartment designed for one family was cut up into multiple separate units. Erecting extra walls between rooms, cutting new doors into public hallways, and providing additional cooking facilities split one living unit into two or more. Several different groups of people could occupy an apartment without having to share private space. Reversing the process through "deconversion" restored a residential unit to its original structure. During World War II, the Chicago City Council encouraged apartment owners to convert their buildings to create housing for the tens of thousands of war workers migrating to the city. After the war ended and migrants continued to crowd into Chicago, the poor living conditions in conversions became increasingly suspect, but remained lucrative. Some property owners who wanted to convert their apartments legally applied for permits for the work. Others converted their units on the sly, hoping to escape the attention of overburdened housing court authorities who could forbid this profitable approach to providing shelter.[41]

The city had far too few housing inspectors to catch all the illegal conversions carried out in the postwar years. But neighbors recognized when construction equipment and debris suggested a subdivision in progress. Conversions often presaged neighborhood racial change. Building owners understood that the combination of racial segregation and the resumption of the Great Migration meant that they could charge blacks premium rents, even for inadequate housing. To white Chicagoans, conversions represented a double whammy of undesirable crowding and the anathema of integration. A resident of a West Side block full of two-flat apartment buildings lamented one that had been converted into twelve separate units. She complained, "The kind of problems presented by that building range from children playing on top of my garage, pulling up my lawn purposely, throwing litter into my property area, loud alcohol drinking parties, to children playing ball in the front streets until after midnight." Black property owners lacked the racial animus that routinely informed white opposition to conversions, but many of them also resented the crowding brought on by the increased capacity of apartment buildings.[42]

Blocking or reversing conversions usually required the involvement of public officials. On the 7200 block of Rhodes Avenue, for example, block club members debated what to do about a conversion underway nearby. One member had already reported "her suspicion" to General Richard Smykal, who served as Chicago's acting building commissioner and was the city's first commissioner of conservation. Her fellow club members were skeptical that a sole report would be sufficient, so another club member agreed to call the property owner to speak with him directly. In addition, the club decided "that a statement of the organization's objections to the conversions be included in the forthcoming news-letter." Such gentle probing was indeed unlikely to get results. By contrast, the 3800–3900 Monroe Block Club's persistent action did push the owner of a neighboring building to request a permit for deconversion. Block clubs were only one of the many kinds of neighborhood organizations that kept an eye out for conversions in the 1950s and 1960s.[43]

Larger organizations that cultivated block clubs sometimes employed staff to systematically track property owners who converted their buildings. The GLCC employed a "housing and zoning officer" to personally inspect properties, report violators to city housing inspectors, and track the disposition of their cases.[44] In conjunction with expert staff, the HPKCC engaged block clubs directly in this work, deploying their members in two ways to help prosecute property owners suspected of violating the housing code. First, it encouraged block clubs to be attentive to potential code violations among their neighbors. Peggy Wireman, the HPKCC's block program director, suggested tactics for one block club leader to deal with houses that lacked back porch lights:

> Perhaps you could send around a block newsletter explaining that block groups have been asked to work on code enforcement and will be giving out information about the code monthly so that owners will know what is required of them, and tenants will know what they are entitled to. You might then say that the code requires such and such about back porch lighting and that you notice some of the buildings are in violation. You might also explain the safety reasons behind the regulations. You can tell them that eventually the city will do an evaluative survey of all buildings in Hyde Park–Kenwood to make sure they meet code requirements. You can suggest they call the Conference, or yourself, if they have any further questions.[45]

Resources at the HPKCC's main office included experienced staff members familiar with the city's building regulations, inspectors, and court procedures. A published list of common housing code violations aided residents in identifying specific problems.[46]

In a second practice that other Chicago community groups later adopted, HPKCC block club members consistently showed up at court hearings. Their presence reminded the building owners and judges about their concerns. They did not participate in the hearings; they simply sat in the audience as mute witnesses to the effects of nonconforming buildings and their desire for judicial remedy. HPKCC staff members expected a clear division of labor among themselves, block club members, and public officials. Staff members reported specific complaints from block clubs to police and inspectors with whom they built working relationships. Grace Tugwell, in her capacity as director of the HPKCC's building and zoning program, insisted that "the function of the block group is to supply the evidence and not try to prosecute the cases." As community members, they should provide information to inspectors and a presence at hearings—but they were not to intercede directly. Under the header "Patience and Durability," a HPKCC guide for block clubs explained, "The danger for the block group lies in neglecting to constantly, and persistently, follow up on the action taken on each building regardless of how many months it will take." Keeping a case in court could lead to victories even on nonlegal grounds. With some glee, HPKCC executive director Julia Abrahamson related the story of a building owner who simply abandoned her own defense. She feared riding elevators, and could no longer tolerate walking up eleven flights of stairs to the courtroom where she was frequently summoned.[47]

Vigilance was not always enough. In many cases, block clubs objected to having commercial enterprises as neighbors. Residential streets usually did not attract the broad range of strangers who frequented commercial districts, so they were easier to maintain and control. Block clubs sometimes were surprised to discover that their streets were not zoned exclusively for residential occupancy. In the spring of 1954, for instance, members of the 7500 Eberhart Block Club worried about a pool room opening up around the corner. Hoping to forestall its anticipated unsavory customers, members of the block club were disappointed to learn that they could not challenge it as a zoning violation. A visiting Chicago Urban League staff member reported that no legal action was possible. As an alternative, "the group discussed the possibility of trying to interest more realiable [sic] types of businesses to move into vacant property when it is available in the neighborhood." Members of the Miller-Carpenter Street Block Club were similarly frustrated the same year by a new automobile repair shop. The minutes of the meeting in which they discussed the topic reported frustration, for there "was nothing we could do about it because this area is a Commercial zone." Without a legal foundation for action, block clubs could not challenge what their neighbors did with their properties.[48]

Block clubs affiliated with the NCO and The Organization of Palmer Square (TOPS) regarded abandoned buildings as a central threat. In the 1970s and 1980s, residents in renter neighborhoods feared concrete dangers from abandoned properties. A shaming letter sent to the suburban neighbors of the owner of an unoccupied and neglected building outlined the threats it presented:

> In Chicago, on the 1700 block of Mozart Street, near Humboldt Park, there is an abandoned house which is causing us lots of problems:
> —The house is abandoned and wide open
> —Two girls, age 12 and 14, were pulled inside and raped
> —Gangs use this house as their hang-out
> This house is in a high arson area—and if it burns, the two adjacent homes will burn as well.
> This house is a blight to our neighborhood, just as it would be a blight to Glenview.[49]

Both assault and fire endangered people who lived near abandoned buildings. A widely read series of 1971 *Chicago Daily News* articles documented how absentee landlords in the Woodlawn neighborhood "milked" as much money as they could out of decaying buildings. Unscrupulous owners allowed buildings to deteriorate without making repairs. They took their final profit from insurance money when they hired arsonists to burn down their properties. As neighborhood residents recognized the milking process at work, they considered block clubs to be a possible firebreak. Such clubs were not structurally positioned to solve and punish crimes once they had been committed, but they could ameliorate the conditions that fostered crime. Block clubs in the West Town area invited neighbors to do something about unoccupied buildings that landlords had stopped maintaining. For example, a flyer calling residents to a meeting of the 1200 & 1300 North Bosworth Block Club exhorted neighbors: "To prevent more abandoned buildings and more fires, we have to stand together!"[50]

TOPS and NCO block clubs tried a variety of public and private means to address the threats presented by abandoned buildings. Each club preferred different tactics; no standard set of approaches described how they tackled their shared concern about the dangers of abandoned buildings. The NCO's origins in Saul Alinsky's IAF meant that confrontational tactics were part of its arsenal, but its staff did not force block clubs to act against their members' inclinations. For instance, participants in the initial meeting of the Charleston-Leavitt Block Club discussed an abandoned building with a "shack in the backyard." Someone, possibly the meeting's organizer, suggested going "to Alderman Gabinski's office to make a demand that he take action on the building." If that approach failed, they could circulate a petition "which would demonstrate that many neighbors are concerned, not just a select few." Meeting participants, however, "felt that they wanted to start in a cooperative manner with the building owners," so they placed a phone call inviting them for a meeting.[51] Similarly, a flyer for the 1200–1300 North Bosworth Block Club raised concerns about two buildings on the block that appeared that they were "about to become abandoned." The flyer explained that they had "a phone number but no address" for the owner, and listed some options for next steps:

> What action shall we take to find out how to contact Raul Diaz?
> —Once we know how to contact him, what action will we take to make sure these buildings don't go abandoned or burn?
> —invite him to a meeting here soon?[52]

Block clubs that made polite overtures to building owners did not usually insist on full rehabilitation of problem buildings. Angrily requiring a prohibitively expensive response could have shut down a tenuous relationship. Instead, clubs requested manageable changes to remedy immediate threats. For example, the 1200 North Cleaver Block Club wrote to one building owner expressing concern that her property was not secured. Although it had no tenants and may have been boarded up following vandalism, footprints in the snow suggested that someone was going in and out. Reboarding the doors could ease the fears of passersby. Similarly, the "neighborhood leader" of the 2600 West Attrill Block Club wrote to the owner of a building at 2617 West Attrill Street asking her plans for the property and inviting her to a block club meeting. The building was already in court proceedings leading to its demolition, which meant that rehabilitation was an unlikely solution. The inquiry letter continued: "As you well know it has already burned twice and we fear it will burn again unless action is taken immediately. The unclean and destroyed condition of your property needs to be corrected as soon as possible." In contrast to the futility of preventing conversions, politely framed overtures about neglected buildings could prompt small-scale change. Representatives of the Julian, LeMoyne, and Paulina Block Club met with the owner of a building at 1445 North Paulina Street, and later reported to their fellow club members that "our visit to the owner got results. He cleaned away the burned garbage and boarded up the building. Now we need to make him sell, fix up, or demolish the building before it gets vandalized again." Another NCO block club, the Dickens-Winchester Block Club, reported two once-vacant buildings that were rehabilitated rather than abandoned.[53]

Reaching a building's owner did not guarantee a response. The Charleston-Leavitt-Dickens Block Club, concerned about the building at 2213 West Charleston Street, invited its owners to attend their meeting. When the owners did not show up, a club member called them and spoke with them on the telephone. The owners answered that they were aware of the invitation as well as the dangers their building presented. They did not attend because "they are presently involved in a lawsuit and their lawyer has advised them not to talk about their property." The block club members planned to follow up by attending the building's court date; they hoped their alderman would join them.[54]

Block clubs were small organizations with few resources. They could not do all the work needed to mitigate the dangers of abandoned buildings. They lacked the supplies, equipment, and skills to board up and rehabilitate buildings, as well as the necessary legal authority. But they could lobby public authorities to take appropriate steps. The 1200–1330 North Bosworth Block Club learned from the publication *Police Community News* that the Chicago Police Department offered help for problem buildings. In 1979 the CPD's services included "district officers and tactical units who stop their vehicles to try the doors and check interiors of abandoned buildings on their beats." The CPD also had an "arson detail of 60 Special Operations Group officers" assigned to patrol abandoned buildings at risk of fire. The agenda for the block club's special meeting on "crime and police protection" asked members to discuss whether "we want patrols to regularly inspect the abandoned buildings on our block, including checking the inside and from the alley."[55] For its part, the Dickens-Winchester Block Club gave an officer from the 14th District Tactical Unit a very specific list of requests. They wanted to "increase the public safety of our blocks in order to cut down on the rash of burglaries, loitering/trespassing, public drinking, and illegal entrance into abandoned buildings on our block." They typed a memo requesting that the police department

1. Please instruct Day-time beat officers to clear loiterers off the doorsteps at the following addresses:

    _____

    _____

    _____

2. Break up crowds of people who are drinking and littering our neighborhood with cans and bottles, especially at the corner of Dickens and Winchester.

3. Put a 'Special Attention' on the abandoned building on the NW corner of Dickens and Winchester.

4. Instruct tactical officers and beat officers about the two youths who are responsible for 2 break-ins on our block that live at 2119 N. Damen.

5. Help our block obtain 'NO LOITERING' and 'NO LITTERING' Signs.

After meeting with both the tactical officer and his commander, the block club found that "our police response has actually gotten worse," and so requested a meeting with the chief of the patrol division.[56] When the CPD initiated a community policing model in the 1990s, beat officers' responsibilities included routing complaints about dangerous buildings to appropriate city departments.

When owners did not cooperate in the rehabilitation of their buildings, block clubs pushed the court system to see to their demolition. The city's housing court's docket was notoriously slow, overcrowded, and corrupt. But the block groups sent their members as court watchers to influence the speed of demolition and encourage the mandated rehabilitation of problem properties. The example of Hyde Park block clubs working in concert with the staff of the HPKCC suggested that court watching was an effective tactic. The 1200–1300 North Greenview Block Club sent five representatives to housing court to track the progress of several cases of abandoned buildings. They reported back to their neighbors that the judge had ordered one building torn down, and for the owner to "to start cleaning . . . and fixing" the other. When members of the 2100 North Point Street Block Club finally succeeded in getting a dangerous building torn down, they counted it as a triumph. The club celebrated with a block party on the newly vacant lot.[57]

Attending housing court sounds like an exercise in tedium, but block club court watchers may have succeeded in pressuring judges to act. Studying Chicago public officials in this period, political scientist Bryan Jones found that "both the chief judge of housing court and the corporation counsel in charge of prosecuting housing cases noted in interviews that the entire process moved more speedily where neighborhood groups and ward organizations intervened in the proceedings." The chief prosecutor admitted to Jones, "If someone is on my back, I'll act to get them off. That sets priorities—the most dangerous cases and those that someone is persistent about complaining about—those are the ones I'll give special attention to." Jones acknowledged that his statistical analysis contradicted the anecdotal evidence offered by his informants. Overall, he found, "community organizations do not generally make a difference in housing-court outcomes in Chicago." But occasional success stories gave block club members reason to believe it was worth their while to make a visible showing at hearings they cared about.[58]

As an alternative to demolition, Chicago's housing court occasionally stripped an owner's title to a property and bestowed it on a third party prepared to invest in its rehabilitation. In the 1970s, block clubs in the NCO's West Town area turned to a nonprofit membership organization, the Bickerdike Redevelopment Corporation, to rehabilitate salvageable properties. The NCO had a formal agreement with the federal Department of Housing and Urban Redevelopment to organize the rehabilitation of local deteriorating properties, and they often channeled this business through Bickerdike. According to the organization's twenty-first-century website, "Bickerdike was founded in 1967 by residents of Chicago's near northwest side and representatives of local community groups who joined forces to fight widespread housing deterioration, abandonment, and arson. . . . Bickerdike was charged in its mission to redevelop West Town, Humboldt Park, Logan Square and Hermosa communities for the benefit of and control by the lower and moderate-income residents of those areas." Bickerdike staff worked with block clubs to determine whether problem buildings were plausible candidates for rehabilitation. For example, in 1976 the chair of the 1700 North Washtenaw Block Club wrote to Bickerdike in anticipation of a meeting because they were "organizing around several abandoned HUD properties on our block." They requested that Bickerdike "write proposed specs for these buildings" and "deliver [them] to the NCO office in care of our staff person."[59]

That NCO-affiliated block clubs systematically relied on the services of the specialized Bickerdike Corporation suggests how difficult it was for small, local, volunteer-driven organizations to influence their built environment on their own. Block clubs could and did use sweat equity to cleanse their territory of garbage, and such efforts successfully attracted the aid of municipal authorities. Their lobbying also pressured the court system to address particularly dangerous buildings. But the block clubs' independent capacities ended there; they could not generate large-scale physical change. They were, however, used as tools in the efforts of larger local organizations to create such transformations through urban renewal and conservation programs. Local activism for improvement demonstrated to municipal authorities that certain areas were good candidates for further attention. Cleanup campaigns such as those of the Miller-Carpenter Street Block Club and the HPKCC's pushes for code compliance showed city officials that their areas were salvageable enough to receive conservation and urban renewal aid. These mid-century urban redevelopment tools were too coarse to apply to one block at a time.

Urban Renewal

The intense effort required to get even one deteriorating building remediated or torn down suggests that such problems were more than residents of a single block could fix. In postwar Chicago, building decay was a matter of deep concern.[60] Chicagoans who worried about the effects of "blight" at midcentury often created neighborhood-level associations to address the issue.

Such organizations worked to attract state and federal urban renewal funding that could be used to clear out sections of deteriorated properties and replace them with new construction. To show that they had community support, larger organizations enlisted block clubs to make their case for renewal. But involving block clubs carried an intrinsic risk. While many Chicagoans agreed that nearby places within their neighborhoods needed redevelopment, no one supported their own displacement.[61]

Urbanists concerned about city decay after World War II worried about "blight." The term, borrowed from agriculture, referred to the physical deterioration of buildings. Left untreated, blight was contagious. Even if property owners maintained their own buildings, neighboring properties with untreated flaws threatened them. Just as loose garbage spread through an alley, building decay could spread to adjacent properties. The assessment of properties for municipal taxation and sale confirmed their fears.[62] Assessors determined a property's worth not only on the basis of its intrinsic merits but also taking into consideration the sale prices of similar properties nearby. A blighted building suppressed its neighbors' property values.

Americans developed new legal mechanisms to cope with such perceived threats in the mid-twentieth century. Conservation provided tools for preserving patches that were not beyond rehabilitation. Urban renewal allowed the clearing and rebuilding of swaths of the landscape that could be repaired only at an expense greater than their estimated sale value. With encouragement from the federal government, Illinois created laws that enabled cities to award quasipublic, local "conservation commissions" the power to enact both forms of redevelopment within their boundaries. The legal and social forms required for implementing urban renewal were pioneered in Chicago's Hyde Park neighborhood.[63]

A perhaps surprising number of Chicago communities sought recognition of their eligibility for urban renewal funding. Because of the drastic ways in which it played out, urban renewal earned its bad reputation. Historians have emphasized urban renewal's disruptions. Neighborhoods with populations of different class levels and varying housing quality were particularly vulnerable. Residents who had been hanging onto homes in poor neighborhoods with inferior, crowded housing stocks were cleared out; many relocated to public housing developments that perpetuated racial segregation. African Americans often bitterly called the process "Negro removal." Although this sobriquet reflected the frequency with which the process destroyed black communities, they were not its only victims. In Lincoln Park, the historian Lilia Fernández shows, urban renewal carefully excised the Latino population. Because it destroyed buildings and moved poor people, urban renewal addressed two perceived problems simultaneously. After being launched in Hyde Park and the Near South Side, full-scale urban renewal occurred in a ring around the Loop, on the Near North Side, on the Near West Side, and in Lincoln Park. Organized stakeholders in a variety of other communities, including Uptown and North Lawndale, bid for urban renewal with less success.[64]

Establishing a conservation commission was a key step in the quest for urban renewal. Large local institutions, such as universities and business interests, typically funded conservation commissions. To bolster their bids, the conservation commissions had to show city authorities that they had community support. To demonstrate that the supporters of urban renewal included ordinary neighborhood residents and not just monied interests, the commissions turned to block clubs. But because block clubs were technically independent organizations, they did not always do what their sponsors wanted. Some surely existed merely as paper organizations that conveniently could be listed in appeals to the city for funding, but which did little.[65]

In Hyde Park, the Southeast Chicago Commission (SECC) and the HPKCC jointly conducted the effort to secure urban renewal. Hyde Park, founded as a genteel commuter suburb in 1853, was aging, and by World War II was facing racial transition. The University of Chicago anchored both prongs of the renewal effort. The SECC provided formal guidance for Hyde Park's urban renewal program, while the HPKCC interpreted its importance to local residents. Although HPKCC director Julia Abrahamson thought the separation of these functions unnecessary, the historian Arnold Hirsch's landmark book about urban renewal in Chicago points out that the divide allowed Hyde Park residents to enjoy the "luxury of their liberalism," accepting integration by race but not by class. Although the HPKCC itself was a cheerleader for area urban renewal, a few of its block clubs protested the plans, some fervently.[66]

The HPKCC kept block clubs informed about the developing plans for urban renewal, and encouraged participants to weigh in. It sponsored meetings where residents could ask questions and share feedback about the plans. Its leaders assumed that most block clubs supported cleansing Hyde Park of the neighborhood's deteriorating pockets, whose residents were disproportionately poor, migrant, and African American. In a memo urging block leaders to testify at a City Council hearing, for example, the HPKCC's Block Steering Committee cautioned, "If you have been lulled into thinking that approval will be a shoo-in, requiring no further effort on our part, you are dead wrong. The opposition forces will be well organized and very vocal before the City Council."[67]

Most Hyde Park block clubs rewarded the HPKCC's assumption that they supported urban renewal, but a few expressed locally informed opposition to the plans. Participants from the 4800–4900 Dorchester block, for example,

observed that not all the buildings designated for demolition on their strip
were in bad shape. They recommended "spot demolition" and "rehabilitation"
instead of the proposed "clearance." The 5000 South Blackstone Block Group
unanimously passed a resolution "vigorously opposed to any plan of redevelopment which would include a wholesale leveling of the area between
50th Street and Hyde Park Boulevard and Dorchester and Harper." It argued
that "destruction of buildings should be limited to those buildings which
have been allowed to deteriorate substantially." Such opposition ultimately
made little difference to the overall program for urban renewal in Hyde Park,
which proceeded largely along the lines envisioned by its sponsors. Members
of the 5300–5400 Kimbark Block Club forlornly advertised a block meeting
for residents looking for advice on how to find new homes, as their entire
strip was condemned.[68]

The HPKCC's approach to urban renewal inoculated it against having to
confront such opposition directly. It never asked its block clubs to vote on
urban renewal or directly advise it of their position; the clubs were instead
asked to testify to officials. Mark Santow points out that the HPKCC was
structured as an organization of individual members rather than of groups.
Block clubs had no official influence on its positions. This approach successfully defused opposition to urban renewal from within the HPKCC's ranks,
allowing it to represent itself as conveying the position of a united community.
As Arnold Hirsch explains, urban renewal was implemented in Hyde Park in
accord with the University's vision.[69]

Proponents of urban renewal for North Lawndale modeled their effort on
Hyde Park's example. The impetus for urban renewal in North Lawndale came
from the retail giant Sears, Roebuck, and Company, whose corporate headquarters building occupied four blocks in the neighborhood. Backed by Sears
and other local companies, the Greater Lawndale Conservation Commission
began seeking urban renewal in 1953.[70] Beginning in 1955, it tried to cultivate block clubs to support its goals. At an early public meeting, the GLCC
explained that block clubs could be simultaneously parallel to and part of its
operations, as they were in Hyde Park:

> Question: Of what value are block clubs and such organizations as the Greater
> Lawndale Conservation Commission in preventing slums?
>
> Answer: Both types of organizations are the city's first line of defense in pre-
> venting the deterioration of an area. Block clubs operating in a limited area are
> the "eyes and ears" of the Conservation Commission. The two groups working
> together can effectively prevent blight in the community and make it a better
> place in which to live.[71]

In contrast to the situation in Hyde Park, however, the conservation commission and block clubs did not cooperate successfully in North Lawndale.

The GLCC lacked the kind of local ties that the HPKCC nurtured so assiduously. While the GLCC represented corporate interests and initially hired a largely white staff, the population of North Lawndale in the 1950s increasingly consisted of African Americans recently migrated from the South. Rather than simply hire a staff member to cultivate relationships with black Lawndale residents, the GLCC attempted to tap into a nascent network of area block clubs. Unfortunately for the GLCC's aspirations, the person at the head of that network was Gloria Pughsley, who was building a network of block clubs in North Lawndale. Pughsley proved to be frustratingly independent. The GLCC made her a vice president on its board, and spent two years attempting to bend her network to its purposes before giving up and hiring a staff organizer.[72]

Multiple accounts suggested that Pughsley was a difficult person to get along with. She was familiar with the Chicago Urban League's block club program and modeled the Greater Lawndale Association of Block Clubs & Organizations on the League's district federation model. But she angrily disparaged Rachel Ridley, who had organized West Side block clubs for the League in the 1950s, as an "Uncle Tom."[73] GLCC staff member Ethel Vrana, who also served as the initial secretary for the Greater Lawndale Association of Block Clubs & Organizations, told a representative of the Welfare Council of Metropolitan Chicago that she

> had gone along with Mrs. Pughsley for some time until she found that it was impossible to deal with her as Mrs. Pughsley tended to be opinionated and strong-willed and suspicious of white people despite what they tried to do. Also, everyone had worked with Mrs. Pughsley along very careful lines attempting to placate her, compliment her, and using every device possible to gain her cooperation.[74]

Pughsley repeatedly clashed with other members of the GLCC board at meetings. To their dismay, she even questioned whether the organization should seek designation as a conservation area—their basic purpose. The exasperation other GLCC board members felt with her was mutual, as Pughsley was "very hostile in her remarks toward Mr. Jerome Braverman who she said had once told her that he knew more about her people than she did. She described him as an avaricious grasping absentee businessman who victimized her people." A staff member of the Welfare Council of Metropolitan Chicago, assigned to look into the problem between Pughsley and the GLCC, seemed to share the views of Pughsley's antagonists. He allowed disparagement of Pughsley's appearance to slip into a report on one meeting: "Mrs. Pughsley appeared on the scene attired in knee-length pedal pushers which I thought gave her oversized figure a somewhat grotesque appearance." In his report, he characterized the Greater Lawndale Association of Block Clubs & Organizations as "a militant Negro residential group."[75]

Despite their conflicts, Pughsley's organization of block clubs and the GLCC coexisted for a few years. The GLCC clearly hoped to use the block clubs to expand its base in North Lawndale, to demonstrate that its conservation effort had the support of large numbers of residents. Although Pughsley clashed with other board members, she seems to have accepted without dispute the GLCC's request that she "'spread the word' about the real meaning and intent of conservation through the block clubs." Following open hostilities, however, the GLCC finally abandoned its relationship with Pughsley in 1957 and hired a community organizer.[76] The GLCC's staff members then built relationships with several networks of block associations on Chicago's West Side, but none held firm.

Nor did urban renewal ever come to fruition in North Lawndale. The deep reasons for this decision lay in the priorities of Mayor Richard J. Daley, who clearly saw urban renewal as a means of stabilizing Chicago's downtown. Because the GLCC failed to connect effectively with North Lawndale's block clubs, the organization could not make the case that it represented a united community. The contrast with the solid organizational relationships in Hyde Park also meant that block clubs in Lawndale lacked a natural ally for promoting smaller-scale improvements as an alternative.

Some block clubs supported urban renewal, while others were working groups whose agendas diverged from or even rejected the plans of their parent groups. Urban renewal was not simply a matter of large institutions destroying established communities. Invited into the process, neighborhood residents expressed contradictory views of the process of clearance and redevelopment. The block clubs' roles in planning for urban renewal underscore the conflicts that occurred among neighbors in Chicago.

Conclusion

Block club members recognized an array of local problems that were beyond their capacity to solve alone. In their quest to protect their surroundings, the clubs often tapped municipal resources. Government services were necessary for some of the problems they hoped to solve. But block clubs were best suited to small, inwardly directed, local actions. Pushing a single property through a housing court complaint required a significant time commitment from members. Club members could do little to influence the direction of adverse urban renewal projects. Some appeals to the municipal government for superficial improvements proved fruitful, but block clubs were not suited to sustained direct engagements with government programs. Larger organizations, with professional staff and more reliable budgets, could build the relationships required to leverage specialized action from Chicago's government. This imbalance made block clubs vulnerable to the parent organizations' agendas.

Block clubs' philosophical attitudes toward the appropriate role of government varied. Julia Abrahamson's book about the HPKCC takes pains to point out that block group members did not want to try to replace government action. In liberal Hyde Park, the clubs often undertook temporary and private efforts to solve problems such as unlit and therefore dangerous streets. But these actions were meant as "temporary relief measures, not as a permanent solution. Citizens united in the conference had no wish to encourage the abdication of public responsibility." On the other hand, the geographer Brian J. L. Berry observed of the Southwest Associated Block Clubs (SWABC) that its participants were suspicious of the federal government, and even more hostile to the city government. Neither, they felt, did enough to deal with "interracial problems," which in their view occurred when African Americans were provided with the financial and legal tools that enabled them to purchase homes near where whites lived. Berry observed that SWABC members "were protesting the subsidizing of home mortgages by [the] FHA that made it 'too easy' for low income blacks to move into white neighborhoods."[77] In their view, government was already doing too much to change their environment, and should not be encouraged to do more. Most block clubs had a simpler, pragmatic view of government; they called upon its existing services for local aid.

As a supplement to environmental transformations, many block clubs tried to regulate their neighbors' actions. Public behavior influenced residents' experience of home as much as the physical streetscape did. When other people made too much noise, loitered on the corner, or committed crimes, block club members took notice. Many such annoyances were too minor to admit legal action, so block clubs turned to moral suasion and social pressure tactics to achieve their vision of a mannered environment. The effort to influence their neighbors' behavior, however, also entangled block clubs with the city government. Attempts to control crime, for example, necessarily connected block clubs with the Chicago Police Department. In the 1990s, with the launch of a new community policing initiative, the CPD institutionalized its relationship with block clubs, making them an official partner in law enforcement.

Regulate

In July 2011, the Magnolia Malden Block Club invited neighbors to participate in an upcoming evening of "positive loitering" at three nearby intersections. A larger North Side group, the Clarendon Park Neighborhood Association, organized the action in response to a trio of nearby shootings. "Loiterers" were to arrive at seven p.m. and spend an hour standing around. The announcement explained that

> Positive Loitering . . . gives us a chance to meet each other, pet each other's dogs, support the police by calling in suspicious activity, making it generally uncomfortable for "negative loitering" to take place, and demonstrate that there is a growing number of people that find these shootings unacceptable. The police support and greatly appreciate these Positive Loitering events. They are non-confrontational and truly demonstrate strength in numbers. Friendly dogs are certainly welcome.

If the chance to counter violence, meet neighbors, and pet friendly dogs was not enough of an incentive, "Amy" promised to bring "chocolate chip cookies" to the positive loiterers at the site of the most recent shooting.[1]

In the early twenty-first century, some Chicagoans turned to positive loitering as a strategy for reclaiming public space for safe and orderly use. Positive loitering signaled to "negative loiterers" and criminals that law-abiding residents intended to use streets and sidewalks without harassment or exposure to danger. In contrast to demonstrations and marches where activists carry signs, chant slogans, and demand change, positive loiterers simply gather and occupy space together. When positive loiterers observe activities they think are criminal, they are supposed to report to police. They are not to engage the suspects directly. The positive loitering tactic, which has received the most publicity in Chicago's North Side neighborhoods, originated in the 1990s. Such activities are often organized by neighborhood associations that draw on constituent block clubs to turn out participants. In the twenty-first century, the Chicago Police Department turned to a community policing strategy that treated block clubs as integral to crime reduction. It embraced a broad definition of positive loitering as a way for residents to contribute to their streets' safety.

The official use of positive loitering activities capped decades of less coordinated efforts by block clubs to regulate their neighbors' behavior. How other people used the street mattered to their neighbors' quality of life. Although individual behavior was more ephemeral than fixed physical features such as vacant lots and abandoned buildings, certain patterns of use troubled block club members. In response, they sometimes tried to regulate their neighbors' actions. Of course, block clubs lacked the legal standing to enforce their desires, but that did not stop them from expressing their views. The authority offered by a block club's existence gave its rules and regulations more weight than a preference expressed by a lone neighbor.

Most early regulatory efforts manifested the long-standing desire of middle-class African American urbanites to influence their poorer neighbors. In the name of racial uplift, established black Chicagoans demanded that recently migrated Southerners modify their public behavior. They wanted their neighbors to use nearby spaces as they did, as places that they enjoyed briefly as they traveled to and from their homes. They rejected the neighbors' right to use public areas for illicit commerce, for boisterous recreation, for loud socialization, and for passing time idly. In her study of the middle-class Groveland area of Chicago, sociologist Mary Pattillo characterized the block club members and the gang leaders who reside there as sharing a desire for a "quiet neighborhood."[2] The housing expert Charles Abrams expressed this orientation succinctly, observing that in the post–World War II city, "'the proper function of the neighbor is to keep his garbage covered, his lawn trim, his children and radio quiet, his house painted, his troubles to himself.'"[3]

Although most block club activity addressed the physical environment, participants also scrutinized the social uses of the street. Extending an early-twentieth-century practice, they forthrightly announced what they considered acceptable public behavior in detailed lists of rules and regulations. Block clubs were particularly concerned about the effects of young people on their neighbors. Efforts to contain youth's noise and visual impact included both preemptive and reactive programming. Some block clubs were also troubled by the public consumption and sale of drugs and alcohol, both of which were subject to legal regulation, which in turn offered reinforcement for the block clubs' unofficial efforts.

In the last third of the twentieth century, many Chicago block groups made tackling local crime a centerpiece of their activity. Although their goal was to decrease crime, they often simply displaced it to other blocks. George Kelling and James Q. Wilson's "broken windows" theory animated such approaches. Kelling and Wilson argued that small imperfections in the environment signal neglect, and therefore invite larger problems.[4] This intellectual link between the physical and social environment encouraged block clubs to increase their surveillance of potential and actual criminal activity. At the turn of the twenty-first century, block clubs worked directly with the CPD's Chicago Alternative Policing Strategy (CAPS) program to address crime. CAPS block clubs built relationships with beat officers, engaged in crime-prevention activities such as positive loitering, and reported legal infractions and building code violations. The clubs lacked the mechanisms and authority to substitute for police functions; they were discouraged from directly engaging dangerous criminals such as armed drug dealers. An active anticrime block club, however, subtly communicated that criminals should seek their targets on the next block over. Block clubs' regulatory programs were structured to alleviate their own localized problems, not to create an absolute citywide reduction in undesirable behavior.

Do's and Don't's

Chicago's African American block clubs routinely directed members, neighbors, and visitors in how to behave in public spaces. The activities examined in previous chapters conveyed the club members' standards for the physical environment. The modeling of their desired aesthetic sensibility was an expression of the block clubs' vision for their area. At least temporarily, clubs made concrete changes to the environment for all neighbors and passersby to see and appreciate. Neighbors who did not belong to the block club sometimes recognized the message, and brought their properties into compliance. For example, one of the sociologist Mary Pattillo's Groveland informants observed that "everyone else on the block had [Christmas decorations] up . . . So we figured we better get some stuff."[5] But the simple modeling of respectable behavior was rarely enough to influence neighbors' deportment. Respectability included keeping oneself off display, invisible to neighbors, for much of the time. So that there would be no mistaking of their views, block clubs spelled out exactly what they expected of their blocks' other denizens.

The rules of block clubs targeted specific nuisance behaviors that neighbors could reasonably adjust. For example, Leroy Whiting, president of the 700–800 S. Kilbourn-Kolmar and Fifth Avenue Block Club used the club newspaper's "Onions and Quinine" column to condemn "those people in our block who allow car horns to be blown in front of their doors every morning. The whole neighborhood is being awakened." Whiting's complaint suggested a belief in the power of a polite reminder to reduce interruptions. Of course, block clubs could not enforce their attempts at behavior modification. They sometimes referenced city ordinances regulating hazardous conditions, but most lacked the personal contacts required to make good on threats to bring in housing inspectors.[6] Realistically, they could only hope that neighbors would recognize the legitimacy of their standards and comply voluntarily. Block clubs' rules described the kind of streets where their members—and people like them—aspired to live.

In publicly defining desirable and undesirable behavior, block clubs continued a venerable black tradition of urban uplift. The historian James Grossman's *Land of Hope* describes lists of "Do's and Don't's" published in the *Chicago Defender* during the First Great Migration of the interwar years. These lists targeted recent Southern migrants with the intent of acculturating them into urban life. The rules aimed to make life more pleasant for their established African American neighbors, while demonstrating to white Chicagoans that blacks were suited for city living.[7] After World War II, community organizations of various sizes continued publicizing lists of acceptable behavior. The *Voice of the Midwest Community Council*, for example, described "good neighbors" in 1959, emphasizing especially how children disrupted the environment:

Good Neighbors (Will you help "to make the West Side the Best Side"?)

1. Let every home have a lawn or window box. (Large or small)
2. Discourage our children from playing on our lawn and the lawn of others.
3. Refrain strangers and guests from throwing bottles or containers from their cars onto our lawns.
4. Endeavor to keep strangers and guests from parking cars or trucks on our lawns or parkways.
5. Teach our children to respect our property and the property of others.
6. Encourage our children to play in front of their own home
7. Discourage our children from riding bicycles across private property.
8. See to it that *our children* are CLEAN and NEAT before they are allowed to play outside.

9. Please refrain your children from making loud unnecessary noises after
7:30 P.M. so as not to disturb your neighbors.

10. Encourage your children to be inside their home before dark unless
they are accompanied by you, their parent.

11. Let us leash our dogs and not allow them to roam the streets.[8]

Many block clubs published similar lists reflecting members' pet peeves (for several block clubs' rules and regulations, presented in their entirety, see appendix 2). Their entreaties routinely mixed together a variety of concerns. The 2200–2300 South Kostner and Kenneth Civic and Improvement Club, for example, began an appeal to neighbors by asking them to protect women and children: "Close your garage doors at all times, leaving doors open is a danger signal. With so many things happening in our City, our girls and boys, also our women could be molested in one of these shelters without our knowledge." The club's request moved from safety to the social and sanitary standards for the block, continuing, "Wash your cars and do other minor repairs in the alley. Will you please keep your *dogs* and *pets* off the lawns."[9]

The 38–3900 Monroe Block Club was forthright about the class-based assumptions behind its efforts to control behavior. Members publicized the views of "the responsible residents of the blocks," explaining that there were "many more people of upper middles [*sic*] class standards, economic and social status, than of lower class. The blocks stand firm on reflecting that image by assuring a majority denomination in representing the block image." In order to project members' standards, the club "selected six areas for concentrating their efforts in lifting the blocks back to their middle class perspective." They resolved

> that action will be employed against anyone: Repairing automobiles in the front street, washing automobiles in the front street, purposely littering the front street, over-crowding living quarters, parking oversize vehicles in front street and ice cream trucks serving children in the center of the streets or sounding charms or bells at irritating volumes.[10]

Although they applied to everyone, these lists of regulations reflected a very particular vision of appropriate use of public and private spaces. Block clubs endeavored to create public space that residents could pass through without encountering untoward noise, visual disruptions, groups of unoccupied people, or even casual clothing. That some neighbors might not have access to private recreation spaces was immaterial to the block clubs' demands.

The rules of the 4100 West Grenshaw Block Club suggested that every space had specific functions that inhabitants should not sully with improper uses. To keep alleys looking tidy, garbage and litter should be "wrap[ped] up" and "pile[d] neatly" in appropriate receptacles until it was collected. While cleanups were a familiar program, these regulations emphasized the appearance of refuse while it awaited removal over the hygienic and health reasons for a clean street. Similarly, food and alcohol were to be consumed only in private places such as homes, although the group also objected to drinking in stationary automobiles. Like other clubs, members of the 4100 West Grenshaw group expected that people who owned cars not repair them on the block. Ethnographer Sudhir Venkatesh explains that rejecting informal automobile repair business did not merely reflect respectable residents' disdain for commerce on the street. Such operations could leave pollutants, oil slicks, and other dangerous detritus in the streets or alleys where mechanics conduct their work. In prohibiting car washing, the block club members might have been dismayed by soap suds and puddles left by overzealous car cleaners, or they might have been trying to discourage an underground car-washing business on the block. Because the homes on the 4100 block of West Grenshaw were primarily single-family residences and two-flat apartment buildings, the block club members might have reasonably expected that car owners had access to off-street facilities for automobile maintenance. But on other streets with larger apartment buildings and fewer private parking spaces, such a rule might have created an impossible dilemma for residents who wanted their cars to be as clean as the private spaces they inhabited.[11]

Block clubs' public rules sought to control the appearance and demeanor of block residents and visitors, young and old. They enjoined children to respect property lines while they played. They wanted denizens to modulate their voices, radios, and televisions to protect the quiet that block club members valued. Property owners were asked to prevent "loud talking or congregating of adults or teenagers in front of your residence." Idling on the sidewalk suggested people with nothing better to do—a hint of unemployment that conflicted with block clubs' aspirations for respectability. The 4100 West Grenshaw Block Club even tried to control how people ate and dressed. In language redolent of the racial uplift message of the interwar years, it admonished residents, "Do not appear on the streets or on front porches improperly dressed, or hang feet out of windows or over porch rails eating watermelons, etc."[12] The reference to outdoor consumption of watermelon—a stereotype associated with Southern African Americans—suggests that the block club members were thinking not only of their own aesthetic standards, but were also sensitive to the possibility of racist white critics happening by.

The Progressive Twin Block Club issued a two-page memo entitled "The

Making of Good Citizenship and Neighborly Conduct." They opened their rules with the assertion that "property and real estate value depends upon the group and not the individual home appearance of the neighborhood. Thus, it is mandatory that every property owner and tenant see that the property is kept up to standards provided by the laws of our city." So that no one could feel exempt from the obligation to "to donate some time and labor to what he or she is best qualified to do," the club's rules carefully attended to the distinct responsibilities that residents took on as property owners, tenants, residents, neighbors, or parents. Property owners were responsible for removing snow and providing covered, painted trash containers, while all residents were to report rodents and cooperate with pest removal operations. The club also emphasized the joint privilege of all residents to decide how to deal with problems: "Where vacant property exits, it shall be up to the neighbors to come to some agreement on its care." Although the rules emphasized the maintenance of property, the club asserted that all neighbors benefited from compliance, enjoying the returns of living on a safe, attractive street.[13]

Some block clubs published their rules on painted signs erected on the parkway, not just in their newsletters. Placing signs in the public thoroughfare reinforced the idea that the rules applied to everyone, not just to block club members. The lists posted on signs were necessarily less elaborate than those published in newsletters. The 70th Wabash Block Club's simple list of public rules was posted on a sign painted in green, yellow, red, and black, echoing the colors of Pan-African solidarity. Like many block club signs, it began with the word "Greetings," welcoming visitors to the block. This club added the plea "Save Our Children," implying that its rules protected young people in particular.[14]

Block club signs were usually homemade affairs, handpainted on wood and erected simply on pairs of wooden posts. One function of the signs was to notify passersby of a block club's existence. The signs also set out simplified versions of the club's expectations for public behavior on the block, typically condemning some combination of illegal drugs, loitering, gambling, unsafe driving, and car repair. The signs themselves reflected different levels of skill and maintenance. A group of photographs archived on the Flickr website in 2007 shows some of the variations. Some signs were neatly stenciled, others lettered in a shaky hand. Many were decorated only with black paint on a white background, while others used several bright colors and illustrations to underscore their point. The Flickr photographers captured images of some signs that looked newly made, while other signs were so neglected as to imply that the block club was no longer paying attention.[15] A rare variation was the sign for the "Block of Unity" at 82nd and Morgan, photographed by David

FIGURE 13. Welcome sign of the 70th Wabash Block Club, painted in the black, green, yellow, and red of Pan-African solidarity. Photograph circa 2011. Courtesy of Dr. Jeannine Hogg.

FIGURE 14. "Welcome & Notice" sign of the 93rd & Throop Block Club. Photograph courtesy of David Salk.

FIGURE 15. Welcome sign of the 900 block of North Monticello Avenue. Photograph courtesy of David Salk.

FIGURE 16. Welcome sign at West 82nd and South Morgan Streets. Photograph courtesy of David Salk.

FIGURE 17. Welcome sign at 7700 South Wolcott Avenue. Photograph courtesy of David Salk.

FIGURE 18. Bilingual welcome sign at 3400 West Hirsch Street. Photograph courtesy of David Salk.

Salk; it showcased a collage of photographs of the trim bungalows that graced the street, illustrating exactly how members expected their block to appear.

At their best, these regulatory signs signaled that residents were looking out for their block as a whole, not just their own properties. They informed neighbors, visitors, and prospective residents of what to expect on the street. Lists of prohibited activities hinted that a block club had experienced some problems in the past but was now on alert, while simpler greetings sent messages of welcome and local pride. The signs also hinted at ongoing informal surveillance, even if a block club's members and activities were not conspicuous at the moment. The sociologist Peter K. B. St. Jean's analysis of Chicago's Wentworth Police District argues that criminals discern carefully—on the level of the block—where to focus their activities. The presence of a well-maintained block club sign bearing the club's regulations communicated a block's specific standards, and also sent a signal that the street's denizens were vigilant. Observing such an environmental clue, a thief or drug dealer might try his luck on a less attentive block.[16]

Civil Defense

The prominent display of block club regulations in Chicago's African American neighborhoods suggested to casual observers that these were black institutions. But at mid-century, many white Chicagoans were also personally familiar with block clubs. As part of the federal government's mobilization of civilian support for the American role in World War II, the Office of Civilian Defense promoted home-front organizing. In Chicago, OCD block clubs capitalized on residents' relationships with the places where they lived. Many Americans received indoctrination about their role in sustaining the war effort through their workplaces, where they were praised for supporting the military and encouraged to buy war bonds. As was explained in chapter 1, in Chicago the OCD also divided the city's residential areas into zones, divisions, and blocks that were all expected to assist domestic materiel, military, and morale goals. The OCD charged Chicago block club leaders with winning their neighbors' cooperation with conservation and safety measures.

Gaining civilian compliance with the war effort required delicacy. In the workplace, the existing hierarchical relationships facilitated the national propaganda program. But neighbors could not appear to command other free citizens. Block club leaders, elected by a subset of their neighbors, could not coerce compliance. Their task was to induce participation. One block captain's greetings implicitly contrasted the constraints of American democracy with Nazi totalitarianism:

> Through a regularly constituted election of residents in your block you have
> elected me to be your BLOCK CAPTAIN for the Office of Civilian Defense.
>
> Therefore I am calling a Block meeting for the purpose of getting better
> acquainted and also to obtain your assistance in carrying on the business of
> Civilian Defense.
>
> Please bear in mind that this is not a GESTAPO COMMAND but a respectful
> request that you be present.

The block captain underscored his point by stressing that attendance was voluntary. It was not necessary to stay for the whole meeting, but any involvement was welcome:

> So won't you please keep this date open, "Sept. 3" for a neighborly get-together
> in the Basement of Benson's Piano Store, rear[.] The meeting will start
> promptly at 8 P.M. and you can feel free to leave as you desire. Come out and
> give us your suggestions. We are doing our best to serve your defense needs
> and I hope it isn't asking too much for your attention and attendance at least
> one evening each month.[17]

OCD block leaders combined courtesy, guilt, and patriotism to persuade their neighbors to participate in the war effort.

To start its civilian mobilization effort, Chicago's OCD sought a bevy of leaders for every block. These volunteers were responsible for enticing their neighbors to bend their domestic practices toward civilian defense projects. In addition to block captains, who served as liaisons with the larger agency, blocks identified "wardens" to supervise sales of government bonds, encourage conservation of fat and grease to make bullets, collect scrap metal and paper, and tend victory gardens. Children could serve as messengers who delivered news in the event of an emergency. Block clubs and their superordinate zones threw parties to entertain participants and furloughed soldiers. They also engaged in the odd local improvement project. One block captain, for example, tried to ease his neighbors' hay fever by trimming weeds in local vacant lots. By 1944, when public enthusiasm for the block club program had waned, a clipping summarized the main goals that OCD block clubs still focused on: "(1) check O.C.D. lists and information for the installation of memorial plaques; (2) conduct paper salvages for the block and stress the importance of saving paper; (3) accelerate the interest in salvage of tin cans to produce arms and ammunition for our armed forces; (4) conduct war loan drives to meet the established quotas."[18]

The minutes of the Hermitage-Wood Block Club, in the Englewood neighborhood, provide a window into how one group prioritized the OCD's directives. In the first years of American involvement in the war, residents actively cooperated with the OCD's desire to keep them thinking constantly about the war effort. In their early meetings, the group devoted much discussion to erecting the OCD-recommended flagpole. They also worked on a public honor roll of block residents in the military and a memorial plaque commemorating soldiers killed in service. For a few months, they sent cards and plants to hospitalized neighbors.[19] This broad range of activity proved too much for the group to sustain.

Quickly, members made their highest priority that of sending Easter and Christmas cards to soldiers from the block, enclosing money orders as holiday gifts. By early 1943 their block's flag was "showing signs of wear" and needed replacement, but the club decided that the Easter gifts were more important. To raise funds, club members held bunco and bingo parties, featuring games of chance that did not advantage skilled players. Women donated baked goods for refreshments, with the money paid for admission to the parties added to the club treasury. Whether out of genuine gratitude or a desire to keep their parents from being shamed in front of their neighbors, the young soldiers sent effusive thank-you notes indicating their appreciation just for being remembered. Fritz Long, for example, wrote: "I think the block is doing a lot for the service men, and I think they all appreciate it. I am sorry I didn't do anything to help the block while I was there, but I guess I just didn't relize [sic] what it was doing to help the war." Despite these thanks, the group's success in fundraising combined with meeting fatigue to inspire fewer gatherings in the war's later years. The members stopped short of formally disbanding themselves in 1945, but they also decided not to meet unless circumstances suggested that they needed to do so.[20]

Block clubs' civilian defense efforts differed substantially from peacetime attempts to regulate behavior. Because the city blocks were not directly threatened by war, the OCD program aimed to keep the importance of the war effort in view of their residents. Only blackout drills implied that participants should regulate themselves for the direct protection of their neighbors. Before and after the war, however, the block clubs appealed to their neighbors to help create a more peaceful environment.

Youth

Block clubs gave special attention to local young people, who both disturbed their neighbors and needed help themselves. From the mid-twentieth century on, Americans expressed particular worries about youth. By World War II, American young people benefited from the universal provision of high school education and the prohibition of child labor. But adults viewed them as being more vulnerable than ever to the lure of crime, gangs, sex, drugs, and other vices that undermined their own future and threatened their neighbors' peace. As was the case with other Americans, block clubs' concerns about the younger generation varied. Sometimes their attention was on elementary school children, at other times on teenagers and young adults. Clubs rarely spelled out their full motivations for youth programming, but they often sponsored projects that corralled troublesome young people and diverted their energy into wholesome directions. In some cases, youth-oriented activities simply extended a block club's general intent to build a sense of community among neighbors. As was explained in chapter 3, block clubs threw parties and held other events catering to children's tastes. Club members hoped this special attention to youth would curb their undesirable behavior, and therefore make their blocks a more congenial environment for all.

In the postwar years, block clubs were certainly not alone in their attention to youth. Block club members shared in the broader cultural sense that young people were both endangered and dangerous themselves. The transformation of street gangs was especially worrisome. Chicago gang members had long flaunted their masculinity on the streets, violently expressed their hostility to outsiders, and engaged in criminal activities. After the 1960s, the gangs became larger and more menacing networks, which the historian Andrew Diamond refers to as "supergangs." Their activities became more systematically criminal as participants sold illegal drugs and carried more sophisticated weapons. Gangs such as the Blackstone Rangers and the Vice Lords dominated several African American neighborhoods on Chicago's South and West Sides. Some, such as Lincoln Park's Young Lords, engaged in political activity that echoed that of their early-twentieth-century predecessors.[21] Although not all young people were involved in them, the influence of the gangs was hard to escape in neighborhoods where they operated. Boys especially felt pressure to affiliate with local gangs to protect themselves. Belonging to a gang often appeared safer than becoming its victim. Block clubs rarely worked directly to intervene in gangs, which were usually too well organized and intimidating for club members to risk confrontation with. But street gangs formed a backdrop to many of the club members' postwar anxieties about youth, and informed club activities that were aimed at younger children.

Block clubs responded to these growing pressures on their young neighbors by engaging them in constructive alternatives. They interpreted young people's excess of unstructured, unsupervised time as a major source of their mischief. In the view of the Merry K Block Club, "the key issue is a youth program. Youths are full of energy. They will utilize that energy one way or another. Without some kind of guidance they normally choose the destructive way." Young people's misbehavior ranged from rudeness and thoughtlessness to endangering themselves and others, but responsible adults could redirect that energy. Chicago has an important tradition of street outreach workers building relationships of trust with gang members, but block clubs do not appear to have used this approach; their limited resources and respectable character caused them to focus on preventing trouble before it happened, rather than fixing it after harm was done. Leading up to Halloween in 1953, for example, a Chicago Urban League staff organizer asked block club participants to "recall the amount of damage and cost stemming from pranks and vandalism on this occasion" in previous years. The League advised "that perhaps cost in vandalism and property damage may be sharpely [sic] decreased through Block Club sponsored Halloween parties for both the youths and adults of your block."[22]

Some adults saw it as their prerogative to correct young people's demeanor. Members of the 3800 Van Buren Block Club agreed with convener Alex Nixon's assertions about "the local and visiting youths in the area" who made trouble. Nixon argued, "The vandalism and vulgar language used by the youths of all ages in the area must cease . . . adults must assume their responsibilities and train their children. We must ask the parent to take firm action against these practices." The club members agreed to split their responsibility for correcting miscreant youth along gender lines. Women were assigned to "promot[e] activities for the smaller children while the men concentrate on the teenage boys." This division of labor assumed that men had the best rapport with almost-grown male youth, while women could preempt trouble by nurturing girls and younger boys who were not yet making malicious trouble. The youths, however, were not always receptive to reproval. Young people swore at members of the 4300 Wilcox Block Club who tried to discipline them.[23]

Unsupervised children playing in front yards and on sidewalks also worried their neighbors. Without fences to contain them, children's games too easily spilled out onto sidewalks, between parked cars, and into oncoming traffic—threatening the children's lives and limbs. Rufford Milton, whose Garfield Community Council Block Club news and comment column appeared regularly in the *Garfieldian*, wrote, "I have witnessed five pedestrian accidents since the start of spring. Each one of them involved a child, who ran between parked cars into a public street." Several block clubs addressed children's safety by trying to regulate them and traffic. The 38–3900 Monroe club forbade "free play for children on front lawns," a practice Milton urged on other clubs. For its part, the 2900 Fillmore Block Club successfully petitioned for "slow" signs to urge caution on drivers, but the Julian-Paulina Block Club found the city's Bureau of Street Traffic unresponsive to its request for stop signs. The Miller-Carpenter Street Block Club was worried about high traffic in an alley adjacent to a children's playlot. It did not specify a remedy, but instead asked the local police captain to work out a solution.[24]

Block clubs corrected the demeanor of children on the street. Members of the 4200 West End Block Club were dismayed daily by students being dismissed from the adjacent Tilton Elementary School. Some of the students left the building fighting; their disputes continued down the sidewalks, and sometimes into neighbors' yards. The block club's president lamented, "It's a shame when residents have to duck for safety on their own property." The club devised a series of proposals for dealing with the situation. Its first choice was for the school to change the children's departure pattern to "eliminate having the entire student body on the same street at the same time." The principal responded that Chicago Public School rules made this suggestion impossible. Instead, he worked with the block club, the Off-the-Street-Club, and the local police to monitor children's behavior at the end of the school day. Both "street workers" and police were deployed to the school at closing time each day to ease neighbors' concerns.[25]

Block clubs had less success dealing with vandalism and minor crimes committed by local youth. Even when club members knew who was disrupting the peace of their blocks, they sometimes lacked the direct leverage needed to address the problem. Anticipating that youths who did not respect private property might mock them or do worse, the club members thought carefully about how to discipline them without alienating them altogether. The 4100 Adams club placed the blame for vandalism on negligent supervision of local youth. Club participants devised a strategy to "visit parents in an attempt to free them from the apathy which in many cases prevents parents from at least scolding children engaged in senseless destruction." In response to a rash of vandalism and false fire alarms, the club also invited boys to join a "junior volunteer fire patrol." Participating boys "were instructed on the expense and danger involved in pulling false alarms," provided with badges, and given the responsibility "to watch the boxes and report their observation to our committee."[26]

In a few cases, block clubs sought to remove troublemaking youths from their territory altogether. A 1998 issue of the EPIC Block Club's newsletter praised several "responsible" local landlords for steps they had taken after the club complained about their tenants. In addition to addressing code violations in their buildings, two of the landlords had evicted families whose children were disturbing their neighbors. One family, consisting of two married adults and seven children—described as "four subteens and three teens"—lost its home because "the minors were vandalizing the neighborhood and threatening motorists and pedestrians." In another building, "children of some tenants also were vandalizing neighborhood properties." The landlord evicted these "problem tenants with numerous children." EPIC's newsletter also celebrated a third landlord whose tenants had "agreed to discourage large numbers of minors from congregating on the Rosedale side of the property."[27] Block clubs could not always induce parents of miscreant youth to respond to their criticisms, but long-standing organizations like EPIC developed enough status and powerful relationships in their neighborhoods so that landlords responded to their pressure.

Alcohol and Drugs

Idle youth might gather in front of any structure, residential or commercial, whose occupants tolerated their presence. Taverns attracted both adult and underage patrons, who troubled their neighbors. Many residential Chicago streets had taverns on their corners. While many Chicagoans enjoyed sociability in these convenient, familiar neighborhood establishments, the effects of taverns spilled out onto the streets. Block club leaders celebrated when a tavern at the intersection of Pulaski Road and Congress Parkway suddenly closed. The tavern, they explained, had given "the block a disgraceful appearance but it also kept away desirable tenants as well as prospective buyers." Patrons often lingered outside a tavern, to the chagrin of passersby. Female neighbors especially resented the consequences; male loiterers urinated against sides of buildings, and harassed women walking by. Block club participants expressed a range of concerns about taverns, and tried various tactics to moderate their effects. One of the most complicated solutions was a "local option" election, which banned alcohol sales.[28]

Black Chicagoans were often bothered by taverns located on streets that were primarily residential. John Ragland offered a succinct expression of the problems created by the Your Friendly Liquors tavern at 1216 South Kedzie, in 1954: "Bad characters hang out here. Rear yard filled with debris." In 1960, the 1800–1900 Property Owners Block Club elaborated on another tavern's threats: "The people leaving our churches, the buses, the elevated trains and other places are faced with the problem of getting by, the foul talking alcoholics, who stand and even sit on chairs on the side walk around the Tavern at the north west side of Lawndale and Ogden Avenues." Gloria Pughsley campaigned on behalf of the Greater Lawndale Association of Block Clubs against an "overabundance" of taverns in the 24th Ward. She complained about one establishment's "lack of separate toilet facilities for men and women, and lack of a clear view into the tavern from the street." Although Pughsley desired to see what was going on behind closed doors, the view inside a tavern presented a problem to the 4400 Van Buren Block Club, whose members were disturbed that it "operate[d] with open doors," exposing its enticements to children walking by. Closing the doors might have made no difference to that tavern's influence on the street, however. The block club president explained that "patrons purchase alcohol from the tavern and occupy passageways between the buildings in the block to talk and consume the liquor, leaving the containers on the sites." Moreover, while hanging around outside, male loiterers conducted themselves so that "ladies could not pass by the place without being molested." In short, the patrons of taverns offended the sensibilities of neighbors who wanted more respectability than sociability on their street.[29]

Block clubs tried to ameliorate the effects of taverns on local street life. The ever-watchful 15th Place Block Club heard rumors in 1968 that a tavern operator was seeking a license to operate on their block. Members deluged the mayor's office with petitions and letters of protest, prompting the denial of the license. Block clubs that started on streets where taverns already operated sought meetings with the owners, hoping that they would moderate their patrons' behavior and clean up their messes. Summoned to a meeting with the 4100 Van Buren Block Club, the Garfield Community Council, and a local police commander, the owner of the Van-Keeler tavern asserted that "his business did not draw the caliber of people described" by the organizations' representatives. He denied serving "wino-gangs" or underaged drinkers. On the contrary, he claimed, his was "an exclusive business" whose staff prevented children from buying alcohol. In response to the complaints, however, he agreed to a "three week cooperative measure."[30]

Not all tavern owners acceded to conciliatory overtures. As a next step, block clubs thus moved to close the taverns down. To enable communities to prohibit alcohol sales, Illinois law allows "local option" elections. This policy enables voters to declare a section of the city "dry," and therefore put neighborhood taverns out of business. Members of the 6800 Indiana Block Club, a "very serious, interested group," investigated a troubling tavern on their block, and learned that it did not present a zoning violation. Members of the club consulted with a Chicago Urban League staff worker about the possibility of shutting down the tavern through a local option vote.[31] League staff organizer Alva B. Maxey outlined in detail the work necessary to use the local option to close a tavern. She explained the commitment required to win the club's fight:

Members must not be easily intimidated, and must wage a continuous, political-type campaign throughout the neighborhood. Legal assistance is usually necessary. Petitions must be drawn up and circulated among the voters in the area, requesting that election officials put the "local option" proposition on the ballot. Literature is distributed in the area, meetings are held prior to the election, and club members conduct house-to-house canvasses, in an effort to persuade the "fence sitters" and disinterested electors. On election day, members escort voters to the polls and watch the canvass of the vote after the polls close.

As one would expect, the taverns also engage in a well-organized counter-campaign, with literature and propaganda, and these are accompanied, not infrequently, with attempts at intimidation and bribery. Such a battle is a real test of the strength and courage of the block organization.[32]

Because local option campaigns could go awry in so many ways, such elections did not always succeed. Gloria Pughsley's antitavern campaign in Lawndale lost two of the three votes it spearheaded; its sole victory was overturned in court. Anticipating that businesses would object to their actions, one block club conducted several local option vote planning meetings "without fanfare, to avoid counter action by tavern owners." The effort required to put local option on the ballot and win the election could easily tax a block club beyond its capacity. Despite such obstacles, however, the number of Chicago precincts that limited alcohol sales increased around the turn of the twenty-first century.[33]

In recent decades, illegal drugs presented residents with a wider set of problems than taverns did. Young men locked out of the conventional economy sometimes turned to drug sales to make a living, usually as part of gang operations. To be sure, some of the effects of drugs were similar to those of alcohol sales: intoxicated customers' appearance, words, and bodily odors made streets unpleasant or intimidating for nonconsuming neighbors. Because drug sales were illicit, often took place on the street, and were inconsistently suppressed by the police, they created several additional concerns for block clubs. Most problematically, drug sellers were legally defined as criminals.[34] Many were actively dangerous, participating in street warfare, carrying weapons, and sometimes exchanging gunfire and injuring innocent bystanders. Mothers worried about the consequences for their sons, who saw drug commerce as exciting and lucrative, and their daughters, who prostituted themselves to pay for drug habits.[35]

In some cases, block clubs mitigated the effects of drug dealing and other illicit activities. In his ethnographic study *Off the Books*, for example, the sociologist Sudhir Venkatesh relates in detail one block club's struggle with a local gang leader, "Big Cat," over control of nearby Homans Park in the 1990s. The block club's president, Marlene Matteson, worked out an understanding with Big Cat over the timing of drug sales in the park. Mothers wanted their children to be able to enjoy the public amenity without exposure to danger, but they were too fearful of the drug dealers to directly assert their right to use the space. As Venkatesh explains, the gang's complete "absence was not even considered a possibility." The block club could not hope to drive the drug dealers from the park altogether. Instead, Matteson and Big Cat agreed that gang members would not conduct their drug sales at the peak times of children's use of the park, before and after school hours and during prear-ranged family reunion events.[36]

Although the arrangement was tenuous, breaking down a couple of times a year, Matteson's status as block club president and her ongoing relationship with the gang enabled her to continuously remind them of the terms of the deal until 1999, when Big Cat decided to expand the range of underground economic activity in the park to include sex work and automobile repair. He asserted his control by deploying his "rank and file around the area: all were armed, they physically searched and harassed passersby, and they drank and smoked marijuana until the early morning hours with loud music blaring from their stereos." Block club members debated how to handle the gang's takeover of the park. Some members recognized sex work as a form of labor, undesirable but necessary to the prostitutes' economic survival. Collectively, the club members recognized that "even if the local traders were threatened with police detection or gang beatings, they would probably just move their operations temporarily, only to return to Homans Park if the other location proved unsuitable." Backed by the block club's authority, Matteson worked strategically with community policing staff and a local pastor to renegoti-ate shared access to the park.[37] The block club empowered one bold resident with the social legitimacy needed to persuade drug dealers to let families use public space. But it did not provide enough of a platform to rid the area of drug sales altogether. The work of block clubs complemented police func-tions without replacing them.

One block club response to drug dealing was to move it temporally, to times when children were not using a playground. Another was to displace it. In "Hurt Me Soul," the rapper Lupe Fiasco praises a block club's success in protecting his immediate neighbors: "Glamorized drug dealing was ap-pealing / But the block club kept it from in front of our building." The lyric suggests a block club that was powerful enough to temporarily wrest con-trol of its immediate public space, but not to eliminate the drug dealing al-together. Statistical evidence begins to bear out Fiasco's impression that the block clubs pushed drug sales to more distant neighbors. For example, early data from the 11th Police District on Chicago's Northwest Side suggested that in the winter of 2003, blocks without clubs had three times as many reports of "drug activity" as those with block clubs. The sociologist Peter K. B. St. Jean's *Pockets of Crime* found that drug dealers and thieves take into consideration microenvironmental differences when they decide where to conduct their operations. St. Jean argues that both the quality of a streetscape and the apparent activism of residents—both of which block clubs affect—can account for street-to-street variations in crime rates.[38] But it is not clear that block club programs prevent overall drug sales or associated violent crimes from occurring elsewhere.

The problem of drug sales throws the limits of block clubs' capacities into sharp relief. Some block club efforts are classic NIMBY ("not in my backyard") politics. They can move problems away, but they do not eliminate them. In this respect, block clubs' efforts against drug dealing resembled their garbage cleanup campaigns. Block clubs could not confront the economic structures that made drug dealing one of the few ways for poor young men to make a living; nor could they remedy the political and social shortfalls in public services that might have improved the overall quality of life in their neighborhoods and made other, legitimate economic opportunities locally viable. One of the largest police forces in the United States had not controlled drug sales in Chicago; how could a small, local, volunteer organization make a dent in the imperatives that drove the underground economy? The best its members could hope for was to move the problems elsewhere.

Crime

Like other problems such as garbage and vacant lots, crime troubled Chicago block club members. During the twentieth century, clubs sporadically incorporated anticrime work into their programs, usually in the form of pleas to the CPD to increase local patrols. Alva B. Maxey explained in her 1957 article about the Chicago Urban League's community organization efforts, "Aiding law enforcement constitutes a major block club activity. A great deal of effort is directed toward securing better police protection, a project which frequently necessitates continuous vigilance and persistent, tactful action. Block clubs often form committees to visit police captains in the district stations, for the purpose of calling their attention to special neighborhood problems arising out of law violations and inadequate law enforcement." As Maxey's comments suggest, block clubs' support of policing primarily consisted of their seeking increased attention to their own territory. It is unlikely that they

affected the overall crime rate, but a sociologist studying the relationship between New York City block clubs and crime in the 1980s suggested that "they
may make people feel safer in an unsafe environment."[39]

For most of the twentieth century, such efforts confronted a Chicago bu-
reaucracy that was largely unreceptive to civilian input. In 1986 the 15th Place
Block Club, whose records reflect little concern about crime, decided that it
wanted to connect with the police officers assigned to its area. Its strategy
involved requesting an appointment with the district's commander in order
to learn their names, thus suggesting the distance between the CPD and civilians.[40] The advent of community policing in the 1990s, however, transformed
the anticrime efforts of block clubs into a central program. For the first time,
the CPD designated officers to liaise with residents. Community policing officers began responding to residents' concerns about crime as well as other
quality-of-life issues. Perhaps more significantly, in the twenty-first century
the CPD has become one of the largest organizers of block clubs in Chicago's
history, as it has systematically attempted to create civilian partners.

Despite Maxey's assertion that Chicago Urban League block clubs tried
to attract police assistance, little concern about violent crime is evident in
League staffers' notes of their interactions with the clubs. League clubs did
ask for police assistance in dealing with nuisances such as vandalism and
intoxicated loiterers, but they did not generally seek remedies for the kinds of
criminal activity that concerned later block clubs. Most of the early evidence
about block club anticrime efforts emerges in the context of white neighborhoods experiencing racial transition. In the 1950s, according to executive director Julia Abrahamson, HPKCC block clubs banded together to petition for
extra protection against a wave of "purse snatchings and burglaries"; the CPD
offered the petitioning blocks extra patrols. But the HPKCC's investigation of
another reported "crime wave" demonstrated that there was no real increase
in crime in that case. Instead, they found, one local resident's rumormonger-
ing had succeeded in whipping up needless fear among the neighbors.[41] Many
white Chicagoans perceived African Americans as criminal, but the nuances
of block club members' attitudes toward race influenced to whom and how
they appealed for protection.

The divergent approaches of two block clubs to crime illustrate how white
members filtered their desire for personal safety through race and politics. As
the Austin neighborhood began to experience racial transition in the mid-
1960s, its residents suspected that the level of crime in the neighborhood was
increasing. The 4600–4700 Adams-Jackson block club was affiliated with the
racially liberal Austin Tenants and Owners Association, a mostly white group
making an effort to welcome African Americans into the neighborhood.

Responding to "disturbances occurring in southeastern Austin," the 4600–4700 Adams-Jackson block club "agreed to contact police at the sight of suspicious persons in an attempt to decrease the number of burglaries and purse snatchings in the area." By contrast, the West Van Buren Street Block Club—which did not use a street number to identify its boundaries—lacked confidence in a police response. The leader of the club, which boasted one hundred members, explained that it was "an organization formed to protect local residents against criminal attacks." In 1970 its members asked a Republican legislative candidate for assistance.[42] Their appeal to an unelected Republican aspirant to state office for help in a city controlled by the legendary Democratic political machine was a sign of thoroughgoing alienation. A political stunt rather than a practical search for protection, such a request was unlikely to yield helpful results.

Despite their divergent tactics, these groups shared a strategic response to crime: seeking aid from public officials who might increase police protection for their street. Block clubs alarmed by crime had few options beyond working with authorities. The alternatives were to fight crime directly themselves, or to do nothing. Taking on crime unilaterally was not feasible; the criminals were too dangerous, while most block clubs were too staid to become vigilantes and too resource-poor to intervene effectively. Yet some block club members found real and perceived crime a serious impediment to a desirable environment, just as garbage in the alley or deterioration of the house down the block threatened their serenity.

Preserving public order was a central concern to the leadership of the anti-black Southwest Associated Block Clubs (SWABC). Fighting crime was one of the SWABC's three main pillars of action, alongside protesting racial integration in the schools and stopping blockbusting. The SWABC saw its interests as being closely aligned with rank-and-file police officers, most of whom were, like its members, working-class whites. In fall 1968, the SWABC demonstrated to praise the actions of the CPD, whose officers were being vilified elsewhere for attacking demonstrators at the Democratic National Convention. The 8th District police commander sent the SWABC a letter of gratitude, thanking its members because, "after working long strenuous hours during the convention week, your support of the Police Department has elevated the morale of all police officers to a high standard of efficiency."[43]

Given their amicable relations with the CPD, the SWABC probably expected favorable responses to their requests. In 1970 its members asked for more patrols to prevent the crimes they believed would inevitably follow from the appearance of African Americans in the neighborhood. The SWABC demonstrated little interest in disguising the racism underlying their

SOUTHWEST ASSOCIATED BLOCK CLUB

NEWS

SOUTHWEST ASSOCIATED BLOCK CLUBS
1725 West 69th Street
Chicago, Illinois 60636
Phones: 778-1395 - 6

September 15, 1968

Vol. 1 No. 11

CHEERS FOR POLICE and Mayor Daley are provided in signs carried by pickets filing past Chicago Lawn police station at 3515 W. 63rd st. Marching with the group, near the Southwest Block clubs' sign is the Rev. Francis X. Lawlor, Block club organizer.
(News-Herald Photo)

FIGURE 19. Members of the Southwest Associated Block Clubs marched in support of the Chicago Police Department following violent clashes between officers and protesters during the 1968 Democratic convention. Source: *Southwest Associated Block Club News*, September 15, 1968. Chicago History Museum. Courtesy of the *Hyde Park Herald*.

call for increased patrols. Under the alarmist headline "Crime Statistics Show Need for Police Help for Southwest Residents," the *ABC News* asserted: "The rights of homeowners and apartment dwellers in a stable, law-abiding community are being challenged by government bureaucrats, biased and incompetent clergymen, unscrupulous real estate speculators and agents, the Administrative Staff and Members of the Chicago Board of Education, leaders of the Black and pro-Black Civil Rights organizations and a highly vocal handful of pseudo-intellectuals, teachers and laymen who erroneously believe that de facto segregation is necessarily evil or an injustice to the Black people." The *ABC News* noted with some frustration: "A major complaint of the committee centered on the fact that there is a noticeable increase in the crime rate in the area but it is almost impossible to obtain additional police protection." The police responded that the number of patrols sent into an area depended on the number of calls. Because West Englewood had a low crime rate, they were not entitled to extra protection.[44]

The SWABC did ask the police for help, but they also took matters into their own hands. The geographer Brian J. L. Berry reported that the SWABC's "block clubs instituted nightly mobile patrols that reported suspicious events to the police, and they regularly demanded increased police protection." One issue of the *ABC News* included a detailed full-page spread encouraging readers to "take these protective measures." The instructions included suggestions for safety at night, in public places, and at home. Half the feature was devoted to tips for babysitters, alerting young women that they might be in danger. Despite such fearmongering, the *ABC News* repeated advice from the CPD that residents should not arm themselves, because "in Illinois it is against the law: To carry pistol or other firearm; tear gas projector; bomb or object containing noxious liquid or gas; or other weapons like bludgeon, blackjack, metal knuckles or switchblade knife." Referring to the SWABC members' assumption that African Americans traveled west into Englewood in order to find vulnerable white victims, one leader in the organization complained: "The youth of our area, and adults as well, are constantly being told not to carry weapons but are asking why that same admonition does not apply to those who come over from east of Ashland for the purpose of robbing and assaulting." The Highburn affiliate of the SWABC (south of Englewood) ran a "Citizens Radio Patrol" group, consisting of "two cars per block, two men per car, assigned one night each month." Patrollers were instructed: "The base operator on duty will be in contact with you and will instruct you if he feels the reports given by your unit are urgent enough to call in the police. He will make the decision[;] your job will be to keep surveillance of a suspicious act until the police arrive."[45]

Highburn was not the only Chicago neighborhood participating in the Citizens Radio Patrol program. In 1971, block clubs in Central Austin also ran a radio patrol and offered a resolution to the annual Congress of the Organization for a Better Austin, urging other groups to join in.[46] The Citizens Radio Patrol resembled the better-known Neighborhood Watch program, which emerged nationally in the late 1960s after the federal government called for civilians to become involved in local crime prevention. The National Sheriffs' Association founded Neighborhood Watch, modeling it after a pilot project in Seattle. The program theoretically works in two ways, deterring crime through the conspicuous vigilance of neighborhood residents, and speeding the arrival of police after a crime has occurred.[47] Police authorities accepted participants from the Citizens Radio Patrol and the Neighborhood Watch program as allies without involving them directly in official law enforcement.

In the late 1970s and early 1980s, block clubs affiliated with the Northwest Community Organization also reached out to the police for assistance. In contrast to the SWABC, which saw police as allies, the Alinsky-style activists in the NCO treated the police as public servants but not as partners. For example, they specifically asked their CPD district commander for immediate responses to members' reports of local abandoned cars, "since these cars are often sites for illegal activity." But they demanded accountability. They asked, "If the cars we report are not removed we request that the police inform us, in writing, why no action was taken." They also sought information about the district staff's ability to communicate with the neighborhood's Spanish-speaking residents, whom the NCO block club organizers were cultivating. They asked a series of questions to ascertain whether the police force had what is now called the "cultural competence" to work in their neighborhood: "How many Latino officers are there in the 14th District? How many 14th District officers are bilingual? How do English speaking officers deal with translation problems?" The 1900 Richmond Block Club's relationship with the police was similarly formal. In a thank-you note for police participation in a public meeting, the club requested that "an increased number of patrols be directed to the Yates School area after recess" to deal with gang activity. They also wanted "increased patrol along Cortland (from California to Humboldt) after dark and on weekends." To demonstrate that they would do their part in the effort to reduce neighborhood crime, the club's letter stressed, "The individuals of the Block Club restated their intention to call 911 immediately whenever a shotting [sic] or gang related crime occurs."[48]

Until the 1990s, when the CPD launched its community policing initiative, efforts like those of SWABC- and NCO-affiliated block groups remained intermittent and isolated. CAPS, however, changed how the city government related to block clubs. For the first time, the CPD systematically welcomed civilian input. CAPS provided a dedicated way for block clubs to bring their concerns about crime and other quality-of-life issues to the attention of appropriate city agencies. To help civilians support law enforcement, in the twenty-first century the CPD employed the largest community organizing staff focused on the creation and maintenance of block clubs in the city's history.

Chicago's community policy strategy emerged in the early 1990s as a way for the recently elected Mayor Richard M. Daley, the son of Mayor Richard J. Daley, to demonstrate that his administration could address the city's crime problem. Crime is a perennial concern in big American cities, but in the 1980s and 1990s crime rates were trending upwards nationally in a way that alarmed observers. Without intervention, Chicago's levels of serious crime seemed doomed to perpetually increase. Many American city leaders turned to community policing, which got police officers out of cars and into foot patrols, as a promising way to address rising crime rates. The idea underpinning community policing was that preemptively familiarizing officers with residents and local institutions would reduce crime and increase police responsiveness.[49]

Criminologists Wesley Skogan and Susan Hartnett, part of an academic research team that conducted several formal evaluations of CAPS, explained, "Community policing assumes that police cannot solve neighborhood problems on their own; to achieve success, it depends on the cooperation of the community and public and private agencies." Rather than meeting members of the public only when responding to 911 emergency calls, police officers walked beats in the neighborhoods, getting to know residents in advance of any incident that required traditional automobile-based policing. Like many of his peers in American urban government, Richard M. Daley embraced community policing, but insisted that it have a name that distinguished Chicago's approach from its earlier implementation elsewhere. The Chicago Alternative Policing Strategy (CAPS) was "prototyped" in five of Chicago's twenty-five police districts beginning in April 1993, and was expanded to the remainder of the city by the start of 1995. Prototyping allowed the CPD to test and evaluate combinations of tactics, an approach that continued even after the program was launched. Such experimentation has since become a hallmark of CAPS, whose methods are continuously in flux. Despite this flexibility, a crucial and stable feature of the CAPS program was the division of the city into thousands of small beats in which police officers could get to know the population and their problems. In addition to becoming acquainted with locals through their patrols, CAPS officers held regular beat meetings at which residents were invited to air their concerns and build relationships with their assigned liaisons.[50]

In Chicago, community policing was deeply informed by Kelling and Wilson's "broken windows theory." The idea behind the theory was that small defects in the physical environment—such as a broken window—signal to criminals that a property is uncared for, and essentially licenses them to prey on it with impunity. Popularized on the national level by an influential 1982 article in *The Atlantic* magazine, the broken windows theory also gained special traction in New York City, which adopted "problem-oriented policing." In an effort to improve the city as a whole, Mayor Rudolph Giuliani (1994–2001) devoted public resources to cracking down on small infractions of New York's municipal code. The city stepped up enforcement of its regulations against "squeegee men," implemented a notorious "stop-and-frisk" policy, and embraced statistically driven resource deployment.[51]

In Chicago, the broken windows theory informed late-twentieth-century block club actions just as the idea of blight informed those operating at midcentury. Under CAPS, police officers' traditional expertise in the handling of crime expanded to include all manner of quality-of-life issues formerly beneath CPD notice. Members of the public were invited to bring broken windows, abandoned buildings, code violations, and other nuisances to the attention of their beat officers, who routed the complaints to the city departments best equipped to handle them.

Launching CAPS required more effort than simply designating beat officers and setting up public meetings. It depended on reorienting the attitudes of police toward being in favor of the program. Persuading the police that their job involved "social work" was a formidable task. Skogan and Hartnett noted that at beat meetings, "citizens called for action against abandoned buildings and cars, garbage-strewn vacant lots, loitering youth, and loud music more frequently than they demanded that police do something about burglaries and robberies." These were precisely the kinds of problems that block clubs routinely cared about. To address this litany of problems and convince Chicagoans that they took the concerns seriously, the CPD had to develop relationships and coordinate with the city agencies responsible for such non-crime nuisance issues. In contrast to the practice in New York City, Chicago's adoption of community policing embraced what scholar Archon Fung calls "empowered participatory governance." Fung argues that in the 1990s, both the CPD and the Chicago Public Schools underwent transformations in governance that made them into "the most participatory-democratic public organizations of their kind in any large American city." As part of a national trend toward "third-party policing," the CPD made block clubs into important partners in Chicago's crime-prevention efforts.[52]

In its early years, CAPS encouraged block clubs to participate in beat meetings and otherwise raise their concerns with the CPD. In the prototyping period, notes Skogan, "residents were frequently reminded of the importance of organizing themselves into block clubs, watches, and patrols." In the mid-1990s, CAPS staff sought to connect with representatives from the block level who would attend meetings and let officers know what issues their neighbors thought needed special attention. The 8th Police District, for example, hoped to "have a representative from each block taking part in the program" within the next five years. CAPS quickly began encouraging residents to organize their own block clubs in order to generate participation in beat meetings. In 1994, an enterprising married couple in one far Southwest Side beat developed a network of approximately forty block captains who distributed flyers announcing CAPS meetings to their neighbors. In 1997, Chicago sponsored a citywide block club convention. Attendees received a binder full of documentation about connecting with the city for services, and heard a keynote address delivered by General Colin Powell.[53]

The CPD's strategy for identifying residents to connect with CAPS officers rapidly shifted from amateur to professional community organizers. Between 1994 and 1996 it contracted with an organization of neighborhood associations, the Chicago Alliance for Neighborhood Safety (CANS), to organize block clubs across the city. Despite receiving funding from the CPD, CANS persistently offered public criticism of Chicago policing. In 1996 the city canceled the $2.3 million program. Around 1998, according to the CPD's Beth Ford, the department began to employ its own full-time professional organizers to create block clubs. By 2013, of forty-nine civilian CAPS staff members, twenty-four were full-time organizers who went from door to door creating block clubs. They hoped to involve more residents in preventing crime, promoting public safety, and increasing "collective efficacy." This level of systematic professional organizing, unprecedented since the OCD's mobilization during World War II, made the CPD one of the largest organizers of block clubs in Chicago's history. In 2011, CAPS counted 463 registered clubs, with another 257 added by the middle of 2012. Lillie Davis, hired as a civilian organizer in Washington Heights because of her enthusiastic promotion of CAPS as an amateur, encapsulated the transformation of block clubs in Chicago: "Block clubs are no longer a social club for neighbors. It's a means of survival. It's a way to get drug houses and gangs off of a block. It's a way to determine crime problems and take care of them."[54]

As Davis suggested, CAPS-organized block clubs focused directly on violations of the law. Block club members told their beat liaisons of problems on their blocks. However, reporting on gangs and abandoned buildings sometimes drew unwanted attention to civilian activists. In December 1997, CAPS volunteer and block club captain Arnold Mireles was killed. An angry landlord whose buildings Mireles had targeted for court attention was convicted in his death along with two other men. Because of the danger dramatized by Mireles's murder, the CPD subsequently encouraged CAPS block clubs to demonstrate community solidarity without confronting criminals directly. When the Lakewood Balmoral Residents Council posted a photograph of gang tags on Facebook, it asked its members only to call the 311 city services phone number and "request to have tagging removed ASAP." Such low-risk activity was typical of twenty-first-century CAPS block clubs.[55]

The term "positive loitering" captured much of the activity that the CPD encouraged of CAPS block clubs. Originally, as suggested by the plans of the Magnolia Malden Block Club to gather at several Uptown intersections in 2011, positive loitering asserted to gang members, other residents, and passersby that public space belonged to everyone. In 1996 a police officer cited an early example of this approach without attaching the label "positive loitering" to it. He told a Chicago Lawn audience about some North Side residents who had been disturbed by public crime in their neighborhood:

> They ultimately formed a block club and set up a phone tree where if something suspicious was happening, one neighbor would call police then call another resident who would report the incident to the authorities. Eventually, when police would arrive on the block after being called, a large group of neighbors would come out of their homes to talk with the officers in a show of strength against the criminal elements. Those who were causing all of the disturbances did move out and never returned.[56]

Positive loitering grew up as an intentional civilian anticrime practice alongside CAPS. In a pre-CAPS effort to prevent gang members from gathering on the streets, in 1992 the Chicago City Council passed a general antiloitering ordinance. However, the law was written so capaciously that it did not pass constitutional muster; it was replaced in 2000 with an ordinance prohibiting loitering as part of criminal street gang activity. After the US Supreme Court ruled in 1999 that the Chicago police could not simply order small groups of loiterers to disperse, CAPS volunteers stepped into the breach. They publicly observed other people gathered on the street and assessed their motives. As the practice evolved, the positive loiterers sought to preempt crimes by staging public walks at prearranged times. They routinely notified police, and sometimes their alderman's office, of their plans ahead of time. Lynn Pierce, who has long been active in the Edgewater area, explained that when she and others engage in positive loitering, they are very careful never to confront those engaging in suspicious behavior. Instead, they always call the police at the 911 emergency telephone number, and then wait a block away to ensure that the troublemakers are dispersed. This classic form of positive loitering became especially prominent on Chicago's North Side in the early twenty-first century.[57]

The ethnographer Candice Rai offers a detailed analysis of a group of CAPS positive loiterers in the Uptown neighborhood. Uptown, historically the most ethnically and economically diverse portion of the North Side, has experienced a spike in housing prices in the twenty-first century. Rai interprets a positive loitering event that occurred in 2007 "within the context of gentrification and decades['] worth of heated contestation over competing visions of urban development in Uptown." Working with the police, a group of positive loiterers decided to focus on men who lingered outside a truck rental shop. The men were waiting for temporary work helping locals move their possessions. While they were not in violation of any laws as long as they remained within certain prescribed areas, their presence and behavior dismayed some residents. CAPS volunteers staged what Rai characterizes as a "passive-aggressive social control" effort to persuade the men to stop soliciting temporary employment. At a prearranged time, a group of positive loiterers, who "sipped Starbucks, pushed strollers, or came with leashed dogs in tow," gathered to confront the "negative loiterers." They admonished the men to "find a real job" and get help from a social worker. The CAPS liaison officer then directed all the loiterers to leave temporarily. Rai analyzes such interchanges as being part of the larger neoliberal project in which functions of the state have been devolved upon nongovernmental actors.[58]

Under CAPS, the term "positive loitering" has taken on a meaning much broader than the early attempts to reclaim the streets from gang members by staking out streetcorners. The term came to encompass a range of outdoor activities that block clubs used to assert their presence, and which occured beyond neighborhoods fractured by gentrification. In an oral history interview, CPD staff member Beth Ford described a block club's "smokeouts" as an example. Members of the block club barbecued meats on grill and cooked hot dogs in a turkey fryer as a way of signaling their claim to the street. Another popular tactic had a block's residents turning on their lawn sprinklers simultaneously. Sending smoke or water through the air made the street less congenial for loiterers without doing them any permanent damage. A 1996 letter to the editor recommending this approach explained, "As soon as all the people appeared with the sprinklers, the gang members left the neighbor-hood for the evening. The neighbors, pleased with the results of this action, decided to gather and sprinkle every Monday night." As a symbolic approach to reclaiming public space in a city on Lake Michigan, watering the lawn is irreproachable. The residents demonstrate their own responsibility and re-spectability while greening their yards, as the water gently implies that "nega-tive" loiterers might be more comfortable elsewhere.[59]

Positive loitering, whether organized through block clubs or through CAPS, cannot possibly turn the tide on Chicago crime. No one expects lo-cally organized volunteers who observe their neighbors and stand on the sidewalk to accomplish what decades of professional policing have not: elimi-nate the harm that urbanites inflict on one another. Instead, just as organized antigarbage campaigns encouraged extra municipal refuse collection, these eyes on the street help police determine how to allocate their resources. The CPD has embraced the organization of residents into block clubs as one strat-egy among many by which they hope to reduce crime. Chicagoans, for their part, appear to have embraced CAPS-organized block clubs as a way to push crime further away from their own homes, if they cannot hope to eliminate it altogether.

Conclusion

Civilian engagement in crime prevention implicated block clubs in law en-forcement policy. Scholars have identified the rise of a carceral state in the United States in the last third of the twentieth century—a government that imprisons large numbers of its citizens, many of them black. When they par-ticipate in CAPS-organized activities such as positive loitering, even block club members who consider themselves socially and racially liberal may find themselves connected to a system in which African Americans are dispro-portionately targeted for police attention and imprisonment.[60] It is similarly tempting to interpret the CPD's cultivation of block clubs as an example of the rise of the neoliberal city in the late twentieth century, as Candice Rai does in her work on positive loitering. Such an explanation understands the state—in this case, the city government—as offloading its proper responsibilities into private hands, where market forces selectively provide for the needs of the citizenry according to their position in the class structure. If block clubs, with their positive loitering and neighborhood watch programs, proactively try to reduce crime and then call in police officers when crimes occur, have they not in some important sense volunteered to become an unpaid arm of the government? Certainly, looking only at policing and only at the recent past makes this analysis appealing.

But viewed from the perspective of block clubs' histories, whose members have sought better protection from real and imagined crime for more than half a century, the story looks different. The CAPS program also represents the first time that the city government has tried systematically to create a partnership with Chicago's block clubs that is responsive to residents' daily concerns—not only about crime, but also about the broad range of quality-of-life issues that affect them. The CPD certainly is encouraging residents to assume responsibility for a policing function. But under the aegis of CAPS, twenty-first-century Chicago block clubs have a one-stop shop for pushing government agencies to do the jobs to which they are already theoretically committed. The problem, of course, is one that has consistently troubled Chicago's urban service provision: Only the squeaky wheel gets the grease. Universal distribution is impossible in a political environment with pressures to keep taxes down and the numbers of public employees low. Government services are unevenly distributed. Places where residents are organized into block clubs or other community groups can ask for attention, while other sections of the city—perhaps those in even greater need—will be left to further decay, with only the indifferent market to improve conditions. An alley-cleaning project can temporarily reduce the overall level of filth in the city, but evidence suggests that a block watch merely shifts criminals to nearby locations.

Preventing crime is one among many arenas of urban life that Chicago block club members have cared about for a century. In addition to regulating their neighbors' behavior, block club members have tried to improve their quality of life by removing garbage, beautifying local properties, and providing communal amenities. In pursuing many of their goals, block clubs have consistently bumped up against the edges of government responsibilities. In some cases it was clear to club participants that city government would never do what they wanted, even though it was formally part of the urban civic compact. So the club participants did it themselves. In other cases, active block clubs that demonstrated their members' concern for their surroundings were just enough to prompt public authorities to live up to their commitments. Through their involvement in CAPS, twenty-first-century block clubs found a collective middle ground between reliance on the state and dependence on individual initiative. Seen in the long view, their cooperation with the CPD was not a new phenomenon, but an extension of their basic role in the city: to prod authorities to improve Chicago, or to do it themselves.

Consider Neighboring

In the summer of 1964, Peggy Wireman reflected on her tenure as the block director for the HPKCC. She concluded that if differences of class and race were carefully managed, block clubs could help neighbors transcend their differences. She explained, "Block groups do help people to meet their neighbors and feel 'at home' on their blocks, but still leave them free to select their personal friends on whatever basis they wish. The distinction between good neighbor and good friend is necessary in a community with as much diversity as this one. There is more than one block in this community where the social distance is too great for them to meet in each others' homes co[m]fortably; yet in a public building they can discuss and solve their mutual problems."[1] In Hyde Park, neighbors did not always want to socialize privately, but if they cooperated they could accomplish mutual goals. Wireman understood that block clubs facilitated positive and productive neighborly relations without imposing additional social obligations. Residents could be neighbors without having to become friends.

When block club members set out to address local problems, they were always working at two levels. First, of course, they were trying to solve particular problems. They counteracted psychological isolation by throwing block parties. They built tot lots for children. They leveraged the power of city officials to clear out dangerous buildings. They instructed residents in how to behave in public. With concentrated effort, they could succeed at turning some problems, like vacant lots, into assets such as gardens. Against other problems, such as the gun violence crisis of the 2010s, they could only try to buffer themselves.[2] Second, at the same time as block club members worked together, they were also developing their relationships as neighbors.

Wireman's key insight was that neighboring is a distinctive human relationship. Being neighbors is different from being kin, spouses, coworkers, employee and employer, client and patron, or, as Wireman suggested, friends. Residential proximity makes strangers into neighbors. The implicit connection between neighbors is severed when one moves away. Neighbors do not choose each other as companions in the way that friends mutually consent to their affiliation. Neighbor is an impermanent status; neighboring is grounded in space.

Neighbors do not always agree on the implications of their relationship. Are renters and children neighbors in the same way that property-owning adults are? Must you greet your neighbors when you pass them on the street? Should adults correct the misbehavior of their young neighbors? What reciprocal obligations does neighboring provide? May your guests make a nuisance of themselves on your private porch, even if their behavior disturbs your neighbors' rest? Do you have to keep your front yard orderly to protect your neighbors' property values? Do former neighbors need to keep in touch? How far away can people live from each other and still count as neighbors? Must you treat all your neighbors with equal kindness and respect?

Such questions implicitly underpinned all block club programs. Participants acted on their shared assumption that neighboring imposes a mutual responsibility to improve environs. Not everyone who lived in the block clubs' territory agreed with this principle, however. Nor did their neighbors necessarily welcome their priorities for improvement. Some residents allowed their trash to spill out of cans into shared alleys, and their children to trample their neighbors' carefully tended flowerbeds. Gang members—who might be strangers or neighbors—carried weapons and dealt drugs on the streetcorners. Block club members spent much of their energy correcting deficits created by people they were stuck with as neighbors. Although club members shared a sense that neighboring meant they should improve their surroundings, their efforts consistently illuminated their neighbors' quite different beliefs and practices.

A small but healthy scholarly literature examines the social significance of the answers that informed block clubs. Such works analyze neighboring and especially its kindred concept, neighborhood. Social scientists in disciplines including archeology, criminology, geography, and sociology have weighed in on the role of neighborhood in urban life. Michael E. Smith's study of ancient neighborhoods, for example, explores how scholars have sorted city districts by size, ranging from the "home area" to the neighborhood to the "district." Margarethe Kusenbach proposes that urbanites experience four nested layers of local space, which she identifies as "microsettings, street blocks, walking distance neighborhoods, and enclaves." Robert Sampson's *Great American City* argues that city neighborhoods are not merely neutral platforms on which urbanites act on one another. Rather, by using multiple analytical methods, scholars can trace how structural forces, urbanites' actions, and neighborhoods themselves interact to create and sustain urban conditions. Historians are part of this conversation. Suleiman Osman unpacks the role of neighborhood in American politics in the 1970s. Benjamin Looker's *A Nation of Neighborhoods* dissects cultural representations of American neighborhoods in the postwar period.[3]

Some of this literature features *neighboring* as a phenomenon worth scrutinizing in its own right. Neighboring emerges as a positive subset of the analytical categories of community and neighborhood. Suzanne Keller, surveying secondary sociological literature in the 1960s, understood neighboring in largely appreciative terms. Neighboring's "manifest functions," she writes, "involve the exchange of moral and material aid, including tools, information, and advice, in times of minor and major crises." Its "latent functions" include exercising "reciprocal social control . . . to supply and spread information . . . [and] the creation and maintenance of social standards." Working from ethnographic research she conducted in Los Angeles, Kusenbach developed a typology of four kinds of neighborly interactions, which she described as "friendly recognition, parochial helpfulness, proactive intervention, and embracing and contesting diversity." Notably, these approaches consider neighboring in the same normative terms of mutual responsibility that animated block club members.[4]

It is tempting to imbue the word "neighbor" with a range of uplifting meanings that imply positive connection and mutual care. But neighbors do not always treat each other well, as Jan T. Gross's *Neighbors* unmistakably demonstrates. Gross unraveled the history of the July 10, 1941, pogrom in the village of Jebwabne, Poland. The Nazi occupation of Poland made it possible for the villagers to blame Germans for generations after the deaths. Gross argues that it was in fact gentile Polish men from Jebwabne who brutally massacred 1,600 of their Jewish neighbors that day, while German soldiers merely observed without interfering. Only seven of Jebwabne's Jews survived, protected by a handful of their neighbors. Those gentiles known to have sheltered Jews from the pogrom were permanently stigmatized by the rest of their neighbors.[5]

Gross's book unleashed anger, guilt, and controversy in Poland. His argument that ordinary Polish citizens committed mass murder shocked a population that preferred to lay responsibility for the Holocaust's atrocities on Nazi occupiers.[6] Gross's invocation of the word "neighbor" in the title and throughout the book rhetorically underscores the horror of his narrative.

Neighbors are supposed to at least tolerate one another, not kill each other because they belong to different groups. But just as sharing residential space prompts mutual obligations, it can also generate antagonisms and allow hostility to fester. Familial relationships are not always loving; they can be brutal. So too can neighbors be adversaries rather than allies.

It is important to acknowledge that neighborly relationships are not always good. Scholars of family and work have spent decades describing the tensions implicit in relationships that we might prefer to idealize. Although employers and employees are mutually dependent, workplaces are not always geared toward cooperative production. Families are not always little islands of harmony, or nations sites of patriotic unity. Scholars have not stopped using the terms family, work, and nation because we recognize them as imperfect and changing institutions. For example, cultural conservatives lament divorce, remarriage, and same-sex weddings as the end of the "traditional" American family. But scholars understand the decline of the two-parent, heterosexual, patriarchal family structure as the transformation of a form rather than its end. As a framework for thinking about how urban dwellers relate to one another, the word "neighbor" enjoys that same elasticity. In this way, the term "neighbor" offers a potential direction for scholarly analysis that its more famous cousin, "community," lacks.

How much community city dwellers experience is a founding question in urban studies. Writing in the nineteenth century, the sociologist Ferdinand Tönnies assumed that the sense of community common to small villages was dauntingly difficult to replicate in the complex, modern city. Since Tönnies, scholars of cities have argued that community sensibility is actually detectable, if not always common, in urban contexts. To cite just two examples from a vast field, Claude Fischer's network theory and Kenneth Scherzer's study of nineteenth-century Manhattan both model how scholars can trace community bonds among urban dwellers. But, as Tönnies suggested, modernization and urbanization seem to keep community continuously under siege. The historian Thomas Bender found that eight different studies of early America, spread out across almost 270 years, repeatedly discovered that community was disappearing. At the turn of the twenty-first century, the political scientist Robert Putnam breathed new life into scholarly discussions of community in *Bowling Alone*, with his analysis of "social capital." Putnam decried the generations of Americans growing up after World War II who spent less and less time engaged with and trusting other people. Community, it seems, is always in decline in comparison to a nostalgic past. Echoing Bender, Robert Sampson has called the propensity of scholars to search for community—only to regret its decline—"the ideology of community lament."[7]

The scholarly analysis of community has special resonance in Chicago. In the early twentieth century, leading sociologists at the University of Chicago understood cities as sharing a common model of development. To provide an empirical foundation for their theories, they drew a map of Chicago and divided it up into a set of distinct "community areas" bounded by fixed elements of the landscape such as railroads and viaducts. Because the US Census Bureau had not yet developed census tracts, these static community areas allowed scholars to track changes in social indicators such as mortality and poverty in defined areas of Chicago. The label "community areas" subtly feeds the notion of perpetual decline. It reinforces the sense that, regrettably, community itself is lost when social indicators trend negatively. Although the community areas mapped awkwardly onto Chicagoans' changing mental maps, almost a century later they remain in wide use by the media, real estate dealers, and city government. Competing maps, such as the popular series published by Big Stick, divide the city into more recognizable units that reflect Chicagoans' shifting notions of the boundaries of their neighborhoods.[8]

Thinking about how urban residents relate as neighbors—for both good and ill—turns our attention away from the well-worn question of the ascent or decline of community. Instead, we can examine how inhabitants actually related to one another and how their actions affected the city around them. Importantly, as the experience of Chicago block clubs suggests, the idea of neighbor is ideologically ambivalent in a way that community is not. Tönnies himself pointed out that "the expression bad Gemeinschaft (community) violates the meaning of the word."[9] Neither "good neighbor" nor "bad neighbor" is the default description; the term neighbor requires some descriptor to define the quality of the relationship. Block clubs enjoyed measures of both success and frustration as they pooled their energies. Because they were neighbors, they felt an obligation to correct local problems. But the problems they addressed were often ones created or exacerbated by other neighbors.

Understanding neighboring as an alternative framework to community allows urbanists to ask new questions about the shape of cities. How did cooperating (and conflicting) neighbors affect their surroundings? Can the strength of neighborly cooperation account for variations within city neighborhoods that are broadly affected by forces such as deindustrialization and municipal disinvestment? How did hostilities among neighbors, such as property-use disputes or gang turf wars, affect residents' quality of life and local attachments? To what extent did concern for the ground-level politics of the street extend outward to the formal political system? Did neighborly ties of affection influence the bonds of domestic life? Neighboring matters. We need to know what it affects and how it works.

When do urban residents invoke their sense of themselves as neighbors? How does the status of urbanites as neighbors articulate with the other social categories that inform and constrain their actions? Consider a black woman renting an apartment in a two-flat on a street where drug dealers conduct operations. Should she call the police, work with her block club to mute their effects, or do nothing? Recognizing one drug dealer as the child of a neighbor whose goodwill she values, she may ignore him. She might aspire to buy the building where she lives, and hope to preserve its value. Perhaps she hopes to keep her elderly neighbors from being trapped in their homes by crossfire. If she calls the police, she risks being singled out as a "snitch," a term that evokes the taint of the "race traitor." Yet she might want to protect her own young son from the lure of the drug trade. Thinking about how city dwellers activate their sense of neighborly responsibility and hostility can help us parse the complex decisions that they make about what urban forces to surrender to, and which to confront.

Thinking about neighbors as urban actors can also shift how historians narrate the past. Since their field's emergence in the late 1960s, urban historians have firmly established that American cities have been unevenly developed by the twin forces of capitalism and the state, as modulated by racial segregation.[10] Less clear, however, is what explains the variations within that development—why government officials and capitalists decided where to channel their resources, and which areas to neglect. This book has shown that as intermediaries between the urban landscape and the resource holders, block club members influenced which places received what aid.[11] Acting collectively as neighbors, urbanites helped define which problems needed attention and which stood out as insoluble. More broadly, neighbors set the day-to-day terms for each other's experiences of urban life by shaping their immediate physical, psychological, and social environments. For example, white urbanites who understood neighboring through a racial lens shaped segregation in cities and suburbs. City dwellers were subject to structural and political forces beyond their direct control, but they did not lack power over each other.

As neighborhoods emerge as a focus of scholarly analysis, the time is also ripe to examine neighboring as an urban practice. In block clubs, small groups of neighbors addressed a broad array of local concerns. Discovering how urbanites dealt with ephemeral but persistently recurring nuisances requires archival sleuthing. The historian Emily Thompson's website The Roaring Twenties, for example, cleverly unpacks the "soundscape" of the early-twentieth-century city by using noise complaints that New Yorkers filed with their Department of Health.[12] If they still exist and are made publicly available for research, parallel records from government departments in Chicago like the Mayor's Office of Inquiry and Information or the CPD's CAPS beat meetings might similarly illuminate what problems bothered Chicagoans on a daily basis. Because Chicagoans so often turned to block clubs, we are able to learn about how they tried to remedy local problems. They worked together privately and sought the attention of city agencies. In the process of forming organizations, discussing their troubles, taking action, and celebrating their successes, block club members dealt with each other—and with troublemakers—as neighbors.

Block clubs could not solve all of their members' problems. Many of those problems, such as crime, were simply too large for them to handle on their own. Other endlessly recurring products of human inhabitation, such as garbage, required perpetual vigilance. The scale of a problem or its source, however, did not determine how significant it was to the people who lived with it every day. In many cases, a block club's most effective approach was to craft a temporary remedy or move it elsewhere—to people who were far enough away to perhaps not count as neighbors. Although their strategies did not always work, for more than a century Chicago block clubs kept trying. And at their best, they hoped to turn bad neighbors into good neighbors.

Researching Block Clubs

Because block clubs are a new topic for historians, this appendix describes the research path underpinning this book. Two decades of teaching and conducting research alongside social scientists have convinced me of the merits of their methodological transparency. The scholarship of historians, whose approaches to research are often veiled by narrative and relegated to footnotes, should include this kind of discussion. Quantitative historians are accustomed to describing their research methods, but qualitative historians usually are not.[1] In this spirit, I offer the following description of this book's research trajectory.

As I developed this project, I looked where the light was good, using sources that I had found in previous work or that my intuition suggested would be fruitful. Anthropologists, criminologists, political scientists, psychologists, sociologists, and scholars of social work have mentioned block clubs in their studies. Unfortunately, their research methods do not routinely produce the kind of documentation that historians can take advantage of, except through the reporting in their published studies. However, Chicago enjoys an embarrassment of archival riches. Because of this intellectual wealth, it is possible that I have overlooked useful sources that other researchers should tap. Scholars interested in Chicago block clubs may want to revisit the sources cited here, or to search out material in repositories where I did not think to look. Researchers focused on block clubs in other cities may read this narrative as a series of suggestions for the kinds of primary sources that might exist elsewhere.

This book has its genesis in other research projects. Early in the process of researching my dissertation in the 1990s and the book it became, I stumbled across materials about block clubs. They seemed interesting and relevant to what I was working on. As a Chicagoan I knew a little about what they were. I took some notes. As I pursued that project, block clubs kept popping up, so I kept taking notes. Around 2003 or 2004, it occurred to me that I had enough material to write something focused on block clubs, so I began to look for primary sources more systematically.

As it turned out, deliberately locating materials about block clubs felt harder than finding them by accident. Because there was almost no historical scholarship on block clubs, I could not follow someone else's trail of footnotes back into the archives. The only dedicated historical scholarship about block clubs that I have been able to locate—a book chapter and an article by Sylvia Hood Washington—relied exclusively on the records of the Chicago Urban League, material with which I was already familiar.[2] As I looked back over the kinds of collections where I had serendipitously learned about block clubs, I realized that if I had begun my research by looking for sources about them, I might not have found them in the first place.

Because block clubs simply have not been a subject of concentrated study, archival records are not usually organized in ways that draw researchers' attention to their presence in a collection. For example, one of the first primary sources from which I learned about block clubs was the records of the Greater Lawndale Conservation Commission, held by the Chicago History Museum. The GLCC was created to attract urban renewal funding for local improvement, an effort that the collection's finding aid emphasizes. However, the GLCC's monthly newsletter, News Notes, included regular activity reports from block clubs in the area. Because the collection is organized chronologically, the only way in which I could have efficiently identified, perused, and understood the significance of those newsletters was by doing what I had originally done— reading through the collection in a linear fashion to understand the larger context. It was fortunate that an existing dissertation about the GLCC also interpreted the relationship between North Lawndale's block clubs and the organization,[3] so that when I read the monthly column in the News Notes I knew that they represented something more than insignificant reports about parties and flower planting.

Materials on block clubs are often hidden, scattered into larger collections, with scant mention of them even in well prepared finding aids. The papers of the Chicago Urban League, for example, were reorganized and reprocessed between my first consultations with them at the Richard J. Daley Library at the University of Illinois at Chicago in the late 1990s and my systematic return to this project in the early 2010s. Although I considered block clubs a focused topic of interest, the materials that documented them were separated into different series within this enormous collection. Most of the folders that have "block club" in the title—and which therefore are relatively easily located with a digital search of the finding aid—ended up in series II, which focused on programs. But only a researcher who knows that in the 1950s the Chicago Urban League encouraged the organization of block clubs into neighborhood-level "improvement councils" might also think to look for those headers, some of which are housed into series I, focusing on administrative files. Finding materials about block clubs in archival collections organized around other topics therefore presents a research catch-22: before you know what to look for in a collection, you must understand the collection's contents well enough to know what to look for in them. Researchers seeking evidence about block clubs in collections that are not primarily about block clubs should therefore plan to use finding aids iteratively. You should circle back to the finding aid as your understanding grows, so that you can pick up hints of nomenclature and organization you might not have recognized on your first pass.

Materials about block clubs lurk in many kinds of archival records, even if they are not flagged in collection names and finding aids. Because block clubs were often networked with each other through larger community and civic organizations, those groups' records may contain materials about efforts to organize them, minutes from their meetings, and ephemera such as announcement flyers. For example, the Northwest Community Organization Collection, whose records at the Chicago History Museum are unfortunately now sealed, reflects the group's efforts to encourage local block clubs. Collections that focus on particular neighborhoods also sometimes contain traces of block club activity among their civic organization records. Important evidence about block clubs in Austin, for example, is maintained in records about the Organization for a Better Austin (OBA), which can be studied through sources housed in the Austin Community Collection of the Chicago Public Library's Special Collections. Archives of activists and careful observers of urban life also sometimes collect materials about block clubs that researchers can harvest. The papers of Faith Rich, also held by the Chicago Public Library, provided one of the richest sources of material for this book. Newspaper clippings files that libraries maintain are also a rich source of concentrated, specialized information. I found it easiest to learn about the Southwest Associated Block Clubs (SWABC) in the clipping files about Father Francis X. Lawlor maintained at the Chicago History Museum. The last portion of this appendix lists the archival collections that contain materials about block clubs, in order to give future researchers in Chicago and other places a sense of the kinds of records in which they might profitably conduct their searches.

Happily, finding information about block clubs in old newspapers has gotten substantially easier since I first started paying attention to them. An early source that taught me about block clubs was the *Garfieldian*, a weekly neighborhood newspaper that served the West Garfield Park community area between the 1920s and the 1960s. As I read through a twenty-year span of hard copies owned by the Chicago Public Library, I found lots of information about block clubs. Since that time, the *Garfieldian* has been digitized by NewspaperArchive, a service to which many libraries subscribe, but the digital files only cover the years 1935–48 and 1967–68. Complete runs of the *Chicago Tribune* and the *Chicago Defender*, both important primary sources, have been digitized by ProQuest Historical Newspapers. A manual search of microfilm versions of these dense daily newspapers would have been a very inefficient and time-consuming process. But by the time I was preparing this book manuscript, I could deploy graduate research assistants to conduct targeted searches in these newspapers (rather than read them page by page) for relevant material.

As this discussion suggests, information about block clubs is not only scattered; it is fragmentary. Only the papers of Faith Rich offer a sustained look over time at a single (and atypically active) block club; the minutes of the Hermitage-Wood Block Club and the records of the Very Good Club, though they cover a shorter period during World War II, offer rare complete coverage of two groups' efforts. Much of the analytical labor for this book involved stitching together small bits of evidence from such divergent sources and understanding how they were connected. Because this is a qualitative project whose research was not conducted in a systematic fashion, I do not try to offer estimates of how many block clubs have existed in Chicago over time. Nor do I assert that they were concentrated in some neighborhoods and not in others; mapping the data I have collected in such an idiosyncratic fashion might well be misleading. When I began to think about this project as a book rather than an article, I attempted to organize my notes on a spreadsheet so that I could count the number of different clubs I had identified; at that point, the number was well over four hundred. I feel confident that this final project rests on information drawn from more than one thousand different Chicago block clubs. But because I have not yet created a professionally acceptable database, I have not included this information in this book's formal analysis. Future researchers who are interested in estimating more accurately the extent to which block clubs cover Chicago may wish to begin with the dataset of the Project on Human Development in Chicago Neighborhoods (PHDCN). A large-scale project featured in Robert J. Sampson's *Great American City*, the PHDCN includes a questionnaire administered across Chicago that asks several questions about respondents' awareness of and participation in block clubs. Because block clubs come into and out of existence so quickly, however, a snapshot of any one moment may be misleading.[4]

Researchers interested in Chicago block clubs may wish to consult the following archival collections. Additional primary sources, such as the newspapers mentioned above and other published materials and clipping files, are not listed here. Readers are referred to the notes for detailed references.

ABC News, Chicago History Museum

Annetta M. Dieckmann papers, Richard J. Daley Library, University of Illinois at Chicago[5]

Austin Community Collection, Harold Washington Public Library

Austin Newspapers Collection, Harold Washington Public Library

Chicago Area Project records, Chicago History Museum

Chicago Regional Office Files, American Friends Service Committee Archives, Philadelphia, PA

Chicago Urban League records, Richard J. Daley Library, University of Illinois at Chicago

Christopher B. Cohen papers, Richard J. Daley Library, University of Illinois at Chicago

Greater Lawndale Conservation Commission records, Chicago History Museum

Greater Lawndale Conservation Commission records, Richard J. Daley Library, University of Illinois at Chicago

Faith Rich Collection, Harold Washington Public Library

Hyde Park–Kenwood Community Conference records, Regenstein Library, University of Chicago

Industrial Areas Foundation records, Richard J. Daley Library, University of Illinois at Chicago

Lincoln Central Neighborhood Association records, DePaul University Library

Lincoln Park Conservation Association records, Chicago History Museum

Marillac House records, Chicago History Museum

Mary Ann Smith papers, Women and Leadership Archives, Loyola University Chicago

Monsignor John Egan papers, Hesburgh Library, Notre Dame University

Near West Side Community Committee records, Richard J. Daley Library, University of Illinois at Chicago

Northwest Community Organization records, Chicago History Museum

Office of Civilian Defense records, Harold Washington Public Library

Old Town Triangle Association records, DePaul University Library

Sheffield Neighborhood Association records, DePaul University Library

Small Collections, Expansion Collections, Chicago History Museum

The Woodlawn Organization records, Chicago History Museum

Thomas A. Gaudette papers, William H. Hannon Library, Loyola Marymount
    University
Uptown Chicago Commission records, Chicago History Museum
Very Good Club records, Chicago History Museum
Washington Heights Community Organization Archives, Vivian G. Harsh Re-
    search Collection, Woodson Regional Library, Chicago Public Library
Welfare Council of Metropolitan Chicago records, Chicago History Museum
Woodlawn Block Club Council Records, Harold Washington Public Library
Woodlawn Social Services Center records, University of Chicago Library

Two other kinds of research supplemented the fragmented archival materials about block clubs. First, I conducted selected oral history interviews. Because block clubs remain so common in Chicago, this approach holds great
promise for both contemporary and historical research. Second, Internet
search engines make finding online materials about block clubs easy. I took
advantage of Google's tools in three different ways. First, I set up a Google
news alert for new postings about block clubs. Interestingly, most of the material that came to me in this manner was about Buffalo, New York. Second,
I periodically conducted keyword searches for information about block clubs.
In some circumstances I used Google's search engine to locate particular websites such as those maintained by municipal governments. Finally, Google's
Street View function was also very helpful for visualizing the context in
which Chicago's block club members acted. The Internet Archive's Wayback
Machine was indispensable for visualizing websites that have disappeared.

Close readers of this book may have noticed that there are other kinds of
evidence I have not consulted. Although in recent years the city of Chicago
has made a great deal of information available online, the operations of its
municipal government are not transparent. Records of the city government's
inner workings in the past are similarly inaccessible. If Chicago should ever
make available records from units such as the Mayor's Office of Inquiry and
Information, the Chicago Police Department (CPD), or the Building Department, these might prove to be a treasure trove of information about block
clubs (and other topics of historical interest). CPD annual reports, archived
online at ChicagoCop.com and in hard copy at the Municipal Reference Collection at the Harold Washington Library Center, do not enable statistical
tracking of their organization of block clubs. In other cities with better records
of municipal government activity, however, block clubs' requests for assistance
may have been preserved for public inspection. Researchers might also look
to federal records to further illuminate the history of block clubs. The most
promising initial directions are probably through explorations of the World

War II period records of the Office of Civilian Defense (OCD) and the records of Great Society's War on Poverty, when the federal government cultivated direct ties with urban communities.

This appendix is meant to be suggestive of possible research paths, rather than definitive. I hope that other researchers intent on expanding our understanding of block clubs will discover new sources of information about block clubs and publish their findings. I encourage scholars of block clubs to contact me by e-mail.

Block Club Rules and Regulations

This appendix provides lists of rules and regulations developed by several Chicago block clubs, as discussed in chapter 6. They are presented here in their entirety so that readers can review the language the block clubs used to regulate themselves and their neighbors.

Rules and Regulations Governing 4100 Block West Grenshaw, 1960[1]

1. No washing or repairing of cars (except flats) on the streets in this block at any time.
2. No throwing of litter on the streets or alleys (pile neatly for collection).
3. No burning of garbage in containers or cans in alleys.
4. Do not let your children play on other people's property.
5. Do not allow loud talking or congregating of adults or teenagers in front of your residence.
6. Do not appear on the streets or on front porches improperly dressed, or hang feet out of windows or over porch rails eating watermelons, etc.
7. No drinking of intoxicating beverages in parked cars.
8. No dirty halls, stairs, garbage outside of containers, dirty front and back yards.
9. No noisy parties, playing loud radio or T.V. after 11 p.m.

"The Making of Good Citizenship and Neighborly Conduct," Progressive Twin Block Club, 1962[2]

Real Estate

1. *Property*: Property and real estate value depends upon the group and not the individual home appearance of the neighborhood. Thus, it is

mandatory that every property owner and tenant see that the property is kept up to standards provided by the laws of our city.

2. *Safety*: No property is to be allowed to become so sub-standard as to create a hazard to tenants or neighbors.

3. *Appearance*: Each building should be such as to instill pride in the owner, the tenants and neighbors.

    (1) Lawns should be sown and properly cared for.

    (2) Where vacant property exits, it shall be up to the neighbors to come to some agreement on its care.

4. *Health*: Each property owner should provide enough refuse containers with covers, for his building and tenants, to prevent refuse being spilled, uncovered into the alley.

    (1) Containers should be painted.

    (2) Rodent Control:

    (a) It shall be the duty of each resident to report to the designated authorities if rodents are seen.

    (3) Pest Control:

    (a) To join with our neighbors or tenants in any plan to rid our neighborhood of pests.

5. *Hardship*: Each neighbor or group of neighbors should be willing to donate some time and labor to what he or she is best qualified to do, to assist.

Children

1. It shall be the responsibility of each parent to see that the conduct of his or her child or children is such that it does not interfere with the rights and property of their neighbors; and, to assume all responsibility for payment of adjustment for losses to property of neighbor or landlord, caused by acts of their child or children.

    A. All small children, for their own safety, should be kept in backyards and off streets and sidewalks unless supervised by an adult.

    B. All curfews to be observed by teenagers as follows:

    (a) Boys and Girls under age 17—curfew time
    Sunday thru Thursday 10:30 PM
    Saturday and Sunday *only* 11:30 PM

    C. *All* acts of vandalism to be reported to the Juvenile Officer, Chicago Police Department—phone PO-5-1313. Promptness in reporting such acts is most essential.

    D. All non-residents and loiterers to be reported to the police at once! Call PO-5-1313 for quick investigation.

Autos

1. All autos, assumed to be abandoned, must be reported to the Police.

2. No car with mechanical trouble which requires it to be hoisted up for major repairs, shall be repaired on the street.
3. It shall be assumed the right of each neighbor to park his auto in front of his respective property.
4. No neighbor, or his guests, should park in a manner which would make it impossible for a fellow neighbor to enter or leave his garage.
5. All autos should be washed in the garage or in the alley.

Snow Removal

1. All property owners to be responsible for the removal of snow and ice from their property and the public sidewalk in front of such property.

Noise And Pets

1. All noise shall be kept to a minimum.
2. No television, radio, Hi-Fi, etc., should be played so loud that it disturbs the neighbors.
3. All guests should be cautioned against loud conversation when leaving, so as not to awaken the neighbors.
4. All guests should be cautioned against blowing auto horns to pick up a rider.
5. All dogs shall be walked on a leash, and not permitted to stop on the lawns of the neighbors, or in back of garages, back gate openings.
6. All commercial vehicles, equipped with sound, should be cautioned to turn off sound when entering neighborhood after 9:00 PM

4600–4700 Monroe Block Club, Rules Proposed for Adoption, 1966[3]

no washing/fixing cars in front of homes
no moving through front entrances
pick up trash from front and back
cut lawns and sweep sidewalks
remove snow
no large gathering or drinking
do not play records and radios "to the extreme"
no ball playing or jumping rope in front of houses
no writing on sidewalks
no running on someone else's lawn
no knotted curtains flying out of windows
no penny tossing in front of someone else's home
no bike riding on sidewalk by bigger kids

2100 South Lawndale Block Club, Undated[4]

We need your wholehearted cooperation in order that we may have a clean and respectable block. Please wrap up all garbage and place in garbage cans. Landlords please supply all tenants with garbage and trash containers. Repair all doors and windows before cold weather arrives. Parents tell your children not to eat in hallways. Teach your children to eat at tables. We want no writing on walls and buildings. Respect other people's property. Don't break glass in streets and sidewalks. Please cooperate in keeping your block clean.

Drexel Square, Undated[5]

These Are Our Aims:
1. To welcome new neighbors into the community and to acquaint them with community standards.
2. To meet and discuss neighborhood problems.
3. To prevent conditions that endanger physical and moral well-being of our neighbors and their children.
4. To encourage the care and maintenance of lawns and flower gardens and the proper maintenance of public and private property in the neighborhood.
5. To encourage the enforcement of housing standards as set by the Chicago Municipal Code in regard to:
   a. Building specifications and repairs,
   b. Water supply and facilities,
   c. Sanitation and health,
   d. Fire protections and heating.
6. To secure adequate police protection and street lighting.

We Insist On . . .
1. Elimination [of] overnight or prolonged parking of trucks on our street.
2. Having commercial deliveries to rear or side entrances.
3. Eliminating the public display of crude signs from buildings.
4. Eliminating the careless dropping of trash in sidewalks, streets and in alleys.
5. Regular and proper disposal of garbage
6. The removal of debris from premises where cars may be washed or cleaned.

Hi Neighbors![6]

We the residents on the 7300 block of Rhodes Avenue are striving to maintain certain standards in the Block. Please cooperate with us by complying with the following Regulations.

1. Lets [*sic*] keep lawns clean—leaving no cans or bottles about.
2. Why not use rear entrance for moving or any large objects.
3. Ask that your goods be delivered in rear.
4. All washing and polishing of cars should be done in our Alleys or Garage. Lets [*sic*] not wash them on the streets.
5. It is safer for children to play in the yard, not on the walk and in the street.
6. Ask your Cab or Ride to ring your bell and please not to Honk and wake a neighbor who works nights and has just dozed off.
7. No trucks, or immoveable cars left on the streets.
8. Please keep your voice, T.V. and Radio at a moderate tone for your pleasure.
9. It is safer to leave that Vestibule light on all night and stay on the alert.
10. Provide proper containers for garbage.
11. Lets [*sic*] air our dogs, but respect our neighbors [*sic*] premises as we do our own. (Cleanliness is next to Godliness.)

Notes

Introduction

1. Letter, Pearlie Mae Robinson, president, and Faith Rich, secretary, West 15th Place Block Club, October 1, 1985, to Mayor Washington, folder 18, box 10; holiday letter, 1973, Ted and Faith Rich, folder 5, box 20; letter, Faith to Nikki, June 9, 1968, folder 3, box 20; letter, Faith to Rhoda, November 27, 1974, folder 10, box 18; "Delicious Asparagus from Kedzie Garden," *West 15th Place Block Club Newsletter* no. 45, May 1976, folder 4, box 9, all in Faith Rich papers, Special Collections and Preservation Division, Harold Washington Library Center, Chicago Public Library (hereafter Rich papers). Note: This collection was processed between the time when I first consulted the papers in the late 1990s and the time when I returned to them to research this book. With the help of librarians Morag Walsh and Roslyn Mabry, I was able to relocate many of the materials, but I was unable to find all of them. In these notes, whenever a document could not be relocated, I provide its location in the collection when it was unprocessed.

2. Letter, Faith to Rhoda, May 18, 1974, folder 10, box 18; "The Men Take To Gardening," West 15th Place Block Club newsletter no. 26, May 1974, box 18, folder 9; letter, Pearlie Mae Robinson, president, and Faith Rich, secretary, West 15th Place Block Club, October 1, 1985, to Mayor Washington, folder 18, box 10; letter, Faith to Rhoda, January 28, 1977, folder 1, box 19; "Delicious Asparagus from Kedzie Garden," *West 15th Place Block Club Newsletter* no. 45, May 1976, folder 4, box 9; letter, Faith Rich and Pearlie Mae Robinson to Honorable R. Cardiss Collins, March 3, 1986, folder 5, box 9; letter, Faith to Rhoda, November 27, 1974, folder 10, box 18; letter, Faith to Andrea, August 17, 1969, folder 6, box 18, all in Rich papers.

3. Akron: Mohan L. Kaul, "Serving Oppressed Communities: The Self-Help Approach," *Journal of Sociology & Social Welfare* 12, no. 1 (March 1985): 205–19. Buffalo: Eyal Press, "Can Block Clubs Block Despair?," *American Prospect* online, May 16, 2007, http://prospect.org/article/can -block-clubs-block-despair, last accessed June 1, 2014; Cassi Ann Meyerhoffer, "Who's Doing What? Gender and Neighborhood Organizing through Block Clubs in Buffalo, NY" (MA thesis, State University of New York at Buffalo, 2006). Judging by the flow of articles from my Google news feed, block clubs are either especially active in Buffalo or local news media are especially attuned to reporting on their activities. Cincinnati: Patricia Mooney Melvin, *The Organic City: Urban Definition and Community Organization, 1880–1920* (Lexington: University Press of Kentucky, 1987). Cleveland: James Borchert, "Visual Landscapes of a Streetcar Suburb," in *Understanding*

Ordinary Landscapes, edited by Paul Groth and Todd W. Bressi (New Haven and London: Yale University Press, 1997), 38; Randy Cunningham, *Democratizing Cleveland: The Rise and Fall of Community Organizing in Cleveland* (Cleveland: Arambala Press and the Michael Schwartz Library at Cleveland State University, 2007), 36–45, 109, http://engagedscholarship.csuohio.edu /clevmembks/17/, last accessed March 9, 2015. Detroit: Heather Ann Thompson, *Whose Detroit? Politics, Labor, and Race in a Modern American City* (Ithaca, NY: Cornell University Press, 2001), 73; Amy Maria Kenyon, *Dreaming Suburbia: Detroit and the Production of Postwar Space and Culture* (Detroit: Wayne State University Press, 2004), 160; George Henderson "Twelfth Street: An Analysis of a Changed Neighborhood," *Phylon* 25 (1964): 91. Kansas City: Mary Ohmer and Elizabeth Beck, "Citizen Participation in Neighborhood Organizations in Poor Communities and Its Relationship to Neighborhood and Organizational Collective Efficacy," *Journal of Sociology and Social Welfare* 33 (1) (March 2006): 195, citing Kansas City Local Initiatives Support Corporation [LISC] (n.d.), "Kansas City Building Blocks: An Approach to Building Physical and Social Capital in Neighborhoods." Los Angeles: Erin Aubry Kaplan, "Hardy Party: Thoughts on an Inglewood Block Party," August 23, 2012, KCET, http://www.kcet.org/updaily/socal_focus /commentary/hardy-party.html, last accessed January 7, 2015. Milwaukee: Records of the Sherman Park Community Association and the West End Community Association, both held by the Archives Department, Golda Meir Library, University of Wisconsin–Milwaukee. Minneapolis: Wesley G. Skogan and Susan M. Hartnett, *Community Policing, Chicago Style* (New York and Oxford: Oxford University Press, 1997), 75. Nashville: Richard C. Rich and Abraham Wandersman, "Participation in Block Organizations," *Social Policy* 14 (12) (1983): 45–47; Abraham Wandersman, Paul Florin, David Chavis, Rich Richard, and John Prestby, "Getting Together and Getting Things Done," *Psychology Today* (November 1985): 64–71. New York City: Roger Sanjek, *The Future of Us All: Race and Neighborhood Politics in New York City* (Ithaca, NY: Cornell University Press, 1998), passim, see map on 264; Wendell Pritchett, *Brownsville, Brooklyn: Blacks, Jews, and the Changing Face of the Ghetto* (Chicago: University of Chicago Press, 2002), 202–3; Rosalyn Baxandall and Elizabeth Ewen, *Picture Windows: How the Suburbs Happened* (New York: Basic Books, 2000), 201–2; Susanne M. Tumelty, "Block Associations, Crime, and the Police," (PhD diss., City University of New York, 1987); Douglas Yatkes, *Neighborhood Democracy* (Lexington, MA: Lexington Books, 1973), 35–39. Philadelphia: Abigail Perkiss, *Making Good Neighbors: Civil Rights, Liberalism, and Integration in Postwar Philadelphia* (Ithaca, NY, and London: Cornell University Press, 2014), 130–31 and 140. Pittsburgh: Arthur J. Edmunds, *Daybreakers: The Story of the Urban League of Pittsburgh, The First Sixty-Five Years* (Pittsburgh: Urban League of Pittsburgh, 1983), 42 and 53. St. Louis: Priscilla A. Dowden-White, *Groping toward Democracy: African American Social Welfare Reform in St. Louis, 1910–1949* (Columbia and London: University of Missouri Press, 2011), chapter 6. St. Paul: Deborah G. Martin, "'Place-Framing' as Place-Making: Constituting a Neighborhood for Organizing and Activism," *Annals of the Association of American Geographers* (2003) 93(3): 730–50, http://www.jstor.org/stable/1515505, and Deborah G. Martin, "Constructing the 'Neighborhood Sphere': Gender and Community Organizing," *Gender, Place and Culture* 9 (4) (2002): 333–50, DOI:10.1080/0966369022000024678. Suburban New Jersey: S. Mitra Kalita, *Suburban Sahibs: Three Immigrant Families and Their Passage from India to America* (New Brunswick, NJ: Rutgers University Press, 2003), 144.

4. Annabelle Bender, "Civilian Defense Block Organization in Hyde Park" (MA thesis, University of Chicago, 1943), 2–4. In the absence of a centralized registration such as one that a government agency might keep, it is difficult to count the number of block clubs at any one time. Delmos J. Jones and Susanne M. Tumelty discussed the problem of counting New York

City block associations in "Are There Really 10,000 Block Associations in New York City?" *Social Policy* (Fall 1986); reprinted in Tumelty, "Block Associations, Crime, and the Police," 93–94.

5. Concepts in Community [O]rganization, folder 2282, box 233, Chicago Urban League records, Special Collections and University Archives Department, Richard J. Daley Library, University of Illinois at Chicago (hereafter Chicago Urban League records).

6. Julia Abrahamson, *A Neighborhood Finds Itself* (New York: Harper & Brothers, Publishers, 1959), passim, especially 23–26 and 34–35.

7. Chicago Urban League, Report for 1951, folder 23, box 1, Chicago Urban League records.

8. Maria Kefalas, *Working-Class Heroes: Protecting Home, Community, and Nation in a Chicago Neighborhood* (Berkeley: University of California Press, 2003), 59–61; Patrick J. Carr, *Clean Streets: Controlling Crime, Maintaining Order, and Building Community Activism* (New York and London: New York University Press, 2005), 64.

9. Evan McKenzie, *Privatopia: Homeowner Associations and the Rise of Residential Private Government* (New Haven: Yale University Press, 1994) and Evan McKenzie, *Beyond Privatopia: Rethinking Residential Private Government* (Washington: Urban Institute Press, 2011), 2.

10. Jane Addams, *Twenty Years at Hull-House, with Autobiographical Notes* (New York: Macmillan, 1910); John Hall Fish, *Black Power/White Control; The Struggle of The Woodlawn Organization in Chicago* (Princeton, NJ: Princeton University Press, 1973); John Hall Fish et al., *The Edge of the Ghetto: A Study of Church Involvement in Community Organization* (New York: Seabury Press, 1968); Sanford D. Horwitt, *Let Them Call Me Rebel: Saul Alinsky, His Life and Legacy* (New York: Knopf, 1989); Thomas J. Jablonsky, *Pride in the Jungle: Community and Everyday Life in Back of the Yards Chicago* (Baltimore: Johns Hopkins University Press, 1993); Peg Knoepfle, *After Alinsky: Community Organizing in Illinois* (Springfield, IL: Sangamon State University, 1990); Zorita Mikva, "The Neighborhood Improvement Association: A Counter-Force to the Expansion of Chicago's Negro Population" (MA thesis: University of Chicago, 1951); Robert A. Slayton, *Back of the Yards: The Making of a Local Democracy* (Chicago: University of Chicago Press, 1986). On the future president's sojourn as a Chicago community organizer, see Barack Obama, *Dreams from My Father: A Story of Race and Inheritance* (New York: Times Books, 1995), part II.

11. Anne Meis Knupfer, *The Chicago Black Renaissance and Women's Activism* (Urbana and Chicago: University of Illinois Press, 2006), 31. Jeffrey Helgeson makes a related argument about the importance of black women's organizing to Chicago politics in *Crucibles of Black Empowerment: Chicago's Neighborhood Politics from the New Deal to Harold Washington* (Chicago: University of Chicago Press, 2014).

12. A large scholarly literature explores these transformations. Good starting points include Peter C. Baldwin, *Domesticating the Street: The Reform of Public Space in Hartford, 1850–1930* (Columbus: Ohio State University Press, 1999); Richard Harris, *Unplanned Suburbs: Toronto's American Tragedy, 1900 to 1950* (Baltimore: Johns Hopkins University Press, 1996); Ann Durkin Keating, *Building Chicago: Suburban Developers and the Creation of a Divided Metropolis* (Columbus: Ohio State University Press, 1988); and Becky M. Nicolaides, *My Blue Heaven: Life and Politics in the Working-Class Suburbs of Los Angeles, 1920–1965* (Chicago: University of Chicago Press, 2002).

13. Elaine Lewinnek, *The Working Man's Reward: Chicago's Early Suburbs and the Roots of American Sprawl* (Oxford and New York: Oxford University Press, 2014), 172; Carl H. Nightingale, *Segregation: A Global History of Divided Cities* (Chicago: University of Chicago Press, 2012), 96.

14. Elaine Lewinnek, "Better than a Bank for a Poor Man?: Home Financing Strategies in Early Chicago," *Journal of Urban History* 32 (2006): 274–301. See also Margaret Garb, *City of American Dreams: A History of Home Ownership and Housing Reform in Chicago, 1871–1919* (Chicago: University of Chicago Press, 2005).

15. On tenants' claims that they had the right to set a local agenda, see Jared N. Day, *Urban Castles: Tenement Housing and Landlord Activism in New York City, 1890–1943* (New York: Columbia University Press, 1999); and Roberta Gold, *When Tenants Claimed the City: The Struggle for Citizenship in New York City Housing* (Urbana: University of Illinois Press, 2014).

16. John R. Logan and Harvey L. Molotch, *Urban Fortunes: The Political Economy of Place* (Berkeley: University of California Press, 1987), 1–2 and 99. See also Nicolaides, *My Blue Heaven*, 29, for a concrete example of their approach at work in the context of a Los Angeles suburb.

17. Evelyn Brooks Higginbotham, *Righteous Discontent: The Women's Movement in the Black Baptist Church, 1880–1920* (Cambridge, MA: Harvard University Press, 1993); Victoria W. Wolcott, *Remaking Respectability: African American Women in Interwar Detroit* (Chapel Hill: University of North Carolina Press, 2001), 38.

18. Clipping, George N. Schmidt, "Faith," *Chicago Reader*, August 5, 1983, folder 1, box 38, Rich papers; Faith Baldwin Rich, "The Activities of C. Asinius Pollio, 42–38 B. C. and Their Connection with the Eighth and Fourth Eclogues of Vergil" (PhD diss., Bryn Mawr College, 1944). For more about the history of North Lawndale and an overview of racial change there, see Amanda I. Seligman, *Block by Block: Neighborhoods and Public Policy on Chicago's West Side* (Chicago: University of Chicago Press, 2005), 19–22 and 30–37.

19. Major historically oriented works in the field include Robert Fisher, *Let the People Decide: Neighborhood Organizing in America* (Boston: Twayne Publishers, 1984); Robert Halpern, *Rebuilding the Inner City: A History of Neighborhood Initiatives to Address Poverty in the United States* (New York: Columbia University Press, 1995); Horwitt, *Let Them Call Me Rebel*; Aaron Schutz and Marie G. Sandy, *Collective Action for Social Change: An Introduction to Community Organizing* (New York: Palgrave Macmillan, 2011); David Walls, *Community Organizing: Fanning the Flames of Democracy* (Malden, MA: Polity Press, 2015), 1 and 55; Mark R. Warren, *Dry Bones Rattling: Community Building to Revitalize American Democracy* (Princeton, NJ: Princeton University Press, 2001).

20. St. Clair Drake, *Churches and Voluntary Associations in the Chicago Negro Community* (Chicago: Works Projects Administration, 1940). Drake's subsequent collaboration with Horace Cayton, the landmark two-volume *Black Metropolis*, reflects the same emphasis on social clubs and omission of block clubs: St. Clair Drake and Horace R. Cayton, *Black Metropolis: A Study of Negro Life in a Northern City*, revised and enlarged edition (New York: Harcourt, Brace & World, 1962; originally published 1945). Anne Meis Knupfer's important scholarship on black Chicago club women similarly leaves out block clubs: Knupfer, *The Chicago Black Renaissance and Women's Activism*, and Anne Meis Knupfer, *Toward a Tenderer Humanity and a Nobler Womanhood: African American Women's Clubs in Turn-of-the-Century Chicago* (New York and London: New York University Press, 1996). Christopher Robert Reed's epic trilogy, *Black Chicago's First Century*, also omits mention of block clubs: Christopher Robert Reed, *Black Chicago's First Century, Volume I, 1833–1900* (Columbia, MO, and London: University of Missouri Press, 2005); Christopher Robert Reed, *Knock at the Door of Opportunity: Black Migration to Chicago, 1900–1919* (Carbondale: Southern Illinois University Press, 2014); and *The Rise of Chicago's Black Metropolis, 1920–1929* (Urbana: University of Illinois Press, 2011). Allan H. Spear, *Black Chicago: The Making of a Negro Ghetto, 1890–1920* (Chicago: University of Chicago Press, 1967), 172, mentions block clubs briefly, relying on Strickland's history of the Chicago Urban League: Arvarh E.

Strickland, *History of the Chicago Urban League* (Columbia, MO, and London: University of Missouri Press, 2001; originally published by University of Illinois Press, 1966).

21. Kristin Emery, "'This Is My Home, I Have to Defend It': Preserving Community in Chicago's Lakewood-Balmoral Neighborhood" (MA paper, Loyola University Chicago, 2013); Meyerhoffer, "Who's Doing What?"; Tumelty, "Block Associations, Crime, and the Police"; John Brister Turner, "A Study of the Block Club; an Instrument of Community Organization" (PhD diss., Western Reserve University, 1959).

22. Mary Pattillo-McCoy, *Black Picket Fences: Privilege and Peril among the Black Middle Class* (Chicago: University of Chicago Press, 1999); Mary Pattillo, *Black on the Block: The Politics of Race and Class in the City* (Chicago: University of Chicago Press, 2007); Sudhir Alladi Venkatesh, *American Project: The Rise and Fall of a Modern Ghetto* (Cambridge, MA: Harvard University Press, 2000); and Sudhir Alladi Venkatesh, *Off the Books: The Underground Economy of the Urban Poor* (Cambridge, MA: Harvard University Press, 2006).

23. Daniel P. Doyle and David F. Luckenbill, "Socioeconomic Status, Perceived Need, and the Mobilization of Officials," *Social Science Journal* 30, no. 2 (April 1993): 151–63; Kaul, "Serving Oppressed Communities"; Mohan L. Kaul, "Block Clubs and Social Action: A Case Study in Community Conflict." *Journal of Sociology & Social Welfare* 3 (4) (March 1976): 437–50; Martin, "'Place-Framing as Place-Making'"; Martin, "Constructing the Neighborhood Sphere"; Rich and Wandersman, "Participation in Block Organizations"; Abraham Wandersman, John F. Jakubs, and Gary A. Glamartino, "Participation in Block Organizations," *Community Action* (September/October 1981): 40–47.

24. Sylvia Hood Washington, *Packing Them In: An Archaeology of Environmental Racism in Chicago, 1865–1954* (Lanham, MD: Lexington Books, 2005) and "Mrs. Block Beautiful: African American Women and the Birth of the Urban Conservation Movement, Chicago, Illinois, 1917–1954," *Environmental Justice* 1 (2008): 13–23; Dowden-White, *Groping toward Democracy*, x; Touré F. Reed, *Not Alms but Opportunity: The Urban League & the Politics of Racial Uplift, 1910–1950* (Chapel Hill: University of North Carolina Press, 2008); Helgeson, *Crucibles of Black Empowerment*. An enormous body of scholarly literature documents African Americans' struggle for justice and equality in the United States, including the urban North. Good starting points on this topic include Martha Biondi, *To Stand and Fight: The Struggle for Civil Rights in Postwar New York City* (Cambridge, MA: Harvard University Press, 2003); Jacquelyn Dowd Hall, "The Long Civil Rights Movement and the Political Uses of the Past," *The Journal of American History* 91 (4) (2005): 1233–63; Thomas J. Sugrue, *Sweet Land of Liberty: The Forgotten Struggle for Civil Rights in the North* (New York: Random House, 2008); Jeanne Theoharis and Komozi Woodard, *Groundwork: Local Black Freedom Movements in America* (New York: New York University Press, 2005); and Jeanne Theoharis and Komozi Woodard, *Freedom North: Black Freedom Struggles outside the South, 1940–1980* (New York: Palgrave Macmillan, 2003).

25. Venkatesh, *American Project*; Roberta M. Feldman and Susan Stall, *The Dignity of Resistance: Women Residents' Activism in Chicago Public Housing* (Cambridge and New York: Cambridge University Press, 2004); Rhonda Y. Williams, *The Politics of Public Housing: Black Women's Struggles against Urban Inequality* (New York: Oxford University Press, 2004); D. Bradford Hunt, *Blueprint for Disaster: The Unraveling of Chicago Public Housing* (Chicago: University of Chicago Press, 2009).

26. Flyer, Federation of Building Council, folder: "July–Sept. 1965" and letter, Sister Mary William to Richard, Oct. 11, 1965, folder: "Oct.–Nov. 1965," both in box 3, Marillac House records, Chicago History Museum.

27. David Horton Smith, "The Rest of the Nonprofit Sector: Grassroots Associations as the

Dark Matter Ignored in Prevailing 'Flat Earth' Maps of the Sector," *Nonprofit and Voluntary Sector Quarterly* 26 (2) (June 1997): 114–31. DOI: 10.1177/0899764097262002. I thank John Palmer Smith for referring me to this article.

28. A large literature documents the dominance of the Democratic Party in Chicago politics. Among other works, see John M. Allswang, *A House for All Peoples; Ethnic Politics in Chicago, 1890–1936* (Lexington: University Press of Kentucky, 1971); Roger Biles, *Big City Boss in Depression and War: Mayor Edward J. Kelly of Chicago* (DeKalb: Northern Illinois University Press, 1984); Roger Biles, *Richard J. Daley: Politics, Race, and the Governing of Chicago* (DeKalb: Northern Illinois University Press, 1995); William J. Grimshaw, *Bitter Fruit: Black Politics and the Chicago Machine, 1931–1991* (Chicago: University of Chicago Press, 1992); Keith Koeneman, *First Son: The Biography of Richard M. Daley* (Chicago: University of Chicago Press, 2013); Milton L. Rakove, *We Don't Want Nobody Nobody Sent: An Oral History of the Daley Years* (Bloomington: Indiana University Press, 1979); Gary Rivlin, *Fire on the Prairie: Chicago's Harold Washington and the Politics of Race* (New York: H. Holt, 1992); and Mike Royko, *Boss: Richard J. Daley of Chicago* (New York: Dutton, 1971).

29. Helgeson, *Crucibles of Black Empowerment*, 11.

30. Jane Jacobs, *The Death and Life of Great American Cities* (New York: Vintage Books, 1992; originally published 1961), 133 and 122.

31. Sam Bass Warner, *Streetcar Suburbs: The Process of Growth in Boston, 1870–1900* (New York: Atheneum, [1973]); Martin V. Melosi, *Garbage in the Cities: Refuse, Reform, and the Environment: 1880–1980s* (College Station: Texas A&M University Press, 1981); Martin V. Melosi, *The Sanitary City: Urban Infrastructure in America from Colonial Times to the Present* (Baltimore: Johns Hopkins University Press, 2000); Joel A. Tarr, "The Search for the Ultimate Sink: Urban Air, Land, and Water Pollution in Historical Perspective," *Records of the Columbia Historical Society, Washington, D.C.* 51 (1984): 1–29; Louis P. Cain, *Sanitation Strategy for a Lakefront Metropolis: The Case of Chicago* (DeKalb, IL: Northern Illinois University Press, 1978); Craig E. Colten, "Chicago's Waste Lands: Refuse Disposal and Urban Growth, 1840–1990," *Journal of Historical Geography* 20 (2) (1994): 124–42; Keating, *Building Chicago*; Harold L. Platt, *The Electric City: Energy and the Growth of the Chicago Area, 1880–1930* (Chicago: University of Chicago Press, 1991); Kenneth T. Jackson, *Crabgrass Frontier: The Suburbanization of America* (New York: Oxford University Press, 1985); Louis P. Cain, "To Annex or Not? A Tale of Two Towns: Evanston and Hyde Park," *Explorations in Economic History* 20 (1983): 57–72; Arnold R. Hirsch, *Making the Second Ghetto: Race and Housing in Chicago, 1940–1960* (New York: Cambridge University Press, 1983); Seligman, *Block by Block*, chapters 2 and 3; Christopher Klemek, *The Transatlantic Collapse of Urban Renewal: Postwar Urbanism from New York to Berlin* (Chicago: University of Chicago Press, 2011); Seymour I. Toll, *Zoned American* (New York, Grossman Publishers, 1969).

32. Kefalas, chapter 3.

33. Rachel Ridley, to Mrs. Ollie Haddow, 2711 W. Adams St., March 19, 1952, series I, box 220, folder 2184, Chicago Urban League records.

Chapter One

1. 2200 West Maypole Avenue Block Club, March 18, 1952, folder 2304, box 235, series II, Chicago Urban League Records, Special Collections and University Archives Department, Richard J. Daley Library, University of Illinois at Chicago (hereafter Chicago Urban League records).

2. For a general analysis of this process see Amanda I. Seligman, *Block by Block: Neighborhoods and Public Policy on Chicago's West Side* (Chicago: University of Chicago Press, 2005).

3. Robin L. Einhorn, *Property Rules: Political Economy in Chicago, 1833–1872* (Chicago and London: University of Chicago Press, 1991), passim, quote on p. 104.

4. Einhorn, *Property Rules*, passim.

5. Ann Durkin Keating, *Building Chicago: Suburban Developers and the Creation of a Divided Metropolis* (Urbana and Chicago: University of Illinois Press, 2002; originally published Columbus: Ohio State University Press, 1988), 59. Based on sources from 1911 and 1921, Margaret Garb identifies the existence of "block clubs and neighborhood associations" formed in Packingtown in the 1890s. They began as improvement organizations and turned in the twentieth century to protesting black settlement: Margaret Garb, *City of American Dreams: A History of Home Ownership and Housing Reform in Chicago, 1871–1919* (Chicago: University of Chicago Press, 2005), 159 and 190. I thank Chicago History Museum librarian Lesley Martin for helping me check this citation.

6. William M. Tuttle, Jr., *Race Riot: Chicago in the Red Summer of 1919* (New York: Atheneum, 1970); James R. Grossman, *Land of Hope: Chicago, Black Southerners, and the Great Migration* (Chicago: University of Chicago Press, 1989); Will Cooley, "Moving On Out: Black Pioneering in Chicago, 1915–1950," *Journal of Urban History* 36, no. 4 (July 2010): 485–506; Garb, "Drawing the 'Color Line': Race and Real Estate in Early Twentieth-Century Chicago, *Journal of Urban History* 32(5) (2006): 773–87.

7. Beryl Satter, *Family Properties: Race, Real Estate, and the Exploitation of Black Urban America* (New York: Metropolitan Books, 2009), 40; Rose Helper, *Racial Policies and Practices of Real Estate Brokers* (Minneapolis: University of Minnesota Press, 1969), 226.

8. In general on racial restrictive covenants, see Clement E. Vose, *Caucasians Only: The Supreme Court, the NAACP, and the Restrictive Covenant Cases* (Berkeley: University of California Press, 1959). For estimates of the extent to which Chicago was covered with restrictive covenants over time, see Wendy Plotkin, "Deeds of Mistrust: Race, Housing, and Restrictive Covenants in Chicago, 1900–1953," (PhD diss., University of Illinois at Chicago, 1999), 17–30.

9. "Conservation Agreement," folder 5, box 107, Hyde Park–Kenwood Community Conference records, Department of Special Collections, University of Chicago Library (hereafter HPKCC records); "Property Owners Agreement" beginning "The following agreement has been signed," folder 7, box 108, HPKCC records. See Mark Santow, "Saul Alinsky and the Dilemmas of Race in the Post-War City," (PhD diss., University of Pennsylvania, 2000), 151–56. On the racial liberalism of Hyde Park, see Arnold R. Hirsch, *Making the Second Ghetto: Race and Housing in Chicago, 1940–1960* (Cambridge and New York: Cambridge University Press, 1983), chapter 5.

10. Patricia Mooney Melvin, *The Organic City: Urban Definition and Community Organization, 1880–1920* (Lexington: University Press of Kentucky, 1987), 21.

11. Mooney Melvin, 69, 75, 87–89, 92–93, and 152. See also Robert Fisher, *Let the People Decide: Neighborhood Organizing in America* (Boston: Twayne Publishers, 1984), 23–27.

12. Oral history interview with Dara Salk, June 10, 2013, Chicago.

13. Nancy J. Weiss, *The National Urban League, 1910–1940* (New York: Oxford University Press, 1974), 29.

14. See the annual reports of the Chicago Urban League, arranged by year in box 1, Chicago Urban League records.

15. One strategy for sorting out the early spread of the idea of block organization work would be to compare the board members of the National Urban League with the supporters of the National Social Unit Organization and look for overlap. Mooney Melvin's *The Organic City* provides the names of the NSUO's supporters on pp. 67–70.

16. Weiss, 137.

17. Walter R. Chivers, "Neighborhood Union: An Effort of Community Organization," *Opportunity* (June 1925): 178–79; Touré F. Reed, *Not Alms but Opportunity: The Urban League and the Politics of Racial Uplift, 1910–1950* (Chapel Hill: University of North Carolina Press, 2008), 14 and 42.

18. Typed manuscript, two pages, "Block Clubs," folder 2138, box 198, series III, Chicago Urban League records; Arthur J. Edmunds, *Daybreakers: The Story of the Urban League of Pittsburgh, The First Sixty-Five Years* (Pittsburgh: Urban League of Pittsburgh, 1983), 16, 42, and 53. Clark informed the broad Urban League audience about the block unit idea in an article in *Opportunity*: John T. Clark, "When the Negro Resident Organizes," *Opportunity* (June 1934): 168–170. On the block unit work of the St. Louis Urban League, see Priscilla A. Dowden-White, *Groping toward Democracy: African American Social Welfare Reform in St. Louis, 1910–1949* (Columbia and London: University of Missouri Press, 2011), 217–42. See also Guichard Parris and Lester Brooks, *Blacks in the City: A History of the National Urban League* (Boston and Toronto: Little, Brown and Company, 1971), 222–24.

19. Arvarh E. Strickland, *History of the Chicago Urban League* (Columbia, MO, and London: The University of Missouri Press, 2001; originally published by University of Illinois Press, 1966), passim, quote on 197; Jeffrey Helgeson, *Crucibles of Black Empowerment: Chicago's Neighborhood Politics from the New Deal to Harold Washington* (Chicago: University of Chicago Press, 2014).

20. Dowden-White, *Groping toward Democracy*, xi.

21. Brief Summary of the Work of the Chicago Urban League, March 1 to August 1, 1917, folder 1–1, series I, Chicago Urban League records; Strickland, *History of the Chicago Urban League*, 45; "Tenth Annual Report of the Chicago Urban League, For the Fiscal Year Ended October 31st, 1926," folder 1–6, series I, Chicago Urban League records.

22. Strickland, *History of the Chicago Urban League*, 114; Chicago Urban League 1916–38, folder 1–13, series I, Chicago Urban League records; "Journal of Negro Life in Chicago," April 1941, pp. 10–11, folder 1–14, series I, Chicago Urban League records. On the policy racket in Chicago, see St. Clair Drake and Horace Cayton, *Black Metropolis: A Study of Negro Life in a Northern City*, rev. ed. (New York: Harcourt, Brace & World, Inc., 1970 [originally published 1945]), 2: 470–494; A more recent work, Nathan Thompson, *Kings: The True Story of Chicago's Policy Kings and Numbers Racketeers, An Informal History* (Chicago: Bronzeville Press, 2003), is, as the subtitle suggests, not a formal work of scholarship.

23. Annual Report, Chicago Urban League, 1916–1947, folder 1–19, series I, Chicago Urban League records; 1916–1952 Annual Report, folder 1–24, Chicago Urban League records; Jeffrey Helgeson, "Striving in Black Chicago: Migration, Work, and the Politics of Neighborhood Change, 1935–1965," (PhD diss., University of Illinois at Chicago, 2008), 368, and his *Crucibles of Black Empowerment*, 146–47. For a fuller accounting of Maxey's life and work, including her experience as a black property owner in Chicago, see Helgeson's dissertation, 361–69, and book, 143–51.

24. 1500 Drake Block Club, Aug. 9, 1950, folder 2298, box 234, series II, Chicago Urban League records; Alva B. Maxey, "The Block Club Movement in Chicago," *Phylon Quarterly* 18(2) (1957): 125, 129, 131; Rebecca Stiles Taylor, "Federated Clubs," *Chicago Defender* (National Edition), p. 7, June 5, 1948, accessed online through ProQuest Historical Newspapers, September 22, 2010, emphasis in the original.

25. Evelyn Brooks Higginbotham, *Righteous Discontent: The Women's Movement in the Black Baptist Church, 1880–1920* (Cambridge, MA, and London: Harvard University Press, 1993), chapter 7, quote on p. 196; Erica Ball, *To Live an Antislavery Life: Personal Politics and the Antebellum*

Black Middle Class (Athens: University of Georgia Press, 2012), 35. Victoria W. Wolcott, *Remaking Respectability: African American Women in Interwar Detroit* (Chapel Hill and London: University of North Carolina Press, 2001), 38.

26. Maxey, "The Block Club Movement in Chicago": 125 and 131; Touré Reed, *Not Alms but Opportunity*, 37.

27. Strickland, *History of the Chicago Urban League*, 184; Berry quoted in Helgeson, "Striving in Black Chicago," 391, see also 394; Parris and Brooks, *Blacks in the City*, 410 and 470; "Block Club Honors Ex-Presidents," *Chicago Defender*, May 21, 1957, accessed through ProQuest Historical Newspapers, September 25, 2013.

28. Christopher Reed, introduction to Strickland, *History of the Chicago Urban League*, xii and xiii.

29. Touré Reed, *Not Alms but Opportunity*, 4–5, 174, and 193.

30. Helgeson, "Striving in Black Chicago," 358 and 369; Dowden-White, *Groping toward Democracy*, x.

31. Sylvia Hood Washington, *Packing Them In: An Archaeology of Environmental Racism in Chicago, 1865–1954*. (Lanham, MD: Lexington Books, 2005), 159.

32. Maxey, "The Block Club Movement in Chicago," 129.

33. Maxey, "The Block Club Movement in Chicago," 130; *1916–1952 Annual Report*, p. 15, folder 1–24, Chicago Urban League records.

34. Chicago Urban League, Report for 1951, folder 1–23, series I, Chicago Urban League records.

35. Civilian Defense Handbook, Public Buildings & Institutions; Office of Civilian Defense, Chicago Metropolitan Area, Edward J. Kelly, United States Coordinator, folder 14, box 2, Office of Civilian Defense Records, Special Collections and Preservation Division, Harold Washington Library Center (hereafter OCD); Mary Watters, *Illinois in the Second World War: Operation Home Front*, vol. 1 (Springfield: Illinois State Historical Society, 1951), 74; Roger Biles, *Big City Boss in Depression and War: Mayor Edward J. Kelly of Chicago* (DeKalb: Northern Illinois University Press, 1984), 91–92 and 116.

36. Biles, *Big City Boss*, 116; Watters, *Illinois in the Second World War*, 76 and 79; Clipping, "West Siders Come Through," *Midwest News* January 28, 1942, folder 2, box 2, OCD; Perry R. Duis and Scott La France, *We've Got a Job to Do: Chicagoans and World War II* (Chicago: Chicago Historical Society, 1992), 35; Clipping, "Community OCD Groups Report on Activities," *Austin News* May 7, 1944, folder 4, box 2, OCD. For an overview of the OCD's work in Chicago, see Watters, *Illinois in the Second World War*, chapter 2, especially 69–86. The Chicago Metropolitan Office of Civilian Defense, which covered not only Cook County but also the Illinois counties of DuPage and Lake and Indiana's Lake County, sought to organize approximately twenty thousand blocks: Annabelle Bender, "Civilian Defense Block Organization in Hyde Park" (MA thesis, University of Chicago, 1943), 2–4.

37. Clipping, "Census Is On of Everybody in this Area," folder 20, box 2; Clipping, "Announce Bond Quotas for Blocks," *WSN*, June 16, 1944, folder 13, box 3; "Major Points about Chicago's 5th War Loan Drive to Incorporate in Your Advertising," folder 12, box 3; Local News Civilian Defense, Division 4–District 5, October 7, 1942, folder 2, box 2, all in OCD. See Duis and La France, *We've Got a Job to Do*, 40.

38. *The Very Good Club News*, February 5, 1945, no. 21, folder 1, the Very Good Club records, Chicago History Museum. For the newsletters, see the Very Good Club records, folder 1.

39. Memorandum, February 1, 1945, "Why Continue Civilian Defense," folder 5, box 1, OCD;

Memorandum, date illegible, Subj. General Information on conversion of O.C.D. to Chicago War Services Corps, folder 5, box 1, OCD; Biles, *Big City Boss*, 133; *The Very Good Club News*, October 11, 1945, no. 29, folder 1, and Minute Book, folder 2, Very Good Club collection; Amanda Seligman, "Old Town," *Encyclopedia of Chicago*, http://www.encyclopedia.chicagohistory.org /pages/927.html, accessed July 10, 2013; Old Town Triangle Association, http://www.oldtown triangle.com/, last accessed September 26, 2013.

40. Herbert A. Thelen, *Dynamics of Groups at Work* (Chicago: University of Chicago Press, 1954), 15; Julia Abrahamson, *A Neighborhood Finds Itself* (New York: Harper & Brothers, 1959), 90.

41. The history of Hyde Park's urban renewal program is best analyzed in Arnold Hirsch's landmark book, *Making the Second Ghetto*. On the founding of the SECC, see p. 136; for the quotation, see 139.

42. "Herbert Thelen, 1913–2008," *UChicagoNews*, March 5, 2008, http://news.uchicago.edu /article/2008/03/05/herbert-thelen-1913–2008, accessed July 9, 2013; minutes of the Chicago Beach Area Group meeting at Surf and Surrey, May 20, 1964, folder 5, box 105, HPKCC; Herbert A. Thelen, Human Dynamics Laboratory, Education 399D, November 27, 1950, "Notes for Formulation of Methodology of the Hyde Park–Kenwood Community Conference," folder 6, box 94, HPKCC; "Report on Training Session for Block Leaders to Work in the Block Organization of the Hyde Park-Kenwood Community Conference, held at Temple Isaiah Israel, 4/4/51, Under Dr. Thelen's Direction," folder 1, box 95, HPKCC; "Block Leaders and Block Steering Committee Members," folder 2, box 95, HPKCC; Thelen, *Dynamics of Groups at Work*, 3–30; Herbert A. Thelen and Bettie Belk Sarchet, *Neighbors in Action: A Manual for Community Leaders* (Chicago: Human Dynamics Laboratory, Department of Education, University of Chicago, 1954); Bettie B. Sarchet, "Block Groups and Community Change: An Evaluation of the Block Program of the Hyde Park-Kenwood Community Conference," Human Dynamics Laboratory, University of Chicago, 1955; "Chronological History of the Development of the Block Program of the Hyde Park–Kenwood Community Conference, May 1956," folder 7, box 92, HPKCC.

43. Abrahamson, *Neighborhood Finds Itself*, 253 and 331 (emphasis in the original). In general on HPKCC block clubs, see chapter 16.

44. Hirsch, *Making the Second Ghetto*, 138.

45. Offprint, "We *Can* Do Something About It!" by Stuart Chase, *Reader's Digest*, 1953, folder 13, box 94, HPKCC; Herbert Thelen counted six Chicago communities that modeled their structure on the HKPCC's block clubs within three years of its founding. Thelen, *Dynamics of Groups at Work*, 26.

46. The literature on the history of urban renewal is too voluminous to list here. Classic works on urban renewal include Herbert J. Gans, *The Urban Villagers: Group and Class in the Life of Italian-Americans* (New York: Free Press of Glencoe, 1962); and Martin Anderson, *The Federal Bulldozer* (New York: McGraw-Hill, 1967). Good starting points in more recent scholarship include Hirsch, *Making the Second Ghetto*; Jon Teaford, *The Rough Road to Renaissance: Urban Revitalization in America, 1940–1985* (Baltimore: Johns Hopkins University Press, 1990); Christopher Klemek, *The Transatlantic Collapse of Urban Renewal: Postwar Urbanism from New York to Berlin* (Chicago: University of Chicago Press, 2011); and the articles focused on urban renewal in the special issue of the *Journal of Urban History* published in spring 2013.

47. "The Chicago Conservation Program," Community Conservation Board of Chicago, pp. 12–13, folder 129, Greater Lawndale Conservation Commission Records, Special Collections and University Archives Department, Richard J. Daley Library, University of Illinois at Chicago

(hereafter GLCC-UIC); Clipping, "Report Calls for Co-operation in Urban Renewal," *Chicago Sun Times*, December 18, 1962, folder: Urban Renewal, Ruth Moore By-Lines 1959–1964, box 7, Ruth Moore Papers, Chicago History Museum.

48. I am indebted to historian Devin Hunter for developing this argument in the context of the Uptown Chicago Commission. Devin Hunter, "Chicken Teriyaki and a Blind Woodcarver with a Fake Southern Accent: Promoting Urban Renewal at Chicago's Uptown Folk Fair, 1959–1962," paper delivered at the Sixth Biennial Conference of the Urban History Association, New York City, New York, October 27, 2012.

49. Claude Peck, President's column, *GLCC News Notes* 3, no. 31 (September 16, 1958), folder "September, 1958," box 7, Greater Lawndale Conservation Commission Records, Chicago History Museum.

50. This organization was also called the West Garfield Community Council and the West Garfield Park Neighborhood Council.

51. This organization was also called the Garfield Park–Austin Community Council.

52. Maxey, "The Block Club Movement in Chicago," 126; clipping, "Blocks Together Gets Tough on Crime," *Extra*, June 15, 1995, folder: CPD–Community Relations, 1993–1995, clipping file, Chicago Public Municipal Reference Library, Harold Washington Public Library, Chicago; Strickland, *History of the Chicago Urban League*, 142; Sudhir Venkatesh, *American Project: The Rise and Fall of a Modern Ghetto* (Cambridge, MA, and London: Harvard University Press, 2000), 33; Beryl Satter, *Family Properties: Race, Real Estate, and the Exploitation of Black Urban America* (New York: Metropolitan Books, 2009), 40; Erica Salem, Jessica Hooberman, and Dinah Ramirez, "MAPP in Chicago: A Model for Public Health Systems Development and Community Building," *Journal of Public Health Management and Practice* 11 (5) (2005): 393–400; Abrahamson, *A Neighborhood Finds Itself*; Helgeson, "Striving in Black Chicago," 314–15; Helgeson, *Crucibles of Black Empowerment*, 221, 226–27; Irving Spergel, Erwin Bloom, Ann Hyman, and Robert Ross, "Block Clubs in Three Chicago Neighborhoods," School of Social Service Administration, University of Chicago, May 1966, folder 2, box 10, The Woodlawn Organization records, Chicago History Museum; letterhead for Southwest Lawndale United Block Club Council, folder 5, box 9, Rich papers. This list omits "Save Our Neighborhood," the pseudonym sociologist Patrick J. Carr uses to describe a block-club organizing group in the "Beltway" area in the 1990s; Patrick J. Carr, *Clean Streets: Controlling Crime, Maintaining Order, and Building Community Activism* (New York and London: New York University Press, 2005), 64.

53. Abrahamson, *A Neighborhood Finds Itself*, 29.

54. Princeton Avenue Civic Club, March 13, 1953, folder 2300, box 234, series II, Chicago Urban League records.

55. Clipping, "Call Special Meeting of Block Clubs," *Community Publications*, January 23, 1963, folder 54, Off the Street Club collection, Department of Special Collections, Richard J. Daley Library, University of Illinois at Chicago; "To Form Block Club North of Madison St.," *Garfieldian*, October 23, 1963; memo, to file from Charlotte Meacham, August 24, 1965, re visit to Chicago, August 4, 1965, folder "Housing Opportunities Program, Correspondence with Philadelphia, Chicago RO 1965," box "Chicago R.O. 1965 (Housing Oppors. Prog.-Coms & Orgs.: Suburban Human Rels. Comm. Com. to Youth Oppors. Prog.)," Chicago Regional Office Files, American Friends Service Committee Archives, Philadelphia (hereafter AFSC); "History and Program of the Urban Affairs Program of the American Friends Service Committee, presented to the Midwest Urban Progress Center Requesting Status as a Program Station, February 6, 1966," folder "Urban Affairs Program, Committees & Organizations: Midwest Urban Progress

Center, Chicago Regional Office, 1966," box "Chicago R.O. 1966 (Pre-Adolescent Enrichment Prog. to Urban Affairs Prog.)," AFSC.

56. Flyer for special block meeting, June 24, 1954, folder 6, box 101; meetings of block groups on final plans, February 1958 to March 10, 1958, folder 6, box 96; Statement of the 5200 Kenwood-Kimbark Block Group to the Conservation Community Council, April 25, 1957, United Church of Hyde Park, folder 5, box 100, all in HPKCC.

57. Detailed responses to the survey can be found in folder 16, box 96, HPKCC. Gary Os-sewaarde, "A Timeline of Block Clubs in Context of HPKCC (Founded in 1949) and SECC (Founded 1952) Code Enforcement and the Impetus towards Urban Renewal," http://www .hydepark.org/hpkcc/whistlestop/HPKCC%20and%20old%20block%20clubs.pdf, accessed July 8, 2013; Jeffrey Bishku-Aykul, "Block Club Workshop Soon," June 19, 2013, http://hpherald.com /2013/06/19/block-club-workshop-soon/; by-laws of the Winona Block Club, adopted September 15, 1962, folder 6, box 49, records of the Uptown Chicago Commission, Chicago History Museum (hereafter UCC); Kay Granberg to Mrs. Joanne Fowler, April 4, 1973, folder 6, box 49, UCC; Uptown Chicago Commission, http://www.uptownchicagocommission.org/about.htm, last accessed September 25, 2013.

58. Seligman, *Block by Block*, passim.

59. See, for example, documentation about 5312–16 Kimbark, a building where residents sued the landlord in an effort to get adequate repairs to the building. Portions of the case can be traced in folder 2, box 100, HPKCC.

60. Zorita Mikva, "The Neighborhood Improvement Association: A Counter-Force to the Expansion of Chicago's Negro Population" (MA thesis: University of Chicago, 1951), 2, 29, 44, 72. On improvement associations, see also Plotkin, 57–84.

61. This kind of mobbing in response to the first African Americans moving into a white neighborhood was so common in this period, yet unreported in the daily newspapers, that Hirsch calls it "an era of hidden violence." See Hirsch, 40–68. On the Hargraves, see Seligman, *Block by Block*, 169–72. On white resistance to black in-migration generally, see Stephen Grant Meyer, *As Long As They Don't Move Next Door: Segregation and Racial Conflict in American Neighborhoods* (Lanham, MD: Rowman & Littlefield, 2000).

62. "Calmness, Resistance to Speculators Stressed," *Garfieldian*, August 12, 1959; Seligman, *Block by Block*, 171–75.

63. "Lawlor to Speak Here Thursday," *Austin News*, November 4, 1970, box 3, Austin News-papers Collection, Department of Special Collections, Harold Washington Public Library (hereafter ANC); Brian J. L. Berry, *The Open Housing Question: Race and Housing in Chicago, 1966–1976* (Cambridge, MA: Ballinger Publishing Company, 1979), 184; clipping, "Father Lawlor: His Kingdom and Power," *Tribune Magazine*, February 21, 1971, Francis X. Lawlor clipping file, Chicago History Museum (hereafter Lawlor clipping file).

64. Clipping, "Fr. Lawlor Coming Back to Chicago," *Chicago Daily News*, March 22, 1968, Lawlor clipping file; Berry, 184 and 186. Berry notes that Lawlor was elected without carrying his own precinct, which had become primarily African American by the time he ran for office.

65. Clipping, "Father Lawlor: His Kingdom and Power," *Chicago Tribune Magazine*, Febru-ary 21, 1971; clipping, "Lawlor in New Move to Get Reinstated," *Chicago's American*, June 12, 1968; clipping, "Dissenting Priest Faces Dismissal," *Chicago Daily News*, August 13, 1968, all in Lawlor clipping file. The claim of 150 member groups is repeated in clipping, "Father Lawlor: His King-dom and Power," *Chicago Tribune Magazine*, February 21, 1971. Another figure given is 186 block clubs by 1969; clipping, *Sun-Times Midwest Magazine*, March 9, 1969, Lawlor clipping file. *ABC News*, July 24, 1970, Chicago History Museum.

66. Clipping, "'Holding the Line' at Ashland Av.," *Chicago Daily News*, April 18, 1968; untitled clipping, *Tribune*, August 29, 1971; both in Lawlor clipping file.

67. "Fr. Lawlor Advises: Unity with Block Clubs," *Austinite*, November 11, 1970, box 9, ANC.

68. Clipping, "Father Lawlor: His Kingdom and Power," *Chicago Tribune Magazine*, February 21, 1971, Lawlor clipping file; *ABC News*, February 27, 1970, and June 12, 1970, Chicago History Museum.

69. Strickland, *History of the Chicago Urban League*, 79; Block Club Meeting, Princeton Ave. 3500 to 3600 South, October 21, 1952, folder 2324, box 235, series II, "Chicago Urban League records; 600–700 Block on 46th Street, Jan. 21, 1953," folder 2299, box 234, series II, Chicago Urban League records.

70. Good starting points for understanding the operations of machine politics in Chicago include Milton L. Rakove, *Don't Make No Waves . . . Don't Back No Losers: An Insiders' Analysis of the Daley Machine* (Bloomington: Indiana University Press, 1976); and William J. Grimshaw, *Bitter Fruit: Black Politics and the Chicago Machine, 1931–1991* (Chicago: University of Chicago Press, 1992).

71. In an unusual move, the block-club organizing 47th Ward alderman Ameya Pawar posted a job announcement for the position of his ward superintendent, rather than hiring a traditional "close affiliate." See "Pawar Selects New Ward Superintendent," *Center Square Journal*, July 22, 2011, http://www.centersquarejournal.com/news/pawar-selects-new-ward-superintendent, accessed September 23, 2013.

72. Letter, Faith to Nikki, June 9, 1968, folder 3, box 20, Faith Rich papers, Special Collections and Preservation Division, Harold Washington Library Center, Chicago Public Library.

73. 43rd Street and Prairie Avenue Block Club, August 14, 1951, folder 2300, box 234, series II, Chicago Urban League records. On the difficulties presented when the self-identified neighborhood activists of the National Association of Neighborhoods tried to organize their coalition around nonlocal political issues, see Benjamin Looker, "Visions of Autonomy: The New Left and the Neighborhood Government Movement of the 1970s," *Journal of Urban History* 38 (May 2012): 590 (DOI:10.1177/0096144211428770); Jessamine Cobb, "Survey of the Field of Local Community Organization," September 1962, folder 4, box 202, Welfare Council of Metropolitan Chicago records, Chicago History Museum.

74. See folder 7, box 96, HPKCC. See also Bettie B. Sarchet, *Block Groups and Community Change: An Evaluation of the Block Program of the Hyde Park–Kenwood Community Conference* (Chicago: Human Dynamics Laboratory, University of Chicago: 1955), 10; "5000 Block Club Adopts Platform," *Garfieldian*, April 29, 1959; "Back 'Sit-Ins' Block Groups," *Chicago Daily Defender*, April 18, 1960; "Park Manor Unit to Meet Tonight," *Chicago Daily Defender*, June 6, 1960; "Plan Help for Boycott Victims," *Chicago Defender*, September 3, 1960; "30,000 More Pounds of Food to Go to Mississippi Friday," *Chicago Daily Defender*, February 14, 1963; "'Operation Rescue' Gets $1,000 for Mississippi," *Chicago Daily Defender*, August 25, 1964 (*Defender* accessed through ProQuest Historical Newspapers); James R. Ralph, *Northern Protest: Martin Luther King, Jr., Chicago, and the Civil Rights Movement* (Cambridge, MA: Harvard University Press, 1993), 106–7; Urban Affairs Report, for weeks ending June 2 and July 3, 1966, p. 2, folder "Urban Affairs Program, Reports, Weekly, Chicago Regional Office, 1966," box "Chicago R.O. 1966 (Pre-Adolescent Enrichment Prog. to Urban Affairs Prog.)," AFSC.

75. The best overviews of the development of the CAPS program have been produced by the criminologist Wesley Skogan, who enjoyed extraordinary access to CPD materials as a result of his status as its official evaluator. See, for example, Wesley G. Skogan and Susan M. Hartnett, *Community Policing, Chicago Style* (New York and Oxford: Oxford University Press, 1997);

Wesley G. Skogan, *Police and Community in Chicago: A Tale of Three Cities* (Oxford and New York: Oxford University Press, 2006); Chicago Community Policing Consortium, "Community Policing in Chicago, Year 10, An Evaluation of Chicago's Alternative Policing Strategy," April 2004, http://skogan.org/files/Community_Policing_in_Chicago_Year_Ten.pdf, last accessed September 26, 2013.

76. George L. Kelling and James Q. Wilson, "Broken Windows: The Police and Neighborhood Safety," *Atlantic*, March 1, 1982, http://www.theatlantic.com/magazine/archive/1982/03/broken-windows/304465/. Collective efficacy theory is promulgated and summarized in Robert Sampson, *Great American City: Chicago and the Enduring Neighborhood Effect* (Chicago: University of Chicago Press, 2012), 149–78.

77. Clipping, Andy Dunning, "CAPS Salutes Local Block Clubs," *Beverly Review*, September 13, 2000, and clipping, Janis Shumac Wilder, "Chicago Woman Upholds Neighborhood Safety," *Daily Southtown*, January 18, 2001, both in folder "C.P.D.–Community Relations 1999–2001," Chicago Public Municipal Reference Library, Harold Washington Public Library, Chicago; "Welcome to Chicago Block Clubs," https://portal.chicagopolice.org/portal/page/portal/Block Club, last accessed September 26, 2013; oral history interview with Beth Ford, June 17, 2013. For example, the 52nd and Kenwood Block Club has an online "spot" that makes CAPS information available. See "BC52Plus: The 52nd and Kenwood Block Club Spot," http://bc52plus.weebly.com/index.html, last accessed September 23, 2013. A Google search conducted on September 26, 2013 suggested that other cities also use the virtual block club tactic. Cerritos, California: "Join the Virtual Block Club," http://www.cerritos.us/NEWS_INFO/news_press_releases/2013/june/virtual_block_club.php. Lino Lakes, Minnesota: "Virtual Block Club Membership," http://www.ci.lino-lakes.mn.us/index.asp?Type=B_BASIC&SEC=%7B8AAE9C0E-E382-4E43-8076-E43988F53A44%7D. St. Paul, Minnesota: "Virtual Block Clubs," http://www.district2.50megs.com/index_files/page0006.htm. "What is a Block Club?," https://portal.chicagopolice.org/portal/page/portal/BlockClub/Resources/WhatIs, last accessed September 23, 2013.

78. Oral history interview, Marilyn Pierce, June 27, 2013, Chicago. BARGE, Top Three Priorities for Our Neighborhood, folder 44, box 2, Mary Ann Smith Papers, addendum 1, Women and Leadership Archives, Loyola University Chicago; and letter, Mary Ann Smith to Block Club President, undated, folder 17, box 29, Mary Ann Smith Papers, 1978–2009, Women and Leadership Archives, Loyola University Chicago. 49th Ward Participatory Budgeting Initiative, http://www.ward49.com/participatory-budgeting/#Intro and 49th Ward Participatory Budgeting Initiative May 4, 2013 Election Results, http://www.ward49.com/site/files/322/86601/473866/658217/Participatory_Budgeting—Election_Results_2013.pdf, both accessed July 10, 2013.

79. E-mail, Ernie Constantino to Amanda Seligman, June 9, 2013, and oral history interviews with Ernie Constantino and Dara Salk, June 10, 2013; "About the Alderman and His Team," http://chicago47.org/the-ward/about-the-alderman/, last accessed July 10, 2013.

80. Eric Klinenberg, *Heat Wave: A Social Autopsy of Disaster in Chicago* (Chicago: University of Chicago Press, 2002), argues that the social isolation of the elderly and poor in neighborhoods like North Lawndale in Chicago made them more vulnerable to death in the heat wave of 1995. The dogged ethnographer Mitchell Duneier, however, called into doubt Klinenberg's claim that the deceased were more likely to have died alone. See Mitchell Duneier, "Ethnography, the Ecological Fallacy, and the 1995 Chicago Heat Wave," *American Sociological Review* (August 2006): 679–88.

81. "Financial Crisis Just a Symptom of Detroit's Woes," *New York Times* online, July 8, 2013, http://www.nytimes.com/2013/07/09/us/financial-crisis-just-a-symptom-of-detroits-woes.html; "In Oregon, a Demand for Safety, but Not on Their Dime," *New York Times* online, July 5, 2013,

http://www.nytimes.com/2013/07/06/us/In-Cash-Starved-Oregon-County-Citizens-Take-Up -Patrols.html; "Police Force Nearly Halved, Camden Feels Impact," *New York Times* online, March 6, 2011, http://www.nytimes.com/2011/03/07/nyregion/07camden.html?pagewanted=all.

82. Erin Aubry Kaplan, "Hardy Party: Thoughts on an Inglewood Block Party," August 23, 2012, KCET, http://www.kcet.org/updaily/socal_focus/commentary/hardy-party.html, last accessed January 7, 2015; 5600 Blackstone Block Group–Mr. Richard Stephens interviewed, folder 16, box 96, HPKCC. Wesley Skogan reports more participation in block clubs by better-off residents in an experiment in Minneapolis. An important difference between the Minneapolis groups and those in Chicago is that the ones in Minneapolis were what he calls "transplant" groups, which were organized for the study, rather than having grown organically out of local concerns and institutions. Wesley G. Skogan, *Disorder and Decline: Crime and the Spiral of Decay in American Neighborhoods* (New York: The Free Press, 1990), 148.

Chapter Two

1. "Future of Block Club Movement Depends on Austin Residents," *Austinite*, May 25, 1966, Austin Newspapers Collection, box 7, Special Collections and Preservation Division, Harold Washington Library Center, Chicago Public Library (hereafter ANC).

2. Alva B. Maxey, "The Block Club Movement in Chicago," *Phylon Quarterly* 18(2) (1957): 126; West 15th Place Block Club Newsletter no. 3, April 1972, folder 5, box 9, Faith Rich Papers, Special Collections and Preservation Division, Harold Washington Library Center, Chicago Public Library (hereafter Rich papers); Kristin Emery, "'This is My Home, I Have to Defend It': Preserving Community in Chicago's Lakewood-Balmoral Neighborhood" (MA paper, Loyola University Chicago, 2013), 15 and 30. I am grateful to Ms. Emery for generously sharing a copy of her thesis with me. See also the group's Facebook page, at Lakewood Balmoral Residents' Council, https://www.facebook.com/Lakewood.Balmoral, last accessed September 30, 2013. Every Person Is Concerned: EPIC Block Club, http://www.epicblockclub.org/, last accessed December 5, 2014; by-laws of the Winona Block Club, adopted September 15, 1962, folder 6, box 49, Uptown Chicago Commission Records, Chicago History Museum (hereafter UCC Records); and WFCW Facebook page, https://www.facebook.com/pages/Winona-Foster-Carmen-Winnemac -WFCW-Block-Club/153638898008748, last accessed September 30, 2013.

3. John Brister Turner, "A Study of the Block Club: An Instrument of Community Organization," (PhD diss., Western Reserve University, 1959), 5.

4. Arvarh E. Strickland, *History of the Chicago Urban League* (Columbia, MO, and London: University of Missouri Press, 2001; originally published by University of Illinois Press, 1966), 37; Julia Abrahamson, *A Neighborhood Finds Itself* (New York: Harper & Brothers, 1959), 94 and 330; monthly report of the executive director, Commission on Human Relations, January 1951, folder 2791, box 272, series I, Chicago Urban League records, Special Collections and University Archives Department at the Richard J. Daley Library, University of Illinois at Chicago (hereafter Chicago Urban League records).

5. January 9, 1953, 5700 South Calumet Street, series II, box 234, folder 2297, Chicago Urban League records.

6. September 14, 1950, 4400 Block on Langley Avenue, series, box 234, folder 2302; December 29, 1952, 600–700 Block on 46th Street, series II, box 234, folder 2299; minutes of 600 and 700 East 46th Street Block Club, January 7, 1953, series II, box 234, folder 2299; all in Chicago Urban League records.

7. Letter, Rachel Ridley, director, to Mr. Durwood Monroe, March 28, 1952, series I, box 220,

folder 2184; January 23, 1953, record of block club meetings, series II, box 235, folder 2323, both in Chicago Urban League records.

8. Block club meeting, Wentworth Avenue 3500 to 3600 South, October 16, 1952, series II, box 235, folder 2324, Chicago Urban League records.

9. Letter, Rachel Ridley, director, to Mrs. Clementine Stewart, 1927 West Washington Boulevard, September 29, 1950, series I, box 220, folder 2184, Chicago Urban League records.

10. Abraham Wandersman, Paul Florin, David Chavis, Rich Richard, and John Prestby, "Getting Together and Getting Things Done," *Psychology Today* (November 1985): 68; block club meeting, Wentworth Avenue 3500 to 3600 South, October 20, 1952, series II, box 235, folder 2324, Chicago Urban League records; Herbert A. Thelen and Bettie Belk Sarchet, *Neighbors in Action: A Manual for Community Leaders* (Chicago: Human Dynamics Laboratory, Department of Education, University of Chicago 1954), 20.

11. Minutes, Westside Community Improvement Council, August 11, 1950, series I, box 268, folder 2716; letter, Joan Dunn, 3514 W. Grenshaw, to Mrs. Ridley, January 27, 1952, series I, box 220, folder 2184; Calumet Neighborhood Improvement Block Club, 5100–5200 Calumet Avenue, series II, box 234, folder 2297; minutes of 600 and 700 East 46th Street Block Club, January 7, 1953, series II, box 234, folder 2299; July 26, 1950, 1500 Drake Block Club, series II, box 234, folder 2298; all in Chicago Urban League records.

12. Peggy Wireman to William Margolin, August 3, 1962, folder 9, box 105, Hyde Park–Kenwood Community Conference Records, Special Collections Research Center, University of Chicago Library, Chicago (hereafter HPKCC Records).

13. "Semi-Annual Report of West Side Activities," p. 4, series II, box 234, folder 2304; August 6, 1954, Civic and Neighborhood Block Club, 5300 Prairie Avenue, series II, box 234, folder 2297; both in Chicago Urban League records. Emphasis in the original.

14. HPKCC, meeting of executive committee, November 23, 1964, folder 21, box 91, HPKCC records.

15. Aaron Schutz and Mike Miller, eds., *People Power: The Community Organizing Tradition of Saul Alinsky* (Nashville: Vanderbilt University Press, 2015), 147–48; transcript of Aaron Schutz interview with Don Elmer, December 18, 2012. I am grateful to Aaron Schutz for generously sharing both a draft of this chapter and his transcript of the interview with me. On Shurna's experience organizing in Austin, see also Rebecca Marchiel, "Neighborhoods First: The Urban Reinvestment Movement in the Era of Financial Deregulation, 1966–1989," (PhD diss., Northwestern University, 2014), 60–62.

16. Julia Abrahamson, *A Neighborhood Finds Itself* (New York: Harper & Brothers, 1959), 73–83, 87–98. A timeline overview of the HPKCC's block organizing efforts between 1949 and 1956 is available in "Chronological History of the Development of the Block Program of the Hyde Park–Kenwood Community Conference," May 1956, folder 7, box 92, HPKCC records.

17. "Ring Door Bells Today in Membership Drive," *Garfieldian*, July 14, 1954; *Garfieldian*, April 7, 1954, p. 15G; "Tells Growth of Civic Council," *Garfieldian*, October 20, 1954; "Over 2,000 Enrolled in New Council," *Garfieldian*, September 9, 1954; Block-Captains' Manual, Garfield Park West Community Council, folder 2, box 31, Monsignor John J. Egan papers, Notre Dame University Archives (hereafter Egan papers). For the GPWCC's history, see Amanda I. Seligman, *Block by Block: Neighborhoods and Public Policy on Chicago's West Side* (Chicago: University of Chicago Press, 2005), 89–93.

18. Block-Captains' Manual, Garfield Park West Community Council, folder 2, box 31, Egan papers.

19. Flyer, "How Long Do We Have to Put Up with Abandoned Buildings on Our Block??" folder 2, box 46, Northwest Community Organization records, Chicago History Museum (hereafter NCO records). Although they once were open, the NCO records have now been closed to researchers.

20. 1700 Francisco, folder 8, box 46; Charleston-Leavitt Block Club, folder 4, box 46, both in NCO records. For an overview of the NCO, see Thomas J. Jablonsky and Paul-Thomas Ferguson, "Northwest Community Organization," *Encyclopedia of Chicago* online edition, ed. Janice L. Reiff, Ann Durkin Keating, and James Grossman (Chicago: Chicago Historical Society, 2005), http://www.encyclopedia.chicagohistory.org/pages/909.html. For Shel Trapp's reflections on his years as director of the NCO, see Shel Trapp, *Dynamics of Organizing: Building Power by Developing the Human Spirit* (Chicago: Shel Trapp, n.d.), 34–43.

21. See, for example, flyer, "Block Groups for Your Neighborhood: An Outline for Block Organization," Association of Community Councils of Metropolitan Chicago, March 1961, folder 5, box 52, Welfare Council of Metropolitan Chicago records, Chicago History Museum; "fighting battalion" quotation in Benjamin Mark Looker, "A Nation of Neighborhoods: Cities, Communities, and Democracy in the Modern American Imagination, 1940–1980," (PhD diss., Yale University, 2009), 36.

22. Neighbors At Work, staff meeting minutes, November 7, 1966, folder "Nov.–Dec. 1966," box 4, Marillac House records, Chicago History Museum, emphasis in the original; clipping, "Kaczmarek, Vivas Laud G.L.C.C." *Lawndale Journal* 2, no. 7 (May 1963), folder 7, box 31, Egan papers; pamphlet, *Block Club Organization in Lawndale*, folder 87-6, box 87, Chicago Area Project records, Chicago History Museum, Chicago. Archivist markings on the pamphlet suggest that it was issued in 1963. Flyer, "What Is a Block Club?" on East Humboldt Park Planning and Conservation Commission letterhead, folder 36, box 3, Industrial Areas Foundation records, Richard J. Daley Library Special Collections and University Archives, University of Illinois at Chicago; pamphlet, *Block Clubs*, by Residents Councils of Midwest Community Council, folder 9, box 35, American Friends Service Committee, accession 67-87, Richard J. Daley Library Special Collections and University Archives, University of Illinois at Chicago; "How to Form a Block Club," folder: CAPS Block Club Convention 1997, box 3, Lincoln Central Neighborhood Association records, Department of Special Collections and Archives DePaul University Library, Chicago (hereafter LCNA).

23. Map and list, http://chicago47.org/wp-content/uploads/Block-Clubs-Map-with-List-of-BCs.pdf, last accessed June 7, 2014; Dan Kleinman, "The New Neighborhood Block Club Manual," http://chicago47.org/wp-content/uploads/the-new-neighborhood-block-club-manual.pdf, last accessed October 30, 2013; Edgewater Community Council, block club contact list, http://www.edgewatercommunitycouncil.org/blkclubcontact, and Edgewater Community Council, block club map, http://www.edgewatercommunitycouncil.org/ClubMap, both accessed June 7, 2014; CLEARpath Block Clubs, "Getting Started," https://portal.chicagopolice.org/portal/page/portal/BlockClub/Resources/Getting%20Started, last accessed June 7, 2014.

24. West 15th Place Block Club Newsletter no. 3, April 1972, folder 5, box 9, Rich papers.

25. Bettie Sarchet defined the term "block strip" as "one side of the street on one city block" (Bettie B. Sarchet, "Block Groups and Community Change: An Evaluation of the Block Program of the Hyde Park–Kenwood Community Conference," [Human Dynamics Laboratory, University of Chicago: 1955], 10). Social science literature refers to this unit as a "face block." See Robert J. Sampson and Stephen W. Raudenbush, "Systematic Social Observation of Public Spaces: A New Look at Disorder in Urban Neighborhoods," *American Journal of Sociology* 105

(3) (November 1999): 607. According to Shel Trapp, block clubs in the Organization for a Better Austin were "each block facing you": Schutz and Miller, 146.

26. Undated clipping, "Organization of Blocks Rushed to Completion: Civilian Defense Lags until This Preliminary Work Is Done," *WSN* [*West Side News*], folder 20, box 2, Office of Civilian Defense records, Special Collections and Preservation Division, Harold Washington Library Center, Chicago Public Library, Chicago (hereafter OCD); clipping, "Announce Bond Quotas for Blocks," *WSN*, June 16, 1944, folder 13, box 3, OCD; Abrahamson, *A Neighborhood Finds Itself*, 82; Priscilla A. Dowden-White, *Groping Toward Democracy: African American Social Welfare Reform in St. Louis, 1910–1949* (Columbia and London: University of Missouri Press, 2011), 218.

27. 7300 South Evans Avenue, December 9, 1953, series II, box 234, folder 2301; 1500–1600 South Central Park Avenue Block Club, March 18, 1952, Series II, box 234, folder 2298; Progressive Civic Club, August 31, 1950, series II, box 234, folder 2302, all in Chicago Urban League records. Elsie C. Krueger to Henry McGee, November 28, 1955, folder 4, box 106, HPKCC records; 4600–4700 Beacon Block Club, minutes, September 18, 1962, folder 4, box 39, UCC records.

28. Leadership Institute Notes, February 24, 1954, folder 527, box 39, Near West Side Community Committee records, Special Collections and University Archives Department at the Richard J. Daley Library, University of Illinois at Chicago; Thelen and Sarchet, "Neighbors in Action," 51.

29. Letter, Faith to Andrea, August 17, 1969, folder 6, box 18; letter, Faith to Nikki, June 9, 1968, folder 3, box 20; October 15th Place Block Club Newsletter 1986, folder 5, box 9; all in Rich papers.

30. Abrahamson, *A Neighborhood Finds Itself*, 85; oral history interview with Beth Ford, June 17, 2013, Chicago; Sudhir Alladi Venkatesh, *American Project: The Rise and Fall of a Modern Ghetto* (Cambridge, MA, and London: Harvard University Press, 2000), 33.

31. Zorita Mikva, "The Neighborhood Improvement Association: A Counter-Force to the Expansion of Chicago's Negro Population" (MA thesis, University of Chicago, 1951), 44, put the improvement associations between eight and eighty blocks in size.

32. For example, the Every Person Is Concerned Block Club explains on its website that it "serves as the voice of the Magnolia Glen neighborhood," with boundaries of "the west side of Broadway, east side of Glenwood, north side of Elmdale, south side of Rosedale and both sides of Magnolia to Ardmore." EPIC Block Club home page, http://www.epicblockclub.org/, last accessed October 9, 2013.

33. East Andersonville Residents' Council Newsletter, July 1994, folder 7, box 30, Mary Ann Smith Papers, 1978–2009, Women and Leadership Archives, Loyola University Chicago, Chicago; EPIC Block Captains, January 26, 1994, folder 9, box 31, Mary Ann Smith Papers, 1978–2009, Women and Leadership Archives, Loyola University Chicago, Chicago; letter, "Dear Gentlemen," Lakewood-Balmoral Residents Council, October 18, 1971, folder 15, box 43, UCC records, Chicago History Museum, Chicago.

34. Oral history interview, Dara Salk, June 10, 2013, Chicago.

35. Dowden-White, 218 and 235; clipping, "Announce Bond Quotas for Blocks," *WSN*, June 16, 1944, folder 13, box 3, OCD; minute book, June 8, 1943, The Very Good Club collection, Chicago History Museum.

36. For an explanation of Chicago's street naming and numbering system, see Christopher Thale, "House Numbering and Street Numbering," http://www.encyclopedia.chicagohistory .org/pages/3876.html; and Paul Michael Wakeford, "Street Naming," http://www.encyclopedia .chicagohistory.org/pages/1205.html, both in *Encyclopedia of Chicago* online, ed. Janice L. Reiff, Ann Durkin Keating, and James Grossman, accessed January 16, 2013.

37. West 15th Place Block Club Newsletter, October 1986, folder 5, box 9, Rich papers. Kevin Lynch developed the idea of the "mental map" to examine urbanites' conceptions of their environs in *The Image of the City* (Cambridge, MA: MIT Press, 1960).

38. Rufford Milton, "Garfield Community Council Block Club News," *Garfieldian*, December 16, 1964; Chicago Beach Area Block Group: Miss Elsa Wolf interviewed, folder 16, box 96, Hyde Park–Kenwood Community Conference records, Special Collections Research Center, University of Chicago, Chicago (hereafter HPKCC); contacts, 4000 S. Vincennes Avenue, November, Series II, box 234, folder 2303, Chicago Urban League records; summary report of the Block Unit Summer Project, August 2, 1962, p. 6; summary report of the Block Unit Program, Marcy Center, August 20, 1964, folder August 1964, box 24, Greater Lawndale Conservation Commission records, Chicago History Museum, Chicago (hereafter GLCC records); Civic and Neighborhood club, 5300 block on Prairie Avenue, series II, box 234, folder 2297, Chicago Urban League records; block club meeting, Princeton Avenue 3500 to 3600 South, October 21, 1952, series II, box 235, folder 2324, Chicago Urban League records. A group in Milwaukee called itself a "block investment club" because the term block club "sounds too much like snitches": Georgia Pabst, "One City Block Reflects Struggle to Overcome Foreclosure Wave," *Milwaukee Journal Sentinel*, October 30, 2010.

39. Dowden-White, *Groping toward Democracy*, 218–19.

40. Draft constitution, series II, box 233, folder 2273; 500 block on East 47th Street, series II, box 234, folder 2299; 6800 Prairie, series II, box 234, folder 2301, Chicago Urban League records; Alva B. Maxey, "The Block Club Movement in Chicago," *Phylon Quarterly* 18(2) (1957): 126; 4800 Prairie Avenue [B]lo[c]k Improvement Club, series II, box 234, folder 2299, Chicago Urban League records.

41. Abrahamson, *A Neighborhood Finds Itself*, 78; Drexel Strip Block Group, Mr. Ernest Clark interviewed, folder 16, box 96, HPKCC.

42. Argyle Glenwood Magnolia Block Club, Bezazian Library, June 11, 1974, p. 2, folder 13, box 38, UCC records, Chicago History Museum, Chicago; 600–700 block on 46th Street, January7, 1953, series II, box 234, folder 2299, Chicago Urban League records; Civic and Neighborhood Block Club, 5300 Prairie Avenue, July 19, 1954, series II, box 234, folder 2297, Chicago Urban League records; 500 Block on East 47th Street, series II, box 234, folder 2299, Chicago Urban League records; Charleston-Leavitt Block Club, first meeting, folder 4, box 46, NCO. The criticism of block club leaders as "domineering" also appears in the worker's notes about other clubs. See 7200 South Michigan Avenue and 7300 South Calumet Block Club, both in series II, box 234, folder 2301, Chicago Urban League records.

43. 7100 Eberhart Block, January 21, 1954, series II, box 234, folder 2301, Chicago Urban League records; 4000 block on Prairie Avenue, October 12, 1950, series II, box 234, folder 2300, Chicago Urban League records. Typographical errors in source corrected in this quotation.

44. Letter, Faith to Tommy, January 1, 1971, box 19, folder 3, Rich papers. In contract sales, the seller retained title to a property until the buyer paid off the full value of the transaction. If the buyer was late on or missed a payment, the seller could revoke the sale without returning the equity. Most contract buyers could not complete the terms of the agreement and lost their homes. Mrs. Robinson's ability to pay off her contract was testimony to an unusual combination of individual stability and determination that spoke to her leadership capacity. Robinson began studying for her GED in her eighties. See Mary Mitchell, "Octogenarian Proves It's Never Too Late to Return to School: Mitchell," *Chicago Sun-Times*, January 29, 2014, http://www.suntimes .com/news/mitchell/25264780–452/octogenarian-proves-its-never-to-late-to-return-school -mitchell.html#.U6YUDfldWSo. For more on contract buyers, see Beryl Satter, *Family Properties:*

Race, Real Estate, and the Exploitation of Black Urban America (New York: Metropolitan Books, 2009), 3–7 and passim.

45. Single sheet, handwritten testimonial about Faith Rich, undated, beginning, "Faith is now visiting in her home state of Vermont," Rich papers. When I used the unprocessed collection, this document was held in an envelope labeled "1982 Tax & 1983 Tax," in a brown box labeled "Rich 5."

46. News release, November 16, 1953, series I, box 220, folder 2185, Chicago Urban League records; 5700 South Calumet Street, March 12, 1953, series II, box 234, folder 2297, Chicago Urban League records; report on housing and zoning, Jean Wehrheim, July 19, 1964, folder "July 17–31, 1964," box 24, GLCC records.

47. Letter, "Dear Gentlemen," Lakewood-Balmoral Residents Council, October 18, 1971, folder 15, box 43, UCC records. See also West 15th Place Block Club Annual Report, General Not for Profit Corporation Act, folder 4, box 9, Rich papers. In 1974, the cost of the state charter was $25. See Wilson Avenue Block Club, Both Sides of Wilson Ave. from Sheridan Rd. to the Lake, September 23, 1974, folder 5, box 49, UCC records.

48. The 70th Place and Crandon, Oglesby, Paxton Block Club Inc., *COP ByLaws*, Chicago History Museum; "How to Form a Block Club," folder, CAPS Block Club Convention 1997, box 3, LCNA records; oral history interview with Beth Ford, June 17, 2013, Chicago, IL.

49. Jane Kwiatkowski, "Improving Life, Block by Block, in Buffalo Neighborhoods," *Buffalo News*, http://www.buffalonews.com/city-region/buffalo/improving-life-block-by-block-in-buffalo-neighborhoods-20130917, last accessed October 9, 2013.

50. Richard C. Rich and Abraham Wandersman, "Participation in Block Organizations," *Social Policy* 14 (12) (1983): 46; Susanne M. Tumelty, "Block Associations, Crime, and the Police" (PhD diss., City University of New York, 1987), 17.

51. Madrue Chavers-Wright, *The Guarantee: P. W. Chavers: Banker, Entrepreneur, Philanthropist in Chicago's Black Belt of the Twenties* ([New York]: Wright-Armstead Associates New York, 1985), 326.

52. Calumet Avenue, 4000 South, November 6, 1952, series II, box 235, folder 2309; record of block club meetings, page 5, series II, box 235, folder 2323, both in Chicago Urban League records; Jeffrey Helgeson, "Striving in Black Chicago: Migration, Work, and the Politics of Neighborhood Change, 1935–1965," (PhD diss., University of Illinois at Chicago, 2008), 70 and 90; 7200 South Calumet, series II, box 234, folder 2301, Chicago Urban League records.

53. William M. Rohe and Mark Lindblad, "Reexamining the Social Benefits of Homeownership after the Housing Crisis," Joint Center for Housing Studies, Harvard University (August 2013), http://www.jchs.harvard.edu/sites/jchs.harvard.edu/files/hbtl-04.pdf, last accessed October 21, 2013.

54. 200 North California, May 28, 1954, series II, box 235, folder 2304, Chicago Urban League records.

55. Andrew W. Kahrl, *The Land Was Ours: African American Beaches from Jim Crow to the Sunbelt South* (Cambridge, MA, and London: Harvard University Press, 2012) and Satter, *Family Properties*. Other works that explore the significance of home ownership in Chicago include Margaret Garb, *City of American Dreams: A History of Home Ownership and Housing Reform in Chicago, 1871–1919* (Chicago: University of Chicago Press, 2005); and Elaine Lewinnek, "Better than a Bank for a Poor Man? Home Financing Strategies in Early Chicago," *Journal of Urban History*, 32 (2006): 274–301. Elaine Lewinnek, *The Working Man's Reward: Chicago's Early Suburbs and the Roots of American Sprawl* (New York: Oxford University Press, 2014). On tensions

between black property owners and tenants, see also N. B. D. Connolly, *A World More Concrete: Real Estate and the Remaking of Jim Crow South Florida* (Chicago: University of Chicago Press, 2014).

56. Activity sheet, November 8, 1955, folder 6, box 110, HPKCC.

57. For a sense of superiority deriving from migrants' "year consciousness," depending on the timing of their arrival in Los Angeles, see Gerard Horne, *The Fire This Time: The Watts Uprising and the 1960s* (Boston: Da Capo Press, 1997; originally published Charlottesville, VA: University of Virginia Press, 1995), 33.

58. Wendy Plotkin, "Kitchenettes," *Encyclopedia of Chicago* online, ed. Janice Reiff, Ann Durkin Keating, and James Grossman (Chicago: Chicago History Museum, 2005), http://www.encyclopedia.chicagohistory.org/pages/692.html. On conversions, see Seligman, *Block by Block*, chapter 2, "Housing Codes."

59. 7200 South Calumet, series II, box 234, folder 2301; 7400 Indiana block, series II, box 234, folder 2301; both in Chicago Urban League records.

60. James R. Grossman, *Land of Hope: Chicago, Black Southerners, and the Great Migration* (Chicago: University of Chicago Press, 1989), 145; Mary Pattillo, *Black on the Block: The Politics of Race and Class in the City* (Chicago: University of Chicago Press, 2007), 91, 261, and 288.

61. Letter, Frayser T. Lane to Mrs. Ruth Pertiller, August 29, 1955, folder July–September 1955, box 2, GLCC records; Calumet Avenue, 4000 South, November 6, 1952, series II, box 235, folder 2309, Chicago Urban League records; 4300 Block Club on Champlain, September 9, 1950, series II, box 234, folder 2312, Chicago Urban League records.

62. Venkatesh, *American Project*, 33 and 229; letter, Faith to Nikki, June 9, 1968, folder 3, box 20, Faith Rich papers. See generally the records of the Northwest Community Organization, box 35.

63. *Voice of the Midwest Community Council*, vol. III, no. 4, May 1960, p. 3, folder 2, box 35, Egan papers.

64. Text of speech, handwritten date April 12, 1955, p. 7, folder April–June 1955, box 1, GLCC records; Jessamine Cobb, assistant director, Area Welfare Planning Department, Welfare Council of Metropolitan Chicago, "Community Area 29–North Lawndale," October 1955, folder "Oct. Dec. 1955," box 2, GLCC records; Aaron Schutz interview with Don Elmer, December 18, 2012, transcript p. 4, courtesy of Aaron Schutz; council report, series II, box 234, folder 2304, Chicago Urban League records; board of directors, May 26, 1959, p. 4, folder "May 20–31, 1959," box 10, GLCC records; board of directors meeting of January 17, 1956, p. 3, folder "Jan. 1956," box 2, GLCC. The sociologist Albert Hunter reported his belief that "block clubs are more prevalent in the black communities of Chicago than in white areas." Albert Hunter, *Symbolic Communities: The Persistence and Change of Chicago's Local Communities* (Chicago and London: University of Chicago Press, 1974), 145.

65. Abrahamson, *A Neighborhood Finds Itself*, 34–36, credited Thelen with giving the key speech (p. 35). Thelen himself provided the date of January 1950 and the identification of the block, where he and his wife lived at 5655 S. Drexel. Block leaders and block steering committee members, folder 2, box 95, HPKCC records.

66. Sarchet, "Block Groups and Community Change," 79–81, quote on p. 80; Abrahamson, *A Neighborhood Finds Itself*, 34–36, quote on p. 36; Stuart Chase, "We *Can* Do Something about It!" offprint from *Reader's Digest*, 1953, folder 13, box 94, HPKCC records; report from ACTION, "Organization of Block Groups for Neighborhood Improvement: The Hyde Park–Kenwood Community Conference" (New York City, September 1956), folder 10, box 64, HPKCC records;

minutes of the Chicago Beach Area Group meeting at Surf and Surrey, May 20, 1964, folder 5, box 105, HPKCC records; Thelen, 10–11. On ACTION, see Benjamin Looker, *A Nation of Neighborhoods: Imagining Cities, Communities, and Democracy in Postwar America* (Chicago: University of Chicago Press, 2015), 91–97.

67. Francis X. Lawlor, "Panic-Peddlers and Violence Threaten to Destroy Community; South Lynne Area Doomed Unless Blocks Organize Now," *ABC News*, February 27, 1970, Chicago History Museum.

68. Letter, Mrs. Pearlie Mae Robinson, pres., and Faith Rich, corr. sec'y, West 15th Place Block Club, to "Dear Neighbor," April 18, 1969, folder 6, box 18, Rich papers; 1200 block South Springfield Avenue Block Club, Mar. 18, 1952, series II, box 234, folder 2298, Chicago Urban League records; Robert S. Abbott Neighborhood Club (3600 block on South Wells), series II, box 234, folder 2300, Chicago Urban League records; 5100–5200 Michigan block, October 29, 1954, series II, box 234, folder 2297, Chicago Urban League records; Herbert A. Thelen and Bettie Belk Sarchet, "Neighbors in Action: A Manual for Community Leaders" (Human Dynamics Laboratory, Department of Education, University of Chicago 1954), 28; letter, Julia Abrahamson to Mr. Herbert Thelen, Miss Bernice Rogers, and Mr. and Mrs. Kale Williams, March 9, 1951, folder 6, box 98, HPKCC records.

69. Annabelle Bender, "Civilian Defense Block Organization in Hyde Park" (MA thesis, University of Chicago, 1943), 34; Sarchet, "Block Groups and Community Change," 90.

70. 1500 Drake Block Club, Wednesday, July 12, 1950, series II, box 234, folder 2298, Chicago Urban League records; minutes of the meeting of the information committee of the 5000 Drexel Boulevard Block Organization at the Blacks' apartment, 5036 Drexel Blvd., May 13, 1952, folder 5, box 109, HPKCC; flyer, "Your Block Club is Having a Real Party and Its [*sic*] a Good Neighbor Party," series II, box 234, folder 2304, Chicago Urban League records.

71. Joseph P. Schwieterman and Dana M. Caspall, *The Politics of Place: A History of Zoning in Chicago* (Chicago: Lake Claremont Press, 2007), chapter 3; CLEARpath Block Clubs, Getting Started, https://portal.chicagopolice.org/portal/page/portal/BlockClub/Resources/Getting%20 Started.

72. The Friendly Neighborhood Club (5800 block on Indiana Avenue), series II, box 234, folder 2297, Chicago Urban League records; flyer, "How Long Do We Have to Put Up with Abandoned Buildings on Our Block??," folder 2, box 46, NCO; Charleston-Leavitt Block Club: first meeting, folder 4, box 46, NCO; "ATOA Block Club News," *Garfieldian*, April 13, 1966, p. 9.

73. Neighbors At Work central staff minutes, May 25, 1965, folder April–May 1965, box 2, Marillac House records, Chicago History Museum; Sarchet, "Block Groups and Community Change," 59; 4000 block on Prairie Avenue, June 27, 1950, series II, box 234, folder 2300, Chicago Urban League records.

74. Record of Block Club meetings, January 28, 1953, p. 7, series II, box 235, folder 2323; 1300 block Lawndale, February 1, 1954, series II, box 234, folder 2298; 7300 South Calumet Block Club, November 2, 1953, series II, box 234, folder 2301, all in Chicago Urban League records; letter, Mrs. Pearlie Mae Robinson, pres., and Faith Rich, corr. sec'y, West 15th Place Block Club, to "Dear Neighbor," April 18, 1969, folder 6, box 18, Rich papers; letter, Faith to Andrea, August 17, 1969, folder 6, box 18, Rich papers; Thelen and Sarchet, "Neighbors in Action," 27. Tumelty, 31, suggested that dues payments also helped members commit to the group.

75. Letter, David Church et al., to Hello Neighbor, folder 3, box 45, NCO records; record of block club meetings, first meeting, January 28, 1953, p. 7, series II, box 235, folder 2323, Chicago Urban League records; 4300 S. Vernon Avenue block, January 15, 1953, series II, box 234, folder 2303, Chicago Urban League records; letter, Faith to Papa, July 24, 1969, folder 6, box 18, Rich papers; Thelen and Sarchet, "Neighbors in Action," 26–27.

76. 4300 block on St. Lawrence Avenue, series II, box 234, folder 2302, Chicago Urban League records. See also Maxey, "The Block Club Movement in Chicago," 125; 7200 S. Michigan Avenue, January 18, 1954, series II, box 234, folder 2301, Chicago Urban League records.

77. "Lawlor: Block Clubs Good for Community," *Austin News*, November 11, 1970, box 3, ANC; memo to block club presidents and temporary presidents, from Tom Jenkins, assistant C.O. secretary, Chicago Urban League, series II, box 234, folder 2304, Chicago Urban League records; Dowden-White, 217, notes that in St. Louis and New York City, neighborhood organizing was conducted primarily by women in the interwar years, although "men had dominated the work of the earlier period."

78. 1300 block Lawndale, series II, box 234, folder 2298, Chicago Urban League records. According to Arvarh Strickland's analysis, for the first half century of its existence, the League relied on large donations from philanthropists to sustain its operations. In 1919, for example, 707 of the 900 donations to the League came in the amount of one dollar. The organization's entire budget for the year was $15,008.49, most of which was provided in much larger donations. Chicago Urban League, annual report for the fiscal year ended October 31, 1919, folder 1–2, series I, box 1, Chicago Urban League. However, African American Chicagoans were increasingly encouraged to provide small donations within their means. See Strickland, 34, 74, 96–97, 114, and 206–7.

79. Abrahamson, *A Neighborhood Finds Itself*, 138; 2900 West Fulton Street Block Club, series II, box 235, folder 2304, Chicago Urban League records; letter, Ethel Estelle, chairman, to block club president, February 2, 1953, series I, box 220, folder 2185, Chicago Urban League records; Evelyn Brooks Higginbotham, *Righteous Discontent: The Women's Movement in the Black Baptist Church, 1880–1920* (Cambridge, MA, and London: Harvard University Press, 1993), 59, 162, 220.

80. Memorandum to Ed Chambers from Lorraine Johnson, dictated June 8, 1963, folder 11, box 42, Egan papers.

81. Tumelty, 47, in New York City, concluded that the continued involvement of the founding president was crucial to the ongoing activity of a block club. Thelen and Sarchet, "Neighbors in Action," 13; 2100 West Maypole Avenue Block Club, March 18, 1952, series II, box 235, folder 2304, Chicago Urban League records; Rufford Milton, "West Garfield Park News and Comment," *Garfieldian*, July 7, 1966; Civic and Neighborhood Block Club, 5300 Prairie Avenue, August 6, 1954, series II, box 234, folder 2297; 5300 S. Prairie Block, November 12, 1954, series II, box 234, folder 2297; 60th–61st Street Neighborhood Club, October 29, 1954, series II, box 234, folder 2297; East 56th Street Improvement Club, July 14, 1954, series II, box 234, folder 2297; 5700 South Calumet Street, July 21, 1954, series II, box 234, folder 2297; all in Chicago Urban League records.

82. Tumelty, 20.

83. Contacts, Vincennes Avenue 4300 block South, November 11, 1952, series II, box 234, folder 2303, Chicago Urban League records; 5200 Drexel Block Group, Mrs. Oscar Davis interviewed, box 96, folder 16, HPKCC records.

84. Frank T. Cherry, "Southern In-Migrant Negroes in North Lawndale, Chicago, 1949–59: A Study of Internal Migration and Adjustment" (PhD diss., University of Chicago, 1965), p. 83, note 2.

Chapter Three

1. 3100 block on 15th Street, December 17, 1951, and 3100 West 15th Street Block Club, March 18, 1952, both in series II, box 234, folder 2298, Chicago Urban League records, Department of Special Collections, Richard J. Daley Library, University of Chicago at Illinois (hereafter Chicago Urban League records).

2. The hostility white urbanites expressed toward African Americans in the twentieth century has been widely examined. Useful introductory works in this literature include Stephen Grant Meyer, *As Long As They Don't Move Next Door: Segregation and Racial Conflict in American Neighborhoods* (Lanham, MD: Rowman & Littlefield, 2000), and Jeannine Bell, *Hate Thy Neighbor: Move-In Violence and the Persistence of Racial Segregation in American Housing* (New York: New York University Press, 2013).

3. Chicago Fact Book Consortium, *Local Community Fact Book: Chicago Metropolitan Area, 1980* (Chicago: Chicago Review Press, 1984), 80.

4. Ferdinand Tönnies, *Community and Society (Gemeinschaft und Gesellschaft)*, trans. and. ed. Charles P. Loomis (New York: Harper & Row, 1965; edition originally published in 1957 by Michigan State University Press; originally published in German in 1887); Thomas Bender, *Community and Social Change in America* (Baltimore: Johns Hopkins University Press, 1982; originally published by Rutgers University Press, 1978); Robert D. Putnam, *Bowling Alone: The Collapse and Revival of American Community* (New York: Simon and Schuster, 2000); Robert J. Sampson, *Great American City: Chicago and the Enduring Neighborhood Effect* (Chicago: University of Chicago Press, 2012).

5. Robert D. Putnam *Bowling Alone: The Collapse and Revival of American Community* (New York: Touchstone Books, 2001), 22–24.

6. Clipping, "Kaczmarek, Vivas Laud G.L.C.C.," *The Lawndale Journal* 2, no. 7 (May 1963), box 57B, folder 2, Monsignor John J. Egan papers, University of Notre Dame Archives (hereafter Egan papers); "Future of Block Club Movement Depends on Austin Residents," *Austinite*, May 25, 1966, box 7, Austin Newspapers Collection, Special Collections and Preservation Division, Harold Washington Public Library, Chicago Public Libraries, Chicago (hereafter ANC); "Lawlor: Block Clubs Good for Community," *Austin News*, November 11, 1970, box 3, ANC; "Fr. Lawlor Advises: Unity with Block Clubs," *Austinite*, November 11, 1970, box 9, ANC; memo, to File from Charlotte Meacham, August 24, 1965, re visit to Chicago, August 4, 1965, folder, Housing Opportunities Program, correspondence with Philadelphia, Chicago RO 1965, box Chicago R.O. 1965 (Housing Oppors. Prog.-Coms & Orgs.: Suburban Human Rels. Comm. Com. to Youth Oppors. Prog.), Chicago Regional Office Files, American Friends Service Committee Archives, Philadelphia.

7. Sampson, *Great American City*, 45. Sampson's Project on Human Development in Chicago Neighborhoods database contains survey questions about the existence of block organizations that could be used to study their effects on neighborhoods for the years in which the data was gathered. See Felton J. Earls, Jeanne Brooks-Gunn, Stephen W. Raudenbush, and Robert J. Sampson, "Project on Human Development in Chicago Neighborhoods: Community Survey, 1994–1995," http://www.icpsr.umich.edu/files/PHDCN/community-survey.pdf, pp. 11, 17, and 30 (last accessed December 4, 2013).

8. Report from ACTION, "Organization of Block Groups for Neighborhood Improvement: The Hyde Park–Kenwood Community Conference" (New York City, September 1956), p. 7, folder 10, box 64, Hyde Park–Kenwood Community Conference records, Special Collections Research Center, Regenstein Library, University of Chicago (hereafter HPKCC); "Visit to a Block Club Meeting," *Garfieldian*, November 20, 1963; 5000 South Calumet block, October 29, 1954, series II, box 234, folder 2299, Chicago Urban League records; *Voice of the Midwest Community Council* 3 no. 3 (February 1960): 3, folder 2, uncatalogued box 22, Metropolitan Housing and Planning Council, accession 74-20, Department of Special Collections, Richard J. Daley Library, University of Illinois at Chicago; *The Volunteer, the Voice of the Federation of Block Units and Neighborhood Groups*, December 1951, vol. 3, series II, box 235, folder 2314, Chicago Urban League records.

9. "Block Party," *Austin News*, September 16, 1970, box 3, ANC; Wendell Phillips Improvement Club (3900 South Prairie Avenue), November 1, 1954, series II, box 234, folder 2303, Chicago Urban League records; 7100 Eberhart block, January 21, 1954, series II, box 234, folder 2301, Chicago Urban League records; *GLCC News Notes* 4, no. 9 (November 1960), folder 3, box 10, Rich papers; Aaron Schutz interview with Don Elmer, December 18, 2012, p. 4, transcript courtesy of Aaron Schutz.

10. 500 Bowen Improvement Club, September 21, 1950, series II, box 234, folder 2302; Cosmopolitan Neighborhood Improvement Association, series II, box 234, folder 2297; both in Chicago Urban League records. Cover photos, "The WFCW Block Club Presents Our 2012 Holiday Gathering," http://www.facebook.com/photo.php?fbid=474639319242036&set=a.365336903505 612.80442.153638898008748&type=1&theater, accessed March 4, 2013.

11. 4300 South Vernon Avenue block, series II, box 234, folder 2303, Chicago Urban League records; letter, Frances Morano, chairman, block committee, to block members, Miller-Carpenter Street Block Club, May 17, 1955, and letter, Frances Morano, chairman, block committee, to block members, Miller-Carpenter Street Block Club, May 26, 1955, both in folder 531, Near West Side Community Committee records, Department of Special Collections, Richard J. Daley Library, University of Chicago at Illinois (hereafter NWSCC records); memo to McCurine from Mr. Leslie Simmons, activities for the week of November 8–14, 1964, folder 74, GLCC-UIC; Neighbors At Work, staff meeting minutes, November 21, 1966, folder "Nov.–Dec. 1966," box 4, Marillac House records, Chicago History Museum.

12. Newsletter, West Side Community Improvement Council of the Chicago Urban League, undated, series I, box 268, folder 2734; minutes of the Westside Community Improvement Council, July 6, 1950, sSeries I, box 268, folder 2716, both in Chicago Urban League records; letter, McCurine to board members, September. 21, 1965, folder 101, Greater Lawndale Conservation Commission records, Special Collections Department, University of Illinois at Chicago Library (hereafter GLCC-UIC); GLCC Association of Block Clubs, 3rd annual dinner-dance, Sept. 8, 1967, "An Evening in Paradise," program, folder 54-6, box 54, Marcy-Newberry Association records, Special Collections and University Archives Department at the Richard J. Daley Library, University of Illinois at Chicago; "An Evening in Venice," GLCC Association of Block Clubs, souvenir program, folder 5 box 25, Egan papers. A community-wide tea held in West Garfield Park in 1966 attracted representatives from twenty-four block clubs. See "West Garfield Community News and Comment," *Garfieldian*, May 25, 1966; letter, James M. Walton to McCurine, September 25, 1965, folder 101, GLCC-UIC; letter, Hyman Levine to McCurine, September 29, 1965, folder 101, GLCC-UIC.

13. Julia Abrahamson, *A Neighborhood Finds Itself* (New York: Harper & Brothers, 1959), 219; report from ACTION, "Organization of Block Groups for Neighborhood Improvement: The Hyde Park-Kenwood Community Conference" (New York City, September 1956), p. 10, folder 10, box 64, HPKCC records; see also Herbert A. Thelen and Bettie Belk Sarchet, "Neighbors in Action: A Manual for Community Leaders" (Human Dynamics Laboratory, Department of Education, University of Chicago 1954), 51.

14. West 15th Place Block Club Newsletter no. 79, November 1981, folder 4, box 9, Rich papers; *Chips off Our Block*, May 1957, folder 5, box 96, HPKCC records. For Chicago Urban League newsletters, see series II, box 235, folder 2314, Chicago Urban League records.

15. *Street Scene* newsletter, 3100 West 15th St., April, no. 1, series II, box 235, folder 2314, Chicago Urban League records.

16. Newsletter, Greater Progressive Property Owners Club of Millard Avenue, January 1962 edition, folder: January 1962, box 18, Greater Lawndale Conservation Commission records, Chicago History Museum (hereafter GLCC-CHM records).

17. *Block Club News*, 700–800 South Kilbourn-Kolmar and Fifth Avenue Block Club, folder 50, GLCC-UIC.

18. For examples of newsletters, see series II, box 235, folder 2314, Chicago Urban League records. Copies of the *GLCC NewsNotes* newsletter are held in the GLCC-CHM records, passim.

19. *Southwest Associated Block Club News*, September 15, 1968, vol. 1, no. 11, p. 15; *ABC News*, Friday July 24, 1970; *ABC News*, February 27, 1970; "As I See It," *Southwest Associated Block Club News*, September 15, 1958; all held at Chicago History Museum.

20. Richard A. Schwarzlose, "Newspapers," *Encyclopedia of Chicago*, edited by Janice Reiff, Ann Durkin Keating, and James R. Grossman (Chicago: Chicago History Museum, 2005), http://www.encyclopedia.chicagohistory.org/pages/889.html; "Calmness, Resistance to Speculators Stressed," *Garfieldian*, Aug. 12, 1959; Rufford Milton, "Garfield Community Council Block Club News," *Garfieldian*, December 16, 1964; letter, Thomas E. Hummons, chairman of publicity, to Block Club presidents, Aug. 8, 1964, folder August 1964, box 24, GLCC-CHM records.

21. Dear Julia and Elsi, from Pat [Schmenoff?], September 6, 1954, folder 6, box 92, HPKCC.

22. Block Club Federation, http://blockclubfederation.org/, last accessed June 7, 2014; "Block Clubs of the 48th Ward," provided to the author via e-mail by Ernie Constantino, June 10, 2013; BARGE Block Club, http://www.edgewaterbarge.com/, last accessed November 11, 2013; NET Block Club, A Block Club for Neighbors of Elmdale and Thorndale, http://netblockclub.com/, last accessed June 7, 2014; Winona Foster Carmen Winnemac (WFCW) Block Club, http://www.facebook.com/pages/Winona-Foster-Carmen-Winnemac-WFCW-Block-Club/153638898008748, last accessed June 7, 2014; Lakewood Balmoral Residents' Council, https://www.facebook.com/Lakewood.Balmoral, last accessed June 7, 2014; Bob Fioretti, 2nd Ward alderman, "Forming a Block Club," http://bobfioretti.com/residents/forming-a-block-club/, last accessed June 7, 2014; oral history interview with Beth Ford, June 17, 2013, Chicago.

23. For an introduction to the topic of American youth cultures, see Joe Austin and Michael Nevin Willard, *Generations of Youth: Youth Cultures and History in Twentieth Century America* (New York and London: New York University Press, 1998).

24. Report of Executive Director, GLCC general meeting, November 18, 1957, p. 3, folder: November 16–30, 1957, box 4, GLCC-CHM, emphasis in the original; Alva B. Maxey, "The Block Club Movement in Chicago," *Phylon Quarterly* 18(2) (1957): 129.

25. 2600 West Adams Street, series II, box 235, folder 2304, Chicago Urban League records; "Residents Council Report," *Voice of the Midwest Community Council*, vol. 3, no. 4, May 1960, p. 3, folder 2, box 35, Egan papers; Board of Directors, May 26, 1959, p. 4, folder, "May 20–31, 1959," box 121, GLCC-CHM .

26. 5600 South Prairie Avenue, April 20, 1953, series II, box 234, folder 2297, Chicago Urban League records; residents council report, "The Voice of the Midwest Community Council," vol. 11, no. 7, October 1958, folder 524, NWSCC records 356.1–2; 7200 South Calumet, series II, box 234, folder 2301, Chicago Urban League records; 6800 South Prairie, July 24, 1954, series II, box 234, folder 2301, Chicago Urban League records; unlabeled sheet, first entry on page is "10/16/50—500 Bowen Club," October 31, 1950, series II, box 234, folder 2302, Chicago Urban League records; letter, Christopher M. Edwards, ass't. C.O. secretary, to Mrs. Rachel Ridley, May 7, 1953, series I, box 220, folder 2185, Chicago Urban League records. West 15th Place Block Club newsletter no. 47, July 1976, folder 4, box 9, Faith Rich papers, Special Collections and Preservation Division, Harold Washington Public Library, Chicago Public Libraries, Chicago (hereafter Rich papers); West 15th Place Block Club Newsletter no. 49, September 1976, box 19, folder 4, Rich papers.

27. "Teens All Out for Cleanup," *Garfieldian*, September 28, 1966; Whaley Operation Pride Report, June 21, 1963, folder "June 1963," box 21, GLCC-CHM.

28. Summary report of the block unit program, Marcy Center, August 20, 1964, p. 5, folder August 1964, box 24, GLCC-CHM; Sister Jane, "Marillac Unit of Block Clubs," *Voice of the Midwest Community Council*, vol. 11, no. 7, October 1958, p. 3, folder 524, NWSCC; Craig L. Pfannkuche, "Libertyville, IL," *Encyclopedia of Chicago*, Janice L. Reiff, Ann Durkin Keating, and James R. Grossman (2005), http://www.encyclopedia.chicagohistory.org/pages/740.html; Stan Barker, "Amusement Parks," *Encyclopedia of Chicago*, http://www.encyclopedia.chicagohistory.org/pages/48.html; 4700 South Evans Avenue, October 29, 1954, series II, box 234, folder 2299, Chicago Urban League records. On racial conflict in recreational facilities such as Riverview, see Victoria Wolcott, "Recreation and Race in the Postwar City: Buffalo's 1956 Crystal Beach Riot," *Journal of American History* 93 (1) (2006): 63–90, and *Race, Riots, and Roller Coasters: The Struggle over Segregated Recreation in America* (Philadelphia: University of Pennsylvania Press, 2012).

29. "West Garfield Community News and Comment," *Garfieldian*, August 10, 1966; 5600 South Prairie Avenue, January 9, 1953, series II, box 234, folder 2297, Chicago Urban League records; Michael Westgate interview with Shel Trapp, Chicago, October 23, 2003, p. 5. Interview transcript generously provided by Aaron Schutz (hereafter Trapp interview); Thelen and Sarchet, 14.

30. Abrahamson, *A Neighborhood Finds Itself*, 81, 85, and 92. Many of these sample documents were also reproduced as appendices to Abrahamson's book.

31. Abrahamson, *A Neighborhood Finds Itself*, 82 and 93. Report on block organization activities, June 3, 1951, folder 20, box 91; Chronological History of the Development of the Block Program of the Hyde Park–Kenwood Community Conference, May 1956, folder 7, box 92; letter, John Edward Smith, chairman, block steering committee, to Mr. Irving M. Gerick, executive director, HPKCC, May 27, 1963, folder 4, box 94; letter, Mrs. Michael Wireman, block director, to Dear BSC Member, November 27, 1963, folder 21, box 91, all in HPKCC.

32. Princeton Avenue Civic Club, March 13, 1953, series II, box 234, folder 2300, Chicago Urban League records.

33. Mrs. Rachel Ridley, director, West Side activities, to Mrs. Gertrude Elmore, 124 North California Avenue, January 18, 1950, series I, box 220, folder 2183; letter, Tarlease Bell, president, and Rachel Ridley, director, to Dear member, January 4, 1951, series I, box 220, folder 2184; minutes, Westside Community Improvement Council, August 11, 1950, series I, box 268, folder 2716; all in Chicago Urban League records.

34. Priscilla A. Dowden-White, *Groping toward Democracy: African American Social Welfare Reform in St. Louis, 1910–1949* (Columbia and London: University of Missouri Press, 2011), 229–33; form letter, West Side Community Improvement Council of the Chicago Urban League, Allan Lewis, president, Daisy Grisham, secretary, and Rachel Ridley, director, Westside activities, to Dear Council Member, July 31, 1950, series I, box 220, folder 2183; letter, Robert E. Williams, ass't. sec., community organization department, to Dear Block Club member, October 29, 1953, series I, box 220, folder 2185; March 18, 1952, 3100 West 15th Street Block Club, series II, box 234, folder 2298; newsletter, West Side Community Improvement Council of the Chicago Urban League, series II, box 234, folder 2304; form letter (with name space left blank) from Rachel Ridley, Tarlease Bell, and Hester Estelle, February 1, 1952, series I, box 220, folder 2184, all in Chicago Urban League records.

35. 500 Bowen Improvement Club, July 21, 1950, series II, box 234, folder 2302; Washington Park Court Property Owners Association, 4900 block on Washington Park, series II, box 234,

folder 2299; 4900 Vincennes Avenue Improvement Club, series II, box 234, folder 2299; 3200 West Fulton Block Club, February 26, 1954, series II, box 235, folder 2304, all in Chicago Urban League records.

36. Letter, L. Montgomery, asst. sec., to Chicago Urban League, July 15, 1953, and letter, A. B. Maxey, director, community organization department, to Mrs. L. Montgomery, July 21, 1953, both in series I, box 220, folder 2185, Chicago Urban League records.

37. Princeton Avenue Civic Club, March 13, 1953, series II, box 234, folder 2300, Chicago Urban League records; memo to staff from JC, July 1956, folder 5, box 92, HPKCC.

38. Form letter (with name space left blank), from Rachel Ridley, Tarlease Bell, and Hester Estelle, February 1, 1952, series I, box 220, folder 2184; Christopher M. Edwards, ass't. C.O. secretary, to Mayor Martin H. Kennelly, June 16, 1953, series I, box 220, folder 2184; 4800 Block Calumet Club, October 29, 1954, series II, box 234, folder 2299; letter, Christopher M. Edwards, ass't. C.O. secretary, to Mrs. Rachel Ridley, May 7, 1953, series I, box 220, folder 2185, all in Chicago Urban League records.

39. *The Volunteer*, March 1951, p. 5, series II, box 235, folder 2314; 5300–5400 Indiana Avenue Improvement Club, series II, box 234, folder 2297; both in Chicago Urban League records.

40. "History and Program of the Urban Affairs Program of the American Friends Service Committee, presented to the Midwest Urban Progress Center Requesting Status as a Program Station, February 6, 1966," folder "Urban Affairs Program, Committees & Organizations: Midwest Urban Progress Center, Chicago Regional Office, 1966," box "Chicago R.O. 1966 (Pre-Adolescent Enrichment Prog. to Urban Affairs Prog.)." For a tabular representation of the GLCC's structure, see Albert Hunter, *Symbolic Communities: The Persistence and Change of Chicago's Local Communities* (Chicago and London: University of Chicago Press, 1974), 164.

41. Gordon L. Mattson, "UPG Starts Member Drive," *Garfieldian*, December 2, 1959; "Block Clubs Reject SCC," *ABC News*, February 27, 1970, Chicago History Museum.

42. Sanford D. Horwitt, *Let Them Call Me Rebel: Saul Alinsky—His Life and Legacy* (New York: Alfred A. Knopf, 1989); Nicholas von Hoffman, *Radical: A Portrait of Saul Alinsky* (New York: Nation Books, 2010).

43. Confidential memo to Julia Abrahamson from Elsie C. Krueger, "Observations on the Response of Block Organizations to the Membership Drive—1954," folder 10, box 92, HPKCC records.

44. Saul Alinsky, *Reveille for Radicals* (Chicago: University of Chicago Press, 1945); Saul Alinsky, *Rules for Radicals* (New York: Random House, 1971). On these organizations in general, see Horwitt, 110–14 and 125–26 (ANC), 114–19 and 125–26 (South St. Paul Community Council), 458–66 and 484–505 (FIGHT), and also 531–532. Robert Slayton, *Back of the Yards: The Making of a Local Democracy* (Chicago: University of Chicago Press, 1986); Thomas J. Jablonsky, *Pride in the Jungle: Community and Everyday Life in Back of the Yards Chicago* (Baltimore: Johns Hopkins University Press, 1993); John Hall Fish, *Black Power/White Control: The Struggle of The Woodlawn Organization in Chicago* (Princeton, NJ: Princeton University Press, 1973); Thomas J. Jablonsky and Paul-Thomas Ferguson, "Northwest Community Organization," *Encyclopedia of Chicago*, http://www.encyclopedia.chicagohistory.org/pages/909.html; John Fish et al., *The Edge of the Ghetto: A Study of Church Involvement in Community Organization* (New York, Seabury Press 1966); Amanda I. Seligman, *Block by Block: Neighborhoods and Public Policy on Chicago's West Side* (Chicago: University of Chicago Press, 2005), 194–201; Mark Santow, "Saul Alinsky and the Dilemmas of Race in the Post-war City" (PhD diss., University of Pennsylvania, 2000). See also Mark Santow, "Running in Place: Saul Alinsky, Race, and Community Organizing," in

Transforming the City: Community Organizing and the Challenge of Political Change, ed. Marion Orr (Lawrence: University Press of Kansas, 2007), 28–55.

45. See letter, Deton J. Brooks, to Gilbert A. Harrison, editor, *New Republic*, May 21, 1965, p. 4, folder, June 1965, box 2, Marillac House Records, Chicago History Museum; Horwitt, *Let Them Call Me Rebel*, 275–76.

46. Santow, "Saul Alinsky and the Dilemmas of Race in the Post-War City."

47. Text of an address given by Thomas A. Gaudette, president, Chatham-Avalon Park Community Council, at the Fourth National Community Council Leaders Workshop, Ohio State University, 1959, folder 3, box 1, Thomas A. Gaudette papers, Loyola Marymount University, Los Angeles; Trapp interview, p. 5; Shel Trapp, *Dynamics of Organizing: Building Power by Developing the Human Spirit* (Chicago: Shel Trapp, n.d.), 20 and 21.

48. For further insight into how American Roman Catholics handled parish status, see John T. McGreevey, *Parish Boundaries: The Catholic Encounter with Race in the Twentieth-Century Urban North* (Chicago and London: University of Chicago Press, 1996), and Gerald Gamm, *Urban Exodus: Why the Jews Left Boston and the Catholics Stayed* (Cambridge, MA: Harvard University Press, 1999).

49. Santow, "Saul Alinsky and the Dilemmas of Race in the Post-War City," 25–26 and 199–200.

50. Article VI, Constitution of the Organization for a Better Austin, folder 25, box 3, Austin Community Collection, Special Collections and Preservation Division, Harold Washington Public Library, Chicago Public Libraries, Chicago (hereafter ACC).

51. Clipping, "Austin Group Elects 1st Woman President," *Chicago Tribune*, May 1, 1969, and clipping, David Sutor, *New World*, June 19, 1970, both in clipping file, Organization for a Better Austin, Chicago History Museum; "New Block Clubs Bustin' Out All Over," *Austinite*, May 25, 1966, ANC; "Block Clubs in Woodlawn," Urban Problems Seminar, February 17, 1969, Bette Jo Row, p. 3, folder 20, box 9, Woodlawn Social Services Center records, Department of Special Collections, University of Chicago Library; typescript field notes, first page says "Meeting of the Housing and Planning Committee of the City Council, July 16, 1966, 10:30 a.m.," folder 6, box 2, The Woodlawn Organization records, Chicago History Museum. On The Woodlawn Organization in general, see Fish, *Black Power/White Control*.

52. Report of the GRA nominating committee, Justin McCarthy, chairman, June 11, 1967, folder 23, box 3, Austin Community Collection; clipping, "OBA Convention Elects McCarthy, Adopts Resolutions," *Austinite*, June 14, 1967, oversize 1.6, oversize box, ACC; 5th OBA Convention Resolutions, May 1, 1971, Austin Town Hall, folder 23, box 3, ACC; "155 Picket Realty Office," *Austin News*, February 18, 1970, box 1, ANC; "OBA Pickets Oak Park Home of Realty Dealer," *Austin News*, June 9, 1971, box 4, ANC.

53. See Horwitt, *Let Them Call Me Rebel*, and Santow, "Saul Alinsky and the Dilemmas of Race in the Post-War City."

54. For examples of such requests, see Faith Rich to Arkansas Department of Health, October 10, 1977, and Mrs. Pearlie Mae Robinson to Bureau of Vital Statistics, Little Rock, AK, May 2, 1975, both in folder 10, box 18, Rich papers. There are also more examples in folder 2, box 17, Rich papers.

55. Benjamin Looker, "Visions of Autonomy: The New Left and the Neighborhood Government Movement of the 1970s," *Journal of Urban History* 38 (3) (2012): 578, 590.

56. Minutes of the West 15th Place Block Club Meeting, July 7, 1986, at 3158 W. Roosevelt Rd., apt. 405, folder 5, box 9, Rich papers; letter, Faith Rich to Senator Paul J. Simon, October 7, 1987,

Rich papers. When I went through the unprocessed collection this letter was in a folder labeled "NAACP—West. Educ. Comm. 1987," which was in box 3; Winona Foster Carmen Winnemac (WFCW) Block Club, https://www.facebook.com/pages/Winona-Foster-Carmen-Winnemac -WFCW-Block-Club/153638898008748, posts between April and August 2013. Last accessed June 7, 2014.

57. Jeffrey Helgeson, *Crucibles of Black Empowerment: Chicago's Neighborhood Politics from the New Deal to Harold Washington* (Chicago: University of Chicago Press, 2014).

Chapter Four

1. For the history of alleys in Chicago, see Michael P. Conzen, "Alleys," *Encyclopedia of Chicago*, http://www.encyclopedia.chicagohistory.org/pages/38.html. See also Grady Clay, *Alleys: A Hidden Resource* (Louisville, KY: Grady Clay and Company, 1978).

2. Report from ACTION, "Organization of Block Groups for Neighborhood Improvement: The Hyde Park-Kenwood Community Conference" (New York City, September 1956), p. 9, folder 10, box 64, Hyde Park–Kenwood Community Conference Records, Special Collections Research Center, Regenstein Library, University of Chicago (hereafter HPKCC).

3. Carl H. Nightingale, *Segregation: A Global History of Divided Cities* (Chicago: University of Chicago Press, 2012), 96.

4. Kenneth Jackson, *Crabgrass Frontier: The Suburbanization of the United States* (New York: Oxford University Press), chapter 11.

5. The belief that property owners' actions are governed by resale value neglects the circumstances of foreclosure and bankruptcy that make property abandonment a viable financial tactic. Matthew Desmond's ethnography of Milwaukee during the early twenty-first century housing crisis shows how property neglect and abandonment may be "interlocked" as part of a landlord's routine approach to business. See Matthew Desmond, *Evicted: Poverty and Profit in the American City* (New York: Crown Publishers, 2016), 354-355, note 16.

6. Becky Nicolaides, *My Blue Heaven: Life and Politics in the Working-Class Suburbs of Los Angeles, 1920–1965* (Chicago: University of Chicago Press, 2002), 29. For an elaboration of the ideas underlying this distinction in the context of housing, see John R. Logan and Harvey L. Molotch, *Urban Fortunes: The Political Economy of Place* (Berkeley: University of California Press, 1987), especially chapter 4.

7. Kevin Lynch, *Image of the City* (Cambridge, MA: MIT Press, 1960); Grady Clay, *Close Up: How to Read the American City* (New York: Praeger, 1973).

8. "Two Block Clubs Buy Snow Plow," *Garfieldian*, December 12, 1962; Drexel Strip Block Group, Mr. Ernest Clark interviewed, folder 16, box 96, HPKCC.

9. Rufford Milton, "West Garfield Community News and Comment," *Garfieldian*, May 11, 1966; blue flyer, 1800 North Mozart/Francisco Residents, "Victory!," folder 8, box 46, Northwest Community Organization Records, Chicago History Museum (hereafter NCO); letter, Dan Russo, chairman, Miller-Carpenter Street Block Club, to Captain Gibbons, Maxwell Police Station, July 29, 1954, folder 529, Near West Side Community Committee Records, Special Collections and University Archives Department, Richard J. Daley Library, University of Illinois at Chicago (hereafter NWSCC); letter, Hazzard Parks, temporary chairman, Springfield Avenue Community Club, to Dear Chairman, January 18, 1954, series II, box 234, folder 2298, Chicago Urban League records; Burnell Brown, 4100 Van Buren Block Club president, letter to the editor, *Garfieldian*, July 7, 1966; minutes, Miller-Carpenter Street Block Club, July 12, 1955, folder 532,

NWSCC; 3200 West Fulton Block Club, series II, box 235, folder 2304, Chicago Urban League Records.

10. 4700–4800–4900 Kimbark Avenue Block Group, Mr. Edwin Taylor interviewed, folder 16, box 96, HPKCC; 7300 Calumet block, March 1, 1954, series II, box 234, folder 2301, Chicago Urban League records; Julia Abrahamson, *A Neighborhood Finds Itself* (New York: Harper & Brothers, 1959), 69; 7300 South Evans Avenue, December 9, 1953, series II, box 234, folder 2301, Chicago Urban League records.

11. Drexel Strip Block Group, Mr. Ernest Clark interviewed, folder 16, box 96, HPKCC.

12. Rufford Milton, "Block Club News and Comment," *Garfieldian*, October 13, 1965; "West Garfield Community News and Comment," *Garfieldian*, March 9, 1966.

13. "Good Neighbors Create Urban Garden," WGRZ, October 14, 2012, http://www.wgrz .com/video/1899571852001/51730457001/Good-Neighbors-Create-Urban-Garden; letter, Faith to Rhoda, May 25, 1972, folder 5, box 19, Special Collections and Preservation Division, Harold Washington Library Center, Chicago Public Library (hereafter Rich papers); "How to Operate Successful Block Club," *Garfieldian*, July 29, 1964.

14. 4400 South Cottage Grove Avenue, December 22, 1952, series II, box 234, folder 2303, Chicago Urban League records; Christopher Thale, "Waste Disposal," *Encyclopedia of Chicago* online, ed. Janice L. Reiff, Ann Durkin Keating, and James R. Grossman (Chicago: Chicago Historical Society, 2005), http://www.encyclopedia.chicagohistory.org/pages/1322.html; letter, Anne Gaynor, 1858 South Springfield, Springfield Avenue Community Club, to Handy Andy, *Chicago Sun-Times*, series II, box 234, folder 2298, Chicago Urban League records; letter, Richmond Humboldt Block Club to the Honorable Richard Mell, July 7, 1980, folder 21, box 46, NCO; letter, [Faith Rich] to Lois Wille, *Chicago Daily News*, April 26, 1970, folder 2, box 17, Rich papers; 5600 Drexel Avenue Block Group, Mr. Charles Olmsted interviewed, folder 16, box 96, HPKCC.

15. 6900 Wabash Avenue block, May 19, 1954, series II, box 234, folder 2301, Chicago Urban League records.

16. Minutes, West Side Community Committee, undated, folder 528, NWSCC records; 2900 block on Walnut, July 27 and August 10, 1950, series II, box 235, folder 2304, Chicago Urban League records; agenda, 1200–1300 North Bosworth Block Club, September 6, 1979, folder 10, box 45, NCO records; flyer, "Attention: Residents of Albany & Moffat Streets," and 2100 N. Point Street Block Club flyer, both in folder 3, box 45, NCO records.

17. "Urge Kids: Play in Back Yards" and "West Garfield Community News and Comment," *Garfieldian*, August 10, 1966; "West Garfield Community News and Comment," *Garfieldian*, August 10, 1966; memo to Mr. Martin Murphy, Department of Planning, from the Dickens-Winchester Block Club, re: Model Block Funding for 2000 Winchester, 2100 Winchester, and 1900 Dickens, March 13, 1981, folder 5, box 46, NCO records; report from ACTION, "Organization of Block Groups for Neighborhood Improvement: The Hyde Park–Kenwood Community Conference" (New York City, September 1956), p. 9, folder 10, box 64, HPKCC records; "Welcome to Drexel Tot Lot," July 1954, folder 6, box 109, HPKCC records; Herbert A. Thelen and Bettie Belk Sarchet, "Neighbors in Action: A Manual for Community Leaders" (Human Dynamics Laboratory, Department of Education, University of Chicago, 1954), 28, 49, and 50. My thanks to Erin Winkler for pointing out the men supervising play. Curiously, HathiTrust Digital Library holds a version of this book that includes a photograph of women supervising children: http:// hdl.handle.net/2027/mdp.39015003593285. For a detailed account of the work of a playground association, see Marie Louise Deutsch, Drexel Maryland Playground Association, folder 3, box 110, HPKCC records.

18. Memo from T. P. Wintersteen, lt. commander, Office of Civilian Defense, 29 S. Crawford Avenue, March 20, 1944, to all zone captains and block captains, folder 1, box 2, Office of Civilian Defense records, Special Collections and Preservation Division, Harold Washington Public Library, Chicago Public Libraries, Chicago; clipping, "Community OCD Groups Report on Activities," *Garfieldian*, April 6, 1944, folder 4, box 2, OCD records.

19. Letter, Faith to Nikki, June 9, 1968, box 20, folder 3; letter, Pearlie Mae Robinson, president, and Faith Rich, secretary, West 15th Place Block Club, October 1, 1985, to Mayor Washington, box 9, folder 5, both in Rich papers.

20. Letter, Faith to Nikki, June 9, 1968, box 20, folder 3; letter, [Faith] to Henry and Evelyn, June 16, 1973, box 18, folder 10; letter, Faith to Rhoda, August 12, 1973, box 20, folder 6; letter, Faith to Paul and Evelyn, March 5, 1975, folder 10, box 18; all in Rich papers.

21. Letter, Faith to Rhoda, August 12, 1973, box 20, folder 6, Rich papers.

22. Holiday letter, 1973, Ted and Faith Rich, box 20, folder 5; holiday letter, 1973, Ted and Faith Rich, box 20, folder 5; West 15th Place Block Club newsletter No. 26, May 1974, folder 9, box 18; Letter, Faith to Rhoda, August 12, 1973, box 20, folder 6, all in Rich papers.

23. Letter, Faith to Rhoda, September 27, 1972, box 19, folder 5; holiday letter, 1973, Ted and Faith Rich, box 20, folder 5; letter, Faith to Rhoda, May 18, 1974, box 18, folder 9; letter, Faith Rich and Pearlie Mae Robinson to Honorable R. Cardiss Collins, March 3, 1986, folder 5, box 9, Rich papers; "Wreckers: Leave Some Good Topsoil," West 15th Place Block Club newsletter no. 84, April 1983; all in Rich papers. The location for this newsletter when the collection was unprocessed was folder "Corr.-1983 Westside NAACP Educ. Comm. 3.35," which was in box 3.

24. Letter, Faith to Paul and Evelyn, March 5, 1975, folder 10, box 18; letter, Faith to Rhoda, May 18, 1974, box 18, folder 9; letter, Faith to Rhoda, November 27, 1974, box 18, folder 10; West 15th Place Block Club newsletter no. 26, May 1974, folder 9, box 18; minutes of April 3, 1987 West 15th Place Block Club meeting, folder 4, box 9; all in Rich papers.

25. Letter, Faith to Rhoda, 11/27/74, box 18, folder 10, Rich papers.

26. Letter, Faith to Paul and Evelyn, March 5, 1975, folder 10, box 18; West 15th Place Block Club newsletter no. 26, May 1974, folder 9, box 18; letter, Faith to Rhoda, May 18, 1974, box 18, folder 9; letter (handwritten copy only), Faith Rich to Mr. Schroeder, July 6, 1987, box 9, folder 4; all in Rich papers.

27. Holiday letter, 1973, Ted and Faith Rich, box 20, folder 5; letter, Faith to Rhoda, November 27, 1974, box 18, folder 10; West 15th Place Block Club newsletter no. 45, May 1976, box 9, folder 4; letter, Faith to Rhoda, January 28, 1977, box 19, folder 1; letter, Pearlie Mae Robinson, president, and Faith Rich, secretary, West 15th Place Block Club, October 1, 1985, to Mayor Washington, folder 18, box 10; letter, Faith Rich and Pearlie Mae Robinson to Honorable R. Cardiss Collins, March 3, 1986, folder 5, box 9; all in Rich papers.

28. Letter, [Faith Rich] to Jane Riley, October 24, 1983, box 17, folder 2; letter, Faith to Rhoda, November 27, 1974, box 18, folder 10; letter, Faith Rich, sec'y, and Pearlie Mae Robinson, pres., West 15th Place Block Club, to Mayor Harold Washington, May 1, 1983, folder 5, box 9; all in Rich papers.

29. Benjamin Mark Looker, "A Nation of Neighborhoods: Cities, Communities, and Democracy in the Modern American Imagination, 1940–1980" (PhD diss., Yale University, 2009), 135; Benjamin Looker, *A Nation of Neighborhoods: Imagining Cities, Communities, and Democracy in Postwar America* (Chicago: University of Chicago Press, 2015), 90, 99, and 103. For an overview of federal housing policy, see John F. Bauman, Roger Biles, and Kristin M. Szylvian, *From Tenements to the Taylor Homes: In Search of an Urban Housing Policy in Twentieth-Century America* (University Park: Pennsylvania State University Press, 2000).

30. 4800 South Forrestville, October 29, 1953, series II, box 234, folder 2299, Chicago Urban League records; Wilma L. Moore, "Everyday People: Mattie Coney and the Citizens Forum," *Traces of Indiana and Midwestern History* 22 (1) (Winter 2010): 31.

31. 7100 Eberhart block, January 21, 1954, series II, box 234, folder 2301, Chicago Urban League records; *Voice of the Midwest Community Council*, vol. IV, no. 1, January 1961, folder 2, box 35, Monsignor John J. Egan papers, University of Notre Dame Archives ; 5300–5400 Indiana Avenue Improvement Club, October 29, 1954, series II, box 234, folder 2297, Chicago Urban League records; "Christmas Lighting Contest Announced," *Garfieldian*, November 11, 1959.

32. Looker, "A Nation of Neighborhoods," 154–55.

33. "Two Decades of Service: 1916–1936," Chicago Urban League annual report, folder 1-12, box 1, series 1; "American Teamwork—Works": January 1, 1948 to December 31, 1948, 1916–48, p. 6, folder 1-20, box 1, series 1; "Together . . . the Reporter of the Chicago Urban League, August 1950," folder 1-22, box 1, series 1; letter, Christopher M. Edwards, ass't. C.O. secretary, to Mrs. Rachel Ridley, May 7, 1953, series I, box 220, folder 2185; all in Chicago Urban League records; Washington, *Packing Them In*, 171 and 183; Sylvia Hood Washington, "Mrs. Block Beautiful: African American Women and the Birth of the Urban Conservation Movement, Chicago, Illinois, 1917–1954," *Environmental Justice* 1 (2008): 13–23.

34. Memorandum, Rachel Ridley to persons interested in Better Homes and Yards Contest, May 18, 1951, folder 31; Midwest Community Council, Better Homes and Yards, September 21, 1950–August 15, 1952; clipping, "Vie for Better Homes and Yards," *Mid-West Herald*, April 27, 1950, folder 54; Midwest Community Council 1951 Summer Bulletin, August 21, 1951, folder 30; clipping, "Announce Winners of Homes Contest," *West Town Herald*, September 28, 1950, folder 54; all in Off the Street Club collection, Department of Special Collections, Richard J. Daley Library, University of Illinois at Chicago.

35. "American Teamwork—Works": January 1, 1948 to December 31, 1948, 1916–48, p. 6, folder 1–20, box 1, series 1; "1916–1952," annual report, series 1, box 1, folder 24, both in Chicago Urban League records.

36. Neighbors At Work, staff meeting minutes, November 28, 1966, folder November–December 1966, box 4, Marillac House records, Chicago History Museum; Progressive & Improvement Block Club (5100–5200 blocks on Indiana Avenue), October 29, 1954, series II, box 234, folder 2297; Washington Park Court Property Owners Association, 4900 block on Washington Park, October 29, 1954, series II, box 234, folder 2299; Robert S. Abbott Neighborhood Club (3600 block on South Wells), series II, box 234, folder 2300); 7100 Rhodes block, February 1, 1954, series II, box 234, folder 2301; letter, Allan Lewis, Warren Jones, R. Ridley, to Dear Block Club President, December 27, 1950, series I, box 220, folder 2184; all in Chicago Urban League records.

37. "Real Estate Notes," *Chicago Daily Tribune*, October 26, 1957; "485 Chicago Blocks Seek Title of Better Neighborhood," *Chicago Daily Tribune*, May 15, 1958; Ernest Fuller, "Realtors Act to Conserve Areas of City," *Chicago Daily Tribune*, May 23, 1957, p. N10; "Put 485 Blocks in Competition: Neighborhoods Vie for $20,000," *Chicago Daily Tribune*, March 13, 1958, p. N1; all accessed through ProQuest Historical Newspapers.

38. Letter, Vivas to Jack W. Kleeman, Chicago Real Estate Board, August 5, 1959, folder, August 1959, box 11, GLCC-CHM; "Lawndale Trims, Primps for 'Pride': Officials Expect Clean Sweep in Contest," *Chicago Daily Tribune*, August 9, 1962, pg. W3, accessed through ProQuest Historical Newspapers. On tensions among African Americans around Chicago's housing code, see Amanda I. Seligman, *Block by Block: Neighborhoods and Public Policy on Chicago's West Side* (Chicago: University of Chicago Press, 2005), 65–67.

39. "54 Prize Winners in Big Fix-Up," *Chicago Daily Tribune*, September 30, 1962, WA9,

accessed through ProQuest Historical Newspapers; Alphine Wade Jefferson, "Housing Discrimination and Community Response in North Lawndale (Chicago), Illinois 1948–1978" (PhD diss., Duke University 1979), 135–39; Greater Lawndale Association of Block Clubs, entry beginning at April 22, 1957, interview with Mrs. Pughsley and Mrs. Rayner, folder 324-8, box 324, Welfare Council of Metropolitan Chicago Records, Chicago History Museum; Looker, *A Nation of Neighborhoods*, 101; letter, J. W. Young, public relations, Sears to Jerome Braverman, March 11, 1958, folder, March 1–17, 1958, box 6, GLCC-CHM records; Greater Lawndale Conservation Commission, excerpts from weekly log of George Klein, folder 324-9, box 324, Welfare Council of Metropolitan Chicago Records, Chicago History Museum.

40. Letter, Allan Williams to unnamed Gentlemen, August 5, 1955, folder, July–Sept. 1955, box 2, GLCC-CHM; Juliette Buford, "Report on Adult Program" to GLCC board of directors, March 28, 1961, folder, March 1961, box 16, GLCC-CHM records; "Lawndale Trims, Primps for 'Pride,'" *Chicago Daily Tribune*, August 9, 1962, W3; "'Operation Pride' Brings Out Best in Lawndale Homes," *Chicago Tribune*, October 2, 1966, U8; "$600 Will Go to Winners of Home Contest," *Chicago Tribune*, September 22, 1963, W5. Churches and businesses were added as categories in 1965. "Pride Campaign Begins," *Chicago Tribune*, July 1, 1965, W2, and "The People's Link to the Mayor," *Chicago Tribune*, April 11, 1965, 127. "Plan Annual Youth Salute in Lawndale," *Chicago Daily Tribune*, May 31, 1962, W3; "'Pride' Event to be Staged in Lawndale," *Chicago Tribune*, August 22, 1963, W3; "Clean Up Is Slogan of Groups," *Chicago Tribune*, June, 1966, 113; all accessed through ProQuest Historical Newspapers.

41. "Lawndale Offers Prizes for Upkeep of Property," *Chicago Tribune*, July 4, 1963, W2, accessed through ProQuest Historical Newspapers.

42. "Plan Annual Youth Salute in Lawndale," *Chicago Daily Tribune*, May 31, 1962, W3; "'Operation Pride' Brings out Best in Lawndale Homes," *Chicago Tribune*, October 2, 1966, U8; "$600 Will Go to Winners of Home Contest," *Chicago Tribune*, September 22, 1963, W5, all accessed through ProQuest Historical Newspapers.

43. The newly inaugurated Mayor Richard J. Daley established the Mayor's Office of Inquiry and Information to provide a high-profile center where Chicagoans could register complaints and request city services. For more details, see "The People's Link to the Mayor," *Chicago Tribune*, April 11, 1965, 127, accessed through ProQuest Historical Newspapers; and "Go Tell it to City Hall," *Chicago Tribune*, March 9, 1969, F1, accessed through ProQuest Historical Newspapers.

44. "The People's Link to the Mayor," *Chicago Tribune*, April 11, 1965, 127, accessed through ProQuest Historical Newspapers.

45. "Neighbors Will Parade with 'Pride,'" *Chicago Tribune*, July 5, 1964, NA1; "Neighborhood Is Given a Boost by Big Program," *Chicago Tribune*, September 27, 1964, N1; "Annual Cleanup Set for Uptown; Prizes Offered," *Chicago Tribune*, April 29, 1965, NA6, "The People's Link to the Mayor," *Chicago Tribune*, April 11, 1965, 127; "Cleanup Program," *Chicago Tribune*, May 16, 1965, NW5, "The People's Link to the Mayor," *Chicago Tribune*, April 11, 1965, 127; "Sheffield Group Inspires Owners," *Chicago Tribune*, August 1, 1965, N6, "The People's Link to the Mayor," *Chicago Tribune*, April 11, 1965, 127; "City Aid Given to Program," *Chicago Tribune*, September 16, 1965, W1; "Parade Today in Woodlawn to Open Drive," *Chicago Tribune*, October 30, 1965, A9; "Launch Cleanup Campaign in Wicker-Humboldt Area," *Chicago Tribune*, November 12, 1967, WA8; "Lawndale Residents' Group Joins City's Operation Pride Coalition," *Chicago Tribune*, December 8, 1968, "Launch Cleanup Campaign in Wicker-Humboldt Area," *Chicago Tribune*, November 12, 1967, WA8; "Woodlawn Parade to Begin Cleanup," *Chicago Tribune*, April 20, 1969, SCL3; "Community Cleanup Starts Tomorrow," *Chicago Tribune*, April 2, 1972, S14; all accessed

through ProQuest Historical Newspapers. "Call Community Meeting on 'Operation Pride,'" *Garfieldian*, June 9, 1965.

46. "Go Tell it to City Hall," *Chicago Tribune*, March 9, 1969, F1; "City Aid Given to Program," *Chicago Tribune*, September 16, 1965, W1; "Even Garbage Trucks Bloom in Spring," *Chicago Tribune*, April 16, 1973; "City Program Covers Area with Pride," *Chicago Tribune*, July 4, 1967, 11; all accessed through ProQuest Historical Newspapers. In 1987 the *Chicago Tribune* ran several articles about a program called Operation Pride that paid Chicago Housing Authority residents to work as custodians. It is unclear from the newspaper coverage whether this was a new program under Mayor Harold Washington or a transformed version of the older effort. See, for example, Patrick Reardon, "CHA Will Extend Resident Work Plan," *Chicago Tribune*, October 9, 1987, accessed through ProQuest Historical Newspapers.

47. "Antiques Expected to Lure Crowd to Park West Fair," *Chicago Tribune*, May 30, 1966, C10; "City Aid Given to Program," *Chicago Tribune*, September 16, 1965, W1; "Uptown Begins Pride Campaign, Cleanup," *Chicago Tribune*, June 8, 1972, N2; "Neighbors Will Parade with 'Pride,'" *Chicago Tribune*, July 5, 1964, NA1; "Lawndale to Parade for 'Operation Pride,'" *Chicago Tribune*, September 10, 1964, WA1; "Marchers to Mark Flag Day," *Chicago Tribune*, June 13, 1965, NWA2, "The People's Link to the Mayor," *Chicago Tribune*, April 11, 1965, 127; "Woodlawn Parade to Begin Cleanup," *Chicago Tribune*, April 20, 1969, SCL3; "Lawndale Will Parade its 'Pride,'" *Chicago Tribune*, September 9, 1965, W1, all accessed through ProQuest Historical Newspapers.

48. "Pride Rides High in Cleanup Drive," *Chicago Tribune*, September 20, 1964, W16; "Launch Cleanup Campaign in Wicker-Humboldt Area," *Chicago Tribune*, November 12, 1967, WA8; "Lawndale Group Begins Summer Cleanup Campaign," *Chicago Tribune*, O2, all accessed through ProQuest Historical Newspapers.

Chapter Five

1. Memo from the Dickens-Winchester Block Club to Mr. Martin Murphy, Department of Planning, re: Model Block Funding for 2000 Winchester, 2100 Winchester, and 1900 Dickens, March 13, 1981, folder 5, box 46, Northwest Community Organization Records, Chicago History Museum (hereafter NCO).

2. Julia Abrahamson, *A Neighborhood Finds Itself* (New York: Harper & Brothers, 1959), 72; Leon M. Despres, 5th Ward alderman, "New Procedure for Sidewalk Repairs," folder 21, box 91, Hyde Park–Kenwood Community Conference records, Special Collections Research Center, University of Chicago Library, Chicago (hereafter HPKCC Records); letter, Chuck Prentice, Community 21 Staff, to Mrs. Florence A. Rhoda, Rural Route 9, Box 51, May 30, 1978, folder 14, box 45, NCO.

3. Martin V. Melosi, *Garbage in the Cities: Refuse, Reform, and the Environment: 1880–1980s* (College Station: Texas A&M University Press, 1981), and Martin V. Melosi, *The Sanitary City: Urban Infrastructure in America from Colonial Times to the Present* (Baltimore and London: Johns Hopkins University Press, 2000). On the problem of urban pollution, see also Joel A. Tarr, "The Search for the Ultimate Sink: Urban Air, Land, and Water Pollution in Historical Perspective," *Records of the Columbia Historical Society, Washington, DC*, 51 (1984): 1–29.

4. Craig E. Colten, "Chicago's Waste Lands: Refuse Disposal and Urban Growth, 1840–1990," *Journal of Historical Geography* 20, no. 2 (1994): 124–42, quotation on p. 132.

5. The best overview of early-twentieth-century tenement conditions is provided in Edith Abbott, *The Tenements of Chicago, 1908–1935* (Chicago: University of Chicago Press, 1936).

Suellen Hoy, *Chasing Dirt: The American Pursuit of Cleanliness* (New York and Oxford: Oxford University Press, 1994), 76–77, 102–4, quotation on p. 103; Melosi, *Garbage in the Cities*, 114; Maureen A. Flanagan, *Seeing with Their Hearts: Chicago Women and the Vision of the Good City, 1871–1933* (Princeton, NJ: Princeton University Press, 2002), 96–98. For more detail on this topic, see Maureen A. Flanagan, "Gender and Urban Political Reform: The City Club and Woman's City Club of Chicago in the Progressive Era," *American Historical Review* 95 (October 1990): 1036–39.

6. The split in public and private responsibility for garbage pickup depending on the size of the building dates to December 1945, when the Chicago City Council passed an ordinance overhauling the city's approach to refuse collection. The relevant paragraph specified, "Except in the case of a multiple dwelling containing less than five living units, a multiple dwelling producing less than thirty-two gallons of refuse per week, or a multiple dwelling each living unit of which is individually heated by the tenant, it shall be the duty of the owner of every multiple dwelling to cause to be removed at his own cost and expense at least once each week all refuse produced therein." *Journal of the Proceedings of the City Council of the City of Chicago for the Council Year 1945–1946*, §99–18 (p. 4604); passed December 17, 1945. See "City Officials Draft Garbage Law with Teeth," *Chicago Daily Tribune*, December 13, 1945; and "City Council Approves New Garbage Law," *Chicago Daily Tribune*, December 18, 1945, both accessed through ProQuest Historical Newspapers. This law did not anticipate the rise of condominium living in Chicago, an arrangement in which residential units in large buildings were individually owned. Condominium owners paid property taxes that supported garbage pickup, but their boards had to contract privately for scavenger services. This practice prompted an effort to get the city to refund condominium owners the fees associated with garbage collection.

7. Clipping, Jessica Pupovac, "City Pushes Overhaul of Trash Collection System," *News-Star*, October 9, 2008, folder, clipping file, "Refuse Collection—CHGO 1993-," Municipal Reference Collection, Harold Washington Library Center, Chicago Public Library.

8. Garbage Collection, presentation to the LPPAC meeting of January 18, 1986, by the West 15th Place Block Club, folder 5, box 9, Rich papers.

9. Willing Willie column, *Austin News*, May 17, 1972, box 4, Austin Newspapers Collection, Special Collections and Preservation Division, Harold Washington Library Center, Chicago Public Library (hereafter ANC); "Hit Austin's Lack of Black Teachers," *Austin News*, February 4, 1970, box 1, ANC; minutes of March 3, 1986 West 15th Place Block Club meeting at 1514 South Albany Avenue, folder 5, box 9, Rich papers; See also letter, Faith Rich, sec'y, and Pearlie Mae Robinson, pres., West 15th Place Block Club, to Mayor Harold Washington, May 1, 1983 (with West 15th Place Block Club newsletter no. 84, April, "Suggestions for the Mayor and his Departments: The City Should Control All Garbage Collection" on the back), folder 5, box 9, Faith Rich papers, Special Collections and Preservation Division, Harold Washington Library Center, Chicago Public Library (hereafter Rich papers); Garbage Collection, presentation to the LPPAC meeting of January 18, 1986, by the West 15th Place Block Club, folder 5, box 9, Rich papers; City of Chicago, service, residential garbage collection, http://www.cityofchicago.org/city/en/depts /streets/provdrs/streets_san/svcs/residential_garbagecollection.html, last accessed July 31, 2015; Wesley G. Skogan, *Disorder and Decline: Crime and the Spiral of Decay in American Neighborhoods* (New York: The Free Press, 1990), 43–46.

10. Flyer, "Protect the Health of Your Family by Keeping Your Alleys Clean," folder 527, Near West Side Community Committee records, Special Collections and University Archives Department at the Richard J. Daley Library, University of Illinois at Chicago (hereafter NWSCC).

11. Miller-Carpenter Block Club report, undated, folder 527; Draft Block Club agenda, January 21, 1954, folder 527; letter, John Romano, president, West Side Community Committee, to

James Bourjekos, 1023 West Polk Street, March 18, 1954, folder 528; Miller-Carpenter Block Club report, undated, folder 527; letter, Frances Morano, for Miller-Carpenter Street Block Club, to Mr. Louis Farina, April 12, 1956, folder 533; all in NWSCC.

12. Fact sheet, West Side Community Committee, undated, folder 527; minutes, West Side Community Committee, undated, folder 528, emphasis in the original; letter, Frank Seriano, president, Miller-Carpenter Street Block Club, to Mr. John D'Arco, alderman, 1st Ward, March 30, 1955, folder 530, NWSCC, and letter, John D'Arco, alderman, to Mr. Seriano, April 1, 1955, folder 531, all in NWSCC.

13. Julia Abrahamson, *A Neighborhood Finds Itself* (New York: Harper & Brothers, 1959), 71.

14. "Block Group Launches Cleanup Attack Tonight," *Austinite*, May 4, 1960, box 6, ANC.

15. 1200 Block Springfield Club, May 1, 1954, series II, box 234, folder 2298, Chicago Urban League Records, Special Collections and University Archives Department at the Richard J. Daley Library, University of Illinois at Chicago (hereafter Chicago Urban League records).

16. "Cut Weeds, Pick up Litter Block Committees Urge," *Garfieldian*, September 10, 1959; letter, For the Block Club, 2100 West Crystal Block Club, c/o Peoples Baptist Church, to Mr. Dan Madori, 847 North Hoyne, March 29, 1982, folder 2, box 46, NCO; minutes, Ohio-Ashland Block Club, August 11, 1977, folder 17, box 46, NCO; Clean-up Newsletter, 5400 University Block, folder 23, box 109, HPKCC.

17. "Rules and Regulations Governing 4100 Block West Grenshaw," folder "May 1–12, 1960," box 13, Greater Lawndale Conservation Commission Records, Chicago History Museum (hereafter GLCC–CHM).

18. Dickens-Winchester Block Club, block cleanup party, folder 5, box 46, NCO, emphasis in the original; West 15th Place Block Club newsletter no. 45, May 1976, box 9, folder 4, Rich papers.

19. Note, September 17, 1958, from officers of the 1300 Kedvale-Keeler Block Club to "Landlords-Tenants," folder September, 1958, box 7, GLCC–CHM; report from ACTION, "Organization of Block Groups for Neighborhood Improvement: The Hyde Park–Kenwood Community Conference" (New York City, September 1956), p. 9, folder 10, box 64, Hyde Park–Kenwood Community Conference Records, Special Collections Research Center, Regenstein Library, University of Chicago (hereafter HPKCC); clipping, "Longtime Neighbors Form Block Club, Aim to Improve Their Area," *West Town Herald*, July 27, 1977, folder 17, box 46, NCO; letter, Rachel Ridley, director, West Side Activities, to Alderman Louis London, August 17, 1950, series I, box 220, folder 2184, Chicago Urban League records.

20. "Review at the Ending of the Year by Mrs. Pearlie Mae Robinson," Rich papers. When the collection was unprocessed, this document was in a folder labeled "UN and Vista PMG," in a box whose top folder was labeled "Westside."

21. Holiday letter 1970, box 20, folder 5, Rich papers.

22. "Marillac Unit of Block Clubs," *VOICE of the Midwest Community Council*, vol. 11, no. 10, March-April 1959, folder 524, NWSCC; "Residents Council Report," folder 2, box 35, Monsignor John J. Egan papers, University of Notre Dame Archives (hereafter Egan papers); "History and Program of the Urban Affairs Program of the American Friends Service Committee, presented to the Midwest Urban Progress Center Requesting Status as a Program Station, February 6, 1966," folder, "Urban Affairs Program, Committees & Organizations: Midwest Urban Progress Center, Chicago Regional Office, 1966," box, Chicago R.O. 1966 (Pre-Adolescent Enrichment Prog. to Urban Affairs Prog.), Chicago Regional Office Files, American Friends Service Committee Archives, Philadelphia (hereafter AFSC); "West Garfield Community News and Comment," *Garfieldian*, April 20, 1966.

23. 7200 Rhodes Avenue, January 12, 1954, series II, box 234, folder 2301, Chicago Urban

League records; minutes, Ohio-Ashland Block Club, July 23, 1977, folder 17, box 46, NCO; clipping, "Church Group Comes 200 Miles to Help Ohio-Ashland Clean-up," *West Town Herald*, August 17, 1977, folder 17, box 46, NCO.

24. Clipping, "Longtime Neighbors Form Block Club, Aim to Improve Their Area," *West Town Herald*, July 27, 1977, folder 527, NWSCC; clipping, "W. Side Area to Get Rat Control Teams," *Daily News*, March 1, 1966, box 5, folder 3, Metropolitan Housing and Planning Council Records, Special Collections and University Archives Department at the Richard J. Daley Library, University of Illinois at Chicago; Benjamin Mark Looker, "A Nation of Neighborhoods: Cities, Communities, and Democracy in the Modern American Imagination, 1940–1980" (PhD diss., Yale University, 2009), 298; Arnold R. Hirsch, *Making the Second Ghetto: Race & Housing in Chicago, 1940–1960* (Chicago: University of Chicago Press, 1983), 25.

25. 1500 West Erie Block Club Meeting, folder 6, box 46; green flyer, "We Want Our Alley Clean!" folder 10, box 46; minutes, Ohio-Ashland Block Club, July 23, 1977, folder 17, box 46; letter, Margaret Kay to Francis Degnan, commissioner of streets and sanitation, October 12, 1978, folder 1, box 45; flyer, "Shakespeare-Dickens-McLean Block Club and Mozart-Francisco Block Club Present a Public Meeting on Rats," folder 22, box 46; blue flyer, 1800 North Mozart/Francisco Residents, "Victory!," folder 8, box 46; all in NCO.

26. Rufford Milton, "Block Club News and Comment," *Garfieldian*, May 19, 1965; Wells-Princeton Neighborhood Improvement Club, April 2, 1952, series II, box 234, folder 2300, Chicago Urban League Records; West 15th Place Block Club newsletter no. 26, May 1974, folder 9, box 18, Rich papers.

27. Melosi, *Garbage in the Cities*, 127 and 129. On cleanup campaigns in general, see 125–33.

28. Unidentified clipping, April 26, 1951, "Hundreds March in Cleanup Parade," folder 54; clipping, *West Town Herald*, April 14, 1949, "Cleanup Week to Open Here Apr. 25," folder 54; letter, L. M. Johnson, commissioner of streets & electricity, Bureau of Sanitation, to A. Mathien [*sic*], May 26, 1952, folder 33; unidentified clipping, June 5, 1952, "Parade on Jackson," folder 54; all in Off the Street Club records, Special Collections and University Archives Department, Richard J. Daley Library, University of Illinois at Chicago.

29. *Community Reporter*, March 16, 1949, Department of Special Collections, Harold Washington Library Center, Chicago Public Library; "Kennelly Asks Public to Help Clean Up City," *Chicago Daily Tribune*, March 10, 1949; "Mayor to Scrub State St. for Cleanup Drive," *Chicago Daily Tribune*, April 29, 1949; "Cleanup March Inspires Mayor to Grab Broom," *Chicago Daily Tribune*, April 22, 1951; "Leader Named in Drive for Cleaner City," *Chicago Daily Tribune*, March 20, 1949; "Kennelly Says Garbage Pickup Is Much Better," *Chicago Daily Tribune*, June 7, 1950. *Tribune* accessed through ProQuest Historical Newspapers.

30. "War on Dirt to Begin with Alley Attack," *Chicago Daily Tribune*, May 8, 1949; "Mayor Fires 1st Gun in War on Ragweeds," *Chicago Daily Tribune*, July 1, 1949; "Lush Ragweed in City Defies Cleanup Drive," *Chicago Daily* Tribune, August 24, 1949; "Cleanup Queen for West Side Is Being Sought," *Chicago Daily Tribune*, January 15, 1950; "2 West Side Homes Will Get New Faces—For Free," *Chicago Daily Tribune*, April 30, 1953; "City Will Urge Civic Groups to Buy Trash Cans," *Chicago Daily Tribune*, July 18, 1949; "N.W. Side Group Leads in Drive for Cleaner City," *Chicago Daily Tribune*, April 16, 1950; "Waste Baskets Being Put Up in Hyde Park," *Chicago Daily Tribune*, December 11, 1949. All accessed through ProQuest Historical Newspapers. Alva B. Maxey, "The Block Club Movement in Chicago," *Phylon Quarterly* 18 (2) (1957): 130.

31. "Civic Leaders Plan Cleaner City Campaign," *Chicago Daily Tribune*, October 10, 1954; "Garbage, Litter Is Target of New Cleanup Committee," *Chicago Daily Tribune*, March 4, 1956; "Half Million Pupils to Join in Annual Cleanup Drive," *Chicago Daily Tribune*, April 17, 1961;

"10,000 Will March in Loop Clean-Up Parade Saturday," *Chicago Daily Tribune*, May 21, 1956; "June Is Named Good Garden Month," *Chicago Defender*, June 17, 1958; "Wage War on Traffic Accidents and Littering," *Chicago Daily Tribune*, June 29, 1961; all accessed through ProQuest Historical Newspapers.

32. "Cleanup Drive Gets No. 1 Priority," *Garfieldian*, Feb. 1, 1956.

33. The National Clean Up-Paint Up-Fix Up Bureau was best known for its propaganda documentary, "The House in the Middle," which claimed that residents of a tidy, well-painted house were more likely to survive an atomic blast than their slovenly neighbors. Mark Byrnes, "In 1954, Americans Were Told to Paint Their Houses to Increase Their Chances of Surviving an Atomic Bomb," *Atlantic Cities*, May 8, 2013, http://www.theatlanticcities.com/arts-and-lifestyle/2013/05/1954-americans-were-told-paint-their-houses-increase-their-chances-surviving-atomic-bomb/5523/, accessed March 19, 2014.

34. "Chicago Takes Third Place as Cleanest Town," *Chicago Daily Tribune*, February 20, 1955; "Chicago Snags Title of 'Cleanest' Large City," *Chicago Defender*, February 18, 1960; "The Nation's Best Clean-Up Program," *Chicago Daily Tribune*, May 21, 1961; "It's Official: Chicago Cleanest and Safest," *Chicago Daily Tribune*, March 30, 1962; "Chicago Wins Second in U.S. Cleanup Race," *Chicago Tribune*, February 5, 1964; "Daley to Get 'Cleanest Big City' Trophy," *Chicago Tribune*, April 4, 1965; "Name Chicago for National Cleanup Prize," *Chicago Tribune*, February 5, 1967; "Daley Gets 'Cleanest' Award,' *Chicago Defender*, April 1, 1967; "City Trophy Awards Displayed at Luncheon," *Chicago Daily Defender*, April 5, 1969; all accessed through ProQuest Historical Newspapers.

35. Melosi, *Garbage in the Cities*, 132.

36. Kenneth B. Clark, *Dark Ghetto: Dilemmas of Social Power* (New York, Evanston, and London: Harper & Row, 1965), 56. I am grateful to Benjamin Looker's scholarship for highlighting this quotation.

37. Looker, "A Nation of Neighborhoods," 217–18.

38. Daily report, Carol Honnold, folder "Youth Opportunities Program-Staff Reports (C. Honnold) Chicago RO 1963," box "Chicago R.O. 1963 (Peace Ed. Newsletter to Youth Oppors. Program)," AFSC.

39. Mr. Lewis James, 6356 South Ingleside, October 20, 1952, folder 6, box 92, HPKCC.

40. Richard Harris, "The End Justified the Means: Boarding and Rooming in a City of Homes, 1890–1951," *Journal of Social History* 26 (2) (Winter, 1992): 331–58; Elaine Lewinnek, "Better than a Bank for a Poor Man? Home Financing Strategies in Early Chicago," *Journal of Urban History* 32 (2) (2006): 292–93.

41. On wartime and postwar housing strategies in Chicago, see Laura McEnaney, "Nightmares on Elm Street: Demobilizing in Chicago, 1945–1953," *Journal of American History* 92 (4) (2006): 1265–91. For an overview of the history and legality of conversions, see Amanda I. Seligman, *Block by Block: Neighborhoods and Public Policy on Chicago's West Side* (Chicago and London: University of Chicago Press, 2005) 45–46, 48–51, 55–58, 61–64. On kitchenette apartments, see Wendy Plotkin, "Kitchenettes," *Encyclopedia of Chicago* online, ed. Janice L. Reiff, Ann Durkin Keating, and James Grossman (Chicago: Chicago History Museum, 2005), http://www.encyclopedia.chicagohistory.org/pages/692.html.

42. Seligman, *Block by Block*, 157; Rufford Milton, "West Garfield Community News and Comment," *Garfieldian*, June 29, 1966. And 7300 South Evans Avenue, December 9, 1953; 7200 Vernon Block, December 1, 1953; and 6800 Prairie Block, March 26, 1954, all in series II, box 234, folder 2301, Chicago Urban League records.

43. "Gen. Smykal, Chicago Blight Foe, Dies at 57," *Chicago Daily Tribune*, April 5, 1958, C5,

accessed through ProQuest Historical Newspapers; 7200 Rhodes Avenue, January 12, 1954, series II, box 234, folder 2301, Chicago Urban League records; Rufford Milton, "West Garfield Community News and Comment," *Garfieldian*, June 29, 1966.

44. See, for example, report of William Bonner, May through September, 1960, folder September 1960, box 14, June 21–November 1960, Greater Lawndale Conservation Commission Records, Chicago History Museum.

45. Letter, Mrs. Michael Wireman, block director, to Russell J. Donnelly, December 6, 1962, folder 3, box 101, HPKCC.

46. Abrahamson included the pamphlet's contents as an appendix of her book. *A Neighborhood Finds Itself*, 344–46.

47. Abrahamson, *A Neighborhood Finds Itself*, 34–36, 38, and 144–66; Hyde Park–Kenwood Community Conference, 5506 Harper Avenue, activity sheet, June 10, 1955, folder 1, box 100, HPKCC; memorandum for JA, from GFT, April 13, 1955, folder 14, box 94, HPKCC; "A Guide for Block Group Action in Maintaining Physical Standards," folder 12, box 96, HPKCC. For an overview of the operations of Chicago's Housing Court, see Mary B. Wirth "Chapter I: The Housing Court-Obstacle to Housing Progress?," folder 8, box 1, Mary Bolton Wirth papers, Department of Special Collections, University of Chicago Library.

48. 7500 Eberhart block, May 24, 1954, series II, box 234, folder 2301, Chicago Urban League records; minutes, West Side Community Committee, September 16, 1954, folder 529, NWSCC records.

49. Flyer, "An Appeal to the Residents of Glenview—from Your Neighbors in Humboldt Park," folder 23, box 46, NCO.

50. "The Blitz of Woodlawn" series ran in the *Chicago Daily News* from July 6 to July 11, 1971 (July 6, pp. 1 and 8; July 7, pp. 1 and 16; July 8, pp. 1 and 8; July 9, p. 7; and July 10 and 11, pp. 1, 22, and 23); flyer, Albany-Moffat-Kedzie Area Residents, folder 1, box 45; flyer, 1200 & 1300 N. Bosworth Block Club, folder 10, box 45, both in NCO; Skogan, *Disorder and Decline*, 40–43.

51. Thomas J. Jablonsky and Paul-Thomas Ferguson, Northwest Community Organization, in *The Encyclopedia of Chicago*, http://www.encyclopedia.chicagohistory.org/pages/909.html; Charleston-Leavitt Block Club: first meeting, folder 4, box 46, NCO.

52. Agenda, 1200–1300 North Bosworth Block Club, July 5, 1979, folder 10, box 45, NCO.

53. Letter, block club representatives, 1200 North Cleaver Block Club, to Mrs. Hermenegildo Esparza, 1314 West Cornelia, January 30, 1978, folder 14, box 45; letter, Ester Nelson, neighborhood leader, 2600 W. Attrill Block Club, to Adeline Cygan, August 18, 1976, folder 3, box 45, NCO; flyer, Julian, LeMoyne and Paulina Block Club, folder 5, box 45; memo to Mr. Martin Murphy, Department of Planning, from the Dickens-Winchester Block Club, re: model block funding for 2000 Winchester, 2100 Winchester, & 1900 Dickens, March 13, 1981, folder 5, box 46, all in NCO.

54. Charleston-Leavitt-Dickens Block Club meeting: 2nd Meeting, June 25, 1981, folder 4, box 46, NCO.

55. Agenda, 1200–1330 N. Bosworth Block Club, September 13, 1979, meeting on crime and police protection, folder 10, box 45, NCO.

56. Letter, Joan Semmerlig, for the 1900 W. Dickens/2100 N. Winchester Block Club, to Chief Fred Rice, Patrol Division, Chicago Police Department, October 3, 1980; agenda, Dickens/Winchester Block Club, August 6, 1980; both in folder 5, box 46, NCO.

57. Flyer, 1200–1300 North Greenview block, "Victory for Greenview," folder 9, box 46; letter, David Church et al., to Hello Neighbor, folder 3, box 45, both in NCO.

58. Bryan D. Jones, *Governing Buildings and Building Government: A New Perspective on the Old Party* (University, AL: University of Alabama Press, 1985), 161–62, 176.

59. Bickerdike Redevelopment Corporation, Mission and History, http://www.bickerdike .org/About%20Bickerdike/mission_and_history.php?statusFlag=1, accessed February 14, 2013; 1700 N. Washtenaw/2600 W. Cortland Block Meeting, November 22, 1976, folder 11, box 44. See also flyer, 1200–1300 Greenview Block Club, "What's Going to Happen with the 5 Abandoned Buildings on the 1300 Block?!" folder 9, box 46, both in NCO.

60. Seligman, *Block by Block*, chapters 2 and 3.

61. I am grateful to Alexander von Hoffman, whose comments at the 2013 meeting of the Society for American City and Regional Planning History helped me express this idea.

62. Wendell E. Pritchett, "The 'Public Menace' of Blight: Urban Renewal and the Private Uses of Eminent Domain," *Law and Public Policy Review* 21 (1) (2003): 1–52; Robert A. Beauregard, *Voices of Decline: The Postwar Fate of US Cities*, 2nd ed. (New York: Routledge, 2003), 57–62; Seligman, *Block by Block*, 54.

63. Hirsch, *Making the Second Ghetto*, chapter 5.

64. Hirsch, *Making the Second Ghetto*, chapter 5, and Arnold R. Hirsch, "Urban Renewal," *Encyclopedia of Chicago*, http://www.encyclopedia.chicagohistory.org/pages/1295.html. On urban renewal in Lincoln Park, see Lilia Fernández, *Brown in the Windy City: Mexicans and Puerto Ricans in Postwar Chicago* (Chicago: University of Chicago Press, 2012), chapter 4. The scholarly literature on urban renewal is too voluminous to list comprehensively here. Key works include John F. Bauman, *Public Housing, Race, and Renewal: Urban Planning in Philadelphia, 1920–1974* (Philadelphia: Temple University Press, 1987); Ronald H. Bayor, *Race and the Shaping of Twentieth-Century Atlanta* (Chapel Hill: University of North Carolina Press, 1996); Robert A. Caro, *The Power Broker: Robert Moses and the Fall of New York.* (New York: Vintage Books, 1975); N. D. B. Connolly, *A World More Concrete: Real Estate and the Remaking of Jim Crow South Florida* (Chicago: University of Chicago Press, 2014); Herbert J. Gans, *The Urban Villagers: Group and Class in the Life of Italian-Americans* (New York: Free Press of Glencoe, 1962); Christopher Klemek, *The Transatlantic Collapse of Urban Renewal: Postwar Urbanism from New York to Berlin* (Chicago: University of Chicago Press, 2011); Thomas H. O'Connor, *Building a New Boston: Politics and Urban Renewal, 1950–1970* (Boston: Northeastern University Press, 1993); Joel Schwartz, *The New York Approach: Robert Moses, Urban Liberals, and Redevelopment of the Inner City* (Columbus: Ohio State University Press, 1993); Jon Teaford, *The Rough Road to Renaissance: Urban Revitalization in America, 1940–1985* (Baltimore: Johns Hopkins University Press, 1990); June Manning Thomas, *Redevelopment and Race: Planning a Finer City in Postwar Detroit* (Baltimore: Johns Hopkins University Press, 1997); Samuel Zipp, *Manhattan Projects: The Rise and Fall of Urban Renewal in Cold War New York* (New York: Oxford University Press, 2010). See also articles in the May 2013 *Journal of Urban History*, a special issue entitled "Thinking through Urban Renewal."

65. Devin Hunter, "Chicken Teriyaki and a Blind Woodcarver with a Fake Southern Accent: Promoting Urban Renewal at Chicago's Uptown Folk Fair, 1959–1962," paper delivered at the meeting of the Urban History Association, October 27, 2012, pp. 11–12.

66. Max Grinnell, "Hyde Park," *Encyclopedia of Chicago*, http://www.encyclopedia.chicago history.org/pages/622.html. Abrahamson, *A Neighborhood Finds Itself*, 328; Hirsch, *Making the Second Ghetto*, 138.

67. Report, block organization program, March 1956, folder 14, box 92; see examples of flyers from particular block clubs in folder 6, box 96; activity sheet, September 27, 1956, folder 11,

box 99; flyer for Special Block Meeting, June 24, 1954, folder 6, box 101; 5300–5400 Drexel Block Club special bulletin, November 16, 1960, folder 8, box 102; memo from Block Steering Executive Committee to all block leaders, September 11, 1958, folder Block Group Steering Committee, 1958–59, box 93; all in HPKCC records.

68. Recommendation of the 4800–4900 Dorchester block, December 12, 1957, folder 6, box 99; resolution, folder 7, box 99; flyer, "Looking for a Home?" folder 11, box 99, all in HPKCC records. See also clipping, "Block Group Hits Renewal Plan," *Hyde Park Herald*, November 17, 1954, folder 12, box 107, HPKCC records.

69. Mark Santow, "Saul Alinsky and the Dilemmas of Race in the Post-War City" (PhD diss., University of Pennsylvania, 2000), 199; Hirsch, *Making the Second Ghetto*, chapter 5.

70. Meeting, October 29, 1953, at Sears YMCA, folder: 1953, box 1, GLCC-CHM.

71. Meeting of February 8, 1955, sponsored jointly by GLCC and Triangle Neighbors Club at Arnold Memorial Methodist Church, 1330 South Fairfield Avenue, folder January–March 1955, box 1, GLCC-CHM.

72. Board of directors meeting of December 20, 1955, folder, October–Dec. 1955, box 2, GLCC-CHM.

73. Greater Lawndale Association of Block Clubs, begins at April 24, 1957, interview with Mrs. Pughsley over the telephone, p. 10, folder 324-8, box 324, Welfare Council of Metropolitan Chicago Records, Chicago History Museum (hereafter WCMC Records).

74. Greater Lawndale Conservation Commission, entry beginning at April 25, 1957, folder 324-9, box 324, WCMC records.

75. Board of directors meeting, October 16, 1956, folder October 1956, box 3, GLCC-CHM; Greater Lawndale Association of Block Clubs, entry beginning at April 24, 1957, interview with Mrs. Pughsley over the telephone, p. 3, folder 324-8, box 324, GLCC-CHM; First Annual Report of the Citizens Participation Project, Welfare Council of Metropolitan Chicago, stamped August 20, 1958, p. 6, folder 52-4, box 52, WCMC records. For a detailed look at Pughsley's relationship with the GLCC, see Alphine Wade Jefferson, "Housing Discrimination and Community Response in North Lawndale (Chicago), Illinois 1948–1978" (PhD diss., Duke University, 1979).

76. Board of directors meeting, September 25 1956, p. 3, folder, September 1956, box 3; press release, October 7, 1957, folder, October 1–24, 1957, box 4, both in GLCC-CHM. Jeffrey Helgeson's dissertation suggests that Pughsley went on to become a founder of the Contract Buyers League, which is notable for its success in overturning the land contracts that were the one of the only mechanisms that enabled African Americans denied conventional bank mortgages to purchase property. Helgeson, however, refers to the Contract Buyers Association, and the salient endnote is missing from the dissertation. Jeffrey Helgeson, "Striving in Black Chicago: Migration, Work, and the Politics of Neighborhood Change, 1935–1965" (PhD diss., University of Illinois at Chicago, 2008), 314. On the Contract Buyers League, see Beryl Satter, *Family Properties: Race, Real Estate, and the Exploitation of Black Urban America* (New York: Metropolitan Books, 2009), passim.

77. Abrahamson, *Neighborhood Finds Itself*, 181; Brian J. L. Berry, *The Open Housing Question: Race and Housing in Chicago, 1966–1976* (Cambridge, MA: Ballinger, 1979), 188.

Chapter Six

1. "More on Positive Loitering," Magnolia Malden Block Club web page, July 29, 2011, http://magnoliamalden.wordpress.com/2011/07/29/more-on-positive-loitering/, last accessed April 9, 2014.

2. Mary Pattillo-McCoy, *Black Picket Fences: Privilege and Peril among the Black Middle Class* (Chicago: University of Chicago Press, 1999), chapter 4.

3. Charles Abrams, *Forbidden Neighbors: A Study of Prejudice in Housing* (New York: Harper & Brothers), 267. I am indebted to Benjamin Mark Looker's dissertation for pointing out this quotation. Benjamin Mark Looker, "A Nation of Neighborhoods: Cities, Communities, and Democracy in the Modern American Imagination, 1940–1980" (PhD diss., Yale University, 2009), 189.

4. George L. Kelling and James Q. Wilson, "Broken Windows: The Police and Neighborhood Safety," *Atlantic*, March 1982, http://www.theatlantic.com/magazine/archive/1982/03/broken-windows/304465/.

5. Pattillo-McCoy, *Black Picket Fences*, 42.

6. Leroy Whiting, "Something for Nothing," in "Block Club News," 700–800 South Kilbourn-Kolmar and Fifth Avenue Block Club, folder 50, Greater Lawndale Conservation Commission, Special Collections Department, University of Illinois at Chicago Library (hereafter GLCC-UIC); "Rules and Regulations Governing 4100 Block West Grenshaw," folder, May 1–12, 1960, box 13, Greater Lawndale Conservation Commission Records, Chicago History Museum (hereafter GLCC-CHM).

7. James R. Grossman, *Land of Hope: Chicago, Black Southerners, and the Great Migration* (Chicago: University of Chicago Press, 1989), 145–46. See also Touré F. Reed, *Not Alms but Opportunity: The Urban League & the Politics of Racial Uplift, 1910–1950* (Chapel Hill: University of North Carolina Press, 2008), 35; Nancy J. Weiss, *The National Urban League, 1910–1940* (New York: Oxford University Press, 1974), 171–120; Anne Meis Knupfer, *Toward a Tenderer Humanity and a Nobler Womanhood: African American Women's Clubs in Turn-of-the-Century Chicago* (New York and London: New York University Press, 1996), 43; Allan H. Spear, *Black Chicago: The Making of a Negro Ghetto, 1890–1920* (Chicago: University of Chicago Press, 1967), 168. On the deeper history of "black conduct literature," see Erica Ball, *To Live an Antislavery Life: Personal Politics and the Antebellum Black Middle Class* (Athens: University of Georgia Press, 2012), especially chapter 1.

8. *Voice of the Midwest Community Council* vol. 11, no. 11, June 1959, folder June 25–30, 1959, box 10, GLCC-CHM. Emphasis in the original.

9. Meeting notice, 2200–2300 South Kostner and Kenneth Civic and Improvement Club, July 19, 1965, folder, July 1965, box 26, GLCC-CHM, emphasis in the original.

10. "West Garfield Community News and Comment," *Garfieldian*, August 10, 1966.

11. "Rules and Regulations Governing 4100 Block West Grenshaw," folder, May 1–12, 1960, box 13, GLCC-CHM; Sudhir Alladi Venkatesh, *Off the Books: The Underground Economy of the Urban Poor* (Cambridge, MA, and London: Harvard University Press, 2006), 73; 4100 West Grenshaw observed through Google Maps Street View; image capture dated June 2011, https://www.google.com/maps/@41.867026,-87.729038,3a,75y,270h,90t/data=!3m4!1e1!3m2!1s8sTI615mn18e7G0V-H62lg!2e0!6m1!1e1, last accessed April 28, 2014. On differences of class and cultural orientation within a given block, see Mary Pattillo, *Black on the Block: The Politics of Race and Class in the City* (Chicago: University of Chicago Press, 2007), 91–92.

12. "Rules and Regulations Governing 4100 Block West Grenshaw," folder, May 1–12, 1960, box 13, GLCC-CHM.

13. "The Making of Good Citizenship and Neighborly Conduct," two-page memo for Progressive Twin Block Club, September 28, 1962, folder, September 1962, box 19, GLCC-CHM.

14. I am grateful to Jeannine Hogg for providing this photograph. The position of the sign on the corner of the parkway is visible in the Google Street View image of the street:

Intersection of 70th and Wabash, Google Street View, https://www.google.com/maps/@41.76736 ,-87.623351,3a,75y,180h,90t/data=!3m4!1e1!3m2!1sGmSvmqRNtbhP1J5muLlhfA!2e0!6m1!1e1, image capture dated July 2011, last accessed April 24, 2014. See also Pattillo-McCoy, *Black Picket Fences*, 34.

15. Public Phenomena, Block Club Signs—Chicago, all uploaded October 27, 2007, https:// www.flickr.com/photos/15564781@N04/sets/72157602738209842/, last accessed August 3, 2015.

16. Peter K. B. St. Jean, *Pockets of Crime: Broken Windows, Collective Efficacy, and the Criminal Point of View* (Chicago: University of Chicago Press, 2007), passim. For an illustration of a poorly maintained block club sign, see p. 81.

17. Our Block, division no. 4, zone no. 12, community no. 11, block no. 8, folder 1, box 2, Office of Civilian Defense Records, Department of Special Collections, Harold Washington Library Center, Chicago Public Library.

18. Memo from T .P. Wintersteen, lt. commander, Office of Civilian Defense, to all zone captains and block captains, March 20, 1944, folder 1, box 2; clipping, *Midwest News*, May 5, 1943, folder 3, box 2; clipping, "One Last Good Sneeze," *Garfieldian*, August 5, 1943, folder 3, box 2; clipping, OCD Activity Notes, July 19, 1944, folder 4, box 2; all in OCD.

19. Minute book, folder 5, box "Small Collections: Expansion Collections, Geographic: United States, World War II: (Hermitage-M)," Chicago History Museum (hereafter Small Collections).

20. Minute book, folder 5; and Fritz Long to Dear Block Captain, folder 1, both in Small Collections, CHM. The Very Good Club also sent Christmas gifts to soldiers from the block. See minute book, November 14, 1944, The Very Good Club collection, Chicago History Museum.

21. For an introduction to the history and culture of gangs in Chicago, see Andrew J. Diamond, *Mean Streets: Chicago Youths and the Everyday Struggle for Empowerment in the Multiracial City, 1908–1969* (Berkeley: University of California Press, 2009) and Sudhir Venkatesh, *Gang Leader for a Day: A Rogue Sociologist Takes to the Streets* (New York: Penguin Books, 2008). See also Eric C. Schneider, *Vampires, Dragons, and Egyptian Kings: Youth Gangs in Postwar New York* (Princeton, NJ: Princeton University Press, 1999).

22. Rufford Milton, "West Garfield Community News and Comment," *Garfieldian*, April 6, 1966; Rufford Milton, "West Garfield Community News and Comment," *Garfieldian*, March 9, 1966. For his graduate work at the University of Chicago, which led him into community organizing, Saul Alinsky did gang outreach work. See Sanford D. Horwitt, *Let Them Call Me Rebel: Saul Alinsky and His Life* (New York: Alfred A. Knopf, 1989), chapter 3, especially pp. 20–27; letter, R. E. Williams, ass't C.O. secretary, to Dear Block Club Member, October 19, 1953, series I, box 220, folder 2185, Chicago Urban League records.

23. "West Garfield Community Council Block Club News and Comments," *Garfieldian*, September 9, 1965; Rufford Milton, "West Garfield Community News and Comment," *Garfieldian*, May 11, 1966.

24. "Garfield Community Council Block Club News & Comment," *Garfieldian*, April 28, 1965; executive committee meeting, June 9, 1964, folder, June 1964, box 24, GLCC-CHM; Anna Stefanowiz, Julian-Paulina Block Club, to Mr. Dorn, Bureau of Street Traffic, August 19, 1980, folder 5, box 45, Northwest Community Organization Records, Chicago History Museum (hereafter NCO records); letter, Dan Russo, chairman, Miller-Carpenter Street Block Club, to Captain Gibbons, Maxwell Police Station, July 29, 1954, folder 529, Near West Side Community Committee Records, Department of Special Collections, Richard J. Daley Library, University of Illinois at Chicago (hereafter NWSCC records).

25. Rufford Milton, "West Garfield Block Club News and Comment," *Garfieldian*, November 10, November 17, and December 1, 1965.

26. "Visit to a Block Club Meeting," *Garfieldian*, November 20, 1963; "West Garfield Community Council Block Club News," *Garfieldian*, January 27, 1965.

27. EPIC newsletter, January 18, 1998, folder 10, box 31, Mary Ann Smith papers, 1978–2009, Women and Leadership Archives, Loyola University Chicago.

28. Perry R. Duis, *The Saloon: Public Drinking in Chicago and Boston, 1880–1920* (Urbana: University of Illinois Press, 1983); On public urination, see Mitchell Dunier, *Sidewalk* (New York: Farrar, Straus, and Giroux, 2000), 186–87; Rufford Milton, "Garf. Community Council Block Club News," *Garfieldian*, December 22, 1964.

29. John M. Ragland to D. E. Mackelmann, report on rear porches and yards with street addresses, November 22, 1954, folder, January–November 1954, box 1, GLCC-CHM; letter, 1800–1900 [S. Lawndale Ave.] Property Owners Block Club, to Bonner, re Tavern on Lawndale and Ogden Avenues, August 26, 1960, folder "August 1960," box 14, GLCC-CHM; clipping, *Daily News*, March 1, 1957, folder, February–March 1957, box 3, GLCC-CHM; "West Garfield Community Council Block Club News and Comment," *Garfieldian*, February 24, 1965. For a detailed account of how block organizations in an unidentified city (probably Akron, Ohio) addressed the problems associated with a local tavern, see Mohan L. Kaul, "Block Clubs and Social Action: A Case Study in Community Conflict," *Journal of Sociology & Social Welfare* 3, no. 4 (March 1976): 437–50.

30. Letter, Faith to Nikki, June 9, 1968, folder 3, box 20, Faith Rich Collection, Department of Special Collections, Harold Washington Library Center, Chicago Public Library; Rufford Milton, "West Garfield Council Block Club News & Comment," *Garfieldian*, June 16, 1965.

31. For a succinct statement of how local option has changed over time in Chicago, see Rachel E. Bohlmann, "Local Option," *Encyclopedia of Chicago*. http://www.encyclopedia .chicagohistory.org/pages/759.html; 6800 Indiana block, December 1, 1953, series II, box 234, folder 2301, Chicago Urban League records.

32. Alva B. Maxey, "The Block Club Movement in Chicago," *Phylon Quarterly* 18(2) (1957): 128.

33. "What's Happening in North Lawndale," *Citizens of Greater Chicago Civic News* 4, no. 4, (October 1957), folder "October 1–24," 1957, box 4, GLCC-CHM; weekly report to executive director from Helen L. Johnson, week ending November 15, 1963, folder 72, GLCC-UIC; Bohlman, "Local Option." The Red Line Project has mapped locations of dry precincts in Chicago against assaults in April 2014: Kenny Reiter, "Searchable Maps: Assaults in Chicago's Dry Precincts," http://redlineproject.org/dryneighborhoodsmap.php (last accessed December 26, 1914). To visualize only the locations of dry districts, click on "searchable map" and uncheck the assaults box.

34. For an excellent history of heroin in US cities, see Eric C. Schneider, *Smack: Heroin and the American City* (Princeton, NJ: Princeton University Press, 2008). For an overview of how the late-twentieth-century "War on Drugs" criminalized black men and affected their life chances, see Michelle Alexander, *The New Jim Crow: Mass Incarceration in the Age of Colorblindness* (New York and London: The New Press, 2010). For the internal logic of gang operations and economy, see Venkatesh, *Gang Leader for a Day*.

35. Archon Fung, *Empowered Participation: Reinventing Urban Democracy* (Princeton, NJ: Princeton University Press, 2004), 85.

36. Venkatesh, *Off the Books*, 67.

37. Venkatesh, *Off the Books*, 62–90, 292–302, quotations on p. 73, 71, and 75.

38. "Hurt Me Soul Lyrics," MetroLyrics, http://www.metrolyrics.com/hurt-me-soul-lyrics-lupe-fiasco.html, last accessed April 30, 2014. I would like to thank my colleague Robert Smith for drawing this song to my attention. Chloé Mister, "Blocking Crime: How Strong Block Clubs Are Saving Chicago's Neighborhoods," *Shelterforce Online* 132 (November/December 2003), http://www.nhi.org/online/issues/132/blockclubs.html; St. Jean, *Pockets of Crime*, passim. See also Nicole Robinson, "What Can We Learn from Public Health? An Example of Sharing Law Enforcement Spatial Data with Community Partners," *Geography and Public Safety* 3 (2) (August 2012): 11–15.

39. Maxey, "The Block Club Movement in Chicago": 127; Susanne M. Tumelty, "Block Associations, Crime, and the Police" (PhD diss., City University of New York, 1987), 84.

40. Minutes of August 4, 1986 meeting of the West 15th Place Block Club at 1514 S. Albany, folder 5, box 9, Rich papers.

41. Petition, August 6, 1954, series I, box 220, folder 2186, Chicago Urban League records; Julia Abrahamson, *A Neighborhood Finds Itself* (New York: Harper & Brothers, 1959), 69–70.

42. On the Austin Tenants and Owners Association, see Amanda I. Seligman, *Block by Block: Neighborhoods and Public Policy on Chicago's West Side* (Chicago: University of Chicago Press, 2005), 186–90. "Block Club to Work with Police on Crime," *Austinite*, December 7, 1966, box 7, Austin Newspapers Collection, Special Collections and Preservation Division, Harold Washington Public Library, Chicago Public Library (hereafter ANC); letter to the editor from Bruce J. Finne, Republican candidate, 18th Senatorial district, *Austin News*, April 29, 1970, box 2, ANC.

43. *Southwest Associated Block Club News*, September 15, 1968, Chicago History Museum. For an introduction to the events outside the 1968 Democratic National Convention, see David Farber, *Chicago '68* (Chicago: University of Chicago Press, 1988).

44. "Crime Statistics Show Need for Police Help for Southwest Residents," *ABC News*, February 27, 1970, and "Southwest Community Requests Additional Help from Police," *ABC News*, June 12, 1970; both in Chicago History Museum.

45. Brian J. L. Berry, *The Open Housing Question: Race and Housing in Chicago, 1966–1976* (Cambridge, MA: Ballinger, 1979), 187; "Take These Protective Measures," *ABC News*, February 27, 1970, Chicago History Museum; "Police Patrol a Deterent [*sic*]," *ABC News*, June 12, 1970, Chicago History Museum.

46. 5th OBA Convention resolutions, May 1, 1971, Austin Town Hall, folder 23, box 3, Austin Community Collection, Department of Special Collections, Harold Washington Library Center, Chicago Public Library.

47. Joseph P. Linskey, "Neighborhood Watch," in *Encyclopedia of Social Problems*, Vincent N. Parillo, ed. (Thousand Oaks, CA: Sage Publications, 2008), 616–17; Dennis P. Rosenbaum, "Neighborhood Watch," in *Encyclopedia of Community: From the Village to the Virtual World*, ed. Karen Christensen and David Levinson (Thousand Oaks, CA: Sage Publications, 2003), 971–73; Dennis P. Rosenbaum, "Neighborhood Watch Programs," in *Encyclopedia of Crime and Punishment*, vol. 3, ed. David Levinson (Thousand Oaks, CA: Sage Publications, 2002), 1084–87. According to Wesley Skogan, the Ford Foundation sponsored a $550,000 block watch program in Chicago in the 1980s. See Wesley G. Skogan, *Disorder and Decline: Crime and the Spiral of Decay in American Neighborhoods* (New York: The Free Press, 1990), 137–45. For an ethnographic description of a Neighborhood Watch program in Chicago, see Patrick J. Carr, *Clean Streets: Controlling Crime, Maintaining Order, and Building Community Activism* (New York and London: New York University Press, 2005), 113–14 and 126–32.

48. Mozart-Francisco Block Club, October 16, 1979, folder 15; letter, the 1900 Richmond Block Club, to Com[m]ander Jankowski, April 23, 1980, folder 21; and letter, Beth Katsaros, 1942 North Richmond, to Assistant Deputy Superintendent William F. Mahoney, Narcotics and Gang Crimes Division, April 16, 1980, folder 21; all in box 46, NCO records.

49. For a compact account of the historical changes in the Chicago Police Department across the twentieth century that culminated in the emergence of community policing, see Fung, 44–56.

50. Wesley G. Skogan and Susan M. Hartnett, *Community Policing, Chicago Style* (New York and Oxford: Oxford University Press, 1997), 55; Wesley G. Skogan, *Police and Community in Chicago: A Tale of Three Cities* (Oxford and New York: Oxford University Press, 2006).

51. Fung, 12; Kelling and Wilson, "Broken Windows: The Police and Neighborhood Safety."

52. Skogan and Hartnett, *Community Policing, Chicago Style*, 162; Fung, 3; Matthew Desmond and Nicol Valdez, "Unpolicing the Urban Poor: Consequences of Third Party-Policing for Inner-City Women," *American Sociological Review* 78 (1) (2012): 117-141.

53. Skogan and Hartnett, *Community Policing, Chicago Style*, 115; clipping, "Community Policing Assembly Features Outlook of Optimism," *Southwest News Herald*, May 18, 1995, folder "C.P.D.—Community Relations, 1993–1995," clipping file, Municipal Reference Collection, Harold Washington Library Center, Chicago Public Library (hereafter Municipal Reference Collection); clipping, "Cops 'n' Neighbors: Community Policing in Beverly-Morgan Park," *Chicago Reader*, October 14, 1994, folder "C.P.D.—Community Relations, 1993–1995," clipping file, Municipal Reference Collection. Copies of the materials distributed at the convention can be found in folder: CAPS Block Club Convention 1997, Lincoln Central Neighborhood Association Records, Department of Special Collections and Archives, DePaul University Library, Chicago.

54. Clipping, Ben Joravsky, "Trading Community Policing for Public Relations," *Chicago Reader*, June 28, 1996; clipping, Chinta Strausberg, "Police Pull Funding for CAPS Training Program," *Chicago Defender*, August 8, 1996; and clipping, Molly Sullivan, "Neighbors Rally for CANS Funding," *Sunday Southtown*, June 2, 1996, all in folder "C.P.D.—Community Relations 1996–1998," clipping file, Municipal Reference Collection; Fung, 91–92; Carr, *Clean Streets*, 115; Author oral history interview with Beth Ford, Chicago, June 17, 2013. For an explanation of collective efficacy, see Robert J. Sampson, *Great American City: Chicago and the Enduring Neighborhood Effect* (Chicago: University of Chicago Press, 2012), chapter 7; Lolly Bowean and Jeremy Gorner, "Blocking Crime, One Club at a Time," *Chicago Tribune*, September 27, 2012; Clipping, Janis Shumac Parker, "CAPS Program Continues to Grow," *Daily Southtown*, 12/18/97, Folder: C.P.D.—Community Relations 1996–1998, clipping file, Municipal Reference Collection.

55. Clipping, "Tougher Laws Sought for Crimes against CAPS Members," *Suburban Leader*, January 11, 1998, folder: "C.P.D.—Community Relations 1996–1998," clipping file, Municipal Reference Collection; Jennifer Peltz, "3 Are Convicted in the Killing of Activist Mireles Prosecutors, Defense Claim Victory; Death Penalty Is Averted," *Chicago Tribune*, February 10, 2000; Lakewood Balmoral Residents Council Facebook page, October 14, 2013, https://www.facebook.com/Lakewood.Balmoral?hc_location=stream. Patrick J. Carr points out that "court advocates and CAPS volunteers rarely face intimidation and physical danger." Patrick J. Carr, *Clean Streets: Controlling Crime, Maintaining Order, and Building Community Activism* (New York and London: New York University Press, 2005), 134.

56. Clipping, Candy Nolan, "New Human Relations Officer Speaks to Community Group," *Southwest News Herald*, May 23, 1996, folder "C.P.D.—Community Relations 1996–1998," clipping file, Chicago Public Municipal Reference Library, Harold Washington Library Center,

Chicago Public Library. Rai's research dates the first appearances of the term "positive loitering" to 1993. Candice Rai, "Positive Loitering and Public Goods: The Ambivalence of Public Goods and Community Policing in the Neoliberal City," *Ethnography* 12 (1) (2011): 71–72.

57. Rai, "Positive Loitering and Public Goods": 85–86, note 6; Marilyn Pierce, Living Treasures [of Edgewater] menu, Edgewater Historical Society, http://www.edgewaterhistory.org/ehs /treasures/4a, last accessed May 7, 2014; author oral history interview Marilyn "Lynn" Pierce, Chicago, June 27, 2013; "Rogers Park Positive Loiterers Mark Second Anniversary," web page of Alderman Joe Moore, September 6, 2013, http://www.ward49.com/site/epage/146434_322.htm; Dorothy Tucker, "With 'Positive Loitering,' Residents Gather to Send Messages to Criminals," CBS Chicago, July 25, 2013, http://chicago.cbslocal.com/2013/07/25/with-positive-loitering -residents-gather-to-send-messages-to-criminals/; "Loitering for a Reason," *Chicago Tribune*, October 20, 2009; Patty Wetli, "Albany Park Neighbors Group Prepares for First 'Positive Loitering' Event," DNAinfo Chicago, http://www.dnainfo.com/chicago/20130612/albany-park /albany-park-neighbors-group-prepares-for-first-positive-loitering-event; Jake Malooley, "Stand in the Place Where You Live," *Time Out Chicago*, September 8, 2009, http://www.timeout.com /chicago/things-to-do/stand-in-the-place-where-you-live; all last accessed April 9, 2014. For a serious criticism of positive loitering that appeared on a satirical website, see "Uptown's Positive Loiterers: Useless," March 1, 2010, http://rogersparkbench.blogspot.com/2010/03/uptowns -positive-loiterers-awol-last.html, last accessed May 5, 2014.

58. Rai, "Positive Loitering and Public Goods": 65–88; quote on p. 66.

59. Author oral history interview with Beth Ford, Chicago, June 17, 2013; clipping, letter from Tyron K. Smith to the editor, *Beverly Review*, September 25, 1996, folder: C.P.D.—Community Relations 1996–1998, clipping file, Municipal Reference Collection, Harold Washington Library Center, Chicago Public Library.

60. I am indebted to doctoral student William I. Tchakirides for illuminating this point in a seminar paper written for History 971 at the University of Wisconsin–Milwaukee in fall 2012. The literature on the carceral state is burgeoning. Good starting points include Alexander, *The New Jim Crow*, and Heather Ann Thompson, "Why Mass Incarceration Matters: Rethinking Crisis, Decline and Transformation in Postwar American History," *Journal of American History* 97 (3) (December 2010): 703–34.

Conclusion

1. Memo to Irv Gerick from Peggy Wireman, re Committee Goals for 1964–1965, August 17, 1964, folder 21, box 91, Hyde Park–Kenwood Community Conference Records, Special Collections Research Center, Regenstein Library, University of Chicago.

2. "Crime & Public Safety: Tackling Gangs, Criminal Housing and Restoring Peace to our Streets & Public Places," Graceland-Wilson Neighbors Association, e-news, July 24, 2015, https:// gwna.wordpress.com/, last accessed 8/7/15.

3. Michael E. Smith, "The Archaeological Study of Neighborhoods and Districts in Ancient Cities," *Journal of Anthropological Archaeology* 29 (2010): 137–54; Margarethe Kusenbach, "A Hierarchy of Urban Communities: Observations on the Nested Character of Place," *City & Community* 7(3) (2008): 225–49, DOI: 10.1111/j.1540–6040.2008.00259.x; Robert J. Sampson, *Great American City: Chicago and the Enduring Neighborhood Effect* (Chicago: University of Chicago Press, 2012); Suleiman Osman, "The Decade of the Neighborhood," in *Rightward Bound: Making America Conservative in the 1970s*, Bruce J. Schulman and Julian E. Zelizer, eds. (Cambridge, MA, and London: Harvard University Press, 2008), 106–127; Benjamin Looker, *A Nation of*

Neighborhoods: Imagining Cities, Communities, and Democracy in Postwar America (Chicago: University of Chicago Press, 2015). See also John R. Hipp and Adam Boessen, "*Egohoods* as Waves Washing across the City: A New Measure of 'Neighborhoods,'" *Criminology* 51 (2) 2013: 287–327, DOI: 10.1111/1745-9125.12006; Ocean Howell, *Making the Mission: Planning and Ethnicity in San Francisco* (Chicago: University of Chicago Press, 2015); David J. Madden, "Neighborhood as Spatial Project: Making the Urban Order on the Downtown Brooklyn Waterfront," *International Journal of Urban and Regional Research* 38 (2) (2014): 471–97, doi:10.1111/1468-2427.12068; Rebecca Marchiel, "Neighborhoods First: The Urban Reinvestment Movement in the Era of Financial Deregulation, 1966–1989," (PhD diss., Northwestern University, 2014); and Alexander von Hoffman, *Local Attachments: The Making of an American Urban Neighborhood, 1850 to 1920* (Baltimore: Johns Hopkins University Press, 1994). A special issue of the *Journal of Urban History* edited by David Garrioch and Mark Peel focused on "The Social History of Urban Neighborhoods." See David Garrioch and Mark Peel, "Introduction: The Social History of Urban Neighborhoods," 663–76; David Rosenthal, "Big Piero, the Empire of the Meadow, and the Parish of Santa Lucia: Claiming Neighborhood in the Early Modern City," 677–92; Jill Burke, "Visualizing Neighborhood in Renaissance Florence: Santo Spirito and Santa Maria del Carmine," 693–710; Nicholas A. Eckstein, "Addressing Wealth in Renaissance Florence: Some New Soundings from the *Catasto* of 1427," 711–28; Jane Garnett and Gervase Rosser, "Miraculous Images and the Sanctification of Urban Neighborhood in Post-Medieval Italy," 729–40; Graeme Davison, "From Urban Jail to Bourgeois Suburb: The Transformation of Neighborhood in Early Colonial Sydney," 741–60; Alain Faure, "Local Life in Working-Class Paris at the End of the Nineteenth Century," 761–72; and Margaret Garb, "Drawing the 'Color Line': Race and Real Estate in Early Twentieth-Century Chicago," 773–87; all in *Journal of Urban History* 32 (5) (July 2006). The material collected in Ronald H. Bayor, ed., *Neighborhoods in Urban America* (Port Washington, NY: Kennikat Press, 1982), provided a useful introduction to leading secondary sources a generation ago. Emily Talen's book on neighborhoods is expected to synthesize the recent literature (Chicago: University of Chicago Press, forthcoming).

4. Suzanne Keller, *The Urban Neighborhood: A Sociological Perspective* (New York: Random House, 1968), 44–45; Margarethe Kusenbach, "Patterns of Neighboring: Practicing Community in the Parochial Realm," *Symbolic Interaction* 29 (3) (2006): 279–306.

5. Jan. T. Gross, *Neighbors: The Destruction of the Jewish Community in Jedwabne, Poland*, with a new afterword (New York: Penguin Books, 2001; originally published by Princeton University Press, 2001).

6. Jennifer Altman, "Respect the Grievous History of This Place," *Princeton Alumni Weekly*, September 12, 2012, http://paw.princeton.edu/issues/2012/09/19/pages/0221/index.xml?page=1&; last accessed May 28, 2014.

7. Ferdinand Tönnies, *Community and Society* (*Gemeinschaft und Gesellschaft*), trans. and. ed. Charles P. Loomis (New York: Harper & Row, 1965; edition originally published in 1957 by Michigan State University Press; originally published in German in 1887); Claude S. Fischer, *Networks and Places: Social Relations in the Urban Setting* (New York: Free Press, 1977); Kenneth A. Scherzer, *The Unbounded Community: Neighborhood Life and Social Structure in New York City, 1830–1875* (Durham, NC: Duke University Press, 1992); Thomas Bender, *Community and Social Change in America* (Baltimore: Johns Hopkins University Press, 1982; originally published by Rutgers University Press, 1978); Robert D. Putnam, *Bowling Alone: The Collapse and Revival of American Community* (New York: Simon and Schuster, 2000); Sampson, *Great American City*, 44–46.

8. Amanda Seligman, "Community Areas," *Encyclopedia of Chicago*, ed. Janice L. Reiff, Ann

Durkin Keating, and James R. Grossman (Chicago: Chicago History Museum, 2005), http://www.encyclopedia.chicagohistory.org/pages/319.html; Sudhir Alladi Venkatesh, "Chicago's Pragmatic Planners: American Sociology and the Myth of Community," *Social Science History* 25 (2) (Summer 2001): 275–317; Joseph J. Salvo, "Census Tracts," *Encyclopedia of the U.S. Census*, 2nd ed., Margo Anderson, Constance Citro, and Joseph Salvo, eds. (Washington: CQ Press, 2011), 82–84; City of Chicago, Chicago Maps, http://www.cityofchicago.org/city/en/depts/doit/supp_info/citywide_maps.html, last accessed May 28, 2014; Neighborhood Ties Inc., Everyone's Got to Be Somewhere, http://www.bigstickinc.com/chicago3_map_large.html, last accessed May 28, 2014.

9. Tönnies, 34.

10. The urban historical literature is too voluminous to cite here. For an introduction to the scholarship of the 1980s and 1990s, see Timothy J. Gilfoyle, "White Cities, Linguistic Turns, and Disneyland: The New Paradigms of Urban History," *Reviews in American History* 26 (1) (1998): 175–204. For effective recent overviews of the field's shape, see Raymond A. Mohl and Roger Biles, "New Perspectives on American Urban History," in *The Making of Urban America*, 3rd edition, Raymond A. Mohl and Roger Biles, eds., 343–448 (Lanham, MD: Rowman & Littlefield, 2012) and "Forum: From Site to Place? Michael B. Katz's Reflections on a Changing Field," *Journal of Urban History* 4 (4) (July 2015): 559–602. Contributors include Daniel Amsterdam, Michael B. Katz, Lilia Fernandez, Timothy J. Gilfoyle, N. D. B. Connolly, Lynn Hollen Lees, Michael Frisch, and Mark J. Stern.

11. Matthew Desmond argues that landlords' decisions about tenant screening also significantly account for variations of block characteristics within poor neighborhoods. See Matthew Desmond, *Evicted: Poverty and Profit in the American City* (New York: Crown, 2016), 89.

12. Emily Thompson and Scott Mahoy, "The Roaring Twenties," http://vectorsdev.usc.edu/NYCsound/777b.html, last accessed May 28, 2014.

Appendix One

1. Exceptional works that do narrate the qualitative historical research process include Antoinette Burton, *Archive Stories: Facts, Fictions, and the Writing of History* (Durham, NC: Duke University Press, 2006), and James M. Banner Jr. and John R. Gillis, *Becoming Historians* (Chicago: University of Chicago Press, 2009).

2. Sylvia Hood Washington, *Packing Them In: An Archaeology of Environmental Racism in Chicago, 1865–1954* (Lanham, MD: Lexington Books, 2005), chapter 6, and Sylvia Hood Washington, "Mrs. Block Beautiful: African American Women and the Birth of the Urban Conservation Movement, Chicago, Illinois, 1917–1954," *Environmental Justice* 1 (2008): 13–23.

3. Alphine Wade Jefferson, "Housing Discrimination and Community Response in North Lawndale (Chicago), Illinois 1948–1978," (PhD diss., Duke University 1979).

4. Project on Human Development in Chicago Neighborhoods, http://www.icpsr.umich.edu/icpsrweb/PHDCN/, last accessed May 29, 2014; Robert J. Sampson, *Great American City: Chicago and the Enduring Neighborhood Effect* (Chicago: University of Chicago Press, 2012); Delmos J. Jones and Susanne M. Tumelty, "Are There Really 10,000 Block Associations in New York City?" *Social Policy* (Fall 1986), reprinted in Susanne M. Tumelty, "Block Associations, Crime, and the Police" (PhD diss., City University of New York, 1987), 93–94.

5. The University of Chicago Regenstein Library's Special Collections Research Center also holds papers of Annetta M. Dieckmann, but they cover her work with the American Civil Liberties Union.

Appendix Two

1. "Rules and Regulations Governing 4100 Block West Grenshaw," folder, May 1–12, 1960, box 13, Greater Lawndale Conservation Commission Records, Chicago History Museum (hereafter GLCC-CHM).

2. "The Making of Good Citizenship and Neighborly Conduct," two-page memo for Progressive Twin Block Club, September 28, 1962, folder, September 1962, box 19, GLCC-CHM.

3. "ATOA Block Club News," *Garfieldian*, September 8, 1966.

4. Meeting announcement for November 26 [1966], 2100 South Lawndale Block Club, folder, July 1966–March 1967, box 27, GLCC-CHM.

5. "This Is Our Block," folder 13, box 109, Hyde Park–Kenwood Community Conference Records, Department of Special Collections, Regenstein Library, University of Chicago.

6. "Hi Neighbors!" Series I, box 220, folder 2180, Chicago Urban League Records, Special Collections and University Archives Department, Richard J. Daley Library, University of Illinois at Chicago.

Index

HISTORICAL STUDIES OF URBAN AMERICA

Edited by Lilia Fernández, Timothy J. Gilfoyle, Becky M. Nicolaides, and Amanda I. Seligman